T0312010

My mother was a social worker who said to me one day, "Whatever you do, go and make a difference in someone's life." Hence, I entered and spent my career in healthcare, a most noble field. I, along with the women highlighted in this book, spent much of our careers trying to help others through health information and technology. The stories in this book are powerful examples of why, how, and what women can do to make a difference for those they serve.

We learn of women who have overcome workplace and domestic challenges and regardless, they have overcome them to achieve success. This book demonstrates what I call a "Mobile Operations Manager" (MOM). A MOM is someone who, with respect, dignity, resilience, and tenacity, uses all their knowledge and skills to keep going with the goal of making a difference for others, the true definition of success. The book is for early careerists or anyone continuing their journey of life learning.

**Mary P. Griskewicz, HIMSS,
Most Influential Woman in Health IT**

Raised in part by a strong mother and three older sisters, I grew up knowing the power of women. I watched my sisters go to school, graduate, and become powerful leaders in their industries. When I entered the workforce and healthcare technology specifically, I was disappointed in what I saw: a lack of women in leadership roles. This book helps solve this injustice. Packed with inspirational examples of women, their stories at once motivate and give hope to the reader.

For women, you will get a front-row seat learning how pioneering women before you were able to break through this challenge with knowledgeable and practical ideas to make more informed decisions on the best ways to navigate forward. For men, you will see opportunities to help ensure equity within your organization and how you can increasingly ally with women to reduce disparities in leadership. The stories will illuminate and give birth to new ideas you can leverage and share with colleagues.

I have been blessed to be a part of amazing world-class organizations that transformed their communities. Hands down, my best teams were diverse and led by amazing women leaders. Fair warning: buckle up because you are in for a beautiful journey and you will not be able to stop reading.

**Ed Marx, Principal/CEO Marx Advisory, Series Editor,
Taylor & Francis, Board Member, Summa Health System &
Mary Crowley Cancer Institute**

# A Woman's Guide to Navigating a Successful Career in Healthcare Information Technology

This book features over 50 of the industry's brightest female pioneers who share insightful lessons backed by several years of experience, as well as tips for navigating a successful career in HIT. The intent of this book is to provide the opportunity to capture stories from highly successful women to inspire the next generation who want to pursue a career in HIT and to inspire those already working in the field who are eager to advance in their careers. This book also provides insights on industry opportunities, ways to deal with harassment, the history of female tech innovators, and negotiating competitive salary and employment agreements. Additional industry experts provided guidance on tapping into venture capital funding and tools for career development. A comprehensive resource guide and glossary of industry terms are also included. Co-authors included: Amy Sabillon, MSI, Ayanna Chambliss, CAP, SHRM-CP, Lindsay Rowlands, MHA, and Stacey B. Lee, JD.

# A Woman's Guide to Navigating a Successful Career in Healthcare Information Technology

Jeffery Daigrepont

Foreword by Sherri Douville, CEO at Medigram

Routledge
Taylor & Francis Group

A PRODUCTIVITY PRESS BOOK

First published 2024
by Routledge
605 Third Avenue, New York, NY 10158

and by Routledge
4 Park Square, Milton Park, Abingdon, Oxon, OX14 4RN

Routledge is an imprint of the Taylor & Francis Group, an informa business

ISBN: 9781032432809 (hbk)
ISBN: 9781032432793 (pbk)
ISBN: 9781003366591 (ebk)

DOI: 10.4324/9781003366591

Typeset in Garamond
by codeMantra

*This book is dedicated to my two amazing daughters,
Taylor and Chloe, and the many inspiring women who
have had a profound influence on my career and life.*

# Contents

# Foreword

Foreword by **Sherri Douville**, CEO at Medigram | Series editor, Taylor & Francis

It is my honor and privilege to provide the foreword for this special book, *A Woman's Guide to Navigating a Successful Career in Healthcare Information Technology*. Because of the influence of medical ethics and a desire to align with their partner clinicians, leaders in healthcare IT are honest in their efforts to transform healthcare IT. They act with purpose, conviction, and drive real results. This includes embracing what young people expect, which is to see teams and organizations that better reflect them. At the same time, we live in a great paradox in that many positions and levers of power continue to be held in homogeneous networks. This has to be discussed; it's human nature. We are all tribal. We do business with people we like and trust, and we like and trust people who are like us. This tribalism doesn't just apply to the classic categories; it is at play where IT intersects with medicine and even between different factions of medicine and technology, as the term "holy wars of programming languages" describes. This is why I think the natural "onboarding" to allyship is actually allyship between different disciplines or domains (medicine, law, IT, and cybersecurity, for example). Extending and creating value beyond ourselves is the great test of leadership. The more types of domains a leader can connect and drive value from collectively, the more effective we become. These bear strategic and operational challenges requiring what are often ill-understood skills to solve modern complexity in general, for which workforce and patient population diversity is one of many complexity-related challenges that every leader faces.

Because of long-standing power structures, while women should, can, and do help one another, we cannot succeed without the allyship of men. We have to recognize that an act of allyship comes at personal cost and risk; we have to spread the risks and costs by working in teams and networks to do what we know is right and to enable the greater collective courage required to modernize what leadership looks like.

We can't make it as women leaders with real impact and influence without the partnership of powerful men. That's why I love the spirit of this book, as what Jeffery Daigrepont has created with his team is the ultimate act of allyship, a guide for women to pursue a career in healthcare IT.

I was approached to advise Jeffery in this effort due to my position as CEO of Medigram, an early stage Healthcare IT, Mobile Medicine company that drives safety, efficiency, and profitability in healthcare; as IEEE co-chair of Trust for the industry's technical standard; and as an advisory committee member to the College of Healthcare Information Management Executives. I have built the team behind and edited two long-term best-selling, industry-shaping books and have contributed to six books with industry leaders. I also serve on the CHIME certification for digital health in cybersecurity. I am honored but not satisfied to be one of a very small number of women STEM series editors for elite academic book publishers, Taylor & Francis, and the only woman editor in the best-selling cohort of books in medical informatics and medical technology listed on Amazon. I am honored to be one of the top-ranked tech executives on Crunchbase worldwide. I got here unusually as a woman in partnership with both women and men. What I'm most proud of is the consortium we've built, which has been referred to by many industry insiders as the "best of the best" 50 coauthors and 50 editorial reviewers (100 total) across all the required domains that drive healthcare IT: medicine, medical education, regulatory, informatics, cybersecurity, IT, engineering across the whole technical stack, and product marketing and management fielded from the best organizations in their categories including internationally across health systems, medical devices, and precision medicine.

Partners in the journey included my late Father, my brother, many teachers, professors, my academic advisor, family friends, mentors, investors, friends, and colleagues.

On a recent Saturday morning, my hard-working husband, Dr. Art Douville, who is eminent in his own career as a groundbreaking stroke neurologist and repeat CMO, including for Medigram, seemed truly delighted to drop me off at the Board Leadership Academy held by my alma mater, Santa Clara University, where I serve in various formal and informal advisory roles.

When I counted the people involved in that moment, I lost count as I was filled with gratitude.

The stories of the women in this book serve as living role models to help you blaze your trail or provide you with tangible intellectual support if you are mentoring a woman in a space where few role models have existed in the past. I love the concept of this book. I think we overemphasize personal relationships at the expense of representation. Personal relationships are absolutely critical for emotional support, ongoing professional and personal development, and access to highly relevant, specific coaching. However, transformation can come from someone you have never even met. Some of my biggest impacts came from seeing the example of someone I've never met personally, Dr. Lisa Su, CEO at AMD. Prior to accepting my IEEE position and leaning into publishing opportunities, I had noticed that Dr. Su was always introduced on stage as a speaker with more than 40 IEEE publications (whereas publications are chapter equivalents in academic publishing). From seeing Lisa's example, I saw the value of and embraced being a leader in IEEE as well as publishing, and I have reached her publishing numbers. Many allies were instrumental in the success of our books, including Ed Marx, the super sponsor who graces the back cover of this book as a fellow series editor.

These activities, and more importantly, the communities of practice behind them, have transformed our teams intellectually, emotionally, and mentally, as well as impacted many around us. It is my sincere hope that in the pages of this book, you find your own Lisa Su example or, as an ally, you embrace these examples for the women you are committed to developing into the leaders our industry needs for a promising tomorrow. Enjoy!

# Executive Summary

It is no secret that the field of healthcare information technology (HCIT) has been an industry largely composed of men. This continues to be the case, despite the latest information from the U.S. Bureau of Labor Statistics that reports women make up 47% of all U.S. employees.[1] While HCIT is an ever-growing field and the reality is that new roles will continue to emerge with the continued advances made in technology, many women have yet to capitalize on this market. Having worked in HCIT for over 25 years, I find that it is still possible to be misinformed on several issues pertaining to matters of diversity, equity, and inclusivity (DEI), especially as it relates to women in the HCIT space (or lack thereof). For instance, I used to assume that the reason HCIT was so lacking in diversity was contributable to women being less interested in joining this field. However, when I would listen to my female colleagues describe HCIT, they did so with great enthusiasm and passion for what they do, with expertise backed by decades of professional experience, showing me unique ways of thinking and unique areas of interest that I find some men like me would not typically focus on. I later also understood that there are several factors that come into play that influence the decisions made by career-driven women in selecting their desired field, and some of this is impacted by the culture of an organization as well as representation in the workforce. While there are studies to support the idea that greater diversity and inclusivity in the workforce is good for business, studies also show that when it comes to their own workplace, there are mixed opinions as to the value of these initiatives.[2]

Then there is this book. Why did it become so important for me to have something like this written? The answer is very simple and personal: my daughter decided to follow in my footsteps and now wishes to work in HCIT. Did I ever expect my daughter to follow in my footsteps? Never. In fact, as a child, she would always complain about family vacations being combined with work conferences and having to help me pack up a booth after a long weekend of exhibiting and entertaining clients. So, to be perfectly honest, I was unprepared for how to respond. As a father, I was honored and proud to have my daughter walk a similar path, but it also led me to be concerned, knowing she would be in the minority. While my wife and I have raised our daughters to be discerning and strong, it was at this moment that I found I needed to find a better way to guide my daughter in this incredibly rewarding but also challenging field. Therefore, I went in search of strong female mentors that I knew in the industry for guidance. I am in a unique position to be surrounded by numerous successful and intelligent women in my HCIT network, and they have demonstrated a great willingness to mentor my daughter. The knowledge these women have shared is invaluable, and it is where I received the inspiration for this book.

The highlight of the publication and what sets this book apart from others is that it will include features and/or interviews of extremely successful women who are considered experts in the industry and who would ordinarily be difficult to access. From tech companies to health systems to private practices and more, and from highly ranked titles such as Chief Executive Officers (CEOs), Chief Information Officers (CIOs), Directors, and Client Software Managers, insights will be obtained from diverse perspectives of women who are willing to share their lessons backed by several years of experience, as well as tips for navigating a successful career in HCIT. The intent of the publication will be to provide the opportunity to capture stories from highly successful women and inspire the next generation who desire to pursue a career in HCIT on a much larger scale. The information will be beneficial to many, and it will bring reassurance and greater understanding to concerned fathers like me. This book is also comprised of chapters that focus on such areas as HCIT career readiness, existing programs and certifications available for HCIT, a general overview of career options available in HCIT, what it means to be a male ally, the human resources angle of employment in HCIT, as well as chapters contributed by authors such as Stacey B. Lee, JD, Professor of Law and Ethics at the Johns Hopkins University Carey Business School, with additional information focused on legal aspects of employment contracts and negotiation skills.

The goal of this publication is therefore twofold. First, it is to provide the information and resources necessary for women interested in pursuing a career in HCIT to make a more informed decision and to have the means of knowing how best to move forward. Second, it is to encourage future generations of women pursuing careers in HCIT by sharing impactful stories from trailblazing women who have so graciously decided to participate in this endeavor, as well as to encourage greater diversity in our industry by discussing matters that are of great importance as they relate to DEI initiatives.

I would be remiss not to include a direct acknowledgment to all the men and women who made this publication possible. From my co-authors to our featured HCIT women (with a special thanks to Karen Jaw-Madson, principal of Co.-Design of Work Experience and a successful author herself, for permitting us to include her mentoring strategy template in our book), to Stuart Bracken, Managing Director, Ed Marx, Principal/CEO, and Mary P. Griskewicz, HIMSS, it has been such an honor and privilege to work with all of you. An added (and unexpected) bonus was gaining a mentor myself with the introduction to Sherri Douville, CEO of Medigram, Inc. Sherri has been published extensively and is passionate about the topic of allyship and has experienced the power of allyship firsthand. I will always be grateful for her guidance, input, and encouragement.

Jeffery Daigrepont is a senior vice president at Coker, specializing in healthcare automation, system integration, cybersecurity, operations, and deployment of enterprise information systems for large integrated delivery networks and medical practices.

Jeffery Daigrepont
Senior Vice President

# Notes

1 Bureau of Labor Statistics. (2023, September 1). *The employment situation – August 2023*. BLS. https://www.bls.gov/bls/newsrels.htm
2 Minkin, R. (2023, May 17). *Diversity, equity, and inclusion in the workplace.* Pew Research Center. https://www.pewresearch.org/social-trends/2023/05/17/diversity-equity-and-inclusion-in-the-workplace/

# About the Authors – Jeffery Daigrepont

 **Jeffery Daigrepont,** senior vice president of Coker, specializes in healthcare automation, system integration, operations, and deployment of enterprise information systems for large integrated delivery networks. A popular national speaker, Jeffery is frequently engaged by highly respected organizations across the nation, including many non-profit trade associations and state medical societies.

Jeffery authored a top-selling book, *Complete Guide and Toolkit to Successful EHR Adoption*, published by HIMSS in 2011, and was a contributing author to Coker's book, *The Healthcare Executive's Guide to ACO Strategy*, published in March 2012. Mr. Daigrepont is often interviewed by various national media outlets and is frequently quoted in publications.

For FY09, Jeffery chaired the Ambulatory Information Systems Steering Committee of HIMSS. In addition, as the Ambulatory Committee liaison for FY09 to the ACEC Planning Committee, he represented the HIMSS Ambulatory and AISC members. Daigrepont is credentialed by the American Academy of Medical Management (AAMM) with an Executive Fellowship in Practice Management (EFMP).

Jeffery also serves as an independent investor advisor to many of the nation's top health care venture capitalist firms such as Kleiner Perkins Caufield & Byers (KPCB) and Silver Lake Partners.

# About the Authors – Stacey B. Lee, JD

**Stacey B. Lee** is a Professor of Law and Ethics at the Johns Hopkins University Carey Business School (with a joint appointment at the Bloomberg School of Public Health). She teaches courses in business law, health law, and negotiations. Her research and writing focus on pharmaceutical manufacturers' international and domestic influence on access to medicines, transformative healthcare negotiations, and the impact of COVID-19 on the employer-employee relationship.

Stacey is the Academic Program Director for the flagship Full-time MBA program at Carey Business School. In 2019, she founded the Teaching Excellence Initiative at Carey Business School to coach faculty and enhance the pedagogy provided to students. She is an Executive Education faculty at the Academy for Women and Leadership at Carey Business School.

Stacey is a Fulbright Specialist for her expertise in negotiations and healthcare law. She has received numerous research grants and fellowships for her teaching innovations. Her most recent research focuses on how the COVID-19 pandemic and accompanying laws and policies have affected the employer-employee relationship. Stacey has received several awards for Faculty Excellence, including the Excellence in Teaching Award, year after year, at both Bloomberg School of Public Health and Carey Business School.

Stacey was a featured TEDx speaker on "Patient Voices." Her work has also been featured in several prominent law reviews and peer-reviewed journals such as the *Journal of Business Ethics, Yale Journal of Health Policy and Ethics, Annals of Health Law, Aesthetic Surgery Journal, Journal of Legal Medicine,* and *Health and Human Rights International Journal.* Stacey routinely provides legal analyses to news outlets regarding the Supreme Court, Congress, and current events of national importance. Her interviews, quotes, and writings have appeared in the Washington Post, CBS, CNN, CBC, Bloomberg Radio, USA Today, NPR, TODAY.com, and Voice of America, among other media outlets.

Stacey is currently a Maryland court-appointed Transformative Mediator. Before entering academia, Stacey practiced law for over ten years. She began as a securities litigator and later became in-house counsel for two of the country's largest healthcare corporations. Stacey also served as the senior regulatory specialist for the United States' largest national healthcare trade association.

Stacey is a much sought-after keynote speaker and negotiations guru. She regularly delivers experiential workshops to diverse audiences, including hospitals, academic medical centers, and business corporations, to equip them with actionable negotiation strategies.

Stacey is the Founder and Chief Executive Officer at Praxis Pacisci, a negotiations training institute. She is also the author of "Negotiation Matters," a monthly LinkedIn Newsletter that serves as her vehicle to share actionable negotiation tips with her audience. Stacey is currently authoring a book on healthcare negotiations, which provides a negotiation framework designed specifically for the healthcare landscape.

# About the Authors – Ayanna Chambliss, CAP, SHRM-CP

**Ayanna Chambliss,** CAP, SHRM-CP, is the vice president of administration at Coker. She is a seasoned professional with over 20 years of experience in operations and administration at the executive level. She is responsible for developing and implementing comprehensive operation strategies across the organization, which have proven to be instrumental in improving overall employee engagement and retention. Throughout her career, Ayanna has been passionate about supporting high-performing teams and driving organizational change. She is committed to leading initiatives that create an inclusive work environment where diversity and equity are valued and celebrated. As a result of her efforts, Ayanna has earned a reputation as a trusted advisor and mentor. She leads by example and is dedicated to creating a workplace culture where every employee feels valued and supported in their professional growth and development. Ayanna's extensive knowledge of employment law, compensation, and benefits is an asset to the organization. Her proficiency in these areas ensures that the company remains in compliance with regulations while providing competitive compensation packages and benefits that attract and retain top talent. In addition to her professional accomplishments, Ayanna is a Certified Administrative Professional (CAP) and holds a Society for Human Resource Management Certified Professional (SHRM-CP) certification. These credentials demonstrate her commitment to ongoing learning and professional development.

# About the Authors – Lindsay Rowlands, MHA

**Lindsay Rowlands,** MHA, is a project coordinator at Coker. She supports various project initiatives including EHR implementation, vendor vetting, and performance improvement assessments. Lindsay is well-known for her attention to detail, determination, as well as her ability to empathize with healthcare executives. She is passionate about driving home the value of patient and provider experience within an EHR to provide quality care. She has over ten years of knowledge and experience in healthcare operations within the post-acute industry where she served as a Licensed Nursing Home Administrator. Lindsay holds a Master's in Healthcare Management from Sage Graduate School of Albany, NY. She is also an alumnus of the State University of New York of Oneonta, NY. In her free time, she enjoys spending time on the lake with her family, reading, creating new recipes, and volunteering with the elderly.

# About the Authors – Amy Sabillon, MSI

**Amy Sabillon,** MSI, is the document specialist at Coker. Her role involves working extensively with documents and requires a meticulous approach to accomplishing tasks. Her experience covers work in the academic, legal, and healthcare consultative sectors. She obtained her Master's in Information Science (MIS) from Florida State University, which has equipped her with the necessary skills and knowledge for various information-related tasks encompassing information architecture, technology, and information needs and services.

# 1

# Is a Career in HCIT Right for Me?

## Introduction

Deciding upon which career to embark on or which career to change to is a momentous resolution. It requires a deep understanding of yourself, your values, your skills, your ideal work environment, and other factors that ultimately contribute to effectively deciding on a career that most resonates with you. Oftentimes, however, you may not have sufficient guidance and direction in this endeavor. If you are reading this book, that likely means that you are open to considering a career in healthcare information technology (HCIT), but you may desire or need further guidance in understanding what this will likely entail. It is not easy to enter into a unique industry that is a hybrid of both healthcare and technology and for most women, HCIT is like venturing into uncharted territory. When something is unfamiliar, it becomes especially daunting to know how best to proceed. That is why, in our undertaking to make this book, we decided that in order to make the content as practical and authentic as possible, we reached out to women already in the industry, many with decades of experience in their respective roles, to offer their first-hand accounts and insights into what the career has been like for them. We highly recommend you take the time to review these accounts in the chapter of this book, "Featured Successful Women of HCIT," at any time you wish to do so.

For now, we will begin by defining HCIT, providing a high-level overview of the history of HCIT, reviewing some of the prospective benefits of considering a career in HCIT, as well as its disadvantages, and we hope that by doing so, it will enable you to gain some degree of clarity as to whether this

DOI: 10.4324/9781003366591-1

is the right career path for you. While this book will later provide a broad overview of the prospective job opportunities specific to this niche industry, it will only truly matter if it resonates with you and the vision you have for your future. Our goal is to consolidate the existing industry information to enable you to make an informed decision, and should you choose to embark on this rewarding career, we seek to provide you with relevant resources and information that will facilitate this chapter in your life and to empower a generation of women in their successful career in HCIT.

## What Is HCIT?

There are multiple organizations that provide their own definition of HCIT, but all point towards a similar description. One of the most prominent ones is provided by the Office of the National Coordinator for Health Information Technology (ONC), which defines HCIT as "the application of information processing involving both computer hardware and software that deals with the storage, retrieval, sharing, and use of health care information, data, and knowledge for communication and decision making."[1] Another definition, provided by the U.S. Department of Health and Human Services (HHS), is that HCIT is "the processing, storage, and exchange of health information in an electronic environment."[2] The fundamental component of HCIT is thus the use of computers and related technologies to manage data and information in the context of the healthcare space. The end-users of this technology include a wide variety of individuals, including physicians and patients, public health agencies and pharmaceutical companies, health insurance corporations, and more. These technologies are therefore critical for the delivery of care and the advancement of diverse goals in the healthcare sector on a significantly large scale. Those who wish to pursue a career in HCIT will therefore need to have a desire to improve the quality of care for patients and have sufficient skills working with technology. If you have a passion for both healthcare and IT, this will be an excellent career for you to consider.

## The History of HCIT: A High-Level Overview

One of the largest and most complex industries in the United States is undoubtedly the healthcare industry. Vital in its support of people's health and well-being, it is an essential component of daily life and, as such, must function in a manner that is conducive to a healthy population and society. In addition to this, it is an industry with an incredibly high impact on the economy, especially as it relates to government spending on health. According to the National Health Expenditure (NHE) Fact Sheet, it is expected that national health spending will grow at an average annual rate of 5.4% from the period of 2019 to 2028.[3] There are several factors impacting this growth rate, some of which include a growing aging population that will experience a greater need for healthcare services, as well as new health services and technologies that are becoming available, including advances made in the area of HCIT.

We will delve into a brief overview of the history of HCIT in order to contextualize the evolution of technology and its impact on patients, healthcare professionals, providers, and the overall healthcare system. Women who are interested in joining the HCIT field should be knowledgeable of crucial historical information for personal growth and career insight, and to gain an understanding of the origins of the industry in which they wish to be a part of as well as to broaden their insight on the existing technologies, systems, and policies for informed decision-making and to be an asset to those that will ultimately be impacted by their contribution to the field.

# HCIT Advancements in the Early 20th Century

The introduction of technology into healthcare is one that occurred as a gradual byproduct of the advances in technology that primarily occurred throughout the 1960s and 1970s, but the maintenance of medical records and the significance of this have been in place since the 1920s. Prior to this, there was no set standard for the maintenance of clinical records, though it was clear that the documentation of patient information was essential in order to reference the history of a patient's health and keep track of symptoms. Today, the collection of data is used for an even greater variety of purposes, as healthcare technology allows for an effective and far-reaching scope of data analysis that can be used in research, planning, and more. The turning point occurred in the 1920s. Health information management (HIM) became more standardized through the initiative of the American College of Surgeons (ACOS), founded in 1913, to further the education of practicing surgeons.[4] In 1928, the ACOS established the American Association of Record Librarians (AARL), which later came to be known as the American Health Information Management Association (AHIMA) in 1938.[5] Through this, health records were standardized not only in hospitals but in other medical institutions as well.

This would continue throughout the 1960s, but all this was still taking place via paper-based records. The creation of computers would change this.

The creation of the very first computer was conceptualized in the early 19th century by Charles Babbage, but what we would consider to be the first modern digital electronic computer was not developed until 1942 by John Vincent Atanasoff, a physics professor at Iowa State College (now Iowa State University), and his graduate student, Clifford Berry.[6] It was not until around the 1960s that physicians began to contemplate its use in healthcare. One would think that the decision to implement the use of computers would be immediately accepted, but in fact, this was not the case. Though certainly it was expected that possible integration of technology would enable greater efficiency, one must also take into consideration the fact that this technology was all very new, and so there were many grounds for hesitancy with regard to its function and reliability. In addition, costs needed to be taken into consideration. While the introduction of computers opened up the possibility of preserving records electronically, the cost of purchasing the computers as well as the cost of data storage meant that only larger systems with sufficient capital would be able to afford this implementation.

In 1964, El Camino Hospital worked collaboratively with Lockheed Corporation on its initiative to develop a hospital information system that included medical records.[7] However, given the information noted above, most computer manufacturers did not understand the needs of the healthcare industry, as it was still primarily uncharted territory. Medical records were stored in the form of paper records up until this period, as technological innovations were still quite new. While this was the case, it was becoming more apparent that standardization would be essential as a way of improving healthcare practices and ensuring proper documentation of sensitive patient health information (take into consideration that HIPAA became enacted in the 1990s, so there were no standards for the management of this information at this time). It must be noted that a central figure in the effort to standardize the sharing of medical records was Dr. Lawrence Weed, a professor of medicine and pharmacology at Yale University. After noticing that students were experiencing difficulty attempting to discern doctors' notes during hospital rounds, Dr. Weed created the problem-oriented medical record (POMR) to record and monitor patient information.[8] POMR utilized the subjective, objective, assessment, and plan (SOAP) system as a way to systematically document patient notes. In the future, POMR would be coupled with software and would enable doctors to have access to an entire database of information relative to diagnosis and treatment options derived from existing journal articles.[8]

Around this period, the advent of Medicare and Medicaid, approved by President Lyndon B. Johnson in 1965,[7] propelled healthcare information systems forward as precise record-keeping became a top requirement for compensation. It became a necessity for patient information to be documented for reimbursement eligibility, and as such, this led to a shift in the way information was stored. Universities began partnering with large healthcare facilities, and the use of computers for medical record storage began to increase. However, the information that would be generated and electronically recorded could only be accessible in that specific healthcare location and facility,[9] which of course limited the usefulness of the software's integration in the medical space. Nevertheless, these were the initial steps to the integration of technology, and the interest in incorporating this technology continued to increase over time, so much so that by the end of that year, there were around 70 hospitals employing the use of electronic medical records (EMRs).

# HCIT Advancements in the Late 20th Century

It was in the 1970s that we would begin to see the shift towards the integration of information management systems as technology became more advanced. One of the first instances of an attempt to implement a comprehensive, integrated health records system occurred in 1971 in a gynecology department at the University Medical Center in Burlington, Vermont.[10] The system was patient-centered and took the POMR approach to gather patient information across different disciplines. This initiative did not gain immediate traction in the medical field, however, in large part owing to the hesitation in sharing information across different departments. However, this would largely begin to change in the 1980s as technology would further begin to advance, and it quickly became apparent that data interchange would become inevitable and necessary to the increasingly growing and complex industry. The year 1971 also saw the creation of Eclypsis, a computerized physician ordering system by Lockheed Corporation at El Camino Hospital.[11] This would be greatly influential for future models, as it enabled several users to access the system simultaneously. In addition, the University of Utah worked collaboratively with a company called 3M to develop one of the first clinical decision support systems called Health Evaluation through Logical Processing (HELP), while another system called the Computer Stored Ambulatory Record (COSTAR) was developed at Massachusetts General Hospital in collaboration with Harvard.[12]

As the advances became more widely accepted, this led to very specific developments that would further the movement toward digital integration. Desktop computers became available in the 1980s and improved significantly by this time. A major turning point was the creation of an international set of standards called Health Level Seven (HL7), founded in 1987 by Health Seven International, a non-profit organization that included members from more than 50 countries.[13] This arose out of a need to have a framework in place that would provide standards for the exchange of data and electronic health information. Around this time, diagnosis-related groups were created. DRGs were introduced by the government-run Medicare program in 1983 to halt the rise in healthcare costs. The result was the imposition of hierarchical management over previously independent service providers, which thereby increased hierarchical control over service providers in the private, market-based healthcare system.[14] This made the creation of HL7 essential, and it also further solidified the need to have systems in place that would enable the effective gathering of data necessary for reimbursement.

There were, however, challenges that delayed widespread adoption of EMRs. Namely, financial barriers limited the ability for hospitals to quickly adopt these new measures. This would continue until the early 1990s, when hardware started to become more affordable. In the meantime, further progress was being made in other areas. The 1980s would see the creation of the master patient index (MPI), which "identifies patients across separate clinical, financial, and administrative systems and is needed for information exchange to consolidate the patient list from the various RPMS databases."[15] Technology attributed to advancements across virtually all departments in the healthcare industry, and these advancements propelled the formation of health systems as integration of systems began playing a more prominent role.

In the 1990s, what billions of people now use today to interact with the internet, known as the World Wide Web (WWW) or simply the Web, was created. A British scientist by the name of Tim Berners-Lee had originally invented this with the goal of being able to share information among scientists and universities (he was employed at the European Organization for Nuclear Research, also known as CERN).[16] While this did not immediately affect the healthcare industry, over time (as we are well aware), this would impact the world in an unprecedented way. This would revolutionize the way in which information was shared and the ease of accessibility with which information would be distributed. In no other period before this were patients, as well as doctors and other relevant parties, able to communicate and cooperate as it related to matters of health records and other such health matters.

As this new information system began to proliferate and vast amounts of data exchange became the norm, it became necessary for new standards to be adopted relative to the security and confidentiality of patient information. In fact, over a period beginning in the mid-1980s, a non-profit organization known as the Institute of Medicine (IOM) began studying health records, including the benefits as well as the challenges of adopting EMRs.[17] On matters concerning health and medicine, IOM is a leading authority figure and has continued to provide a source of rigorous and trustworthy studies for a little over half a decade. In 1991, IOM published the *Computer-Based Patient Record: An Essential Technology for Health Care*, which documented 12 functions for the EMR and focused more on the patient than primarily on technology.[18] This was incredibly significant, as it would set the stage for the standards we now have for electronic health record (EHR) systems.

Nearly concurrently, another significant standard would soon be adopted, initiated by an organization known as the World Health Organization (WHO). Founded in 1948, WHO is a United Nations agency established with the mission of globally achieving efforts to promote health by connecting nations and partners in this endeavor.[19] Recognizing that there needed to exist a system of classification for diagnosing and documenting diseases in such a way that it would be comparable nationally, WHO developed such a system. This came to be known as the International Classification of Diseases, otherwise known as ICD. According to WHO, "Clinical terms coded with ICD are the main basis for health recording and statistics on diseases…these data and statistics support payment systems, service planning, administration of quality and safety, and health services research."[20] These codes are revised periodically in order to remain accurate and viable for the ever-changing field of healthcare.

Additionally, 1996 would prove to mark another turning point that continues to play a vital role in our health system today. In order to protect certain health information, "the U.S. Department of Health and Human Services (HHS) issued the Privacy Rule to implement the requirement of the Health Insurance Portability and Accountability Act of 1996 (HIPAA)."[21] HIPAA is a federal law enacted for the purpose of creating standards to protect and secure confidential patient information. As part of HIPAA, the National Committee on Vital and Health Statistics (NCVHS) was also developed. According to NCVHS, it "serves as the statutory [42 U.S.C. 242k(k)] public advisory body to HHS for health data, statistics, privacy, and national health information policy and HIPAA."[22] This committee would thus promote greater dependable and secure interconnectedness amongst health systems.

# HCIT Advancements in the 21st Century

At the turn of the century, the healthcare industry would see a predominant shift towards the integration of EHRs. This was further advocated by then-President George W. Bush in his 2004 State of the Union Address. In his speech, President Bush stated, "By computerizing health records, we can avoid dangerous medical mistakes, reduce costs, and improve care."[23] He outlined a 10-year plan for Americans to have EHRs, with the goal of addressing the longstanding challenges of preventable errors and rising costs in health care spending, with the initiative led by David Brailer, MD, PhD, as National Health Information Technology Coordinator. One of several key initiatives was a certification requirement that would set minimal standards of functionality, security, and interoperability that would enable physicians to make informed purchasing decisions.[24] The following year, two associations—the American Medical Informatics Association (AMIA) and the AHIMA—shifted their focus to preparing a workforce throughout this transition to digital healthcare. They hosted a work force summit meeting in 2005 and issued a report the following year entitled *Building the Work Force for Health Information Transformation*,[25] which later culminated in the development of a task force to define basic competencies for working with EHRs.

In 2009, President Barack Obama passed the American Recovery and Reinvestment Act (ARRA) and, as part of this act, signed the Health Information Technology for Economic and Clinical Health (HITECH) Act.[26] Through this, physicians and hospitals were incentivized to adopt EHRs by achieving "meaningful use" of the technology over the next few years. The three requirements specified were using "certified EHR technology in a meaningful manner, using the electronic exchange of health information to improve the quality of care, and using certified EHR technology to submit clinical quality measures (CQMs)."[27] ARRA also required the adoption of EHRs by 2014, which inevitably necessitated the quick migration toward digital health informatics. Coinciding with this was the growth and development of cloud computing services by major industries, including healthcare, which would further expand the efforts to increase the efficiency of electronic networks. By 2015, "96 percent of hospitals and 87 percent of physician practices were using electronic health records."[28] Therefore, in the span of only seven years, from ARRA's enactment to 2015, the use of EHRs had doubled. While progress was being made, there were still areas that needed to be improved, namely with respect to system interoperability and seamless sharing of information. While this was still in progress, five years later, COVID-19 began.

The COVID-19 pandemic would force robust changes to occur as they relate to the role of technology in healthcare. State-wide and local stay-at-home policies emerged during this time in an effort to contain the spread of the coronavirus as well as to alleviate the strain felt by hospitals that were being overwhelmed by COVID-19 patients. As a result, we would see a sharp rise in telehealth, remote monitoring of health, and other virtual service renderings. Hospital-at-home services increased in response to this public health emergency (PHE). CMS also issued waivers related to COVID-19 to enable these services for the first time in locations other than rural areas. Specifically, according to a report prepared by the Assistant Secretary of Planning and Evaluation (ASPE), pandemic telehealth flexibilities were made possible through the passage of the Coronavirus Aid, Relief, and Economic Security (CARES) Act, allowing telehealth to be delivered at the same payment level as in-person visits for the duration of the pandemic.[29] Prior to the pandemic, this would not have been possible. The report would also reveal evidence of disparities both by ethnicity as well as location. Additionally, it would report that the number of Medicare fee-for-service (FFS) beneficiary telehealth visits increased 63-fold in 2020, from approximately 840,000 in 2019 to nearly 52.7 million in 2020.[30] Needless to say, the pandemic has left a profound impact on the way technology is utilized in healthcare, and it is likely that some of the changes that occurred in response to COVID-19 may be here to stay.

## The Future of HCIT

With all this in consideration, there is still much progress to be made, but we have come a long way over the past century. Overall, historically we have seen significant progress in healthcare technology, with the widespread adoption of EHRs having led to better quality of care and a reduction in healthcare costs. As it stands, interoperability and data sharing are the areas that arguably require further attention. In addition, new and revolutionary technologies are emerging. AI, EHRs, and telehealth and virtual care services are only a few examples of such advances that will undoubtedly change the way technology further impacts the healthcare industry. Healthcare information management and process improvements will continue to play a critical role in the industry, and while the future is uncertain, it can be expected that technology in healthcare will continue to see breakthroughs and advancements in the years to come.

# Specific Impact of HCIT on Different Facets of the Healthcare Industry

With the above information as a brief backdrop to the major histori-cal advances and achievements of HCIT over the course of the past few decades, the following section will involve more specific considerations of the impact technology has on different facets of the health industry, includ-ing patient safety, access to care, and the cost of healthcare delivery, as a few notable examples. Technology has significantly transformed the ways in which medical services can be offered to patients, but it also presents challenges that impact such things as patient security and privacy, system interoperability, and other ethical considerations. The following impacts are documented below.

## Access to Care

The advent of technological integration into healthcare has enabled indi-viduals who typically do not have access to the appropriate resources to now be able to seek these resources and the information they require for their healthcare needs. Technology has helped to narrow the unavailability of adequate healthcare,[31] especially for individuals from lower socioeco-nomic statuses as well as those who reside in farther, more remote locations. According to an article published in Diversity & Equality in Health and Care, health professionals and workers rely on medical devices to provide effective preventive, diagnostic, therapeutic, and rehabilitative services,[32] and notably, EHRs have largely changed the way providers work with sen-sitive patient data. According to the Office of the National Coordinator for Health Information Technology (ONC), as of 2021, nearly four in five office-based physicians (78%) and nearly all non-federal acute care hos-pitals (96%) adopted a certified EHR.[33] A decade ago, this number was substantially lower, and it is expected that this upward trend will continue to rise. Along the point of access to care, EHRs enable patients to access their records more quickly, and for practices, they enable many processes to become automated, thereby increasing the efficiency of tasks and, in turn, the efficiency of care. Medical professionals are able to exchange informa-tion in real-time, and there is a reduced chance of medical errors in com-parison to paper records.

# Cost of Healthcare Delivery

One of the major challenges in the United States is the rising cost of healthcare. In 2021, U.S. healthcare spending reached \$4.3 trillion,[34] while healthcare spending was half as much in other countries. One of the reasons for this may result from the implementation of healthcare technology in hospitals. As the cost of healthcare technology is not in decline, so too is the cost of healthcare, which is not decreasing. For practices with limited resources, this is a significant issue. While the costs of complex medical devices such as MRI machines, CT scanners, and systems used for surgical procedures can easily bring healthcare expenditure into the millions, the cost of digital technologies such as EHRs will vary based upon the size of the healthcare facility, the type of EHR system implemented, and whether additional software features are included in the software package. According to a report prepared by Software Path, the average budget per user for EHR software is \$1,200.[35] This does not factor in other expenditures such as EHR training, data migration, and maintenance, nor does it factor in whether the EHR deployment method will be on-premise versus cloud based. More accurate and personalized information would need to be determined directly through the EHR vendor via a request for information (RFI) or a request for proposal (RFP) to inquire about the specific products and services offered. Some examples of major EHR vendors include the following:

- Allscripts
- athenahealth
- Cerner
- eClinicalWorks
- Epic
- Meditech
- ModMed
- NextGen
- NexTech

While there are significant benefits to EHR implementation, every organization must closely examine the budgeting allocations available for this initiative as well as determine whether the cost of EHR implementation is a justifiable investment. Typically, this is accomplished through a return on investment (ROI) calculation that considers both quantifiable (such things as revenue and provider productivity increases) and non-quantifiable (such things as patient as well as personnel satisfaction) benefits, but this in itself is not straightforward and can be challenging. Nevertheless, it is imperative to carefully calculate this as it is an incredibly significant project to undertake, and it will lead to far-reaching impacts within the organization, including improved documentation and automated processes, a reduction in medical errors, improved efficiency of systems management, and a reduction in costs relative to billing and service delivery.

## Patient Safety

According to a study published by the Saudi Medical Journal and accessed from the National Library of Medicine (NLM), health information technology improves patients' safety by reducing medication errors, reducing adverse drug reactions, and improving compliance with practice guidelines.[36] The Agency for Healthcare Research and Quality (AHRQ), an agency within the United States Department of HHS, also expressed a similar position, stating that technological advances have opened new possibilities for improving patient safety, with the potential to increase standardization and efficiency of workflows.[37] However, it must also be considered that while numerous benefits exist when integrating technology for the purposes of improving patient safety, there are also potential risks that arise from implementing these technologies, which include risks to data security and patient privacy. Additionally, the continuous development of new medical devices and surgical technologies, as well as the ever-increasing transformative potential of artificial intelligence applied in healthcare, are also areas that must closely be monitored to ensure that proper user training and integration of these technologies are accomplished. There would need to be more studies to explore and closely analyze the impact that emerging technologies are having on the healthcare industry, especially in terms of patient safety.

## Rural Healthcare

Rural healthcare settings have a significant potential to be positively impacted by healthcare technology in a number of ways. As a result of their more remote location, limited resources, and lower patient populations, rural hospitals frequently confront unique challenges. With the rise in available healthcare technologies over the past few decades, these can be implemented for the benefit of rural hospitals to address some of the challenges and improve the quality of care for patients. Some of the key issues experienced by rural hospitals include worker shortages, limited access to physician specialists and specialized services, financial constraints, transportation challenges, and, in most cases, a higher aging population. According to an article published by the Journal of Medical Internet Research, a strong majority of the available data leads to the conclusion that HIT positively supports medical outcomes, with at least one improved medical outcome identified in 81% of research studies that met the inclusion criteria of the systematic review.[38] That being said, one of the major challenges that act as a barrier towards certain HIT measures involves the limited access to broadband that can hinder the implementation of healthcare technologies such as EHRs and telemedicine, as well as financial limitations that would impede a hospital's ability to invest adequately in technological measures that would improve the existing technology infrastructure. Therefore, rural healthcare facilities must plan to address these challenges by establishing strategic partnerships, developing innovative solutions, and obtaining government support to ensure quality healthcare services can be provided to their community.

Additionally, there are valuable HIT resources specific to the needs of rural healthcare facilities that are worthy of note, including the National Rural Health Resource Center (NRHRC) which features a wide range of resources trusted by industry leaders; the National Rural Health Association (NRHA), which provides a section dedicated to health information technology resources; and the Office of the National Coordinator for Health Information Technology (ONC), the principal entity for the entire HIT initiative nationwide. Another resource that consolidates specific information as it relates to healthcare technology in rural healthcare is the Rural Health Information Hub (RHIhub), which is supported by the Health Resources and Services Administration (HRSA) of the U.S. Department of HHS. Ultimately, the state of healthcare information technology in rural healthcare settings continues to evolve, especially with such developments as telehealth advancements, EHR implementations, and integrated health information exchange networks. Improvement in the technological resources utilized by rural systems is critical to both equitable care and increased accessibility to health services by the community.

# Telehealth and Telemedicine

Telehealth enables healthcare professionals to remotely deliver clinical and non-clinical services via healthcare communication technology. These technologies include videoconferencing, the internet, store-and-forward imaging, streaming media, and terrestrial and wireless communications.[39] The COVID-19 pandemic accelerated the adoption and acceptance of telehealth services, supporting long-distance communication and the provision of services during a precarious period that also presented serious ethical concerns as it relates to the disclosure of protected health information (PHI). In response to the PHE presented by COVID-19, certain HIPAA rules were temporarily relaxed to facilitate the rapid implementation of telehealth services. For example, the Office of Civil Rights (OCR) at the Department of HHS issued the Notification of Enforcement Discretion during this nationwide PHE, exercising its enforcement discretion to not impose penalties for noncompliance with the HIPAA Rules in connection with the good faith provision of telehealth using such non-public-facing audio or video communication products.[40] This technology was critical during this time, and many of these telehealth services are likely to continue shaping the future of healthcare.

While telehealth and telemedicine are sometimes referred to interchangeably, there is a difference between the two. In contrast to telehealth, telemedicine refers strictly to remote clinical services. While telehealth may encompass training, administrative meetings, and other non-clinical services, telemedicine solely focuses on health communications, which can, for example, include helping a remote practitioner present a patient to a specialist for consultation.[41] Nonetheless, both have been instrumental in enabling healthcare professionals to continue to support their patients and provide the continuation of services even in a remote capacity. The continued development and integration of telehealth and telemedicine with traditional healthcare systems will likely shape the future of medicine and improve health outcomes for patients worldwide.

# Clinical Decision Support

According to the ONC, clinical decision support (CDS) provides clinicians, staff, and patients with knowledge and specific information that is intelligently filtered or presented at appropriate times with the purpose of enhancing health and health care.[42] Clinical decision support systems (CDSS) are therefore a significant component of healthcare information technology as they encompass the tools or software to support clinical-making decisions. CDSSs today are primarily used at the point-of-care for the clinician to combine their knowledge with information or suggestions provided by the CDSS.[43] Examples of such tools include generated alerts (including prescription drug interaction alerts) and reminders to help prevent medical errors, clinical guidelines, and protocols that aid physicians in following best practices for specific medical conditions or procedures, the creation of document templates to facilitate the clinical process, and the development of tools that support the clinical workflow.

# Artificial Intelligence and Integration into Healthcare

Artificial intelligence (AI) leverages computers and machines to mimic the problem-solving and decision-making capabilities of the human mind.[44] It is becoming increasingly prevalent in business, and no less so than in healthcare. Most notably, key categories of applications for AI involve diagnosis and treatment recommendations, patient engagement and adherence, and administrative activities.[45] Some specific areas wherein AI and healthcare information technology intersect include areas such as AI algorithms for medical imaging and diagnostics, predictive analytics, personalized medicine, and virtual health assistance, in addition to their use for extracting relevant information to be used in EHRs. While there is much promise in incorporating AI into the industry, there are challenges and issues that must be addressed in order to ensure AI is deployed ethically and responsibly. Challenges that need to be addressed include data privacy concerns, regulation of AI algorithms, and other issues relating to accountability and transparency. AI must be integrated in such a way that it maintains a focus on enhancing patient care and improving healthcare outcomes.

# Overview of the Benefits of a Career in HCIT

This section will focus more on the benefits of pursuing a career in HCIT. Please note that for the purposes of this book, we will consider both healthcare information technology and health technology and systems under the same umbrella, though they may be viewed under a separate lens according to a subtle distinction in their focus.[46] We do so in order to cover a broader spectrum of roles available to women in HCIT and to present as many job prospects as possible throughout the course of this book. Some of the women featured in this book will remark that they themselves did not consider a career in HCIT, to begin with, and that it was instead a special set of circumstances in their lives that led them to where they are today. Many remark that they wish they were aware of the existing opportunities in HCIT sooner, as this industry is not something that is commonly considered when women are deciding on a career. Women will often think of careers in healthcare that typically include the roles of a registered nurse, nurse practitioner, physical therapist, doctor, etc., but they do not consider prospective IT roles that are also very much in demand in the healthcare industry. Typically, when one thinks of IT, some roles that come to mind may include ones such as software developer, data scientist, network administrator, and computer technician, to name a few, but there are other types of IT roles that a woman can take on if these do not align with their preferences. Women should take advantage of the opportunities available, and there is no limit as to who is able to consider this career. Whether it is a woman who is just beginning her career or a woman who wishes to change her current career and is interested in HCIT, it is never too late to join this industry. Some of the advantages of pursuing a career in HCIT include the following:

# Projected Job Growth: Faster than Other Occupations

In comparison to other career growth outlooks, jobs in the HCIT space are growing faster than others, which provides an additional sense of security for women who seek not only well-paying opportunities but a secure career that will likely withstand difficult periods in the employment landscape, with the most recent COVID-19 being an example of this type of impact. In fact, the pandemic led to a surge in the need for developing remote solutions for providing patient care and other healthcare services in order to reduce the risks of transmitting infection, which led to an increase in the digital shift in healthcare. Telemedicine and other digital technologies enabled physicians to connect with patients and, as a whole, technologies enabled businesses across diverse sectors to remain connected during this turbulent period. As HCIT will continue to play a central role in healthcare, women can be confident that this is an industry that will provide job stability and ample opportunities for employment, whereas other industries may not be fairing as well in the market and are in fact being negatively disrupted by the rise in technology, with some jobs being at risk of being replaced by machines and other online technology.

According to the U.S. Bureau of Labor Statistics, employment for individuals in health information technology is projected to grow by 16% from 2022 to 2032, which is well above the average growth rate of 5%–8% in other career sectors.[47] For that reason, women should take advantage of the prospective job stability to be expected in this prospective career path. There is a rising need for qualified workers in this industry as EHRs, telemedicine, health informatics, and other digital technologies become more widely used. As it currently stands, HCIT continues to be a male-dominated industry, but there is a plethora of opportunities available that women may find are in line with some of their career expectations and desires, which they simply have not been made aware of. Therefore, women can take advantage of entering a thriving industry with ample career prospects and contribute to shaping the future of healthcare technology and improving patient outcomes.

# Healthcare IT Professionals Make a Higher Average Salary

Typically, professionals in HCIT earn a greater salary on average than in other occupations. While salaries in HCIT will vary as a result of the various roles that exist and additional factors such as location, education, years of experience, etc., the medium annual wage for health information technologists and medical registrars is $55,560, with the highest 10% earning over $98,490.[48] Additionally, considering information technology professionals as a whole, the average salary in the information technology industry is $97,430.[49] A further snapshot of varied salary ranges, according to the information from the U.S. Bureau of Labor Statistics, includes the following:

### National Average Salaries by Occupation

- Medical Records Specialist: $46,660
- Health Information Technologists and Medical Registrars: $55,560
- Computer Support Specialist: $57,910
- Compliance Officer: $76,980
- Systems Analyst: $99,270

- Medical and Health Services Manager: $101,340
- Information Security Analyst: $102,600
- Computer and Information Systems Manager: $159,010

In other words, when compared to other industries, a woman is more likely to make a more profitable salary and therefore have a stronger return on investment, which increases the likelihood of living a comfortable lifestyle, even on a single-person income. Especially for women who are uncertain of what they would like to pursue, financial factors are critical in making a career determination. Given more research on a specific job opportunity under consideration, there is much to be said about the advantages for women who venture into this field.

## Diverse Roles to Choose from

Women can choose from a variety of career routes and areas of specialization within HCIT, such as designing and implementing software solutions, overseeing health information systems, maintaining data security and privacy, and using technology for research and analysis. The variety of roles means that women have many choices and can find positions that align with their skillsets, interests, and career aspirations. Women are therefore able to explore diverse paths in HCIT that most closely suit their strengths and preferences. This book will provide a general overview of these prospective roles in Chapter 4.

## Varied Educational Backgrounds for Success

When pursuing any career, there are generally rigid educational requirements that need to be considered. Some careers will require a minimum of a bachelor's degree, while others require a master's degree or other specific criteria. When it comes to careers in HCIT, one of the advantages is that the educational background requirements tend to be more fluid. While a bachelor's degree is a typical requirement, some job opportunities will accept alternative educational backgrounds, including an associate degree with a specific certification that is relevant to the job or other existing educational programs that will provide the candidate with certain skill sets desired by the employer. Some of the certifications that should be considered in HCIT include the following (these certifications will be reviewed in greater detail in Chapter 3):

- Certified Health Data Analyst
- Certified Outpatient Coder
- Certified Professional Coder
- Certified Professional in Electronic Health Records
- Certified Professional in Healthcare Information and Management Systems
- Epic Certification
- HealthCare Information Security and Privacy Practitioner
- Healthcare Technology Specialist Certificate
- Project Management Certification
- Registered Health Information Administrator
- Registered Health Information Technician

Networking is also crucial and can open doors for opportunities that otherwise may be unavailable (further information on networking is reviewed in Chapters 2 and 6). However, it is always advantageous to align your professional background as closely as possible to the job specifications when possible.

# HCIT is in High Demand

A career in HCIT will almost always guarantee a constant stream of workflow. Part of the reason for this demand results from government regulation mandates, which require certain compliance measures to be followed by healthcare organizations. Some of the regulations that have resulted in the healthcare industry's rapid transition to EHR systems include the following:

- **ARRA**: The American Recovery and Reinvestment Act was signed into law during the Obama administration in 2009. This law included the HITECH Act, which was intended to quicken the pace at which the EHRs were adopted. This was accomplished through a program under Medicare and Medicaid called "meaningful use," incentivizing payments for those organizations that met the requirements of the program.
- **Medicare Access and CHIP Reauthorization Act (MACRA)**: MACRA established the quality payment program (QPP), rewarding

high-value, high-quality Medicare clinicians with payment increases via either the alternative payment model (APM) or the merit-based incentive payment system (MIPS).[50] To qualify for the APM track, certain criteria must be met and involve added risks during patient treatment, while MIPS is performance-based and involves four components. MACRA integrated meaningful use into the four components, thereby consolidating multiple programs, into one.[51]

- *HIPAA*: HIPAA is a federal law passed in 1996 that mandates the development of national standards to prevent the disclosure of sensitive patient health information without the patient's knowledge or consent.[52] In order to, implement this, the US Department of HHS issued the HIPAA Privacy Rule, which establishes national standards that address the way in which protected health information (PHI) should be used and disclosed relative to the covered entities, in addition to ensuring that individuals know their rights when desiring access to health information.[53] In addition to the HIPAA Privacy Rule, there is also the HIPAA Security Rule, a subset of the first more specifically focused on protecting an individual's electronic protected health information (e-PHI).

To maintain compliance, information professionals such as medical coders and compliance officers will be needed to ensure these regulations are adhered to and to ensure data privacy and security across the organization. The services rendered by the women who choose to pursue a career in this profession will be essential to the success and security of the organization.

Additionally, the healthcare industry has been undergoing a significant transition into technological integration, which therefore leads to a greater degree of focus on improving EHR systems and their methods of implementation. A shift towards digital integration also signifies an exponential increase in data management requirements as vast amounts of patient, research, and operational data are generated, which necessitates an HCIT professional that can design, implement, and manage these systems. This requires very specific skill sets that are in high demand, and it is here where women can take advantage of an opportunity that will make their skills in the industry truly sought after and will then allow them to leverage these skills in the form of higher pay and improved benefits.

As mentioned before, COVID-19 accelerated the transformation to technological services provided by HCIT professionals, including telehealth and remote care technology. Post-pandemic reconstruction has been characterized by a growing acceptance of the latest technologies—digital platforms, cloud computing, mobile apps—and other communication tools as central to the organizational architecture.[54] There will need to be individuals that can keep up with the updates to these technologies, which provides an additional prospect for women to consider when pursuing a career in HCIT.

## Flexible Work Environment

Often, women may feel pressured or limited in the options available to them as it relates to the job location and environment. Some of the pressures may have to do with having a family and wanting to work while still being able to spend time with the children. Other women may struggle with the long and frustrating commutes that do not match the efforts they are exerting for their current jobs. When considering a career in HCIT, there are a greater number of options available as it relates to job location. Many professionals who work in HCIT do so remotely or in a hybrid capacity of working remotely some days and working in the office other days. If the work location is in a physical setting, this is often a hospital (be it state, local, or private) or other settings such as healthcare consulting firms, management enterprises, insurance companies, other healthcare agencies, and more. This flexibility is an incredibly important factor in a woman deciding what best suits her needs, and it can be especially beneficial for women who struggle to balance their professional and personal responsibilities. Knowing that there will be several options for work environments available removes a lot of the typical stress involved in job hunting as it relates to flexibility.

## Meaningful Impact

Oftentimes, individuals in general desire to pursue careers that make a meaningful impact on society. It provides a sense of fulfillment and leads an individual to value their roles and responsibilities, leading to greater job satisfaction and, more often than not, a higher level of productivity in the workplace. This is especially the case in the healthcare industry, as women who work in this field will make a significant contribution that will benefit the lives of people, though this contribution can be performed in a variety of different ways. Women who join the HCIT field will be able to partake in the act of improving the technology and processes currently in place, which will lead to a long-lasting and far-reaching impact in the future. According to an article published by *PLOS ONE*, the psychological meaningfulness of work represents the cognitive valuation of work as significant and meaningful by an employee.[55] Though what constitutes meaningful work will vary from individual to individual, most women are likely to find fulfillment in work that involves helping others. Women in general are more likely to thrive in an environment that fosters responsibility towards the patient due to the emotional and social connectiveness they exhibit towards those they care for,[56] and this will be reflected in their choice of occupation as well as their level of job satisfaction.

# Representation

It is well known that women are largely underrepresented in HCIT. While it is known that gender diversity has been linked to positive business results, limited data exists to define the gender landscape in healthcare technology, which typically draws professionals with a background in biomedical engineering and medicine.[57] Further studies are needed to determine accurate statistics as it relates to gender disparity in healthcare technology, but from the perspective of the field of technology as a whole, women make up barely 25% of workers in the technology sector and 11% in leadership positions,[58] according to research from the National Center for Women & Information Technology. In contrast, women make up over 77% of workers in healthcare, according to the U.S. Bureau of Labor Statistics.[59] If more women were interested in a career that included both attributes (healthcare and technology), it would help reduce the current disparity in representation in the HCIT field, and it would allow for an increase in perspective as it relates to healthcare innovation, patient needs and preferences, and a different perspective on the user experience of technology. Additionally, it would allow women to have a greater number of female mentors around them. The absence of female presence in positions of leadership may be detrimental to keeping women in the healthcare IT workforce,[60] which is another crucial matter that should be considered. By becoming a part of this field, women will be able to help bridge the existing gap in representation and contribute towards a future with a more diverse and inclusive workforce.

On another level, representation is important in order to address prospective biases and discrimination in the current HCIT workforce. Some of these may stem from implicit bias, with gender bias being one such example.

Though unintentional, organizations may tend to lean towards a particular candidate based on their gender, and this is reflected in the makeup of the workforce. According to the most recent data from the Gender Social Norms Index (GSNI) from the United Nations, nine out of ten men and women hold fundamental biases against women, based on an index covering 85% of the global population.[61] Biases is also, therefore, a global issue, and it becomes important to identify and address this, particularly within the context of healthcare systems and technologies. By having diverse perspectives involved in decision-making processes, there is a greater chance of recognizing and rectifying biases that impact women, which is why representation is critical in the industry.

## Overview of the Disadvantages of HCIT

To make a more informed decision, some of the disadvantages and challenges a woman should consider when deciding upon a career in HCIT include the following:

## Stressful Deadlines

It is not uncommon for jobs to require employees to meet specific deadlines, but this is especially the case in HCIT. Oftentimes, HCIT projects encompass an extensive range of initiatives at different stages of an initiative, and this is especially true for EHR or other system implementation projects that may necessitate on-call duties in order to support healthcare operations at all hours. This type of demanding and fast-paced work may result in a woman experiencing high levels of stress and difficulty maintaining work-life balance, so it becomes important for women to establish boundaries as it relates to work responsibilities in order to maintain a healthy balance and to prioritize their own needs and self-care processes.

## Continuous Education Needed

HCIT is a field characterized by rapid technological advancements, and while this is essential in order to continue to improve upon the existing systems and processes in place, it presents a challenge to staying up-to-date with the latest technologies and trends in the healthcare industry. An individual in this field may find it tiring and demanding to constantly stay current in the knowledge of the latest technologies available, and this will oftentimes require continuous education and undergoing new training that, again, may be challenging for some.

## Resistance to Change by Healthcare Professionals and/or Stakeholders

There can be trepidation as it relates to implementing new technology and processes in a healthcare setting, especially when healthcare professionals are accustomed to their existing processes. There can also be interoperability issues that exist that can hinder transitional processes. Addressing interoperability challenges requires collaboration and coordination across the organization and vendors involved. Properly communicating the advantages of the change can be a significant challenge, so HCIT professionals will need to exhibit strong interpersonal skills to gain support from stakeholders if the initiative is to move forward.

## Data Privacy and Security Concerns

As can be expected, a professional in HCIT will be working with sensitive patient data, making data privacy and security critical concerns. Therefore, it is essential to ensure that the technologies and systems being implemented in the healthcare setting are designed with robust security measures to protect patient information. There has been an increase in both the frequency and sophistication of cybersecurity threats, which adds to the complexity and importance of safeguarding data. Women who wish to join this field must be aware of this and be prepared to place patient safety and security as a priority in their day-to-day responsibilities.

Despite some of the existing challenges noted above, many may find that the rewards of working in a field that has a positive impact on patient care and that incorporates technology into the job outweigh these disadvantages. Each work environment will be unique, and there are a variety of duties and responsibilities that encompass different roles that exist in HCIT. Given the desire to work in this field while exhibiting the right skills, mindset, and commitment to continuous learning, women who wish to pursue a career in HCIT can overcome these challenges and thrive in their careers.

# Gender Gap Realities

Women face gender gaps within all industries of the workforce. In an article published in 2021 titled "7 Challenges Women Face in Getting Ahead in IT," the author depicts many real-world struggles that women continue to face despite many advances within the work world. Being in the HCIT field creates its own subset of issues that women need to recognize and develop a plan for overcoming. For instance, the article touches on the belief that females tend to be more concerned about being liked than their male counterparts. This can lead to an inability to lead, not being assertive, and therefore likely not being promoted.[62] In fact, this was also touched on by Sheryl Sandberg in *Lean In: Women, Work and the Will to Lead*, stating that "aggressive and hard-charging women violate unwritten rules about acceptable social conduct. Men are continually applauded for being ambitious, powerful, and successful, but women who display these same traits often pay a social penalty. Female accomplishments come at a cost."[63]

Sandberg goes on to expand on certain stereotypes and expectations when it comes to women in the workplace. For example, that women are generally more agreeable, less likely to speak up or negotiate, and like to avoid conflict. She goes on to further explain that often times, when females are recognized for their hard work and accomplishments, they downplay it and do not take full ownership of their success, attributing their successes to the efforts of their team members. Contrastingly, most males willingly take responsibility for their accomplishments and will often times exaggerate their successes.

In a CIO article published in 2023, the author touches on the startling facts of the lack of representation of women in the tech industry. "Only one in four startups have a female founder, 37% have at least one woman on the board of directors, and 53% have at least one woman in an executive position."[64] It goes on to explain that the idea of "bro culture" in technology exists today and often creates an environment that has led to many choosing to leave the industry all together due to the concern of peer pressure and assault. In fact, half of the women in technology exit the industry all together, compared to other industry norms of 20%, according to a report by Accenture.[65]

# How to Recognize If HCIT Is Right for Me

Now that we have covered some of the advantages and disadvantages of pursuing a career in HCIT, it is vital to consider whether this is the right career for you. Although it can be tempting to go headfirst into a career or new job opportunity, the best choices begin with careful planning. Self-assessment is therefore an integral step towards determining whether HCIT is the most suitable career choice for you. Begin by analyzing your interests as well as what you perceive to be your strengths and unique skills. Consider whether you enjoy working with technology and data, have an interest in healthcare and patient care, and possess strong problem-solving abilities. A helpful way to commence a more refined level of introspection can be done by following the flower exercise developed by Richard Nelson Bolles, which targets seven different angles that together present a well-rounded reflection of where your interests and compatibility lie.[66] Consider the following questions as you examine your motivations and interests:

- How much money do I want or need to make?
- What are my current strengths? What are my weaknesses?
- What knowledge do I have so far?
- What are my preferred working conditions?
- Where do I want to work?
- What purpose do I want to serve?
- Who do I want to work with?

In addition to asking yourself the above questions, the following are recommended self-assessment tools to help guide your insight and help identify the things that are most valuable to you as they relate to your career options:

- **Myers-Briggs Type Indicator (MBTI)**: The MBTI questionnaire provides a personality-type report that describes your preferred methods of interacting. It is a useful tool for providing insight on the way your personality type can impact your decision-making and communication with others. A website to take this test for free is 16 Personalities: https://www.16personalities.com/free-personality-test.
- **DiSC**: While not a free assessment tool, DiSC is used to help improve communication, productivity, and teamwork in the workplace. Some companies may utilize this personal assessment tool to make data-driven hiring decisions. The DiSC model stands for dominance, influence, steadiness, and conscientiousness.
- **CareerExplorer**: CareerExplorer is a free assessment tool that strives to match satisfying careers based on your interests, personality types, abilities, career values, and preferred work environments. It takes

approximately 30 minutes to complete, but the investment of time is worth it, especially if you are not sure of the options available to you.

- *CareerOneStop Values Matcher and CareerOneStop Skills Matcher*: Sponsored by the U.S. Department of Labor, Employment and Training Administration, CareerOneStop offers two separate assessment tools that can aid in determining the best careers that match your personal values as well as your skill sets. This is useful no matter what point in your career you are starting from.
- *Keirsey Temperament Sorter*: The Keirsey Temperament Sorter assessment helps you discover what type of temperament you have. It takes approximately 20 minutes to complete and provides a free profile description, although there is a cost if you desire to purchase the full report.

Remember, there is no self-assessment tool that can make the decision for you, but the tools enable you to better understand yourself and the potential career matches that best suit your preferences and strengths. Additionally, and especially if you are currently a student with access to career counseling resources, make sure to take advantage of this. Professional assistance through career counseling can better enable you to explore options, plan your career outlook, and achieve your present goals as they relate to employment opportunities. For more experienced professionals, make the best judgment as to whether pivoting into this career path is advantageous for you based on the above information as well as your understanding of what will provide you with the greatest satisfaction. Ultimately, while a career in HCIT is one filled with numerous opportunities, you need to ensure that it is right for you and that it brings fulfillment in your life above all else.

# Conclusion

The integration of technology into services rendered in healthcare has sought to improve the quality of care given to patients and support health outcomes, and there have been several historical milestones as it relates to the evolution and development of HCIT, spanning decades of progression. From the birth of health informatics, which involved the earliest computers and initiatives to standardize healthcare, to the creation of EHRs and other technological advancements, these developments are only a few examples of notable breakthroughs made in healthcare information technology. In pursuing a career in HCIT, women have the opportunity to enter a thriving industry with ample career prospects. It is never too early nor too late for women to consider this career path, and there are numerous advantages to doing so. Above all else, a career in HCIT is not just about technology but also improving the quality of care provided to patients and supporting evidence-based medicine to support best practices in healthcare. By pursuing a career in HCIT, women will be at the forefront of change in one of the most important and dynamic industries in the world, and they will contribute to the advances in technology that will have a positive impact on the future of the medical field.

# Notes

1  The Office of the National Coordinator for Health Information Technology. (2017). *Glossary*. HealthIT. https://www.healthit.gov/topic/ health-it-and-health-information-exchange-basics/glossary#:~:text=Health% 20Information%20Technology%20(HIT)%20%E2%80%93,for%20 communication%20and%20decision%20making
2  U.S. Department of Health & Human Services. (2022, December 2023). *Health information technology*. HHS. https://www.hhs.gov/hipaa/ for-professionals/special-topics/health-information-technology/index. html#:~:text=Health%20information%20technology%20(health%20 IT,information%20in%20an%20electronic%20environment
3  U.S. Centers for Medicare & Medicaid Services. (2023). *NHE fact sheet*. CMS. https://www.cms.gov/Research-Statistics-Data-and-Systems/ Statistics-Trends-and-Reports/NationalHealthExpendData/NHE-Fact-Sheet#:~:text=Federal%20government%20spending%20for%20 health,the%206.3%25%20growth%20in%202019
4  American College of Surgeons. (n.d.). *A history of high standards*. ACS. https:// www.facs.org/about-acs/acs-history/
5  OpenText. (2017). *The history of health information management – from then to now*. OpenText. https://blogs.opentext.com/history-heath-information-management-now/
6  Jacobson, D. (2019). *What was the first computer?* The Conversation. https:// theconversation.com/what-was-the-first-computer-122164
7  Zippia. (n.d.). *American health information history*. Zippia. https://www.zippia. com/ahima-careers-340750/history/
8  Grimes, W. (2017, June 21). *Dr. Lawrence Weed, pioneer in recording patient data, dies at 93*. The New York Times. https://www.nytimes.com/2017/06/21/ science/obituary-lawrence-weed-dead-patient-information.html
9  Brooks, A. (2015). *Health information management history: Present, past & future*. Rasmussen University. https://www.rasmussen.edu/degrees/health-sciences/blog/health-information-management-history/#:~:text=The%20 health%20information%20industry%20has,electronic%20health%20 records%20(EHR)

10  Ibid.
11  BaytechIT. (n.d.). *The history of healthcare technology and the evolution of EHR.* BaytechIT. https://www.baytechit.com/history-healthcare-technology/
12  Atherton, J. (2011). Development of the electronic health record. *AMA Journal of Ethics, 13*(3), 186–189. https://journalofethics.ama-assn.org/article/development-electronic-health-record/2011-03
13  Sutner, S. (2017). *HL7 (Health level seven international).* TechTarget. https://www.techtarget.com/searchhealthit/definition/Health-Level-7-International-HL7#:~:text=A%20nonprofit%20organization%20with%20members,National%20Standards%20Institute%20in%201994
14  Cacace, M., & Schmid, A. (2009). The role of diagnosis related groups (DRGs) in healthcare system convergence. *BMC Health Services Research, 9*(Suppl 1), A5. https://doi.org/10.1186/1472-6963-9-S1-A5
15  Indian Health Service. (n.d.). *Master patient index (MPI).* Indian Health Service. https://www.ihs.gov/hie/masterpatientindex/
16  CERN. (n.d.). *The birth of the web.* CERN. https://www.home.cern/science/computing/birth-web#:~:text=Tim%20Berners%2DLee%2C%20a%20British,and%20institutes%20around%20the%20world
17  Ibid.
18  Ambinder, E. P. (2005). A history of the shift toward full computerization of medicine. *Journal of Oncology Practice, 1*(2), 54–56. https://doi.org/10.1200/JOP.2005.1.2.54
19  World Health Organization. (n.d.). *About us.* World Health Organization. https://www.who.int/about
20  Ibid.
21  U.S. Department of Health & Human Services. (n.d.). *Summary of the HIPAA privacy rule.* HHS. https://www.hhs.gov/hipaa/for-professionals/privacy/laws-regulations/index.html#:~:text=The%20Health%20Insurance%20Portability%20and%20Accountability%20Act%20of%201996%20(HIPAA,enacted%20on%20August%2021%2C%201996
22  National Committee on Vital and Health Statistics. (n.d.). *About NCVHS.* NCVHS. https://ncvhs.hhs.gov/
23  C-SPAN. (2004). *2004 State of the Union Address.* C-SPAN. https://www.c-span.org/video/?179813-1/2004-state-union-address
24  Ibid.
25  AHIMA, AMIA. (2008). *Joint work force task force: Health information management and informatics core competencies for individuals working with electronic health records.* AHIMA, AMIA. https://bok.ahima.org/PdfView?oid=104073
26  U.S. Department of Health & Human Services. (n.d.). *HITECH Act enforcement interim final rule.* HHS. https://www.hhs.gov/hipaa/for-professionals/special-topics/hitech-act-enforcement-interim-final-rule/index.html
27  Henricks, W. H. (2011). "Meaningful use" of electronic health records and its relevance to laboratories and pathologists. *Journal of Pathology Informatics, 2,* 7. https://doi.org/10.4103/2153-3539.76733
28  Ibid.
29  Samson, L. W., Tarazi, W., Turrini, G., & Sheingold, S. (2021). *Medicare benificiaries' use of telehealth in 2020: Trends by beneficiary characteristics and location.* ASPE. https://aspe.hhs.gov/sites/default/files/documents/a1d5d810fe3433e18b192be42dbf2351/medicare-telehealth-report.pdf

30  Ibid.
31  ChronWell. (2023). *How technology is widening patient access to healthcare.* ChronWell. https://www.chronwell.com/how-technology-is-widening-patient-access-to-healthcare/
32  Abbam, G. (2014). What role does technology play in improving access to healthcare? *Diversity & Equality in Health and Care,* 11(3), 173–175. https://doi.org/10.21767/2049-5471.1000e4
33  Office of the National Coordinator for Health Information Technology. (n.d.). *National trends in hospital and physician adoption of electronic health records.* Health IT. https://www.healthit.gov/data/quickstats/national-trends-hospital-and-physician-adop-tion-electronic-health-records#:~:text=As%20of%202021%2C%20nearly%20 4,physicians%20had%20adopted%20an%20EHR.&text=Measures%20of%20 EHR%20adoption%20differ%20over%20time
34  Peter G. Foundation. (2023). *Why are Americans paying more for health-care?* Peter G. Foundation. https://www.pgpf.org/blog/2023/07/why-are-americans-paying-more-for-healthcare
35  Software Path. (2022). *What practices look for when selecting EHR (2022 EHR report).* Software Path. https://softwarepath.com/guides/ehr-report
36  Alotaibi, Y. K., & Federico, F. (2017). The impact of health information tech-nology on patient safety. *Saudi Medical Journal,* 38(12), 1173–1180. https://doi.org/10.15537/smj.2017.12.20631
37  Gale, B., Mossburg, S., Holmgren, A. J., & McBride, S. (2023). *Technology as a tool for improving patient safety.* PSNet. https://psnet.ahrq.gov/perspective/technology-tool-improving-patient-safety
38  Kruse, C. S., & Beane, A. (2018). Health information technology continues to show positive effect on medical outcomes: Systematic review. *Journal of Medical Internet Research,* 20(2), e41. https://doi.org/10.2196/jmir.8793
39  Office of the National Coordinator for Health Information Technology. (2023). *Telemedicine and telehealth.* HealthIT.gov. https://www.healthit.gov/topic/health-it-health-care-settings/public-health/telemedicine-and-telehealth
40  U.S. Department of Health and Human Resources. (2021). *Notification of enforcement discretion for telehealth remote communications during the COVID-19 nationwide public health emergency.* HHS. https://www.hhs.gov/hipaa/for-professionals/special-topics/emergency-preparedness/notifica-tion-enforcement-discretion-telehealth/index.html
41  Office of the National Coordinator for Health Information Technology. (2020). *The ONC health IT playbook.* HealthIT.gov. https://www.healthit.gov/playbook/patient-engagement/#Telehealth
42  Office of the National Coordinator for Health Information Technology. (2023). *Clinical decision support.* HealthIT.gov. https://www.healthit.gov/topic/safety/clinical-decision-support
43  Sutton, R. T., Pincock, D., Baumgart, D. C. et al. (2020). An overview of clinical decision support systems: Benefits, risks, and strategies for success. *NPJ Digital Medicine,* 3(17), 1–17. https://doi.org/10.1038/s41746-020-0221-y
44  IBM. (n.d.). *What is artificial intelligence.* IBM. https://www.ibm.com/topics/artificial-intelligence
45  Davenport, T., & Kalakota, R. (2019). The potential for artificial intelligence in healthcare. *Future Healthcare Journal,* 6(2), 94–98. https://doi.org/10.7861/futurehosp.6-2-94

46 Tressler, K. (2017). *Healthcare information technology: Career and job growth.* UMA Ultimate Medical Academy. https://www.ultimatemedical.edu/blog/intro-to-hit-hts/

47 U.S. Bureau of Labor Statistics. (2023). *Occupational outlook handbook.* U.S. Bureau of Labor Statistics. https://www.bls.gov/ooh/healthcare/health-information-technologists-and-medical-registrars.htm#tab-5

48 Ibid.

49 U.S. Bureau of Labor Statistics. (2022). *Occupational outlook handbook.* U.S. Bureau of Labor Statistics. https://www.bls.gov/ooh/computer-and-information-technology/home.htm

50 The Office of the National Coordinator for Health Information Technology. (2023). *Health IT legislation.* HealthIT. https://www.healthit.gov/topic/laws-regulation-and-policy/health-it-legislation

51 Ibid.

52 U.S. Department of Health & Human Services. (2022). *Health insurance portability and accountability act of 1996 (HIPAA).* CDC. https://www.cdc.gov/phlp/publications/topic/hipaa.html#:~:text=The%20Health%20Insurance%20Portability%20and,the%20patient's%20consent%20or%20knowledge

53 Ibid.

54 Amankwah-Amoah, J., Khan, Z., Wood, G., & Knight, G. (2021). COVID-19 and digitalization: The great acceleration. *Journal of Business Research*, 136, 602–611. https://doi.org/10.1016/j.jbusres.2021.08.011

55 Van Wingerden, J., & Van der Stoep, J. (2018). The motivational potential of meaningful work: Relationships with strengths use, work engagement, and performance. *PloS One*, 13(6), e0197599. https://doi.org/10.1371/journal.pone.0197599

56 Sharma, N., Chakrabarti, S., & Grover, S. (2016). Gender differences in caregiving among family - caregivers of people with mental illnesses. *World Journal of Psychiatry*, 6(1), 7–17. https://doi.org/10.5498/wjp.v6.i1.7

57 Denend, L., McCutcheon, S., Regan, M., Sainz, M., Yock, P., & Azagury, D. (2020). Analysis of gender perceptions in health technology: A call to action. *Annals of Biomedical Engineering*, 48(5), 1573–1586. https://doi.org/10.1007/s10439-020-02478-0

58 TechFunnel. (2023). *International women's day: The latest women in tech statistics to know in 2023.* TechFunnel. https://www.techfunnel.com/information-technology/women-in-tech/#:~:text=The%20proportion%20of%20funding%20raised,workers%20in%20the%20technology%20sector

59 U.S. Bureau of Labor Statistics. (2022). *Over 16 million women worked in healthcare and social assistance in 2021.* U.S. Bureau of Labor Statistics. https://www.bls.gov/opub/ted/2022/over-16-million-women-worked-in-health-care-and-social-assistance-in-2021.htm

60 Ibid.

61 United Nations Development Programme. (2023, June 12). *2023 Gender Social Norms Index (GSNI): Breaking down gender biases: Shifting social norms towards gender equality.* UNDP. https://hdr.undp.org/content/2023-gender-social-norms-index-gsni#/indicies/GSNI

62  Wood, C. (2021, March 9). *7 challenges women face in getting ahead in IT.* CIO.    https://www.cio.com/article/191432/7-challenges-women-face-in-getting-ahead-in-it.html

63  Sandberg, S. (2013, March 12). *Lean in: Women, work, and the will to lead.* Knopf.

64  White, S. K. (2023, March 13). *Women in tech statistics: The hard truths of an uphill battle.* CIO. https://www.cio.com/article/201905/women-in-tech-statistics-the-hard-truths-of-an-uphill-battle.html

65  Accenture. (2020). *Resetting tech culture.* Accenture. https://www.accenture.com/us-en/about/corporate-citizenship/tech-culture-reset

66  Bolles, R. (2022). *What color is your parachute?* Ten Speed Press.

# 2

# What Do I Need to Do to Begin a Career in HCIT?

## Introduction

If you have made it to Chapter 2, that means you are likely interested in pursuing a career in healthcare information technology (HCIT), a growing industry with rewarding contributions toward the entire healthcare sector. As you will be playing a vital role in your community, it becomes critical to make sure you are fully prepared to enter the workforce, but as anyone who is experienced in the job search process would know, this can be a daunting process. It must be noted that there is no single path that would enable a woman to successfully begin a career in HCIT. Each woman will have her own background and life experience; each will be at a different point in her career; and each will have unique motivations behind pursuing a career in HCIT. Therefore, this chapter will provide information on foundational components that are necessary before the job search, strategies for success during the job search process, and strategies for successfully completing the job interview.

## Being in Control of the Job Search

First and foremost, we recognize that job hunting may be a daunting task, especially for individuals just beginning to enter the job market. We want

DOI: 10.4324/9781003366591-2

to first assure you that rather than viewing yourself in a position of having less power and being at the whim of the job market, control is always in your hands. This is about you seeking an opportunity that corresponds to your definition of what a successful career opportunity is. Your definition of success will be different, your desired criteria for a job will be different, and the amount of experience you bring will greatly determine what opportunities are acceptable and desirable for you. At the heart of it all must be your unequivocal understanding of the power and control you have over the entire process.

The mindset you have going forward is important. Research shows that aside from the more common elements of a successful job search process that include such things as goal setting and improving the way you present yourself, the psychological aspect of self-compassion has been shown to be invaluable toward not only your health and wellbeing but also your career success.[1] According to Dr. Kristin Neff, self-compassion is composed of three elements: mindfulness, common humanity, and kindness.[2] The first acknowledges discomfort, the second acknowledges human imperfections, and the third acknowledges generosity and consideration toward oneself. Collectively, this is essential to taking care of yourself throughout the entire job search process. It is very easy to become discouraged and to have a nagging voice in your mind comparing yourself to others and trying to rationalize whether you should even apply for a given job, but setting up goals and taking action, being forgiving to yourself and encouraging yourself to press onward, and even seeking support from others will help you focus on the positives rather than the frustration points, and the correct mindset will save you undo harshness and negativity that you may self-direct but are not at all warranted.

At the center of it all, you must do your research in advance to master the skills of job searching. Throughout the process, the guiding element should be to ensure that you have the skills (and the degree of this will vary based on the different stages of the career you are in) necessary to be employable. Learning is a lifelong commitment, so as you grow in your career, what you may have initially felt to be a sense of inadequacy or inability to satisfy the requirements of a role will change, and you will find that you have more to offer than you think. The following sections will provide information to further support your endeavors, and it is our goal to provide you with information that will improve your chances of success.

# Networking

While initially this section was going to start with the content on document preparedness, it is imperative to stress the significance of networking.
This strongly has to do with the way in which the hiring process is truly
handled. Employers will typically seek to hire an individual with whom they
are acquainted, and that is where networking comes in. Networking is an
essential component in any step of your career, regardless of whether you are
beginning to enter the workforce or whether you are an established professional with several years of experience under your belt. Establishing professional connections and building relationships over time will enable you to get
ahead, and it will open the door to opportunities that you may not have even
considered or to opportunities that may not be even made available to the
public. And this makes sense, as inherently, people will want to do business
and work with individuals they know and have strong connections with. In
fact, some estimates suggest that up to 70% of all jobs are not published on
publicly available job search sites, and research has long shown that anywhere
from half to upward of 80% of jobs are filled through networking.[3] For those
who are experienced in the workplace, you likely have experienced this firsthand, wherein opportunities for upward mobility and job recommendations
begin from within the organization before flowing outward. Networking is
a way to gain access to the "hidden job market," but doing so requires intentional efforts on your part to create this network by gathering information
about the industry and building connections that can help you gain access to
the desired industry. It is a skill that must be developed, but by doing so, you
will find that it will be instrumental in your career endeavors.

One important component of this is that there is such a thing as a "network gap." While two equally qualified professionals should ideally be able
to thrive in a similar manner, the reality is that there are certain individuals
who will have an advantage based on who they know, which will be based on
a variety of factors that may be largely outside of the control of that individual. For instance, such factors as where an individual grows up, where they
go to school, and where they work can give them up to a 12-fold advantage in
gaining access to opportunity.[4] Individuals that lived in areas with a median
household income above $100k were likely to have three times the prospect
of stronger networks,[5] while those who attended top schools and those who
worked at leading companies were unsurprisingly also more likely to have
stronger networks.

In consideration of this gap, there are network-focused nonprofit organizations that exist to create economic opportunities for all members of the workforce, especially as it relates to young adults. Such organizations include the following:

- **Basta**: Project Basta is a nonprofit organization with a mission to close the employment gap for first-generation students of color.[6] Basta partners with such organizations as LinkedIn for Good, Arrow Impact, Bloomberg LP, and the Bill & Melinda Gates Foundation, to name a few.

- **Beyond 12**: Beyond 12 is a national technology-based nonprofit organization with the central goal of increasing the number of students from under-resourced communities who graduate from US colleges and universities and translating their degrees into meaningful employment opportunities.[7] Beyond 12 partners with institutions and helps address systematic barriers through personalized coaching solutions grounded in an evidence-based curriculum.

- **Braven**: Braven's mission is to empower promising, underrepresented individuals, including first-generation college students, students from low-income backgrounds, and students of color, with the skills, experiences, and networks necessary to transition from college to strong first jobs.[8] Braven partners with universities such as Rutgers, National Louis University, and Spelman College, embedding innovative career and networking solutions into the undergraduate experience.

- **COOP**: COOP's mission is to overcome underemployment for underemployed first-generation college graduates through digital skills and peer connections.[9] COOP connects underemployed college graduates with alumni cohorts to support them in building the networks needed to thrive in their careers.

- **MENTOR**: MENTOR was created over 30 years ago to expand the opportunity for young adults experiencing systemic inequity as gaps in networks by building a youth mentoring field and movement, serving as the expert and go-to resource on quality mentoring.[10] MENTOR works in collaboration with its partner affiliates to offer more than 5,000 mentoring programs.

- **Year Up**: Year Up's mission is to close the opportunity divide by ensuring that young adults gain the skills, experiences, and support necessary to empower them to reach their potential through careers and higher education.[11] In addition to strategic partnerships with employers and talent providers, Year Up works with Grads of Life and YUPRO Placement to assist young adults in successfully launching their careers.

While it is very clear that networking is important, some people still tend to underestimate how vital this is and may not realize the significant disparity and social stratification that result from unequal networks. For those who find it difficult to communicate with others, the best place to begin would be with known personal connections, including friends and family (this is otherwise referred to as "informal networking"). Sending out invitations to connect with extended family members, fellow alumni, and (if presently employed or prior work experience is available) other employees is one way to gradually become comfortable with engaging in meaningful and proactive measures to connect with others. In addition, networking via community organizations and relevant social events are small steps toward getting comfortable with the process of intentionally broadening one's social capital.

When it comes to formal networking, which includes such things as attending career center events, conferences, internships, and becoming involved with or a member of professional associations or other industry-specific affiliations, these are all ways to begin increasing your network that is more tailored toward your specific choice of career. Some of these organizations that are especially geared toward women in the technology industry include the following (refer to Appendix A for a more exhaustive list of resources):

- ***Healthcare Information and Management Systems Society (HIMSS)***: HIMSS is a not-for-profit organization dedicated to being a global advisor and thought leader committed to transforming the global health ecosystem through information and technology. It is made up of more than 120,000 individuals, 430 provider organizations, 500 nonprofit partners, and 550 health services organizations,[12] which undoubtedly would be a valuable source for collaboration for women. Additionally, the HIMSS Women in Health IT Community partners with organizations to offer opportunities to engage, empower, and collaborate with women making a difference in health IT.[13] Becoming a member of HIMSS is therefore an excellent way for women to begin networking with other women who have similar values and who are better qualified to provide support and guidance.
- ***ISACA—SheLeadsTech***: ISACA is an international professional organization that focuses on IT governance. It has a specific program called

SheLeadsTech, which seeks to engage the representation of women in the technology workforce through mentorship, professional development, and leadership training.[14] SheLeadsTech regularly holds events that would provide excellent opportunities for networking, and the program provides excellent resources and toolkits for women who desire to join this profession. Additionally, this program is a subset of a larger one called One In Tech, which also offers excellent scholarship opportunities—not only US-based scholarships but international ones as well.

- *Society for Information Management (SIM) Women*: SIM Women is a program that provides networking opportunities focused on mentorship and career development for women. The society is comprised of approximately 5,000 technology leaders, and SIM Women members are able to benefit from programs such as Ladies Who Launch, Call a Coach, and 1:1 Mentoring.[15] In addition, SIM Women holds events such as national summit meetings focused on thought leadership and professional development opportunities.

- *Springboard Enterprises*: The mission of Springboard Enterprises is to provide women entrepreneurs in the technology and life sciences industries with a powerful global network to ensure access to essential resources for success. To date, this global network has led to the growth of over 850 women-led companies and has generated $36 billion in value.[16] Springboard works in collaboration with investors and corporate partners to provide relevant education programs and access to a robust networking community.

- *Women's Executive Network (WEN)*: WEN's mission is to connect women with likeminded organizations to support emerging leaders by creating networking opportunities to solve unmet needs in healthcare.[17] As a part of AdvaMed, WEN provides education and tools to ensure women have access to the necessary resources to support this mission.

- *Women in Global Health (WGH)*: WGH is a not-for-profit organization with a mission of supporting and empowering women in global health leadership. At the heart of its movement are chapters that provide an environment for women from many countries and continents to engage in advocacy, policy development, and leadership at the national level.[18] WGH has also worked with organizations and partners to lead initiatives such as the Gender Equal Health and Care Workforce Initiative (GEHCWI), the Heroines of Health, and the Gender Equity Hub (the Hub) in collaboration with the World Health

Organization (WHO). Finally, WGH also prepares reports backed by research and analysis committed to promoting women's leadership in global health, as well as providing relevant resources and news in support of its mission.

- **Women in Healthcare IT (WHIT)**: WHIT was founded in 2015 with the mission to help women achieve success in healthcare IT by leveraging their networks and expertise to deliver mentoring programs, events, and career counseling.[19] The WHIT Committee includes leaders from multiple healthcare disciplines, including healthcare associations, healthcare consulting firms, and healthcare providers.

Ultimately, the greater and more meaningful your network becomes, the greater the career advancement opportunities and prospective professional long-term relationships will be. To network in the most efficient way possible, it is important to plan ahead whenever possible, especially if the networking opportunity requires you to be present at a scheduled meeting. When appropriate, have copies of your clean and current resume ready for events such as career fairs, or have your business card ready to distribute when establishing connections with others in appropriate circumstances. Be mindful of the way you present yourself, demonstrating professional conduct while also attentively considering your choice of attire for any occasion. It is advantageous to research ahead of a networking event to know the type of information to be presented and the prospective speakers and attendees that are likely to be in attendance, while yet another reason is to simply be aware of the events in your surrounding area that may be relevant to you. Also consider that webinars and other virtual events are also a great way to connect with others as they provide greater accessibility and reach, in addition to being largely cost-effective in most instances.

Adapting to different situations in effective ways is a skill that can be developed over time with greater exposure to events and opportunities, whether these opportunities are in person or online. You will have more chances to constantly improve your interpersonal communication skills, including the practice of active listening and asking open-ended questions to facilitate conversations, as well as improving your body language skills to convey confidence and poise through such actions as maintaining a tactful amount of eye contact and having good posture (e.g., sitting straight, not fidgeting). However, of all the information provided thus far, it is of utmost importance to recognize that networking is not just about expanding your contacts. Networking requires building meaningful relationships with colleagues, mentors, and individuals in your field and nurturing these relationships over the years. It also requires attentiveness on your part to be active in maintaining these connections, both in person and via your online presence on popular networking platforms such as LinkedIn. Be willing to ask for advice from professionals in your network, and always be willing and desirous to learn, as these are characteristics that will take you very far. Collectively, these actions will greatly contribute toward the success of your career goals, and networking can only serve to strengthen your support system and presence in the job market.

# Document Preparedness: The Cover Letter and Building Your Resume

To help differentiate yourself from the competition and to substantiate your expertise and areas of strength suitable for the desired role, cover letters are important and instrumental to the job application process, regardless of whether they are actually reviewed by the recruiter or hiring manager. Regardless of whether they are read, cover letters are often expected to be submitted (some companies will require them), and in some instances, they may be the deciding factor between two candidates with similar qualifications. Cover letters serve as a self-introduction and allow your prospective employer to learn more about your capabilities and motivations behind your desire to work for their company. It is therefore important to analyze the job description requirements to tailor the cover letter and to closely match the contents to the main job criteria, ideally keeping the cover letter to one page or approximately three to four paragraphs. The cover letter should be precise and to the point, clearly stating your position (your reason for applying and your experience relative to the job requirements), demonstrating your familiarity with the company's values (which indicates prior research and thus further confirms the degree of your interest in the role), and describing the ways in which you will be directly contributing to the company's needs. Be sure to proofread the cover letter and end it on a professional and respectful note, expressing gratitude for their time and consideration.

Then there is the resume. A properly crafted resume is essential to effectively showcasing your skills, experience, and qualifications, and you must be able to tailor the resume to fit the requirements for a specific opportunity in the job you are interested in. The average initial screening time for a candidate's resume by an employer based on an eye tracking study is 7.4 seconds, with 80% of resumes not making it passed an initial screening,[20] though this number will vary from company to company. Since this is the case, you need to ensure that your resume will stand out in that very limited amount of time and make it to the remaining 20%. Organization and format are key to this initiative.

Refer to the following page for a resume criteria checklist for your consideration and use (Figure 2.1). Strive to keep the contents within one page, as employers will likely not spend more time on longer resumes (though two pages may be appropriate for professionals with over ten years of professional experience). One important factor to note is that before your resume even reaches the hands of a recruiter or hiring manager, it is likely to be processed by an applicant tracking system (ATS). An ATS is a type of software used by recruiters and employers during the hiring process to collect, sort, scan, and rank the job applications they receive for their open positions, and today, approximately 99% of Fortune 500 companies utilize this software to streamline the applicant interview process. Today, many companies also make use of this software, not just Fortune 500 companies and other large companies. Since this is the case, it is important to understand how an ATS works and what it tracks for when parsing out resume contents.

One of the most important elements of a resume is the incorporation of keywords that typically deal with essential job-related skills that are likely explicitly mentioned in the job posting. If you are still uncertain of what keywords to incorporate in your resume, take some time to review skills and keywords by industry or by specific job title. Another way to make your resume more likely to pass the ATS scan is to keep it as uncluttered as possible. This means making the resume tailored to the job, keeping relevant accomplishments (in addition to the incorporation of the keywords mentioned above), and making sure the layout of the resume is clean with a simple design. Sometimes, there may be candidates who wish to include graphic elements or even charts in their resume, but this is not recommended as the ATS will likely be unable to read it. Therefore, unusual formats are strongly discouraged as it relates to resume formatting. Finally, if you would like to be sure of whether your resume is ATS-friendly, you are able to run your resume through ATS resume scanners for free on different websites, and some of these will provide a rating depicting how great a match your resume is to a specific job posting, which can be extremely helpful to those who would like to receive a numerical representation of the comparability of your resume to a given opportunity.

**FIGURE 2.1**
**Resume Criteria Checklist Example**

## RESUME CRITERIA

| Criteria | Yes | Refine | No |
| --- | --- | --- | --- |
| Clean Format, ATS-Friendly | | | |
| Standard Fonts (11pt or 12 pt) | | | |
| Resume Tailored to Opportunity | | | |
| Logical Ordering by Category | | | |
| Contact Information | | | |
| Objective or Summary | | | |
| Professional Experience | | | |
| Education* | | | |
| Leadership** | | | |
| Professional Memberships** | | | |
| Professional Credentials** | | | |
| Community Engagements** | | | |
| Skills | | | |
| Proofread/Edit for Grammar | | | |
| Consistent Formatting | | | |
| Length (One Page Ideal)*** | | | |

\* List education first if less work experience

\*\* If applicable

\*\*\*Two pages may be appropriate *10 years of work experience

In addition to ensuring that you have a well-crafted and tailored resume, there are other factors to consider that can help improve your ability to stand out from other candidates. Being one of the earliest candidates to respond to the job opportunity is especially important. Ideally, responding within the first few days of the job posting will allow your resume to be one of the first to be reviewed by the hiring manager or recruiter before they are overwhelmed by many applications. If your resume is properly tailored to the job opportunity and your qualifications align well with the role, it is more likely to make a stronger first impression while there are still fewer applicants in the pool. Timing is another factor to consider when applying for a role. According to a study by TalentWorks, the best time to apply for a job is between 6:00 a.m. and 10:00 a.m.[21] Applying within this window and in combination with being one of the earliest to apply will enable a greater likelihood of being invited to an interview for the role.

As for specific statistics about women during the job search process, one that is very important has to do with the number of requirements women believe they need to fulfill in order to apply for a given position. While there are many women who may not apply for a position if they do not meet all the requirements, statistics show that once a candidate meets 40% of job requirements, interview chances are roughly the same as they would be if they met a higher percentage of job requirements.[22] Ian Siegel, the CEO and Co-Founder of ZipRecruiter, similarly encourages applicants to apply for roles even when they meet as few as 40% of the requirements.[23] Therefore, women should have more confidence in themselves and be willing to apply for roles even when they feel they are lacking in certain components of the job criteria. By not applying, they may be missing out on an opportunity for a prospective interview because of the false belief that they are not qualified for the role.

## Job Search Strategies

Now that we have covered the most advantageous mindset to have throughout this process and discussed document-preparedness essentials, we will focus on covering the job search strategies that will give you a better prospect of getting that interview and then getting hired. Many people applying for a job will have the qualifications the employer is looking for, but the interview process will determine who the employer perceives to be the most compatible candidate. The person who knows more about getting hired is in a better position than one who does not, and therefore, the following will provide invaluable information to best prepare you for the job search:

- **Conduct research on the jobs that are in line with your skills and your interests in the field of HCIT:** While this may seem obvious, it is important to note as there are countless individuals who start to send their resumes and cover letters in mass to as many companies and across as many diverse roles as possible to "cast a wider net." However, this is a disservice to yourself in most cases. To begin, you must always frame the prospective job as something that will ultimately be good for you. While a traditional strategy of scouring through numerous job boards and searching for any open positions might at first seem like a good idea to get started, it is not well planned, and planning and goal setting are what we constantly encourage if you truly want to target an opportunity that will be in line with your interests as well as your strengths. The field of HCIT is broad, and the types of jobs that fall under HCIT will require very different types of skill sets, have different work conditions, offer varied salaries, etc. We will cover a broad range of prospective jobs in HCIT in Chapter 4, but for now, we stress the importance of applying exclusively for opportunities where you see yourself enjoying the role and where your skills will make you a competitive candidate.

  The question you would then ask yourself is: How can you verify whether a job is right for you? This is where networking can be a very powerful tool. If you know of someone who is already working in a position you are interested in (or better yet, in the company you are interested in), either you can be sought after internally if that individual recommends you to the hiring manager or recruiter (this is the strongest way to gain entry as employers will be more likely to hire someone with a good recommendation), or that person can provide you with greater insight as to what working in that position is actually like. Alternatively, take advantage of networking platforms to see if it is possible to reach out to someone who is willing to discuss their experiences in working in the position you have your eyes set on. This will help you get a better sense of what a "day in the life" is without even setting foot in the job, and this will help you make a better determination as to whether to proceed with the job application process. In addition to the above, make sure to thoroughly review the key responsibilities and qualifications listed for the given role that you are interested in to help you make this determination.

- **After determining the jobs that are of interest to you, conduct research on the companies that offer these jobs and take the time to learn about their mission and values.** Now that you have determined the jobs that suit your preferences and that are in line with your skill sets, you need to determine which companies offer these jobs. While you may expect all HCIT roles to be in a hospital setting, that is not an accurate conclusion. In addition to healthcare organizations, HCIT roles can be offered in such companies as healthcare consulting firms, law offices with a concentration in healthcare or technology law, electronic health record vendor companies, and other organizations that focus on healthcare technology. In addition, while most individuals seek employment in very large companies, smaller companies should not be disregarded and, in fact, can offer greater advantages in the sense that they are likely to have fewer applicants, reducing the applicant pool and thereby increasing your likelihood of obtaining an interview in these companies. Considering all of the above will also enable you to narrow down your options to a particular setting that is most in line with your interests.

  Once you have determined the companies you are interested in, the next step is to perform more in-depth research about each of these companies' mission and values. First and foremost, it will always be important to frame your search in terms of having values that align with your own, so you need to know what those values are. In addition, after consulting their website for more information, sites that have company reviews, such as Glassdoor, Career Bliss, and Indeed, may be able to help you determine if working there is right for you. This research will also prepare you for the prospective job interview. It will enable you to ask questions specific to how you can utilize your skills in such a way that it will enhance the needs of the company, but it will also enable you to ask specific questions you need to know to better determine whether you ultimately want to work there, should you be offered the position.

At the heart of the job search process is the recognition that you must successfully be able to market the value of your skill sets to the prospective employer, thereby necessitating the need for you to be sufficiently prepared with adequate education and training to fulfill the desired role that aligns with your interests. While certainly having connections can enable you to land a role without some of the typical qualifications, it is still essential for your current skill set to be in some way in line with the role. An overview of relevant certifications for a career in HCIT will be discussed in greater detail in Chapter 3. The greatest advantage women will have, as discussed in the prior chapter, is that the demand for knowledgeable HCIT professionals is high, much higher than average in comparison to other professions. This means that there will be ample opportunities to apply for a greater range of roles, increasing the likelihood of homing in on a job that suits your preferences. Finally, for a list of helpful web resources to facilitate the HCIT job search process, please refer to Appendix A: Healthcare Information Technology Resources.

## The Interview

To begin, as any job search process goes, you must not become discouraged for the duration of time it takes before you get a "yes." This is absolutely normal and is part of the process. If you treat the job search process as work, invest serious time, and strategically select the places you wish to work for, the rest is a matter of time. For some people, it takes more time, and for others, it takes less. Regardless, if you are well prepared with prior research on the company and have conducted research as to the type of questions you may expect to hear in an interview and are thus prepared to respond to them, eventually the conditions will be such that you will be the person that is most desirable for the role. Several factors are in play here, such as the type of interviewer(s) that will be present, the types of questions that are asked, and the specific needs that the given employer is searching for; all of these will factor into the ultimate decisions that are made.

That being said, let's focus on the ways you can best present yourself during an interview. Though this may be obvious, a strong interpersonal factor is necessary. In other words, likeability will play a significant role, as you need to be able to build rapport during the time spent with the interviewer(s). In the same way that you want to like the people you will be working with, the same is true for those interviewing you. They want to ensure they are hiring not only the most qualified candidate who will be competent in their role, but also the candidate who is the best fit for their team. So, what does this mean? In addition to having conducted sufficient research about the company in advance and coming prepared to highlight specific stories and skills that are applicable to the job that would set you apart from candidates, according to a study by the Harvard Business Review, asking the right questions is a significantly important component as it relates to establishing strong interpersonal relationships.[24] It shows you are interested in the company on a deeper level. Remember, while they are obtaining information about you during this time to make their candidate determination, you also must be making the determination as to whether this is a company you want to be working for. In any interview, you need to be prepared to talk about yourself and be prepared for the basic questions of why you want to work for that company and what prior experience you bring, but you also need to determine the values of the company, the traits they hold as most valuable for their employees, any milestones that have taken place recently, etc. By actively listening and truly being engaged in the conversation, this will take you very far.

In addition to establishing a high degree of likeability, body language also plays a critical role in this factor. According to *The Definite Book of Body Language*, "Body language is an outward reflection of a person's emotional condition. Each gesture or movement can be a valuable key to an emotion a person may be feeling at the time."[25] It is imperative to pay attention to the way you present yourself in the interview process. Interviewers will be paying attention to nonverbal cues such as posture, gestures, and facial expression. Therefore, some key points to consider include the following:

- *Eye Contact*: In order to establish a connection with the other party, steady eye contact is essential. It signifies engagement in the conversation, and it also demonstrates good manners and appropriate business etiquette. Make sure to keep this amount of eye contact appropriate so as not to stare at the other party. Looking away, above, or below the eye from time to time[26] is natural, especially when processing information.
- *Sitting Position*: The way one is seated can indicate the level of engagement exhibited as well as signs of receptiveness. According to an article published by Sage Publications, "When a person leans forward with the back curved, the action indicates liking for the person he or she is with."[27] This body language and posture also communicate a sign of openness. By contrast, slouching is a posture that should be avoided, as it may indicate disinterest, and being stiff should also be avoided, as it indicates tension. Typically, individuals who are not willing to listen may lean back in the chair or protectively fold their arms across their chest,[28] so take note of this during the negotiation process.
- *Mirroring*: Subtly mirroring the other party can help create a sense of connection. According to an article published by the Harvard Business Law School Program on Negotiation, "Mimicry is a sign that you're both striving to build rapport, connect, and find common ground,"

and it "makes us feel comfortable with others and encourage us to trust them."[29] The absence of this "postural echo" may indicate the establishment of boundaries.[30]

- *Facial Expression*: Every part of your interaction will be analyzed, and the other party will be considering whether your facial expression corresponds with the words being stated. Therefore, it is recommended to keep your chin up, your eyes level, and to take the opportunity to smile and nod in agreement whenever possible.[31]

- *Proxemics*: Proxemics refers to the impact personal space has on communication. Being too close to an individual may be inappropriate as well as uncomfortable for the other party. This is a very important component of nonverbal communication that is not often considered, but it can play a critical role in disrupting the negotiation process if not noted. According to a study by Edward Hall as it relates to proxemics, "for two unacquainted persons in the interview situation, four feet is the minimum space needed between parties involved. As for the interviewer, space is used to his advantage-an executive maintains his authority by sitting behind a big desk."[32] Therefore, considering the distance between the parties is also very important to note.

- *Paralanguage*: Paralanguage is a component of communication that revolves around such things as intonation, speed of speech, and other vocal qualities. Silence is also a component of paralanguage, meaning it is appropriate to pause at certain times to properly listen to the other individual. Silence enables you to employ active listening skills such as paraphrasing, inquiring, and acknowledging information presented to you. It is therefore recommended to appropriately take a few seconds (around three) before responding.

While taking into consideration the above, it must be noted that many organizations may now be conducting their interviews via Zoom or a different online videoconferencing software. Much of the above still applies, but in addition to this, make sure to prepare in advance, such as by making sure to conduct an audio and camera test on the platform that will be utilized (there will typically be an option to do this in a "test meeting") and that the connection is adequate. Make sure the video is at a flattering angle, and make sure to dress in typical formal attire as you would if the meeting were held in person. If any technical difficulties happen to occur during the meeting, be prepared to have a backup to connect to the meeting, such as through your phone, if all else fails.

# After the Interview, Continue until Search Is Complete

After the interview has been completed, it is imperative that you prepare a "thank-you" note or email correspondence within 24 hours. According to a survey conducted by TopResume, 68% of hiring managers and recruiters replied that receiving a thank-you email or note did impact their decision-making process.[33] It is proper etiquette to do this, as it allows you to express gratitude for their time and also helps them remember who you are. Make sure it is personalized and to the point and proofread it before finalizing. After this is completed, be proud of yourself for the hard work put in and be prepared to do this again for the next interview. So long as you put in the time and effort, have done sufficient research, and have the skills the company is seeking, it becomes only a matter of time until the right opportunity presents itself to you.

# Conclusion

HCIT is a dynamic and evolving field, and there are numerous opportunities for women to excel and make a positive impact on patient care and healthcare systems. By combining technical expertise and a passion for improving healthcare through technology, a woman who desires to enter this industry will be able to forge a successful career in HCIT. This chapter covered specific strategies to set you apart from other candidates and prepare you for the job search and interview process. Preparedness in combination with competency is key, and you will find that the more experience you obtain, the easier the job search process becomes. In HCIT, you will find that it will become significantly important to build your social network. All of these are ingredients to success, and they will prepare you for the bright career path ahead of you.

# Notes

1 University of Pittsburgh. (2021, December 16). *Women who practice self-compassion are at lower risk of cardiovascular disease: Practicing kindness is good for your body.* ScienceDaily. www.sciencedaily.com/releases/2021/12/211216150034.htm

2  Neff, K. (2021). *Fierce self-compassion: how women can harness kindness to speak up, claim their power, and thrive.* Harper Wave.

3  Fisher, J. (2019). *How to get a job often comes down to one elite personal asset, and many people still don't realize it.* CNBC. https://www.cnbc.com/2019/12/27/how-to-get-a-job-often-comes-down-to-one-elite-personal-asset.html

4  LinkedIn. (n.d.). *Network gap.* LinkedIn. https://socialimpact.linkedin.com/programs/network-gap

5  Cancialosi, C. (2020). *The network gap and its impact on the war for talent.* Forbes. https://www.forbes.com/sites/chriscancialosi/2020/04/02/the-network-gap-and-its-impact-on-the-war-for-talent/?sh=1df72b7120de

6  Basta. (2023) *About.* Basta. https://www.projectbasta.com/about

7  Beyond 12. (2023). *Mission.* Beyond 12. https://www.beyond12.org/about-us/mission

8  Braven. (2023). *Moden and impact.* Braven. https://bebraven.org/model-and-impact/

9  COOP. (2023). *Mission.* COOP. https://coopcareers.org/mission#

10  MENTOR. (2023). *Our mission & vision.* MENTOR. https://www.mentoring.org/who-we-are/mission-vision/

11  Year Up. (2023). *About.* Year Up. https://www.yearup.org/about

12  HIMSS. (2023). *Who we are.* HIMSS. https://www.himss.org/who-we-are

13  HIMSS. (2023). *Women in health IT collaborators.* HIMSS. https://www.himss.org/women-health-it-collaborators

14  ISACA. (2023). *SheLeadsTech.* ISACA. https://engage.isaca.org/events/sheleadstechevents

15  SIM Women. (2023). *About us.* SIM Women. https://simwomen.simnet.org/home

16  Springboard Enterprises. (2023). *About us.* Springboard Enterprises. https://sb.co/about-us/

17  AdvaMed. (2023). *Women's executive network.* AdvaMed. https://www.advamed.org/about/initiatives/womens-executive-network/

18  Women in Global Health. (2023). *Chapters.* Women in Global Health. https://womeningh.org/chapters/#header-section

19  Women in Healthcare Information Technology. (2023). *About.* Women in Healthcare Information Technology. https://www.whittywomen.org/about

20  Resume Worded. (n.d.). *How long do employers look at a resume.* Resume Worded. https://resumeworded.com/how-long-do-employers-look-at-resumes-key-advice

21  Burnett, J. (2019). *Study: It's much better to apply for a job before 10 a.m.* Ladders. https://www.theladders.com/career-advice/its-better-to-apply-for-a-job-before-10-a-m

22  Russi, E. (2019). *The data behind the job search.* Medium. https://medium.com/@erika.russi/the-data-behind-the-job-search-39065bb3cdd7

23  Gotian, R. (2021). *Why you only need to meet 40% of requirements in job descriptions.* Forbes. https://www.forbes.com/sites/ruthgotian/2021/03/23/why-you-only-need-to-meet-40-of-requirements-in-job-descriptions/?sh=31be5f141bee

24  Brooks, A.W. (2018). *The surprising power of questions.* Harvard Business Review. https://hbsp.harvard.edu/product/R1803C-PDF-ENG

25  Pease, B., & Pease, A. (2004). *The definitive book of body language.* Bantam Books.

26  Ibid.
27  Carl, H. (1980). Nonverbal communication during the employment interview. *ABCA Bulletin*, 43(4), 14–19. https://doi.org/10.1177/108005699800430410
28  Zhou, H., & Zhang, T. (2009). Body language in business negotiation. *International Journal of Business and Management*, 3(2), 90–96. https://doi.org/10.5539/ijbm.v3n2p90
29  Harvard Law School. (2023). *Using body language in negotiation: Understanding body language in negotiation helps you become a more effective negotiator.* Harvard Law School. https://www.pon.harvard.edu/daily/negotiation-skills-daily/negotiation-techniques-and-body-language-body-language-negotia-tion-examples-in-real-life/
30  Ibid.
31  Hall, S. (2014). *9 body language tricks to improve your negotiation skills.* Fast Company. https://www.fastcompany.com/3032560/9-body-language-tricks-to-improve-your-negotiation-skills#:~:text=Like%20it%20or%20not%2C%20in,nod%20in%20agreement%20whenever%20possible
32  Ibid.
33  Augustine, A. (n.d.). *The importance of saying "thank you" after an interview.* TopResume. https://www.topresume.com/career-advice/post-interview-thank-you-importance#:~:text=When%20asked%2C%20%E2%80%9CAfter%20interviewing%20a%20candidate%2C%20does%20receiving,a%20thank-you%20email%20or%20note%20after%20an%20interview

# 3

# Overview of Top HCIT Certifications, Courses, and Programs

## Professional Organizations and Associations

The following is a general overview of the major associations that offer professional certifications or programs that serve to validate the skills and knowledge of healthcare information technology (HCIT) professionals (both emerging and seasoned professionals) and which contribute to the overall quality and safety of the healthcare system by ensuring that qualified individuals with the requisite combination of training and education are joining the industry.

## AAPC

The American Academy of Professional Coders (AAPC) is the world's largest training and credentialing organization for the business of healthcare.[1] Individuals who become certified by the AAPC typically work in positions that work extensively with medical coding, clinical documentation, auditing, compliance and security, and more. The following is a list of current certifications offered by the AAPC:

DOI: 10.4324/9781003366591-3

- Certified Documentation Expert Inpatient (CDEI)
- Certified Documentation Expert Outpatient (CDEO)
- Certified Evaluation and Management Coder (CEMC)
- Certified Inpatient Coder (CIC)
- Certified Outpatient Coder (COC)
- Certified Professional Biller (CPB)
- Certified Professional Coder (CPC)
- Certified Professional Compliance Officer (CPCO)
- Certified Professional Medical Auditor (CPMA)
- Certified Physician Practice Manager (CPPM)
- Certified Risk Adjustment Coder (CRC)

# HIMSS

The Healthcare Information and Management Systems Society (HIMSS) is a leading global advisor and member-based association that focuses on being leaders in the global health ecosystem through healthcare information and technology.[2] Currently, the three certifications offered by the HIMMS include Certified Associate in Healthcare Information and Management Systems (CAHIMS), Certified Professional in Healthcare Information and Management Systems (CPHIMS), and Certified Professional in Digital Health Transformation Strategy (CPDHTS). Continuous education activities are also provided by the HIMSS.

- ***CAHIMS***: The CAHIMS credential demonstrates an individual's knowledge of healthcare information and management systems.[3]
  - ***The Exam***: According to the HIMSS website, the examination is comprised of 115 multiple-choice questions, with candidates having two hours to complete the exam.
  - ***Eligibility***: The eligibility requirements to take the exam are for candidates to have a high school diploma as well as a minimum of 45 hours of continuing education in HCIT or related education as noted in the CAHIMS Candidate Handbook (available to download as a PDF from the HIMSS website) or 150 hours of HCIT work, volunteer, or internship experience in place of those 45 hours. Alternatively, candidates may have an associate, bachelor's, or related degree as noted in the CAHIMS Candidate Handbook and 25 hours of continuing education in HCIT or 75 hours of HCIT experience in place of those 25 hours.

- **Location**: The exam is administered at a Pearson VUE Testing Center and select HIMSS events.
- **Resources**: To prepare for the exam, HIMSS offers review materials in a section of their website, which can be located by searching for "CAHIMS Resources." Individuals can also purchase the CAHIMS Self-Assessment Exam, which is comprised of 50 questions with four hours to complete the practice exam, one opportunity to take it, and the ability to review the answers during that four-hour window. Finally, individuals can reference other books and materials available online to prepare for CAHIMS certification.
- **Fees**: According to the HIMSS website, at the time of writing this book, the fee ranges based on whether the candidate is a member of HIMSS ($329 for organizational members and $379 for student and corporate members) or a nonmember ($419), and the fee will also be different if the candidate is extending, retaking, or renewing their certification (the CAHIMS certification is to be renewed every three years). This certification is especially well suited for those who are just beginning to embark on their journey in HCIT, as well as for those seeking continuous education.
- **Application**: Professionals credentialed in CAHIMS work in a variety of job roles across the industry (not only HCIT), including analysts, consultants, nurses, chief information officers, and more.[4]
- **CPHIMS**: The CPHIMS credential demonstrates an individual meets an international standard of professional knowledge and competence in healthcare information and management systems.[5]
  - **The Exam**: According to the HIMSS website, the examination is comprised of 115 multiple-choice questions, with candidates having two hours to complete the exam.
  - **Eligibility**: The eligibility requirements to take the exam are for candidates to have a bachelor's degree and five years of experience in the field. Alternatively, candidates may have a graduate degree and three years of experience in the field or at least ten years of experience in the field to be eligible.
  - **Location**: The exam is administered at a Pearson VUE Testing Center and select HIMSS events.
  - **Resources**: Preparing for the CPHIMS certification is similar to preparing for the CAHIMS certification, with the HIMSS providing review materials in a section of their website that can be located

by searching for "CPHIMS Resources." Similarly, individuals can purchase the CPHIMS Self-Assessment Exam.

- *Fees:* According to the HIMSS website, at the time of writing this book, the fee ranges based on whether the candidate is a member of HIMSS ($499 for organizational members and $549 for student and corporate members) or a nonmember ($659), and the fee will also be different if the candidate is extending, retaking, or renewing their certification (the CPHIMS certification is to be renewed every three years).
- *Application:* This certification is especially well suited for more experienced professionals who desire to maintain a competitive edge in the industry. Of the three certifications currently offered by HIMSS, CPHIMS is the oldest and most active one. Professionals credentialed in CPHIMS work in a variety of job roles across the industry (not only HCIT), including executive-level healthcare professionals, analysts, consultants, nurses, pharmacists, and more.[6]
- *CPDHTS*: The CPDHTS credential demonstrates an individual meets an international standard of professional knowledge and competence in digital health transformation strategy and health strategy and is the first certification marketed for digital health transformation.[7]
  - *The Exam*: According to the HIMSS website, the beta examination is comprised of 150 multiple-choice questions, with candidates being recommended to allot three and a half hours for the testing experience.
  - *Eligibility*: The eligibility requirements to take the exam are the same as the ones for the CPHIMS certification.
  - *Location*: The exam is administered at a Pearson VUE Testing Center and select HIMSS events.
  - *Resources*: Preparing for the CPDHTS certification is similar to preparing for the CPHIMS certification, with the HIMSS providing review materials in a section of their website that can be located by searching for "CPDHTS Resources." At the time of writing this book, there was no CPDHTS Self-Assessment Exam available.
  - *Fees*: According to the HIMSS website, at the time of writing this book, the fee ranges based on whether the candidate is a member of HIMSS ($1,259 [beta: $1,099] for organizational members and $1,369 [beta: $1,199] for student and corporate members) or a nonmember ($1,579 [beta: $1,399]), and the fee will also be different if

the candidate is extending, retaking, or renewing their certification (the CPDHTS certification is to be renewed every two years).

- *Application*: This certification is especially well suited for more experienced professionals who desire to maintain a competitive edge in the industry. Of the three certifications currently offered by HIMSS, CPDHTS is the newest one.

In addition, the HIMSS created an initiative called the Technology Informatics Guiding Education Reform (TIGER), a reform focused on technology and health informatics education. This is especially important for individuals affiliated with specific medical associations geared toward health informatics, discussed in more detail later in this chapter.

# AHIMA

The American Health Information Management Association (AHIMA) is a leader in health information, intersecting healthcare, technology, and business.[8] It is backed by the Commission on Certification for Health Informatics and Information Management (CCHIIM), which serves to ensure and enforce the standards pertaining to certification. The AHIMA offers a number of different certifications to ensure that candidates attain the necessary education required for the numerous roles available to them. The following is an overview of the certifications currently offered by the AHIMA:

- *Certified Coding Associate (CCA®)*: This is a nationally recognized accreditation that demonstrates an individual has successfully exhibited the competencies necessary for coding professionals.
  - *The Exam*: According to the AHIMA website, the examination is comprised of 105 questions, with candidates having two hours to complete the exam.
  - *Eligibility*: The eligibility requirements to take the exam are for candidates to have a minimum of a high school diploma or equivalent.
  - *Location*: The exam is administered at a Pearson VUE Testing Center.
  - *Resources*: The AHIMA offers resources for candidates to prepare for the exam. This includes a downloadable exam content outline

and a content crosswalk. Additionally, the AHIMA also makes available code books, which are mandatory for the examination.

- *Fees*: According to the AHIMA website, at the time of writing this book, the fee is $199 for members and $299 for non-members.

- ***Certified Coding Specialist (CCS®)***: This accreditation demonstrates an individual has mastered coding proficiency.

  - *The Exam*: According to the AHIMA website, the examination is comprised of a range of 115–140 items, with candidates having four hours to complete the exam.

  - *Eligibility*: For this exam, the AHIMA lists recommendations but not requirements. These can be located in the certification overview of AHIMA.

  - *Location*: The exam is administered at a Pearson VUE Testing Center.

  - *Resources*: The AHIMA offers resources for candidates to prepare for the exam. This includes a downloadable exam content outline and a content crosswalk. Additionally, it also makes available code books, which are mandatory for the examination.

  - *Fees*: According to the AHIMA website, at the time of writing this book, the fee is $299 for members and $399 for non-members.

- ***Certified Coding Specialist-Physician-based (CCS-P®)***: This accreditation demonstrates an individual has mastered coding proficiency in physician-based settings, specialty centers, etc.

  - *The Exam*: According to the AHIMA website, the examination is comprised of a range of 97–121 items, with candidates having four hours to complete the exam.

  - *Eligibility*: For this exam, the AHIMA lists recommendations but not requirements. These can be located in the certification overview of the AHIMA.

  - *Location*: The exam is administered at a Pearson VUE Testing Center.

  - *Resources*: The AHIMA offers resources for candidates to prepare for the exam. This includes a downloadable exam content outline as well as a flexible online course for purchase that offers Continuing Education Units (CEU) credits. Additionally, the AHIMA also makes available code books, which are mandatory for the exam.

  - *Fees*: According to the AHIMA website, at the time of writing this book, the fee is $299 for members and $399 for non-members.

- *Certified Documentation Integrity Practitioner (CDIP®)*: This accreditation demonstrates an individual has successfully exhibited the competencies for clinical document integrity.
  - *The Exam*: According to the AHIMA website, the examination is comprised of 140 questions, with candidates having three hours to complete the exam.
  - *Eligibility*: The eligibility requirements to take the exam are for candidates to have a minimum of an associate degree or one of the following: CCS®, CCS-P®, RHIT®, or RHIA®.
  - *Location*: The exam is administered at a Pearson VUE Testing Center or online with OnVUE.
  - *Resources*: The AHIMA offers resources for candidates to prepare for the exam. This includes a downloadable exam content outline as well as an online course guide for purchase.
  - *Fees*: According to the AHIMA website, at the time of writing this book, the fee is $259 for members and $329 for non-members.
- *Certified Health Data Analyst (CHDA®)*: This accreditation demonstrates an individual has successfully exhibited the competencies and expertise in health data analysis.
  - *The Exam*: According to the AHIMA website, the examination is comprised of a range of 130–160 items, with candidates having three and a half hours to complete the exam.
  - *Eligibility*: The eligibility requirements to take the exam are for candidates to have a minimum of a bachelor's degree or one of the following: RHIT* or RHIA®.
  - *Location*: The exam is administered at a Pearson VUE Testing Center or online with OnVUE.
  - *Resources*: The AHIMA offers a downloadable exam content outline.
  - *Fees*: According to the AHIMA website, at the time of writing this book, the fee is $259 for members and $329 for non-members.
- *Certified in Healthcare Privacy and Security (CHPS®)*: This accreditation demonstrates an individual has advanced knowledge of privacy and security in healthcare settings.
  - *The Exam*: According to the AHIMA website, the examination is comprised of 150 items, with candidates having three and a half hours to complete the exam.
  - *Eligibility*: The eligibility requirements to take the exam are varied. One of the requirements is for candidates to have a minimum

of a high school diploma or equivalent and a minimum of six years of working experience in healthcare privacy or security. Please visit the AHIMA website for alternative eligibility requirements.

- *Location*: The exam is administered at a Pearson VUE Testing Center or online with OnVUE.
- *Resources*: The AHIMA offers resources for candidates to prepare for the exam. This includes a downloadable exam content outline. At the time of writing this book, the AHIMA also offered optional online preparatory courses for purchase.
- *Fees*: According to the AHIMA website, at the time of writing this book, the fee is $259 for members and $329 for non-members.

- *Registered Health Information Administrator (RHIA®)*: This accreditation demonstrates an individual has successfully exhibited mastery of knowledge relative to the requirements and standards of healthcare information.
  - *The Exam*: According to the AHIMA website, the examination is comprised of a range of 150 items, with candidates having three and a half hours to complete the exam.
  - *Eligibility*: The eligibility requirements to take the exam are varied. One of the requirements is for candidates to complete the academic requirements at the bachelor level set forth by Commission on Accreditation for Health Informatics and Information Management (CAHIIM). Please visit the AHIMA website for alternative eligibility requirements.
  - *Location*: The exam is administered at a Pearson VUE Testing Center.
  - *Resources*: The AHIMA offers resources for candidates to prepare for the exam. This includes a downloadable exam content outline and a content crosswalk.
  - *Fees*: According to the AHIMA website, at the time of writing this book, the fee is $229 for members and $299 for non-members.

- *Registered Health Information Technician (RHIT®)*: This accreditation demonstrates an individual has successfully exhibited mastery of knowledge relative to ensuring the quality of medical records and health information administration.
  - *The Exam*: According to the AHIMA website, the examination is comprised of 150 questions, with candidates having three and a half hours to complete the exam.

- *Eligibility*: The eligibility requirements to take the exam are for candidates to complete the academic requirements at an associate level set forth by CAHIIM or for candidates to have graduated from a health information management (HIM) program that has an agreement with the AHIMA.
- *Location*: The exam is administered at a Pearson VUE Testing Center.
- *Resources*: The AHIMA offers resources for candidates to prepare for the exam. This includes a downloadable exam content outline and, at the time of writing this book, an online preparatory course for purchase.
- *Fees*: According to the AHIMA website, at the time of writing this book, the fee is $229 for members and $299 for non-members.

In addition to certifications, the AHIMA also offers Microcredentials, which are described on their website as a cost-effective way to demonstrate focused expertise in a particular skill set that is valuable to a given employer.[9] It is skill-based and cost-effective, and there are different Microcredentials available. These Microcredentials include the following:

- **Auditing: Inpatient Coding**
- **Auditing: Outpatient Coding**
- **Clinical Documentation Integrity (CDI)—Outpatient**
- **Patient Identification & Matching**
- **Risk Adjustment Coding (RAC)**
- **Release of Information (ROI)**

# AMIA

The American Medical Informatics Association (AMIA) is a leader in transforming healthcare through trusted science, education, and the practice of informatics.[10] Its members are comprised of subject-matter experts in the field of informatics. As it relates to educational programs, the AMIA offers a distance-learning program called the AMIA 10 × 10 with the goal of training the next generation of informatics professionals. The courses are offered in collaboration with universities, some of which include the American College of Emergency Physicians, Oregon Health & Science University, the University of Alabama at Birmingham, and the University of Utah. In addition to this, the AMIA also provides a directory to help locate informatics academic programs, as well as a career center that includes excellent insights and resources to guide your search.

When it comes to certifications offered by AMIA, two significant ones include the following:

- *AMIA Health Informatics Certification (AHIC)*: According to the AMIA, AHIC is intended for individuals seeking to document mastery of health informatics knowledge and readiness to apply this knowledge to real-world healthcare challenges.[11]
  - *The Exam*: According to the AMIA website, the examination is comprised of 150 items, with candidates having four hours to complete the exam.
  - *Eligibility*: The eligibility requirements to take the exam are dependent on the health informatics degree the candidate has and their years of work experience. Please visit the AMIA website for more information.
  - *Location*: The exam is administered at a Pearson VUE Testing Center.
  - *Resources*: The AMIA offers resources for candidates to prepare for the exam. This includes a downloadable exam content outline and, at the time of writing this book, an online preparatory course for purchase.
  - *Fees*: According to the AMIA website, at the time of writing this book, the fee is $996 for members and $1,322 for non-members.
- *Clinical Informatics Subspecialty (CIS)*: According to the AMIA, the CIS certification is intended for physicians who practice clinical informatics and who desire to become board-certified. However, starting in 2025, the exam will only be open to those who have completed an accredited fellowship.[12] Further information as it relates to the exam and eligibility requirements is available through the American Board of Preventive Medicine (ABPM) website or the American Board of Pathology (ABP).

# Clinical and Nursing Certifications and Associations

Women who have either a clinical or IT background are also in an advantageous position to be considered for a role in HCIT, as they are likely to have transferable skills that are sought after in this industry. The following are some of the major associations that offer education that would be relevant to HCIT:

- *American Nurses Association (ANA)*: The mission of the ANA is to represent the interests of the nation's registered nurses.[13] As it relates to HCIT, the ANA offers the specialty certification called the Informatics Nursing Certification (RN-BC®) through the American Nurses Credentialing Center (ANCC), which is an exam that consists of 150 questions with candidates having three hours to complete it.[14] To be eligible, the individual must have a current Registered Nurse (RN) license and meet other educational and training criteria further described on the ANCC website. Additionally, the ANA maintains alliances with associations such as the Alliance for Nursing Informatics (ANI), AMIA, and HIMSS.
- *Alliance for Nursing Informatics (ANI)*: The mission of the ANI is to advance nursing informatics through a unified voice of nursing informatics organizations.[15] The ANI is sponsored by both AMIA and HIMSS. If you are particularly interested in health informatics, this society is very important to consider.
- *American Nursing Informatics Association (ANIA)*: The mission of the ANIA is to advance nursing informatics through education, research, and practice.[16] It is a not-for-profit organization that provides resources and links for nursing informatics professionals, a featured listing of nursing informatics jobs, guides and toolkits, and more.

## Academic Programs and Degrees

Each given HCIT career will have its own educational requirements, but one of the major advantages is that there are often many ways in which your degree can be applicable. Most jobs will typically list an associate or bachelor's degree as a minimum requirement, but remember that a strong network in connection with relevant educational credentials will often enable you to be a qualified candidate for the role. Consider as well that most HCIT roles will focus on hiring candidates that have the specific skill sets requested in the job posting, so make sure to still apply even if you believe that you did not check all the boxes in that posting. For developing more focused skill sets, look into taking certificate programs that are of interest to you. They typically require less time than a formal program and will likely be more cost-effective. In addition to the certifications covered in the section on professional associations, very specific certifications geared toward IT can be earned through CompTIA, a leading voice and advocate for the global information technology ecosystem.[17]

If you already have an associate degree and are considering continuing education, some of the credits may be transferable as you continue to advance in your education. Degrees in healthcare and IT are very clearly advantageous, but degrees that will prepare you for management roles can also be something to consider if management is something that interests you. For instance, there are degrees available for individuals interested in pursuing HIM, degrees that are more focused on IT, such as management information systems, and more. If your degree is not in either healthcare or IT, do not be discouraged! The educational background of HCIT professionals can tend to vary, and this has more to do with the flexibility and varied scope of knowledge an individual brings in that can still very much be applicable in the industry. In addition, individuals who pursue a master's degree are also likely to pursue management roles, as job postings related to management positions will typically include this degree as a requirement. Finally, while doctoral degrees are often not a requirement in HCIT, it may be likely that this will open greater doors in academia. Please refer to Appendix A: Healthcare Information Technology Resources for more information on certifications, programs, associations, and directories.

## Conclusion

This chapter provided a broad overview of the numerous educational opportunities available to HCIT professionals. From academic and educational programs to certification options and trainings made available through a variety of major professional associations and universities, the intent is to provide the reader with as many resources as possible in a comprehensive and functional manner. When it comes to deciding upon which career to embark upon, the more knowledgeable you are about the types of education and training there are, the more you will be able to make an informed decision. As our readers embark on an incredibly rewarding and challenging career, we hope this material provides greater clarity and confirmation as to the options available to them.

# Notes

 1 American Academy of Professional Coders. (2023). *About us*. AAPC. https://www.aapc.com/about-us
 2 Healthcare Information and Management Systems Society. (2023). *Who we are*. HIMSS. https://www.himss.org/who-we-are
 3 Healthcare Information and Management Systems Society, Inc. (2023). *Certification*. HIMSS. https://www.himss.org/resources-certification/cahims
 4 Daiker, M. (2019, July 16). *HIMSS certifications: What you need to know*. HIMSS. https://www.himss.org/resources/himss-certifications-what-you-need-know
 5 Ibid.
 6 Ibid.
 7 Ibid.
 8 American Health Information Management Association. (AHIMA). (2023). *Who we are*. AHIMA. https://www.ahima.org/who-we-are/about-us/
 9 American Health Information Management Association (AHIMA). (2023). *Microcredentials*. AHIMA. https://www.ahima.org/certification-careers/microcredentials/
10 American Medical Informatics Association. (2023). *About AMIA*. AMIA. https://amia.org/about-amia
11 American Medical Informatics Association. (2023). *AMIA Health Informatics Certification (AHIC)*. AMIA. https://amia.org/careers-certifications/amia-health-informatics-certification-ahic
12 American Medical Informatics Association. (2023). *Clinical informatics subspecialty*. AMIA. https://amia.org/careers-certifications/clinical-informatics-subspecialty
13 American Nurses Association. (2023). *About ANA*. ANA. https://www.nursingworld.org/ana/about-ana/
14 American Nurses Credentialing Center. (n.d.). *Informatics nursing certification (RN-BC®)*. ANCC. https://www.nursingworld.org/our-certifications/informatics-nurse/
15 Alliance for Nursing Informatics. (2023). *About ANI*. ANI. https://www.allianceni.org/about-us
16 American Nursing Informatics Association. (2023). *About us*. ANIA. https://www.ania.org/about-us
17 CompTIA. (2023). *About us*. CompTIA. https://www.comptia.org/about-us

# 4

# Overview of Diverse Roles in HCIT

## Analytics Specialist

Analytics Specialists utilize data to improve the quality of healthcare services. They typically serve as an advisor to management, vendors, etc., to extract and collect data according to organizational requirements and/or required reporting to federal, state, and other official agencies.[1] They may be tasked with maintaining a working knowledge of data used in the organization, enhancing databases, documenting, tracking and delivering reports, maintaining a reliable audit quality, etc.

*Salary Range*: $81,000–$126,000; **Average: $95,094**[2]

*Qualifications*: The typical requirements for this role include a bachelor's degree in information technology or a related field, proficiency in Microsoft Office and related skills, and related experience in data structures.

## Applied Data Scientist

Applied Data Scientists utilize large data sets to find opportunities for product and process optimization.[3] This information will be utilized to support decisions made by the health organization. They may be tasked with designing and testing data models and algorithms, identifying new data sources, analyzing critical issues, communicating findings to leaders, etc.

*Salary Range*: $151,000–$223,000; **Average: $134,949**[4]

DOI: 10.4324/9781003366591-4

*Qualifications*: The typical requirements for this role include a minimum of a degree in applied math, statistics, or a related field, with preference for a master's degree; relevant work experience with big data; and proficiency in programming software such as Statistical Analysis System (SAS) and domain languages (e.g., Structured Query Language (SQL)).

## Assistant or Associate Professor: IT, Informatics

Assistant or Associate Professors are instructors that teach a number of courses as they relate to information technology, informatics, or healthcare technology-related courses. This role is presented as an additional consideration for jobs in the education sector. They may be tasked with teaching courses related to health information technology (HIT), programming, and related materials at the college level for either graduate or undergraduate students, conducting scholarly research, having excellent communication skills, etc.

*Salary Range*: $87,000–$162,000; **Average: $104,910**[5]

*Qualifications*: The typical requirements for this role include a minimum of a master's degree in information technology or a related field. A PhD is preferred. Prior teaching experience is required.

## Chief Clinical Information Officer (CCIO)

CCIOs are exceptional leaders with knowledge of both healthcare and business management and additional working knowledge of information systems, practices, and technologies.[6] They may be tasked with working across various departments to ensure appropriate implementation of healthcare information technology (HCIT) systems and practices, leading health IT decisions and providing strategic oversight as it relates to these systems, developing plans for improvement and communicating these strategies with the organization's business leaders, managing relationships with vendors and stakeholders, leading teams to meet organizational goals, etc.

*Salary Range*: $294,463–$412,623; **Average: $356,873**[7]

*Qualifications*: The typical requirements for this role include a bachelor's degree in medical technology or a related field, with a master's degree in clinical informatics or a related field preferred. Related work experience in both healthcare and IT management is required. Board certification in informatics and certifications such as the Certified Professional in Healthcare Information and Management Systems (CPHIMS) are highly recommended.

# Chief Information Security Officer (CISO)

CISOs are executive members of an organization that oversee and manage the information security policies to ensure that critical information and systems are protected and processes are adequately followed to comply with the appropriate standards and regulatory policies in place.[8] They may be tasked with implementing organization-wide information security programs, maintaining confidentiality and safeguarding IT systems, regulating and monitoring data security, managing incidents, communicating with the appropriate regulatory bodies in the case of a breach, maintaining current knowledge of systems, etc.

*Salary Range*: $213,497–$271,501; **Average: $239,839**[9]

*Qualifications*: The typical requirements for this role include a minimum of a bachelor's degree in computer science, information security, or a related field, with a master's degree in business administration or a related field preferred. Related work experience in healthcare information security is required. Certified Information Systems Security Professional (CISSP) certification is highly recommended.

# Chief Medical Information Officer (CMIO)

CMIOs are top executives that are either practicing physicians or IT professionals with specialized training whose critical role is to oversee an organization's IT systems and assure the safety and security of healthcare patient information.[10] They are also active in the policy sector of healthcare by engaging with issues affecting the delivery of care.[11] They may be tasked with planning, directing, or coordinating assignments related to IT systems, evaluating the organization's IT systems and ensuring the quality of these systems, reporting data findings to executives, participating in system selection, designing software applications, training physicians and staff in IT systems, etc.

*Salary Range*: Under $300k–$550k; **Average: Over $300k***

*The following range is based on data gathered by WittKieffer and AMDIS from a survey of 161 individuals who identified themselves as CMIOs.[12]

*Qualifications*: The typical requirements for this role include possession of an MD or DO, board certification in health informatics, board certification in a medical specialty, over ten years of clinical practice experience, and over eight years of clinical information systems experience. Epic certification or experience is preferred.

# Clinical Informatics Specialist

Clinical Informatics Specialists are professionals that are proficient in the use of HCIT and are essential in any organization as they typically help organizations collect, store, manage, and protect health data such as personal medical information, patient records, and medical images.[13] They may be tasked with implementing new systems, upgrading or modifying existing systems, training staff on workflows as they relate to these systems, working with data to run reports, assisting physicians and staff with system issues, etc.

*Salary Range*: $64,609–$138,871; **Average: $94,722**[14]

*Qualifications*: The typical requirements for this role include a bachelor's or master's degree in healthcare informatics, data analysis, computer science, or a related field. Professional certifications such as the Advanced Healthcare Informatics Certification (AHIC) by the AMIA, the Registered Health Information Administrator (RHIA) by the AHIMA, and the Certified Associate in Healthcare Information and Management Systems (CAHIMS) are highly recommended.

# Clinical Systems Analyst

Clinical Systems Analysts are professionals who install and develop a hospital's information systems.[15] They may be tasked with completing system upgrades, maintaining confidentiality, communicating information to leadership and staff, forming corrective action for any issues found, creating policies and training materials, etc.

*Salary Range*: $76,000–$124,000; **Average: $97,313**[16]

*Qualifications*: The typical requirements for this role include a minimum of a bachelor's degree in information management, computer science, or a related field. A master's degree in health informatics is preferred. CPHIMS or CAHIMS certification is recommended.

# Coding Specialist

Coding Specialists are professionals whose role is to classify medical data from patient records, often in a hospital setting but also in a variety of other healthcare settings.[17] They may be tasked with assigning codes to patient records, reviewing claims, complying with medical coding guidelines and being proficient in ICD-10-CM, ICD-10-PCS, CPT* coding systems, etc.

*Salary Range*: $48,000–$79,000; **Average: $61,323**[18]

*Qualifications*: The typical requirements for this role include a minimum of a bachelor's degree in health information systems or a related field and Certified Professional Coder (CPC) certification. Working experience in medical coding is required. Additional certifications relevant to coding are highly recommended.

# Consultant

Healthcare Consultants provide health organizations with specific subject matter and business expertise, providing project support to meet a particular goal or deliverable.[19] They may be tasked with assisting the organization by providing subject matter expertise, recommending areas for improvement, improving patient satisfaction, improving revenue goals, etc.

*Salary Range*: $97,000–$176,000; **Average: $110,488**[20]

*Qualifications*: The typical requirements for this role include a minimum of a bachelor's degree in business, nursing, or a related field. A master's in health administration is preferred. A clinical degree may be required. Work experience in consulting is required. Additional certifications in informatics, project management, and related credentials are recommended.

# Data Analyst

Data Analysts assist the organization by analyzing and interpreting data and will work within the organization to improve clinical quality, improve patient safety, and streamline operations.[21] They may be tasked with evaluating and retrieving data, developing reports, designing or proposing data solutions, assisting the organizational team in making strategic decisions based on the data, etc.

*Salary Range*: $62,000–$104,000; **Average: $75,440**[22]

*Qualifications*: The typical requirements for this role include a minimum of a bachelor's degree in finance, economics, technology, or a related field. Work experience in analytics is required. Experience with programming languages, data tools, SQL, and other tools relevant to data analytics will be required.

# Database Administrator

Database Administrators manage and maintain software databases, providing secure access and managing solutions to prevent data loss in the event of a system failure.[23] They may be tasked with monitoring an organization's database systems, performing regular analysis and troubleshooting systems, testing new updates, managing technical administrative assignments regularly, creating user accounts, etc.

*Salary Range*: $65,567–$139,244; **Average: $95,550**[24]

*Qualifications*: The typical requirements for this role include a minimum of a bachelor's degree in computer science or a related field, though some may enter the profession with a high school diploma combined with relevant experience in the industry. Knowledge of desktop operating systems, server operating systems, and database languages is required. SQL certification is highly recommended.

# Director of Health Information Management

The Director of Health Information Management is a senior-level professional who oversees the management of patient health information within a healthcare organization and is responsible for the accuracy, completeness, and security of that information.[25] They may be tasked with leading strategic plan initiatives, developing policies and procedures relative to the organization's health information management and its electronic health record (EHR) systems, leading and developing the Health Information Management (HIM) team and training staff on these systems, collaborating with leadership, ensuring compliance with relevant laws and regulations, etc.

*Salary Range*: $90,000–$164,000; **Average: $106,927**[26]

*Qualifications*: The typical requirements for this role include a minimum of a bachelor's degree in health information systems or a related field, and a

RHIA or Registered Health Information Technician (RHIT) certification by the AHIMA is often a requirement. Working experience in HIM operations and management or related roles is required.

## Health System Sales Executive

The Health System Sales Executive is a professional focused on the development and maintenance of a sales project pipeline with healthcare entities.[27] They may be tasked with forming partnerships and working closely with healthcare client entities, communicating closely with management, vendors and related leadership, developing strategies and solutions toward project initiatives, monitoring the status of sales initiatives, etc.

*Salary Range*: $37,156–$177,304; **Average: $81,166**[28]

*Qualifications*: The typical requirements for this role include a minimum of a bachelor's degree in business, healthcare, or a related field. Work experience in management or sales is required.

## Help Desk/Field Services Technician

Help Desk Staff/Field Services Technicians provide direct support to end-users of computers, printers, etc., in the organization.[29] They may be tasked with troubleshooting computer systems, providing user support and taking calls, diagnosing errors and resolving issues, managing software updates, providing routine maintenance, etc.

*Salary Range*: $44,345–$54,448; **Average: $49,080**[30]

*Qualifications*: The typical requirements for this role include a minimum of an associate's degree in information systems or a related field, proficiency in Microsoft Office and related applications, and related work experience in a technical help desk position.

## Information Security Manager

The Information Security Manager, or the Information Systems Security Manager (ISSM), is responsible for the cybersecurity initiatives of an organization and the initiatives that deal with the policies, procedures, and practices that ensure the confidentiality, integrity, and availability of company data and assets.[31] They may be tasked with leading an organization's cyber-security initiatives, assessing security measures and performing routine risk assessments, training staff and leadership on security risks and awareness, ensuring compliance, developing policies, etc.

*Salary Range*: $133,543–$164,250; **Average: $147,974**[32]

*Qualifications*: The typical requirements for this role include a minimum of a bachelor's degree in information systems or a related field. Work experience in information security or related leadership roles is required. Relevant certification, such as the Certified Information Security Manager (CISM) credential or the CISSP credential, is required.

# IT Auditor

IT Auditors ensure the quality of IT systems by conducting IT risk assessments and audits, providing risk and audit education, and consulting services to reduce risk in the organization.[33] They may be tasked with conducting internal audits, communicating issues and recommending appropriate feedback, compiling reports, communicating effectively with leadership and staff, etc.

*Salary Range*: $70,000–$103,000; **Average: $79,360**[34]

*Qualifications*: The typical requirements for this role include a minimum of a bachelor's degree in information systems or a related field. Work experience in system auditing or related roles is required. Certified Risk and Compliance Management Professional (CRCMP), Certified Internal Auditor (CIA), Certified in Risk and Information Systems Control (CRISC), Certified Information Systems Auditor (CISA), or Certified Cyber Security Administrator (CCSA) is required. Experience with AI and cloud systems is preferred.

# Nurse Informaticist

Nurse Informaticists utilize data analytics to improve healthcare delivery and may take on various roles such as practitioner, consultant, educator, and evaluator to maintain and improve system services, as well as mentor clinician users to become better technology consumers.[35] They may be tasked with implementing data systems, educating staff and leadership on the use of technology, providing quality reporting, providing system support, etc.

*Salary Range*: $76,000–$125,000;[36] **Average: $104,651**[37]

*Qualifications*: A current Registered Nurse (RN) license is required. Clinical experience is required. BLS certification is recommended.

# Physician Informaticist

The Physician Informaticist works within the subspecialty of medical informatics and acts as a liaison between HCIT teams, including the EHR, clinical applications and systems, and clinical analytics team, as well as with organizational end-users.[38] They may be tasked with analyzing and designing EHR applications, driving the implementation of EHR resources and systems, supporting the overall technology strategy initiatives of the healthcare organization, etc.

*Salary Range*: $159,659–$206,971; **Average: $185,572**[39]

*Qualifications*: A doctorate in medicine is required. A current license to practice is required (MD or DO). A certification in informatics is required. Clinical experience is required. A fellowship in clinical informatics is highly recommended.

# Privacy Specialist

Privacy Specialists are professionals that focus on maintaining the privacy and security of the organization and preventing the violation of such laws and regulatory policies as Health Insurance Portability and Accountability Act (HIPAA), Health Information Technology for Economic and Clinical Health (HITECH), and other law and organizational policies, procedures, and standards.[40] They may be tasked with ensuring the healthcare organization is adhering to appropriate legal privacy laws and procedures, regularly monitoring and auditing the organization for compliance, updating the company's privacy policy, coordinating training as it relates to privacy and security needs, conducting risk assessments, etc.

*Salary Range*: $72,870–$94,751; **Average: $83,091**[41]

*Qualifications*: The typical requirements for this role include a minimum of a bachelor's degree in business administration or a related field. Work experience in compliance-related roles is required; healthcare experience is preferred. Knowledge of privacy laws is required. Certified in Healthcare Compliance (CHC), CRCMP, or Certified in Healthcare Privacy Compliance (CHPC) is highly recommended.

# Project Manager

Project Managers are professionals that lead IT projects and are responsible for the direction, scope, cost, schedule, quality, and success of the projects.[42] They may be tasked with leading and planning IT project strategies, establishing IT system goals and initiatives, managing project budgets, overseeing IT teams and coordinating resources, communicating with leadership and stakeholders on project status and progress, etc.

*Salary Range*: $81,000–$140,000; **Average: $97,974**[43]

*Qualifications*: The typical requirements for this role include a minimum of a bachelor's degree in information systems, business administration, or a related field. Work experience in project management is required. Project management certification is preferred.

# Quality Analyst

Quality Analysts are professionals who collect, analyze, and maintain data regarding quality of care and health outcomes per regulatory requirements.[44] They may be tasked with analyzing data for quality, preparing reports, documenting findings and troubleshooting issues, participating in committee meetings, etc.

*Salary Range*: $63,000–$110,000; **Average: $77,883**[45]

*Qualifications*: The typical requirements for this role include a minimum of a bachelor's degree in computer science, information systems, or a related field. RHIT, Registered Health Information Administrator (RHIA), Licensed Practical Nurse (LPN), or RN credentials are highly recommended. Work experience in clinical or system maintenance is required. Knowledge of software systems or programming is required.

# Software Developer

Software Developers are professionals who develop, maintain, and enhance software applications in accordance with system requirements.[46] They may be tasked with creating new software applications, performing system maintenance, documenting information, meeting user needs, etc.

*Salary Range*: $71,280–$198,100; **Average: $127,260**[47]

*Qualifications*: The typical requirements for this role include a minimum of a bachelor's degree in computer science or a related field. Work experience in writing commercial software is required. Knowledge of databases and developmental tools and Microsoft proficiency are required.

# System Analyst

System Analysts are professionals who analyze, design, and implement information systems for an organization.[48] They may be tasked with providing analytical support, designing information systems, researching problems, performing ongoing maintenance, working effectively with leadership, etc.

*Salary Range*: $88,000–$136,000; **Average: $102,402**[49]

*Qualifications*: The typical requirements for this role include a minimum of a bachelor's degree in computer science, information systems, or a related field. Work experience in IT or systems maintenance is required. Knowledge of software systems or programming is required.

# System Architect

System Architects are professionals who oversee the operation and maintenance of computer systems as part of organization-wide Enterprise Architecture (EA) initiatives.[50] They may be tasked with designing and implementing complex computer systems, defining goals and strategies for the new systems, ensuring the security of the systems, maintaining and upgrading the systems, etc.

*Salary Range*: $151,436–$177,637; **Average: $164,459**[51]

*Qualifications*: The typical requirements for this role include a minimum of a bachelor's degree in management information systems, computer science, or a related field. Working experience with multiple operating systems is required. Knowledge of network design and software systems is required.

# Vice President/Chief Information Officer (CIO)

The Vice President/CIO serves as the key executive for information services for the health system. This position provides leadership, vision, and oversight for information systems and technology with a focus on service excellence, with overall responsibility for the direction, coordination, and management of all IS/IT business and clinical functions.[52] They may be tasked with leading the information services unit of the organization, providing strategic leadership and building strong partnership with leadership and stakeholders, ensuring compliance with policies and procedures, enhancing and developing information services resources, etc.

*Salary Range*: $250,000–$466,000; **Average: $332,669**[53]

*Qualifications*: The typical requirements for this role include a minimum of a bachelor's degree in management information systems or a related field. A master's degree is preferred. Work experience as an IT leader for a minimum of typically eight years is required. Knowledge of HIT systems, EHR, and relevant health technologies is required.

# Conclusion

This chapter provided a broad overview of career opportunities in the HCIT industry. The breadth and depth of opportunities are vast, but it is essential to have a sense of what a given job requires as it relates to education, experience, certifications, and more, in order for you to become the strongest candidate for a given role. Please note that the descriptions are a very broad generalization, and thus, a specific title in one company may not necessarily list all the same requirements that are presented in this book. Likewise, the salary ranges are an approximation based on salary comparison sites, and over time, these ranges will change. Therefore, once you are ready to embark on locating a job tailored to your preferences, make sure to take the time to further research this information relative to the job you are interested in. Ultimately,. the opportunities for women in the HCIT industry are ever-growing. The information in this chapter is meant to broaden your horizons into the possibilities available to you and to inform you of the prospective requirements that will be expected of you to increase your likelihood of success.

# Notes

1  HIMSS. (2023). *Health information and technology job descriptions*. HIMSS. https://www.himss.org/resources/health-information-and-technology-job-descriptions

2  Glassdoor. (2023, October 5). *Analytics specialist salary in the United States*. Glassdoor. https://www.glassdoor.com/Salaries/analytics-specialist-salary

3 Ibid.
4 Salary. (2023, September 25). *Applied data scientist salaries in the United States.* Salary. https://www.salary.com/research/salary/position/applied-data-scientist-salary
5 Salary. (2023, September 25). *Associate professor.* Salary. https://www.salary.com/research/salary/recruiting/associate-professor-salary
6 Ibid.
7 Salary. (2023, September 25). *Chief clinical informatics officer (CCIO) salary in the United States.* Salary. https://www.salary.com/research/salary/alternate/chief-clinical-informatics-officer-ccio-salary
8 Ibid.
9 Salary. (2023, September 25). *Chief information security officer (CISO) salary in the United States.* Salary. https://www.salary.com/research/salary/benchmark/chief-information-security-officer-salary
10 USF Health. (2023, February 28). *Chief medical information officer: Job description and salary data.* USF Health. https://www.usfhealthonline.com/resources/health-informatics/chief-medical-information-officer-job-description-salary/
11 Ibid.
12 WittKieffer. (2021). *The CMIO role and compensation: 2021 survey results.* WittKieffer. chrome-extension://efaidnbmnnnibpcajpcglclefindmkaj/https://amdis.org/wp-content/uploads/2021/06/AMDIS-CMIO-Survey_Ross.pdf
13 Indeed. (2023, January 23). *What is a clinical informatics specialist? (With duties).* Indeed. https://ca.indeed.com/career-advice/finding-a-job/what-is-clinical-informatics-specialist#:~:text=A%20clinical%20informatics%20specialist%20is%20a%20professional%20with,personal%20medical%20information%2C%20patient%20records%2C%20and%20medical%20images.
14 Indeed. (2023, October 5). *Clinical informaticist salary in the United States.* Indeed. https://www.indeed.com/career/clinical-informaticist/salaries
15 Ibid.
16 Salary. (2023, September 25). *Clinical systems analyst.* Salary. https://www.salary.com/research/salary/recruiting/clinical-systems-analyst-salary
17 Indeed. (2023, January 23). *What is a clinical informatics specialist? (With duties).* Indeed. https://ca.indeed.com/career-advice/finding-a-job/what-is-clinical-informatics-specialist#:~:text=A%20clinical%20informatics%20specialist%20is%20a%20professional%20with,personal%20medical%20information%2C%20patient%20records%2C%20and%20medical%20images.
18 Salary. (2023). *Coding specialist salary in the United States.* Salary. https://www.salary.com/research/salary/listing/coding-specialist-salary
19 Ibid.
20 Salary. (2023). *Healthcare consultant salary.* Salary. https://www.salary.com/research/salary/recruiting/healthcare-consultant-salary
21 Ibid.
22 Salary. (2023). *Data analyst salary in the United States.* Salary. https://www.salary.com/research/salary/listing/data-analyst-salary
23 Indeed. (2023, May 10). *What does a database administrator do?* Indeed. https://www.indeed.com/career-advice/careers/what-does-a-database-administrator-do

24 Indeed. (2023, October 17). *Database administrator salary in the United States.* Indeed. https://www.indeed.com/career/database-administrator/salaries?cgtk =672a24d0-f4f1-4139-b837-3eceda5df12f&from=careeradvice-US

25 University of Arizona Global Campus. (2023, June 19). *What does a director of health information management do?* UAGC. https://www.uagc.edu/blog/ what-does-director-health-information-management-do

26 Salary. (2023). *Director of health information management salary.* Salary. https:// www.salary.com/research/salary/recruiting/director-health-information-management-salary

27 Ibid.

28 Indeed. (2023, October 17). *Medical sales executive salary in United States.* Indeed. https://www.indeed.com/career/medical-sales-executive/salaries

29 Ibid.

30 Salary. (2023). *IT help desk support salary in the United States.* Salary. https:// www.salary.com/research/salary/listing/it-help-desk-support-salary

31 Ibid.

32 Salary. (2023). *Information security manager salary in the United States.* Salary. https://www.salary.com/research/salary/benchmark/information-security-manager-salary

33 Ibid.

34 Salary. (2023). *IT Auditor I salary in the United States.* Salary. https://www. salary.com/research/salary/alternate/it-auditor-i-salary

35 Ibid.

36 HIMSS. (2023). *Nursing informatics workforce survey.* HIMSS. https://www. himss.org/resources/himss-nursing-informatics-workforce-survey

37 Salary. (2023). *Informatics nurse salaries in the United States.* Salary. https:// www.salary.com/research/salary/position/informatics-nurse-salary

38 Ibid.

39 Salary. (2023, September 25). *Physician informatics salary in the United States.* Salary. https://www.salary.com/research/salary/hiring/physician-informatics-salary

40 Ibid.

41 Salary. (2023, September 25). *Privacy specialist salary.* Salary. https://www.salary.com/research/salary/recruiting/privacy-specialist-salary

42 Ibid.

43 Salary. (2023, September 25). *Project management manager salary in the United States.* Salary. https://www.salary.com/research/salary/benchmark/ project-management-manager-salary

44 Ibid.

45 Bureau of Labor Statistics. (2023, September 6). *Occupational outlook handbook: Software developers, quality assurance analysts, and testers.* BLS. https://www. bls.gov/ooh/Computer-and-Information-Technology/Software-developers. htm#tab-5

46 Ibid.

47 Bureau of Labor Statistics. (2023, September 6). *Occupational outlook handbook: Software developers, quality assurance analysts, and testers.* BLS. https://www. bls.gov/ooh/Computer-and-Information-Technology/Software-developers. htm#tab-5

48 Indeed. (2022, June 24). *System analysts vs. data analysts (plus definitions)*. Indeed. https://www.indeed.com/career-advice/finding-a-job/system-analysts-vs-data-analysts

49 Salary. (2023). *Systems analyst salary in the United States*. Salary. https://www.salary.com/research/salary/listing/systems-analyst-salary

50 Ibid.

51 Salary. (2023). *Systems architect V salary in the United States*. Salary. https://www.salary.com/research/salary/benchmark/systems-architect-v-salary

52 Ibid.

53 Glassdoor. (2023, October 8). *Chief information officer salaries*. Glassdoor. http://www.glassdoor.com/Salaries/chief-information-officer-salary

# 5

# Negotiating Salary and Employment Agreements

## Understanding Employment Contract Fundamentals

*Navigating the Core of Your Employment Contract*

Securing a role in the healthcare information technology (HCIT) sector signals a new and exciting career chapter, and it begins with a deep dive into your employment contract. Consider this document as your career guide within HCIT, clearly defining your obligations, rights, and benefits package.

*Decoding Job Descriptions*

Your job description is more than a catalog of duties; it outlines the expectations of your role. It should detail your responsibilities, the breadth of your duties, and the criteria against which your performance will be measured. With HCIT positions often being highly specialized, clarifying any industry-specific responsibilities is imperative. Encounter any terms that aren't clear? It's your responsibility to ask for details. The more precise the job description, the better equipped you'll be to meet and even exceed the company's expectations.

DOI: 10.4324/9781003366591-5

## Understanding Compensation and Benefits Beyond Salary

Compensation involves a range of factors beyond your monthly salary. The complete package typically includes several components:

- **Base Salary**: The fixed annual income you'll receive.
- **Bonuses**: These might be tied to your performance or offered as an incentive when you join.
- **Stock Options**: A share in the company's future, valuable in both burgeoning enterprises and established innovators.
- **Healthcare and Retirement Plans**: Standard offerings may come with health initiatives due to the nature of your work.
- **Relocation Assistance**: Companies may provide financial support or services if you need to move for the job.
- **Professional Development**: Access to industry journals, memberships in professional organizations, and funding for further education or certifications.
- **Work–Life Balance Benefits**: Options might include flexible schedules to mental health support initiatives.

Each of these components represents a potential negotiation point. It's essential to understand their relevance in line with industry norms. Given the specialized nature of HCIT, benefits like professional development opportunities or specific health programs can be particularly relevant and should not be overlooked.

## Delving into Contract Duration and Termination Clauses

Understanding the terms regarding the length and potential end of your employment contract is crucial for job security and career planning. In the HCIT field, these terms can vary widely depending on your role or the project's lifecycle. Here's what you need to watch for:

- **Contract Duration**: Is your position set for a specific timeframe, or is it based on "at-will" employment? Fixed-term contracts typically correspond with the lifespan of a given project. In contrast, "at-will" employment means your job could end at any time, initiated by either you or the employer, usually with no reason required. This factor is incredibly pertinent in the HCIT domain, where working across different states or remotely is common. Research employment laws in your or the project's respective state to understand how they might influence your contract terms.

- **Notice Period**: Regardless of whether it's a fixed-term or "at-will" contract, there's likely to be a clause about the notice period. This clause outlines the time required to notify the other party before ending the contract. For specialized roles within HCIT, longer notice periods may be standard to allow for the orderly handover of complex tasks or information.
- **Severance Packages**: Particularly for high-level or specialized positions, severance agreements might be included within the contract. These are designed to provide continued benefits and compensation if the company ends your employment without cause.
- **Non-disparagement and Confidentiality**: HCIT roles, given their close interaction with sensitive healthcare information, often have strict clauses to prevent sharing confidential data and speaking negatively about the company after your employment ends.
- **Project-Specific Termination Conditions**: When you're hired for a project-based position, the contract might include terms that define how and when the contract could be cut short, such as upon the project's completion or if certain performance benchmarks are not achieved.

Being well versed in these areas can significantly contribute to a fair and transparent employment experience in the ever-evolving world of HCIT.

### Understanding Non-compete Clauses in HCIT Employment

Non-compete clauses carry considerable weight in HCIT, driven by propriety technology and specialized know-how that are often at the core of a company's competitive advantage. These stipulations prevent employees from joining competing firms or starting rival enterprises within a certain timeframe after leaving a company. Here are critical elements to consider when evaluating a non-compete clause:

- **Scope of the Clause**: Examine the reach of the non-compete. Is it narrowly defined to include only direct competitors, or does it encompass a broader range of businesses in the healthcare and technology sectors? The scope can significantly influence your future job prospects.
- **Timeframe of the Restriction**: The rapid advancement of technology in HCIT means that even a short-term restriction can have a lasting

impact on your career development. Consider how long the non-compete aims to limit your professional options.

- **Geographic Reach**: Determine whether the non-compete is localized or expansive in its geographic scope. Some clauses may restrict your employment opportunities within a certain city, state, or even globally.
- **Legal Enforceability**: Non-compete enforceability varies widely by state, with some jurisdictions imposing tight restrictions on their legal validity. Understanding the legal context of your non-compete is crucial, especially if your career path might cross different state boundaries.

These clauses are not merely small print; they are pivotal to your professional path in HCIT. If there's any lack of clarity or if the terms seem overly restrictive, it's advisable to consult with a legal professional. Such terms can often be negotiated to ensure they align with your career goals and legal rights. Your informed approach to these clauses will be invaluable in shaping a robust and flexible career trajectory within the HCIT industry.

# Navigating Intellectual Property in HCIT

*Deciphering Intellectual Property in the
Realm of Healthcare Technology*

As a professional in the dynamic field of healthcare technology, grasping the intricacies of intellectual property (IP) is as vital as the innovations themselves. Whether you're developing the next big data algorithm or pioneering a patient care workflow, the IP you create becomes a valuable asset that requires understanding and protection.

*Diverse Expressions of IP in HCIT*

- **Software and Algorithms**: The sophisticated code that drives health applications, from data analytics platforms to artificial intelligence in medical diagnostics.
- **Data Sets**: The aggregated and anonymized health data used for research and development of new healthcare technologies.
- **Methodologies**: The proprietary procedures or systems devised for optimizing data analysis, managing patient records, or integrating new healthcare services.

*Clarifying Brilliance Ownership: Your Rights and Responsibilities*

Engagements within HCIT may stretch beyond internal boundaries to include external collaborators, such as academic partners or other institutions, potentially complicating the landscape of IP ownership. Understanding where you stand in this complex terrain is imperative to preempt ownership disputes. Here are some pivotal points:

- *Your Employment Agreement*: Typically, your contract will have stipulations that any IP crafted during your tenure is the property of your employer. It's essential to read and understand these terms.
- *Collaborative Ventures*: IP ownership is complex if you collaborate with external partners like universities or research institutions. It's vital to establish ownership rights from the start.
- *Navigating Post-employment IP Use*: Contracts may include provisions that limit your ability to use or develop similar IP after your employment ends. Given the specialized field of HCIT, these restrictions can notably shape your professional journey.

With this knowledge, you can ensure that your intellectual endeavors within HCIT are recognized and protected as you navigate your career path.

*NDAs: Your First Line of Defense*

In the highly competitive and confidential health technology ecosystem, non-disclosure agreements (NDAs) are critical for protecting your IP. These agreements function as a strategic safeguard, crucial for maintaining the confidentiality of sensitive information across various professional interactions. Here's how NDAs provide essential protection in diverse settings:

- *Pitching to Private Equity or Investors*: An NDA is fundamental when presenting innovative concepts to investors or venture capitalists. This agreement is your assurance that your ideas won't be exploited or disclosed without your permission, serving as a safety net for your IP and future career prospects.
- *Collaborating with Healthcare Providers*: An NDA is a protective cornerstone in partnerships involving data transfer or processes with healthcare entities. The sensitivity of patient data in healthcare technology renders the NDA advantageous and essential.

- *Consulting with External Experts*: When engaging medical experts to validate your technology, an NDA is a protective measure that ensures these critical consultations lead to unintended sharing of proprietary information.
- *Data Collaboration Agreements*: An NDA clearly outlines the terms of data usage, ensuring adherence to rigorous healthcare regulations such as the Health Insurance Portability and Accountability Act (HIPAA) and protecting the integrity of shared endeavors.

In these scenarios, NDAs are a key defensive measure, ensuring that your intellectual contributions and innovations are securely managed within the healthcare technology sphere.

## *Strategizing IP in HCIT: Patents, Trademarks, and Beyond*

Protecting your IP with patents and trademarks isn't just about claiming your ideas; it's about establishing your expertise and securing your professional future.

- *Trademarks*: A trademark isn't merely a legal right; it's the identifier of your brand's quality and reputation. A well-chosen trademark becomes an invaluable asset in HCIT, where consumer trust is paramount. It differentiates your product in a crowded marketplace and can become synonymous with cutting-edge solutions in healthcare technology.
- *Patents*: Patents provide a temporary but powerful monopoly on using your inventions. For software, algorithms, and even specific applications of technology in HCIT, patents can prevent competitors from encroaching on your space. The process can provide clear documentation of the invention, novelty, and utility. But the payoff is substantial: exclusive control over your creation and potential revenue streams through licensing.
- *Trade Secrets*: The strategic use of trade secrets can be particularly advantageous in HCIT. This form of IP protection requires no registration and does not expire, making it ideal for protecting proprietary systems or methodologies that give you a competitive advantage. The key is implementing stringent confidentiality agreements and security measures to maintain secrecy.
- *Data Use Agreements (DUAs)*: DUAs are essential, particularly in a sector that relies on sensitive and proprietary data. They're not just

contracts; they're frameworks that govern data use, dissemination, and protection, which is critical in maintaining integrity and trust in HCIT applications.

- *Regulatory Compliance*: In-depth knowledge of legal frameworks like HIPAA for the US market, or the GDPR if operating in Europe, is not just compliance—it's a competitive edge. This compliance ensures that your HCIT operations are ethical and lawful, providing a foundation of trust with users and partners.

By proactively addressing these aspects of IP law, you're protecting your creations and solidifying your position in the HCIT field.

*Practical Considerations*

- *Documentation*: Keep meticulous records of your contributions to any IP. This can be evidence of originality and invention during patent applications or legal disputes over IP ownership.
- *Negotiating Co-development*: If you are in a co-development scenario or contributing significantly to a project, don't hesitate to negotiate for shared IP rights or appropriate recognition, especially if you bring specialized healthcare knowledge to a technological project.
- *Seeking Legal Expertise*: Given the complexity of IP laws and the specialized nature of HCIT, consulting with an attorney experienced in healthcare technology can be invaluable. They can assist in:
  - *Clarifying Complex Clauses*: Such as IP ownership and non-compete agreements, which are common in HCIT contracts.
  - *Negotiating Better Terms*: Offering insight into the market value of your IP and helping you negotiate terms that reflect your contribution's worth.

# Mastering the Art of Negotiation

After dissecting the key components of your employment contract, the next step is to negotiate terms that align with your career goals and personal needs. Negotiation in HCIT isn't just about the salary; it's a multifaceted process that can significantly shape your professional trajectory. Here's a blueprint for your negotiation strategy to ensure your employment terms reflect your value and ambition.

## Strategic Foundations: Setting the Stage

Before you enter negotiations, it's crucial to establish a solid foundation. Begin with these actions:

- **Researching Market Rates**: In the specialized field of HCIT, understanding the market rates for your role is crucial. Utilize platforms like Glassdoor, LinkedIn Salary Insights, and industry-specific salary surveys to gauge the average compensation for your role in your geographic area. This knowledge is not just a confidence booster; it sets the stage for a more equitable negotiation.
- **Knowing Your Value**: Your unique skills, certifications, and experiences are your leverage. Make a list of your achievements and any specialized skills or certifications that make you particularly valuable in the HCIT sector. This isn't just about self-assurance; it's about articulating why you're an asset to the organization.

## The Negotiation Process

Preparation leads to confidence, which is essential when you find yourself at the negotiation table. Here's how to conduct the conversation:

- **How to Initiate the Conversation**: The optimal time to initiate negotiation is after receiving the job offer but before accepting it. A simple yet effective way to segue into the discussion could be: "I'm thrilled about the opportunity to contribute to your team. Could we discuss the terms of the employment package?"
- **Strategies for Effective Negotiation**: Negotiation isn't merely transactional—it's relational. As you discuss your terms, aim to present them in a way that highlights mutual benefits. Instead of stating, "I want a higher salary," consider phrasing it as "A competitive salary would allow me to give my best to the team and the projects we'll be tackling."

## Non-compensatory Items to Negotiate

In HCIT, salary isn't the only variable in play. There are often non-financial terms that can be just as crucial:

- *Title*: A title that reflects your role and responsibilities can be valuable for your career progression.
- *Location*: Whether it's the option for remote work or a preferred office location, this can significantly impact your work–life balance.
- *Specific Projects*: If there are particular initiatives or technologies you're interested in, now is the time to express that interest.
- *Voice within the Organization*: Opportunities for leadership roles or participation in key meetings can be important for your professional development. In negotiating the contours of your role in HCIT, remember that the process is as much about creating a partnership as it is about stipulating terms. It's about showing where your growth and the organization's success are interlinked.

## Special Considerations for Women in HCIT

Women entering the HCIT field bring unique skills and perspectives invaluable for innovation and progress. However, the industry is not without its gender-specific challenges, including the gender–pay gap and work–life balance issues. Being aware of these challenges enables you to address them proactively during negotiations.

- *Be Informed*: Use your market research to understand the average salary for your role and use these data as a baseline for your negotiations.
- *Set High Expectations*: Don't undervalue yourself. Ask for a salary that reflects your skills, experience, and the market rate for your role.

Work–life balance is a universal concern but often disproportionately impacts women, who may also have caregiving responsibilities. Here's how to address it:

- *Flexibility*: If work–life balance is a priority for you, make it a part of your negotiation. Whether it's flexible hours or the option for remote work, articulate how this flexibility can also benefit the organization, such as through increased productivity or job satisfaction.
- *Childcare and Family Benefits*: Some companies offer benefits like on-site childcare or extended family leave. If these are important to you, bring them up during the negotiation process.

# Career Advancement and Professional Development in HCIT

Elevating your professional journey in HCIT transcends beyond initial contract negotiations or protecting your intellectual creations. It's a continuous pursuit of knowledge, strategic relationship building, and purposeful career progression. Clarity in your professional ambitions will help you concentrate your efforts on necessary skills and beneficial opportunities. Let's explore the strategic approach to guiding your career path in HCIT.

## Defining Your Career Path

- **Future Vision**: Envision where you want to be in five years. Whether leading a team, becoming a recognized expert, or initiating your own consultancy, having a clear image of your career prospects is pivotal for informed decision-making.
- **Professional Growth Objectives**: Set achievable milestones that align with your long-term vision. Regularly review and tweak these goals to ensure they remain relevant and achievable.
- **Developing Your Personal Brand**: A strong personal brand is key to distinguishing yourself and attracting advanced opportunities.
- **Enhancing Your Online Profile**: Utilize platforms like LinkedIn to exhibit your accomplishments, participate in thought leadership, and network with industry professionals.
- **Online Presence**: Use platforms like LinkedIn to showcase your skills, projects, and thought leadership and engage with industry professionals.
- **Intellectual Leadership**: To become a true leader in HCIT, you need to contribute intellectually to the field. If your role permits, engage in research projects and aim for peer-reviewed publications. This not only elevates your standing but also enriches the industry.
- **Networking**: Building a strong professional network can open doors to new opportunities and provide valuable industry insights. Attend HCIT conferences, webinars, and workshops to meet industry leaders and peers. Never underestimate the power of a good connection.

*Skill Development*

In the ever-evolving field of HCIT, staying updated with the latest technologies and methodologies is crucial. Here are some strategies:

- **Certifications**: Consider obtaining industry-specific certifications in areas like data analytics, cybersecurity, or healthcare compliance.
- **Educational Reimbursement**: Many employers in HCIT offer tuition reimbursement for courses that can enhance your skill set. Take advantage of this whenever possible to deepen your expertise.

*Mentorship and Sponsorship*

- **Seek Guidance**: Look for mentors within your organization or industry who can provide career advice and open doors for you.
- **Be a Mentor**: As you advance in your career, consider mentoring younger women entering the field. It's a rewarding way to give back and enhance your leadership skills.

# Conclusion

In the fast-paced, ever-evolving landscape of HCIT, starting your career on the right foot and continuously adapting and growing is essential. Every step is crucial, from choosing the role that aligns with your interests and skill set to acquiring the necessary educational qualifications and certifications and developing a career path that offers long-term satisfaction and impact. This chapter has laid down the foundational blocks to guide you through your HCIT career—beginning with the initial preparations and job search, diving into workplace skills and strategies, and finally, focusing on long-term career advancement.

However, remember that each career is a journey shaped by individual experiences, challenges, and opportunities. While this guide provides a comprehensive blueprint, the dynamic interplay of your skills, ambition, and the industry's needs will define your unique career path. Stay updated with industry trends, continuously invest in your personal and professional growth, and be proactive in seizing opportunities that align with your career goals. The HCIT field is ripe with potential; it's up to you to tap into it.

# 6

# Cracking the Code
## *An HR Blueprint for Women in HCIT*

## Introduction

In a former life, I joined an event management firm as a receptionist hoping to use this proverbial foot-in-the-door as a launch pad to a more lucrative and exciting career. We were a small tribe, less than 20 employees all under the direction of the owner, a stern individual whose demeanor often oscillated between rude and cold. I was barely 20 yet determined. Despite the icy work environment, my enthusiasm never waned. About a year into my tenure, an assistant event coordinator position opened up and I leaped at it with gusto. However, I would soon discover that I'd be taking on another role entirely, *motherhood.*

Navigating both a professional ascent and personal joy, I somehow managed to secure the promotion prior to going out on maternity leave and would transition into the new role upon my return. As I marveled at my daughter, caring for her needs and providing her with every possible opportunity became my sole focus and this would only be possible through a stable career and steady income. Rather than the recommended three months of bonding time, I opted instead for six short weeks, determined to jump back in and further prove my value to the firm.

But rather than beginning the transition into the coveted role I had been promised, I was met with the cold reality of replacement. The role that was to be a stepping stone in my career was handed over to an employee who had only been with the firm a short time and who would later marry the firm's owner. The incident wasn't merely a professional setback, but a glaring manifestation of the unspoken biases that often lurk in workspaces.

The narrative isn't an isolated one but echoes the sentiments of many women who find themselves at the crossroads of personal milestones and professional advancement. The experience underscored the glaring need for a supportive work environment, a need that is magnified in male-dominated sectors like technology where the stakes are high, and the impact is profound.

## Section I: Where are the Women?

Healthcare information technology (HCIT) is a bustling intersection where the traditional caregiving roles often associated with women meld with the burgeoning domain of technology. As a woman stands at this crossroads, the statistics often echo a disheartening tune of a cold and unyielding landscape where her presence is notably sparse. Transitioning from the warmth of nurturing roles to the sterile, binary world of technology is akin to crossing an invisible yet palpable boundary. Women make up just 28% of the tech industry workforce and only hold 18% of Chief Information Officer and Chief Technical Officer roles in 1,000 of the largest tech companies in the United States.[1]

### Barriers

The lack of early STEM engagement is akin to a garden bereft of sunshine, where potential ideas and aspirations wither away before they can take root.[2] A study involving over 2,000 students from grades 1 to 12 was conducted in 2017 and 2019 to gauge their perceptions of gender interest in computer science and engineering. The findings revealed a predominant stereotype, with 63% of the participants associating a lower interest in engineering with girls as compared to boys, a belief shared across diverse racial backgrounds. Only 9% felt girls were more inclined toward engineering than boys.

Despite a hearty 74% of young girls harboring aspirations for a flourishing career within STEM, a mere 18% among them attain undergraduate degrees in computer science. This disparity casts a long shadow, especially when forecasts tell us that come 2026, the demand for computer science research roles will burgeon by 19%.[3] The initial zest displayed by these young girls toward the field seems to fizzle out somewhere along the way.

For the small cohort of women who do continue down the path of pursuing a career in technology, they are often subjected to gender bias and discrimination in the workplace. According to a survey conducted by the Pew Research Center, 50% of women said they had experienced gender discrimination at work, while only 19% of men said the same.[4]

The gender–pay gap, that silent specter, continues to haunt the possibility of equal pay for equal work. Women in the tech industry are often paid less than their male counterparts for doing the same job. According to a study by Hired, a job search platform, men in the tech industry earn on average 7% more than women.[5] Negotiation, a key to unlocking fair compensation, often sees a divide, with many women finding themselves on the far side of assertiveness. Performance evaluations, a stage where your efforts seek the spotlight, may sometimes be clouded by biases.

The journey from an entry-level role to a robust tech-savvy professional is often fraught with societal stereotypes. These stereotypes, much like unseen shackles, tether the aspirations of many capable women, confining them to roles deemed "suitable." Women in the tech industry are often stereotyped as being less competent than their male counterparts. A survey conducted by the Pew Research Center found that 48% of women reported seeing discrimination in terms of their technical abilities, compared to only 24% of men.[6]

The barriers are not merely societal or external; they are often internal, woven into the very fabric of language. The gender stereotypes are embedded in whispers of discouragement, subtle discouraging nods, and dismissive glances that often greet a woman as she steps into the domain of technology.

## Advancement

Climbing the professional ladder in HCIT, much like in other sectors, is a journey fraught with challenges. For women, these challenges often morph into barriers: some are blatant, while others are subtly camouflaged in the garb of tradition and societal expectations.

The narrative of women climbing the ladder of promotion trails behind that of men, a tale retold across myriad industries and roles. The figures paint a stark picture—for every 100 men ascending to the mantle of manager, a mere 86 women share the same triumph. Yet, when the lens is narrowed to the domain of technical roles, the chasm yawns wider. In this sphere, the number of women advancing into managerial roles dwindles further, with just 52 women stepping into the shoes of a manager for every 100 of their male counterparts.

Women hold 34% of entry-level engineering and product roles and just 26% of first-level manager positions compared with 48% of entry-level roles and 41% of first-level manager positions in the pipeline overall.[7] The metaphor of the "leaky pipeline" aptly describes the dwindling representation of women as one moves up the hierarchical ladder in HCIT.

The pipeline, robust at the entry level, starts leaking as one ascends, with fewer women visible in senior roles. A myriad of factors contributes to this leakage—lack of mentorship, work–life imbalance, and sometimes, circumstances that should be celebrated but are instead seen as hurdles. The birth of a child, for instance, a profound life-altering joy, often comes tethered to a web of professional compromises. Then there's the celebration of love, marriage—yet another profound commitment, that can, in the working world, be misconstrued as a potential detour from career dedication.

Similarly, the choice to prioritize family is often seen through a lens of professional derailment rather than a noble, humane choice. Each of these life chapters, rich with personal growth and human essence, are often misinterpreted as career stumbles, when in truth, they enrich the individual, fostering a depth of understanding and empathy that can be a priceless asset. The ability to balance personal milestones with professional commitments should be lauded, not misconstrued as a lack of focus. The tapestry of life experiences, after all, molds a well-rounded, empathic professional, capable of navigating the nuanced landscape of healthcare with a blend of expertise and heartfelt understanding.

Regardless of the excuses, in overlooking the elevation and retention of women in the early chapters of their technical careers, companies inadvertently thin the ranks of potential female leaders. Each missed promotion and each overlooked talent is not just a narrative of today, but a precursor to a diluted representation in the boardrooms and decision-making tables of tomorrow. The ripple of today's oversight can thus morph into tomorrow's wave of unequal representation, marring not just the equitable tapestry of the workplace but potentially thwarting a rich harvest of diverse ideas and leadership styles.

# Section II: Navigating Treacherous Waters

*Awareness and Bias Training*

Navigating the vast expanses of the tech industry unveils a landscape filled with subtle yet pervasive nets of unconscious biases. These biases, subtle in their manifestation, have a way of weaving through the fabric of our daily interactions, often unnoticed, yet leaving a trace that can morph into barriers. These barriers, though invisible, cast long shadows over the shimmering potential of aspiring women venturing into the field. It's like sailing through a vast ocean, with hidden currents that can subtly alter your course, often without you realizing it. The first step to untangling these hidden nets is to shine a light on them, to recognize their existence and understand how they subtly influence decisions, interactions, and opportunities within the professional landscape.

The antidote to these elusive biases? Awareness and bias training. This remedy transcends beyond a mere series of mundane workshops or routine training sessions. It's a robust, multifaceted tool aimed at unearthing, unraveling, and understanding the intricacies of these biases. This initiative lays them bare, exposing them to the light of acknowledgment, encouraging dialogues, discussions, and deep introspection. When undertaken with sincerity and an open mind, awareness and bias training can be akin to opening the windows in a long-enclosed space, letting fresh perspectives breeze through, challenging the stale, unexamined notions that often reside unchecked in the corners of our consciousness. It's about nurturing a culture of continual learning, reflection, and conscious action.

The journey of dissecting and dismantling unconscious biases does not end with mere acknowledgment. It extends into fostering a culture of action, where the insights gleaned from awareness and bias training translate into tangible changes in behaviors, attitudes, and organizational practices. It's about creating an environment that not only recognizes the value of diverse perspectives but actively cultivates and celebrates it. It's about laying down the stepping stones that will facilitate the journey of many aspiring women in HCIT, ensuring that the path they tread is free from the shackles of unexamined biases. In this endeavor, each stride taken in unison toward addressing and amending unconscious biases is a stride toward crafting a more inclusive, equitable, and nurturing professional landscape in HCIT. Through this concerted effort, the narrative within HCIT can transition from merely navigating the unseen biases to actively dismantling them, thereby nurturing a workspace that allows the brilliance of aspiring women to shine through unobscured.

## Networking

In the vast echo chamber of the tech world, voices of women often get lost or echoed back in a distorted pitch. The remedy? Solid networking platforms, dedicated to amplifying the nuanced yet powerful voices of women in HCIT. As a budding professional, your network is your beacon in the dense fog of professional challenges.

Gravitate toward women-centric tech events, forums, and online communities. They are your wellspring of knowledge, encouragement, and opportunities.

Here are a few to start:

- *Girls in Tech*: A global nonprofit organization that aims to empower and support women in technology and entrepreneurship.
- *Women Who Code*: A global nonprofit organization that provides resources and support for women pursuing careers in technology.
- *AnitaB.org*: A nonprofit organization that works to promote diversity, equity, and inclusion in the tech industry.
- *National Center for Women & Information Technology (NCWIT)*: A nonprofit organization that works to increase the participation of girls and women in computing.
- *Women Tech Council*: A national organization that provides mentorship, networking, and professional development opportunities for women in the tech industry.

These organizations offer a variety of resources, including mentorship programs, networking events, job boards, and more. They are dedicated to supporting women in the tech industry and promoting diversity and inclusion in the industry. Don't just join, be a vibrant participant. Share your journey and learn from others.

## Emphasizing Work–Life Balance

The scales of work–life balance often find themselves heavily tipped, creating a seesaw of obligations that many women find challenging to stabilize. This imbalance tends to amplify as you venture deeper into the intricacies of this field. However, the antidote lies not in a rigid, inflexible structure but rather in a fluid, adaptable arrangement that acknowledges and respects the myriad roles you juggle daily. The first stride toward achieving this equilibrium is to advocate for a work environment that's receptive to flexible work hours, telecommuting, or part-time work arrangements. The modern workspace is evolving, and it's imperative to ensure that your professional environment is morphing alongside to accommodate your unique needs. It's a progressive step that not only underlines your value but also underscores the essence of adaptability in fostering a balanced life.

The essence of work–life balance transcends beyond mere flexibility in work hours; it's an emblem of a culture that respects individuality and personal life commitments. Your prowess in HCIT is not a reflection of the hours clocked in behind a desk but is manifested through the impact and value you impart to your projects and team. This perspective needs to be shared and understood within your workplace to cultivate a culture that values output over hours, quality over quantity. Moreover, a balanced work–life rhythm is quintessential for nurturing your creativity, innovation, and overall wellbeing. It's about creating a symbiotic relationship between your professional commitments and personal aspirations, ensuring one complements the other rather than competing.

Advocating for a balanced work–life sphere is not a solitary endeavor but a collective movement. Engage in discussions with your peers, share your insights with your supervisors, and be a part of or initiate forums within your organization that aim to address and enhance work–life balance. Additionally, seek mentorship from seasoned individuals in your field who have successfully navigated the balance and are leading fulfilling professional and personal lives. Their experiences can provide invaluable guidance and bolster your advocacy for a balanced work–life environment. It's about creating a narrative that resonates with many, a narrative that elucidates the indispensable nature of a balanced work–life structure in fostering not only individual growth but the collective progression of women. Through a blend of advocacy, awareness, and action, you can contribute to sculpting a work culture that is empathetic to your life's diverse roles, ultimately leading to a fulfilling and impactful career.

## Diversity, Equity, Inclusion, and Belonging (DEIB) Initiatives

The rich fabric of HCIT becomes even more vibrant and effective when it's woven with a multitude of diverse experiences and viewpoints. Initiatives around diversity, equity, inclusion, and belonging (DEIB) aren't just items on a to-do list; they're the very constructs that help us build a truly equitable workplace. It's imperative that we actively champion these causes. I encourage you to work closely with your human resources department, to get involved with diversity committees, and to confidently share your own perspectives on how we can cultivate an environment that welcomes everyone.

There are several impactful DEIB initiatives currently underway in the tech industry, as highlighted by recent reports:[8]

- **Shiseido:** The Japanese cosmetics company has implemented initiatives to accelerate gender parity at the board and executive levels, including inclusive work policies and process redesigns. The CEO and senior business leaders are directly accountable for these efforts, which are reflected in their performance metrics and compensation. The initiative has resulted in a significant increase in the ratio of women leaders within the company.
- **Tata Steel:** The steel manufacturer has introduced an initiative focused on intersectional gender diversity by addressing stereotypes, support structures, legal and geographic constraints, and non-inclusive policies. This has included the launch of the first-ever transgender hiring program in India.
- **Randstad:** The HR consulting firm has rolled out a program to economically empower at-risk women in the United States through upskilling and creating opportunities. The initiative includes rigorous tracking of key performance indicators and has added support services such as childcare and professional clothing after identifying the needs of the participants.

In the wake of the COVID-19 pandemic, we've seen how a crisis can act as a catalyst for transformation. This, alongside the rising tide of social and political movements, has propelled companies into a new era of steadfast commitment to tearing down long-standing barriers of inequality. It's a time of intense reflection and action—a period where our collective efforts can set the stage for meaningful progress. Your role in this cannot be understated; each action you take, each idea you share, becomes a part of the larger narrative shaping our industry's future. Let's embrace this opportunity to redefine the norms and create a legacy of inclusivity and fairness that will resonate for generations to come.

# Conclusion

Within the technology space, specifically in the complex realm of healthcare-focused technology, the essence of diverse representation, *and particularly the inclusion of women*, stands as a fundamental necessity. The modern age of healthcare pivots on the axis of technology, where every data point collected, every system deployed, holds the potential to transcend the boundaries of care, extending a beacon of hope and assurance to the seekers of health. Within this dynamic sphere, your presence, as women of substance, intellect, and fervor, is not merely a need—it is an imperative.

However, the barriers to entry are not unseen. Societal stereotypes, that age-old companion of gender disparity, subtly, and sometimes blatantly, question a woman's qualifications, dedication, and prowess. The whispers of doubt often begin early, muffling the enthusiasm of many bright minds at the dawn of their journey. The lack of early engagement in STEM, the scarcity of mentors who reflect your aspirations, can cast long shadows on the path. Yet, within these challenges lies your cue for defiance, for breaking the mold and forging ahead.

The tableau of gender representation in HCIT, though gradually shifting, still unveils stark contrasts. The tech sector, with its sprawling impact, has made strides in nurturing gender diversity with the trajectory to enhance female representation edging toward the 33% mark, as illuminated by Deloitte Insights. Yet, as we narrow down to the core technical roles—where coding merges with creativity, where data breathe life into decisions—the representation dwindles to a mere 17%.

For those who manage to clear these hurdles and secure a role in the tech industry, advancement opportunities are often just out of reach. The metaphor of the "leaky pipeline" reflects the gradual thinning of female representation as one ascends the ladder of hierarchy. The lack of mentorship, the sparse availability of role models, can often feel like a journey through a maze with no guiding light.

The strategies for fostering a conducive environment are not merely pages of a playbook, but a lived reality. Awareness and bias training, cultivation of networking platforms, emphasis on work–life balance, and continuous stride toward diversity and inclusion stand as your allies. Your voice, your advocacy for pay transparency, your insistence on regular pay audits, and your participation in negotiation skill-building workshops are not whispers in the wind—they are the heralds of a transforming landscape.

The journey of women in the tech industry is not a solitary one. It is a collective endeavor, a narrative of resilience, and an ode to the indomitable spirit that each one of you embodies. The road may have its share of twists, turns, and a few steep slopes, yet with every step, you are not merely walking toward a personal milestone, but you are etching the trail for a future where gender diversity is not the topic of boardroom discussions. In this pursuit of excellence and equality, every dialogue initiated, every bias challenged, every hand extended for mentorship, and every stride toward inclusive practices is a stitch in the fabric of a more equitable reality. The horizon is vast, and the potential boundless. As you embark down the path with dreams that soar high and a resolve of steel, remember, you are the harbinger of a future replete with promise and parity.

# Notes

1  Hupfer, S., Bucaille, A., Mazumder, S., & Crossan, G. (2021, December 1). *Women in the tech industry; Graining ground, but facing new headwinds.* Deloitte Insights. https://www2.deloitte.com/us/en/insights/industry/technology/tech-nology-media-and-telecom-predictions/2022/statistics-show-women-in-tech-nology-are-facing-new-headwinds.html

2  Master, A., Meltsoff, A., & Cheryan, S. (2021, November 24). *Stereotypes about girls dissuade many from careers in computer science.* The Conversation. https://theconversation.com/stereotypes-about-girls-dissuade-many-from-car eers-in-computer-science-172279

3  Kiran, H. (2023, July 7). *Women in technology statistics: What's new in 2023?* Tech Jury. https://techjury.net/blog/women-in-technology-statistics/ #:~:text=The%20latest%20women%20in%20tech%20statistics%20 reveal%20the,of%20girls%20desire%20a%20career%20in%20STEM%20 fields

4  White, S. (2023, March 13). *Women in tech statistics: The hard truths of an uphill battle.* CIO. https://www.cio.com/article/201905/women-in-tech-statis-tics-the-hard-truths-of-an-uphill-battle.html

5  Diehl, A., Stephenson, A., & Dzubinski, L. (2022, March 2). *Research: How bias against women persists in female-dominated workplaces.* Harvard Business Review. https://hbr.org/2022/03/research-how-bias-against-women -persists-in-female-dominated-workplaces

6  Marchant, N. (2021, April 13). *8 charts that show the impact of race and gen-der on technology careers.* World Economic Forum. https://www.weforum.org/ agenda/2021/04/gender-race-tech-industry/

7  Gascoigne, A., Griffits, S., Kubalcikova, P., Shenai, G, & Wright, C. (2022, March 1). *Repairing the broken rung on the career ladder for women in technical roles.* McKindseey & Company. https://www.mckinsey.com/ industries/technology-media-and-telecommunications/our-insights/ repairing-the-broken-rung-on-the-career-ladder-for-women-in-technical-roles/

8  Ellingrud, E., Ellsworth, D., Madner, S., Musallam, R., Sandhu, I., & Yee, L. (2023, January 13). *Diversity, equity, and inclusion lighthouses 2023.* McKinsey & Company. https://www.mckinsey.com/featured-insights/ diversity-and-inclusion/diversity-equity-and-inclusion-lighthouses-2023

# 7

# What to Look for in Male Allyship (and How to Become One)

## Introduction

Originally, I intended to only write the introduction, describing how my daughter inspired me to prepare a proposal for this book. When the proposal was approved, I immediately defaulted to the same strategy I used when my daughter came to me for advice: I turned to my personal network of successful healthcare information technology (HCIT) women for guidance and personal mentoring on this topic. As noted in my introduction, I had a feeling of guilt for not being more concerned about the lack of diversity in the industry until it came to my own daughter. This naturally caused me to question if I was doing enough and if I understood the issues well enough to be a good male ally and to take on a project like this. I also wanted to surround myself with people who had firsthand experiences on this topic to gain the requisite insights and learn more about what it means to be the type of leader who encourages success for underrepresented talent.

Needless to say, this was an opportunity for my own personal development and growth. And to no surprise, I still had a lot to learn. My first lesson came from Sherri Douville, a successful best-selling author and CEO of Medigram, Inc. Sherri introduced me to the concept of calling in the support of male allies in my personal network. She described that while many men desire to be an ally and mentor to not just women but to underrepresented

DOI: 10.4324/9781003366591-7

talent in their organizations, they may feel insecure about admitting they don't know how or even where to start. She also described how people in general often struggle with situational awareness when it comes to gender issues. According to her book, she made the point that a state of unawareness of the prospective inequalities in the workplace can lead to not seeing people's true identities and, inadvertently, not seeing the way in which their identities affect their everyday experiences and opportunities.[1] This state of unawareness can therefore lead to incorrect assumptions and prevent individuals from acknowledging that inequity exists. There have been countless publications and studies on gender differences and how these differences impact both communications and interactions. For example, the gender–pay gap is still very real. According to an analysis of the median hourly earnings of workers by the Pew Research Center, women in 2022 earned an average of 82% of what men earned, which is similar to where the pay gap stood in 2002, when women earned 80% as much as men.[2] This is indicative of the lack of progress made toward closing the pay gap in the past two decades. In addition, according to the latest Women in the Workplace report from McKinsey in partnership with LeanIn.Org, the authors describe the unprecedented number of women leaders leaving their companies and calling it the "Great Breakup," with the underlying factors driving these women to leave being having to face stronger headwinds than their male counterparts, having their diversity, equity, and inclusion (DEI) work underrecognized and being overworked, and seeking a different culture of work that was more committed to the wellbeing of the employees and DEI initiatives.[3]

There are still more factors to consider. In a best-selling book by John Gray, PhD, he described the ways in which men and women have unique ways of responding to one another when communicating. While the book is more focused on relationships between men and women, there is much to be said about the significance of communication theory, which is important in both personal and professional circumstances. According to Dr. Gray, men tend to assume women want help when they bring up issues, when most of the time what women desire from men is for them to listen. The book goes on to describe how men will often retreat and withdraw when they get stressed, whereas women prefer to talk about stressful issues in most instances. This often creates a situation of unbalanced communication.[4] While I do not claim to be an expert on gender studies, according to my wife of 33 years, I am guilty of doing all of this and more, and I assume this holds true for many of my male counterparts.

Ultimately, my conversation with Sherri felt more like a "calling in" as opposed to a "calling out." It was helping me think differently and allowing me to see a blind spot without feeling any guilt or shame. Sherri recommended I enlist men in my network to participate in the nomination process for this book. She also encouraged me to not be afraid of directly asking what men can do to improve our male allyship efforts. This book would therefore not be complete unless we discussed some of the ways in which men can pay it forward as allies.

## What does It Mean to be a Male Ally?

Before going further on this topic, it is important to first set some context for what it means to be a male ally. According to David G. Smith, Associate Professor at the Johns Hopkins Carey Business School, and W. Brad Johnson, Professor of Psychology in the Department of Leadership, Ethics and Law at the United States Naval Academy and Faculty Associate in the Graduate School of Education at Johns Hopkins University, allyship can be defined as actively promoting gender fairness and equity in the workplace by creating supportive and collaborative relationships and participating in public acts of sponsorship and advocacy intended to drive systematic improvements in the workplace culture.[5] In a book that has been the recipient of the Axiom Business Book Awards for Best Human Resources/Employee Training, they discussed in depth the ways in which men can support women by shifting their thoughts away from perceiving gender inequality as a "women's issue" and instead viewing themselves as allies to women and acting as a key proponent of change. They stress the fact that allyship connotes the collaborative nature of partnership toward a common goal, which therefore creates a relationship of interdependence and support rather than a relationship stemming from imbalance.

## Characteristics Women Find to be of Value from Male Allies

With this definition of male allyship as a guide, I therefore sought out women leaders to directly ask about the characteristics they believed to be essential from their allies. The following is a summary of what women in my HCIT network have said about what was most important to them from their male counterparts:

- Being a good listener. (Note: This was the **most** popular response.)
- Taking concerns seriously without interrupting or downplaying the issue.
- Standing up and speaking out against any situations that involve inequality, harassment, or sexism in the workplace.
- Being open to feedback.
- Sharing opportunities by doing what is called "pass up and pass on" when diversity is lacking. For instance, when asked to speak in a panel of all males, suggest a female colleague go in your place or go with you (if possible) to bring in some needed diversity.
- Celebrating accomplishments.
- Sharing the workload and giving credit where credit is due.
- Being a mentor or sponsor. (One person called it being a good "work husband.")
- Being visible. Declaring yourself a male ally and encouraging others to do the same.
- Just staying out of the way. (Though stated in a playful and light-hearted manner, this was my personal favorite.)
- Setting an example. (This comment was the most impactful to me personally.)

Taking in feedback and being a good listener are only part of the solution. The real work comes from living up to these expectations and following through on the commitment to be a positive example of a leader who values being an ally. As mentioned above, the comment about *setting an example* was especially impactful, as I recognized that I was late to the party in terms of my own sense of awareness on this matter. On that note, here is what I am doing to set an example:

- Actively listening, observing, and learning.
- Seeking out opportunities to draw in more diverse voices.
- Taking meaningful action by looking for and acting on opportunities to advance diversity in the workplace and within the HCIT industry.
- Setting an example by speaking up and challenging my male colleagues to also think differently.
- Continuously making the effort to keep learning and improving.

As a sidenote, I am not seeking praise or recognition for any of this. My objective for sharing my personal goals is rooted in the hope that it can inspire others to think differently. Using my influence to advocate for greater representation of women in the HCIT industry is my way of setting an example and living up to these expectations. I understand how my actions can have meaningful benefits for myself and our industry when we all encourage women to grow and thrive. This is truly a win-win situation, as success should be a mutually shared goal and is one that is best achieved through collaborative efforts.

# Benefits of Promoting Gender Equity in the Workplace

There is a growing body of research that supports the financial benefits realized when organizations actively pursue a commitment to DEI initiatives. Some of the existing statistics include the following:

- Companies in the top 25% of gender diversity on their executive teams were more likely to experience above-average profitability.[6]
- Companies in the bottom 25% of gender diversity were less likely to see higher profits than the national industry average.[7]
- On average, companies that increased the share of female partners by 10% also increased revenues by 10%.[8]
- A Policy Brief report derived from the financial records of about 62,000 publicly listed firms in 58 economies over 1997–2017, accounting for more than 92% of global GDP, concludes that gender diversity contributes to superior firm performance.[9]
- The World Economic Forum's Diversity, Equity, and Inclusion 4.0 report suggests that companies with diverse employees have "up to a 20% higher rate of innovation and 19% higher innovation revenues."[10]

While it is certainly acknowledged that a cause-and-effect relationship cannot be deduced simply because of the observed correlation in the information above, these data do reveal that there does appear to be a connection between increasing diversity in an organization and financial performance. Setting aside the financial benefits of increasing inclusivity in the workplace, companies tend to thrive in a culture that promotes DEI, as diversity brings together people from different backgrounds, showcasing a variety of perspectives and leading to innovation and creativity.[11] As I continue to gain further knowledge about the existing information available relative to gender diversity and how it impacts the workforce, I am further determined to learn more about the ways in which I can be a part of the change.

## Considerations for Creating a Sustainable Workplace Culture Supporting Gender Equity

As most organizations tend to have men occupying key stakeholder positions, this section is directed toward those in a position to influence change in their organization, like myself. The following are some considerations with fostering a workplace aligned for gender equity initiatives:

- *Increasing Representation of Women (and Diverse Talent in General)*: It is significantly important for companies to have a better representation of women and diverse talent, and this is especially the case for the HCIT industry. Some research shows that companies with a higher parity in the percentage of women in senior management achieve a lower employee turnover.[12] Representation matters, and a diverse team will also naturally allow for greater creativity when it comes to developing solutions to problems in the organization.
- *Improving Leadership Accountability*: Key stakeholders in positions of power have the most influence and capability to promote DEI efforts, with the focus of this book being geared toward gender equity specifically. It should not just be considered the role of human resources to ensure that the company has strong policies in place to have a zero-tolerance policy against discriminatory behavior or instances of gender bias. To truly be impactful, CEOs and leaders must be able to articulate a compelling vision embedded with accountability that then flows downward into all levels of the organization.[13] When male allies in leadership positions embed DEI initiatives in the workplace culture, it strengthens the company's ability to truly realize a change in the cultural shift toward greater inclusivity.
- *Making DEI Initiatives Data-Driven*: While embedding DEI initiatives in the workplace is important, there needs to be a way to

capture the success (or lack of success) of these initiatives. For this to be captured, there need to be specific, tangible goals in place that can be tracked. Therefore, priorities must be explicitly defined based on what will drive the business growth strategy,[14] and this needs to be tracked over a reasonable period of time. A company will then be able to make more informed decisions moving forward regarding these initiatives.

## Personal Experience: A Picture is Worth a Thousand Words

I will end this chapter with a personal experience to bring home the power of gender diversity. The year was 2019, and I had just finished giving a talk on cybersecurity at one of the major medical association annual conferences in San Francisco. As I was leaving the conference center, I noticed my good friend and colleague Julia Lee, Principal Consultant at NorthStar Vision Partners, LLC, was participating in a panel discussion on private equity in an adjacent room. Excited to see my friend, I took a seat in the back of the room and immediately noticed she was the **only** woman in a panel of nine people. What happened next was nothing short of glorious. Once the panel discussion came to an end, several men from the audience gathered around the stage to discuss and gain more knowledge from the experts on the panel. I will let the picture below tell the rest of the story (Figure 7.1).

The amount of pride I felt for my friend Julia in that moment will forever be cherished and remembered as a powerful example of what female representation can accomplish. Many of those men taking advice from Julia will personally (and financially) benefit from the undoubtedly beneficial information exchanged on that day. As they say, a picture is worth a thousand words.

## Conclusion

This chapter has focused on the significance of male allyship and the way this can promote a successful culture of diversity and inclusivity in the workplace. The author has focused on personal, firsthand takeaways from his desire to gain further knowledge in the matters of female representation in the workplace and, in so doing, has recognized the importance of reaching out to

**FIGURE 7.1**
**A panel of nine people with one female speaker.**
**Photographs by the author.**

female leaders in the industry to validate the insights gained and to learn from the lived experiences of these incredibly talented women. The goal is ultimately to create a collaborative environment that supports the success of an organization while committing to broadening one's perspective on matters of gender equity and the actions male allies can take to partner with women and influence a culture of change in the industry.

# Notes

1  Douville, S. (2023). *Advanced health technology: Managing risk while tackling barriers to rapid acceleration*. Routledge.

2 Aragão, C. (2023, March 1). *Gender pay gap in U.S. hasn't changed much in two decades.* Pew Research Center. https://www.pewresearch.org/short-reads/2023/03/01/gender-pay-gap-facts/#:~:text=In%202022%2C%20women%20earned%20an%20average%20of%2082%25,when%20women%20earned%2080%25%20as%20much%20as%20men.

3 Krivkovich, A., Liu, W. W., Nguyen, H., Rambachan, I., Robinson, N., Williams, M., & Yee, L. (2022, October 18). *Women in the workplace.* McKinsey & Company. https://www.mckinsey.com/featured-insights/diversity-and-inclusion/women-in-the-workplace#/

4 Gray, J. (1993). *Men are from Mars, women are from Venus: A practical guide for improving communication and getting what you want in your relationships.* HarperCollins Publishers.

5 Smith, D. G., & Johnson, W. B. (2020). *Good guys: How men can be better allies for women in the workplace.* Harvard Business Review Press.

6 Hunt, H., Prince, S., Dixon-Fyle, S., & Dolan, K. (2020). *Diversity wins: How inclusion matters.* McKinsey & Company https://www.mckinsey.com/~/media/mckinsey/featured%20insights/diversity%20and%20inclusion/diversity%20wins%20how%20inclusion%20matters/diversity-wins-how-inclusion-matters-vf.pdf

7 Hunt, H., Prince, S., Dixon-Fyle, S., & Yee, L. (2018). *Delivering through diversity.* McKinsey & Company. https://www.mckinsey.com/capabilities/people-and-organizational-performance/our-insights/delivering-through-diversity

8 Gompers, P., & Kovvali, S. (2018). *The other diversity dividend.* Harvard Business Review. https://hbr.org/2018/07/the-other-diversity-dividend

9 Han, S., & Noland, M. (2020). *Women scaling the corporate ladder: Progress steady but slow globally.* Peterson Institute for International Economics. https://www.piie.com/publications/policy-briefs/women-scaling-corporate-ladder-progress-steady-slow-globally

10 World Economic Forum (2020). *Diversity, equity, & inclusion 4.0.* World Economic Forum. https://www.weforum.org/reports/diversity-equity-and-inclusion-4-0-a-toolkit-for-leaders-to-accelerate-social-progress-in-the-future-of-work

11 Tynes, B. (2022, March 3). *The importance of diversity and inclusion for today's companies.* Forbes. https://www.forbes.com/sites/forbescommunicationscouncil/2022/03/03/the-importance-of-diversity-and-inclusion-for-todays-companies/?sh=57b980fc49df

12 Williams, E., & Flaherty, T. (2022, March 31). *Reporting on gender equity is a key step to improving diversity, upward mobility for women.* Morningstar. https://www.morningstar.com/sustainable-investing/reporting-gender-equity-is-key-step-improving-diversity-upward-mobility-women

13 Ibid.

14 Ibid.

# 8

# Influential Women in HCIT

## Section I: Past Women in the Health and/or Technology Industry

*Bessie Blount, Physical Therapist, Inventor, Forensic Scientist*

Bessie Blount was a physical therapist during World War II, where she assisted many wounded soldiers and disabled veterans recuperating from their sustained injuries.[1] She recognized a need for patients unable to feed themselves properly and therefore losing their quality of life. Determined to find a solution, her ideas led to the creation of the feeding tube. She went on to create several other inventions, including the medical basin. Notably, she became close friends with Albert Einstein's son! Later in her career, she became a forensic analyst, working in law enforcement.[2]

*Nina Starr Braunwald, MD, Cardio-thoracic Surgeon, Innovator, Researcher*

Nina Starr Braunwald is the first doctor in medical history to create an artificial heart valve. This discovery led to many other medical advances and paved the way for more research to be conducted. For example, she led the study and research of medical advances for children born with heart defects such as atrial septal defect, more commonly known as the hole in the heart disease. It is important to note that Starr Braunwald was the first woman

DOI: 10.4324/9781003366591-8

doctor to perform open-heart surgery and served as New York's Bellevue Hospital's first female surgeon in 1952.[3]

In an article published by Allen Press, it was noted that "despite her substantial achievements in teaching, research, and clinical care at NIH, UCSD, and Harvard University, she was never honored with an endowed professorship at any of these prestigious institutions."[4] This demonstrates the gender bias existent in that time period, but nevertheless, she persevered despite this to ensure advances were made for the wellbeing of her patients.

## Ada Lovelace, Mathematician

Ada Lovelace's achievements date back to the early eighteenth century when she began her career as a computer programmer. She is recognized as the first female computer programmer and was also the co-developer of an in-flight advanced machine that calculated mathematical sequences, named the Analytical Engine.[5] Ada passed away before the machine was completed in its entirety. However, many of the advancements and discoveries in computer language have been accredited to her to this day.

## Florence Nightingale, Nurse, Statistician

As it relates to advances in healthcare and nursing in particular, Florence Nightingale played a significant role in improving nursing protocols. Referred to endearingly as "The Lady with the Lamp," she treated wounded soldiers on nightly rounds during the Crimean War and improved sanitary conditions so drastically that mortality rates decreased from 40% to 2%.[6] She wrote extensively on the matter of health issues, and much of her books and studies are what modern nursing procedures are based upon. She was also incredibly skilled in working with data, and these data would later lead to the formation of a Royal Commission to improve the health of the British army.[7]

When Nightingale passed away in 1910 at the age of 90, several years after her death, the International Committee of the Red Cross created the "Florence Nightingale Medal," awarded to nurses every two years who are recognized for their "exceptional courage and devotion to victims of armed conflict or natural disaster."[8]

# Section II: Contemporary Women in the HCIT Industry

*Priya Abani, President and CEO, AliveCor, Inc.*

Priya Abani is the President and Chief Executive Officer at AliveCor, a health tech company that utilizes deep machine learning and artificial intelligence (AI) to provide intelligent and sophisticated remote cardiological care. According to their website, the mission of AliveCor is to "save lives and transform cardiology by delivering intelligent, highly personalized heart data to clinicians and patients anytime, anywhere."[9] AliveCor makes use of cutting-edge technology that takes a six-lead personal electrocardiogram (ECG) of remote patients, which enables clinicians (and the patient) to receive their ECG data in real time. The company's goal is to focus on heart health and deliver heart health services at any time. Through her leadership, the company has built the largest AI-driven consumer subscription service in the world for cardiovascular care.[10] AliveCor serves over two million people, and it is expected to continue to grow. According to an interview with *Health Evolution*, Abani stated, "Since becoming CEO in 2019, I have built on the strong foundation established by the AliveCor team by leading the development of new product and service offerings to advance our mission of saving lives and transforming cardiology."[11]

The company is continuing to evolve in order to meet its goals for the near future. At AliveCor, Abani oversees the continued convergence of AI and healthcare to create a trusted, worldwide network for both physicians and patients through the company's personal ECG devices, telehealth services, and technology platform.[12] She has over 20 years of experience in the industry, with her educational background including a Master of Science from Clarkson University as well as a Master of Business Administration from Babson College. She has been recognized as an influential woman in HCIT by several major journals and magazines, including *Medium, The HealthTech Report,* the *Silicon Valley Business Journal, PR Newswire,* and is a recipient of the Sweetwater Leadership and Innovation Award. Additionally, Abani is on the Board of Directors for Jacobs and the Board of Trustees for Teachers Insurance and Annuity Association of America (TIAA).

## Raquel C. Bono, Defense Health Agency (DHS), Vice Admiral (Ret), Former Director of the Defense Health Agency, Senior Advisor

Vice Admiral Raquel paved the way for many initiatives within the US Armed Forces to improve healthcare delivery by improving technological infrastructure. She was one of the key players in developing and implementing a program that allows members to securely manage and track their healthcare online. In 2018, she was recognized by the Healthcare Information and Management Systems Society (HIMSS) as being one of the most influential women in HCIT.[13]

Bono retired from the US Navy as the first female medical officer to achieve the three-star admiral rank. She currently "serves as the Chief Health Officer at Viking Cruises and a senior fellow at the Johns Hopkins University Applied Physics Laboratory" as well as a Senior Advisor for Red Cell Partners, a firm focused on promoting health advancements related to national security.[14]

## Julia Cheek, CEO and Founder, Everlywell

Julia Cheek is the CEO and Founder of Everlywell, a company that produces at-home health testing lab products. She began the company in 2014 and even appeared on Shark Tank in 2017, where she succeeded in having Lori Greiner join Everlywell as an investor.[15] Ms. Cheek's company has been immensely successful, and it emerged from a desire to solve the problem of access to affordable testing results. Since then, her company has grown from 0 to 750-plus employees.[16] When it comes to managing her schedule and leading a demanding life, Ms. Cheek makes sure to make time for her family and prioritizes scheduling breaks to prevent burnout. She also notes that access to childcare is incredibly important for a working woman, stating that access to childcare is an "important element in enabling women in the workforce."[17] In addition to the above, Ms. Cheek is an active individual, and she finds that this is especially important and incorporates this into her morning routine.

## Molly Coye, MD, MPH, Executive in Residence, AVIA

Molly Coye, MD, is an American physician by trade and a pioneer of public health initiatives. She attended the Johns Hopkins University School of Medicine, where she received her degree in 1977. She went on to complete her residency in family practice and later became employed by the Center for Disease Control in San Francisco as a medical investigator. Many years later, Coye went on to be appointed commissioner of health for the state of New Jersey, where she was responsible for a significant budget and a multitude of employees. Dr. Coye furthered her career within the academic world at the University of California and Johns Hopkins University.[18]

At the turn of the century, Dr. Coye shifted her focus to technology and was employed by UCLA Health for many years as the Chief Innovation Officer, where she led many strategic advancements.[19] According to a biography about Dr. Coye, "In 2001, she founded the Health Technology Center, a non-profit group dedicated to advancing the use of beneficial technologies for healthier people and communities, where she is currently CEO."[20]

### Judith R. Faulkner, Founder and CEO, Epic

Judy Falkner is an American businesswoman, a self-made billionaire, and the founder and CEO of Epic Systems Corporation, otherwise known as Epic. Established in 1979, Epic is one of the largest electronic health record (EHR) system providers in the United States. In fact, according to the KLAS US Hospital EMR Market Share 2019 report, Epic (along with Cerner) maintained the largest share of the acute care hospital EHR market.[21] EHRs are one of the most critical health information technologies to exist, as they are the electronic record system that maintains patient medical history. Most notably, Epic was created completely in-house by Faulkner from the ground up, with humble origins in Madison, Wisconsin. She received her bachelor's degree in mathematics from Dickinson College and later earned a master's degree in computer science from the University of Wisconsin. Shortly after receiving her master's degree, she started the company under the name Human Services Computing, which later came to be known as Epic.[22] Their website states that Epic was founded in a basement with 1½ employees,[23] and now it has grown to be an EHR business that serves more than 305 million patients. The company began with a $6,000 investment, part of which came from Faulkner's parents.[24] Faulkner and a dozen individuals made up of colleagues and their family members would invest a total of $70,000.[25] She maintained that in order to not lose control of the company, though it would take more time to build, no venture capital would be taken. This proved to be a decisive choice that ended up being incredibly wise. Today, Epic remains a privately held, employee-owned, and developer-led company that has never taken venture capital.

Epic's EHR is based on a 44-year-old programming language called Massachusetts General Hospital Utility Multi-Programming System (MUMPS).[26] It is one of the most recognized and established EHR healthcare software companies in the United States and is known for its comprehensive features and user-friendly, cloud-based interface. As a fully integrated solution, its suite of products was developed in-house and designed to work together synergistically. This creates economies of scale in developing reporting and analytic solutions using common tools.[27] As it relates to meaningful use (and Health Insurance Portability and Accountability Act [HIPAA] compliance in general), hospitals, health systems, and other health organizations can rest assured that Epic will meet meaningful use certification as it has a strong track record of doing so. Its client base is also incredibly notable as a result of the recognized high performance of the Epic EHR. They include Baptist Health, Cedars-Sinai Health, Cleveland Clinic, Johns Hopkins Medicine, and Mount Sinai Health.[28] Faulkner is constantly recognized as one of the most powerful women in healthcare and regularly tops the lists in magazines such as Forbes as one of the most influential women in business. She is also known for her commitment to advancing healthcare through technology and advocating for patient-centered healthcare.

### Theresa Holstead, Senior Director IT Integration and Project Management, McKesson

Theresa has a tenured career with McKesson, previously with PSS World Medical for over 20 years (later acquired by McKesson), where she served as the Executive Director IT PMO and established a high degree of familiarity with logistics in medical supply distribution. Her career began with McKesson in 2013, where she currently serves as the Senior Director of IT Integration.[29] Most notably, in 2022, Theresa was recognized as one of the top five women transforming healthcare through technology by McKesson.

Holstead is recognized at McKesson as a trailblazer leading the way during the pandemic in 2020, when COVID-19 hit the industry. Holstead and her team developed a program to react to the response needs to COVID-19 testing and were instrumental in distributing the equipment throughout the United States. In the article in 2022, Holstead says, "My team is all about finding the best way to take care of the customer through technology, and if we see a better way to meet their needs, we're going to make it happen."[30]

### April Koh, Co-Founder and CEO, Spring Health

April Koh is the Co-Founder and CEO of Spring Health, a company that offers comprehensive solutions for the mental wellbeing of employers and servicing health plans. Founded in May of 2016, the company now works with more than 150 companies, trusted by leading organizations such as Wellstar Health System, Fortive, and Microsoft. According to *Forbes*, Koh is the youngest woman to run a business with a $2 billion valuation, landing on the Forbes 30 under 30 Consumer Technology List. April explained, "The most expensive problem in the mental health space is trial and error. There was this crazy proliferation of all these apps and solutions that were claiming to help people with their mental health. And there was no guidance around which resource, which app or which therapist would be best for you."[31]

Spring Health uses clinically tested, machine learning technology to match an individual to a personalized health plan. Using machine learning models, the company's solution assesses an individual's needs, and care navigators guide the individual to the right care, whether it's coaching, meditation, therapy, or medication.[32] The demand for mental health services is increasing, and Spring Health sets itself apart by reducing the issues of trial and error and guiding the individual to the right service of care, whether the service is therapy, coaching, meditation, or more. According to April, the founding idea of the company was that "faster access to mental health care is meaningless if the care doesn't actually work for you. We recognize that we have to go beyond faster access to faster recovery, and that is only possible through precision and through personalization."[33] April has received honors from the American Psychiatric Association and has been featured in Apple, *Crain's New York Business, Medium, The Wall Street Journal, National Quality Forum*, and Crew Capital. In addition, she is one of the Business Insider's 30 under 40 leaders in healthcare, a Goldman Sachs 100 Most Intriguing Entrepreneurs in 2019, a World Economic Forum Technology Pioneer, and a Yale Entrepreneurial Institute fellow.[34]

### Tania Saison, Senior Vice President and Chief Compliance Officer/Chief Responsibility Officer, Edwards Lifesciences

Tania Saison serves as the Senior Vice President and Chief Compliance Officer/Chief Responsibility Officer of Edwards Lifesciences, a global medical technology company that specializes in technologies for the treatment of structural heart disease. They are a patient-centered organization that work together with physicians and researchers to achieve their goals, serving almost 100 countries globally. In addition to their focus on structural heart disease, Edwards Lifesciences targets medical innovations for critical care and surgical monitoring. One of their most renowned technologies is the SAPIEN valve, with the SAPIEN 3 valve being "the only valve approved for valve-in-valve procedures in both the aortic and mitral positions, allowing patients at high or greater surgical risk to avoid an additional open heart procedure."[35]

Tania has been featured in "The Top 25 Women Leaders in Medical Devices in 2023" by The Healthcare Technology Report. According to the report, "As CRO, Saison oversees the company's Global Integrity Program with unwavering support from the Board of Directors and executive leadership."[36] She received her Juris Doctor from Columbia Law School and her Masters from Harvard Business School. As a member of the global leadership team, Tania ensures that the company's culture of ethics continues to thrive. According to a message from Tania Saison, "Our shared commitment to integrity and ethics is the foundation for our continued success."[37] Edwards Lifesciences is recognized by Ethisphere as one of the 2023 World's Most Ethical Companies, which is a testament to the success of Tania's leadership in these efforts.

## Conclusion

This chapter provided a brief overview of female leaders who have successfully advanced initiatives in the HCIT sector. Their successes are excellent examples that can be learned from and used to inspire our new generation of female leaders. We have come a long way in the industry, and numerous advancements will likely take place well into the future. From this, we hope that women can consider the contributions other women have made to history, both past and present, and that this may instill a desire to not only join the HCIT industry but excel in it.

## Notes

1 AWIS. (n.d). *Bessie Blount.* AWIS. https://awis.org/historical-women/bessie-blount/
2 Ibid.

3   NIH. (2022, March 01). *Nina Braunwald, M.D.* NIH. https://www.nhlbi. nih.gov/nhlbi-celebrates-women-scientists/nina-braunwald-md

4   Sabharwal, N., Dev, H., Smail, H., McGiffin,D. C., & Saxena, P. (2017, April 1). Nina Braunwald: A female pioneer in cardiac surgery. *Texas Heart Institute Journal*, 44(2), 96–100. https://doi.org/10.14503/THIJ-16-6048

5   Brittanica. (n.d.) *Ada Lovelace.* In Brittanica. https://www.britannica.com/ biography/Ada-Lovelace

6   Health Hive. (2021, March 8). *10 trailblazing women in healthcare.* Health Hive. https://hive.rochesterregional.org/2021/03/history-of-women-in-healthcare

7   NWHM. (n.d.). *Florence Nightingale.* National Women's History Museum. https://www.womenshistory.org/education-resources/biographies/ florence-nightingale

8   ICRC. (2023, November 1). *Care amid conflict: Stories of four Florence Nightingale Medal 2023 recipients.* ICRC. https://www.icrc.org/en/document/ care-amid-conflict-florence-nightingale-medal-2023

9   AliveCore, Inc. (2023). *Mission.* AliveCore. https://www.alivecor.com/ mission/

10  Georgiadis, C. (2022). *Inspirational women in STEM and tech: Priya Abani of AliveCor on the 5 Leadership lessons she learned from her experience.* Medium. https://medium.com/authority-magazine/inspirational-women-in-stem-and-t ech-priya-abani-of-alivecor-on-the-5-leadership-lessons-she-15401235fd9a

11  Health Evolution. (2022). *Innovator CEO profile: AliveCor's Priya Abani.* Health Evolution. https://www.healthevolution.com/insider/innovator-ceo- profile-alivecors-priya-abani/

12  The Healthcare Technology Report. (2022). The top 50 healthcare technology CEOs of 2022. *The Healthcare Technology Report.* Retrieved from https://thehealth- caretechnologyreport.com/the-top-50-healthcare-technology-ceos-of-2022/

13  HIMSS. (2018, January 18). *Meet the 2018 influential women in health IT awardees.* HIMSS. https://www.himss.org/news/meet-2018-most-influential- women-health-it-awardees

14  Bloomberg. (2023, June 1). *Retired vice admiral Raquel "Rocky" C. Bono, former director of the defense health agency, joins Red Cell Partners as a senior advisor and the board of TARA Mind.* Bloomberg. https://www.bloomberg. com/press-releases/2023-06-01/retired-vice-admiral-raquel-rocky-c-bono -former-director-of-the-defense-health-agency-joins-red-cell-partners-as-a

15  Everylywell. (n.d.). *The Everlywell story: From Shark Tank to now.* Everywell. https://www.everlywell.com/blog/news-and-info/everlywell-shark-tank/

16  Machina, Z. (2021). *Julia Cheek: How Everlywell founder and CEO spends her time.* Undock. https://phase.undock.com/julia-cheek-how-everlywell-founder- and-ceo-spends-her-time/

17  Ibid.

18  CF Medicine. (2015, June 3). *Dr. Molly Joel Coye.* CF Medicine. https://cfmed- icine.nlm.nih.gov/physicians/biography_71.html

19  Health Evolution. (n.d.). *Molly Coye, MD.* Health Evolution. https://www. healthevolution.com/bios/speaker/molly-coye-md/

20  Ibid.

21  Drees, J. (2019). *KLAS: Epic, Cerner dominate EHR marketshare.* Becker's Health IT. https://www.beckershospitalreview.com/ehrs/klas-epic-cerner-dominate-emr- market-share.html

22  CEO Connection. (n.d.). *Judy Faulkner, CEO & Founder of Epic Systems*. CEO Connection. https://www.ceoconnection.com/judy-faulkner/
23  Epic. (2023). *About us*. Epic. https://www.epic.com/about
24  Ibid.
25  Moukheiber, Z. (2012). *Epic system's tough billionaire*. Forbes. https://www.forbes.com/sites/zinamoukheiber/2012/04/18/epic-systems-tough-billionaire/?sh=5c56cc6158d9
26  Ibid.
27  Coquerel, J. (2016). *Why hospitals choose Epic over other EHR systems?* Syntrix. https://www.syntrixconsulting.com/blog/why-hospitals-choose-epic-over-other-ehr-systems
28  Ibid.
29  LinkedIn. (n.d.). *Theresa Holstead* [LinkedIn page]. LinkedIn. https://apastyle.apa.org/style-grammar-guidelines/references/examples/linkedin-references
30  McKesson. (n.d.). *5 women transforming healthcare through technology*. McKesson. https://www.mckesson.com/Our-Stories/Five-Women-Transforming-Healthcare-Through-Technology/
31  McGrath, M. (2021). *Spring Health notches a $190 million series C at a $2 billion valuation, making CEO April Koh the youngest woman to run a unicorn*. Forbes. https://www.forbes.com/sites/maggiemcgrath/2021/09/16/spring-health-notches-a-190-million-series-c-at-a-2-billion-valuation-making-ceo-april-koh-the-youngest-woman-to-run-a-unicorn/?sh=13ce33654ced
32  Landi, H. *Spring Health snags $190 million to build out family health mental health services, ramp up health plan partnerships*. Fierce Healthcare. https://www.fiercehealthcare.com/digital-health/spring-health-snags-190m-to-expand-family-mental-health-services-for-global#:~:text=Chekroud%2C%20Koh%20and%20Abhishek%20Chandra,to%20multinational%20Fortune%20500%20corporations
33  Chai, J. (2021). *April Koh, Spring Health, on leading in precision health*. Medium. https://medium.com/wharton-pulse-podcast/april-koh-spring-health-on-leading-in-precision-mental-health-59e9a73eb55e
34  Ibid.
35  Edwards Lifesciences. (2023). *SAPIEN 3 TAVI*. Edwards Lifesciences. https://www.edwards.com/gb/devices/Heart-Valves/Transcatheter-Sapien-3
36  The Healthcare Technology Report. (2023). *The top 25 women leaders in medical devices of 2023*. The Healthcare Technology Report. https://thehealthcaretechnologyreport.com/the-top-25-women-leaders-in-medical-devices-of-2023/
37  Edwards Lifesciences. (2023). *Corporate responsibility*. Edwards Lifesciences. https://www.edwards.com/sg/aboutus/corp-responsibility

# 9

# Featured Successful Women in HCIT

We would like to thank all the following women who made this book possible:

- Tayyeba K. Ali, MD, Physician, Stanford University, Department of Ophthalmology
- Pam Arlotto, MBA, LFHIMSS, President and CEO, Maestro Strategies
- Samantha Baun, Director, Salesforce
- Miranda Bender, Senior Director, Digital Solutions
- Heather Bettridge, Associate Vice President, Practice Management Services
- Durga S. Borkar, MD, MMCi, Vitreoretinal Surgeon and Director of Clinical Data Science at the Duke Eye Center and Assistant Professor of Ophthalmology at Duke University
- Cathy Bryan, Health IT Strategist/Innovator/Collaborator
- Serena Bryson, Senior Information Security Program Manager
- Roz Cordini, JD, MSN, RN, CHC, CHPC, Senior Vice President/ Director of Coding & Compliance, Coker
- Marinda Costabile, Senior Account Executive, AdvancedMD
- Leigh Cox, Business Owner and Founder, Medical Group IT INC
- Aleta Daria, Senior National Sales Director, ModMed
- Jessica Feigen, Director of Provider Success, Geode Health
- Michelle Fox, Director Medical Staff and Information Services
- Linn Foster Freedman, Partner, Chair Data Privacy+Cybersecurity Team, Robinson & Cole LLP

  DOI: 10.4324/9781003366591-9

- Chelsea Gambino, Director of Administration, Comprehensive Family Health
- Leshia Garrett, Director of Health Information Technology
- Mary P. Griskewicz, Director, Federal Government Affairs, MS, FHIMSS
- Lisa Grisim, Vice President and Associate Chief Information Officer
- Marcia Howard, Director, Enterprise Project Management Office, Springfield Clinic, LLP
- Heather Hudnall, BSN, RN, Chief Nursing Informatics Officer, NTT DATA
- Erin Jamal, Senior Manager of Implementations, Mergers and Acquisitions (M&A)
- Karen Jaw-Madson, Principal, Co.-Design of Work Experience
- Leah S. Jones, Chief Financial Officer, Allscripts
- Andrea L. Kamenca, MBA, CEO
- Erica Kaplan, Senior Manager, Clinical Applications
- Rachel Kent, Clinical Informatics Manager, Clarify Health
- Laurice Rutledge Lambert, Founding Partner
- Naomi Lenane, Chief Information Officer, Vice-President, Information Services
- Elise Levine, Director of Business Development, Eye Med Management Solutions
- Marissa Maldonado, CEO, Proda Technology
- Julie McGovern, CEO and Founder, Practice Wise, LLC
- Karen Murphy, PhD, RN, Executive Vice President, Chief Innovation and Digital Transformation Officer, Geisinger
- Robin Ntoh, Vice President, Aesthetics
- Jamie M. Nelson, Senior Vice President and Chief Information Officer, Hospital for Special Surgery
- Anna Nyegaard, MISM, Client Software Manager, BrinsonAnderson Consulting
- Carol Olsen, RN, BSN, MSHI, Retired, Previous Director of Population Health EMR Integration
- Melissa Paczos, Clinical Informatics Supervisor
- Dipti Patel-Misra, PhD, MBA, Professional Certified Coach, Principal Consultant
- Katie Pellish, Venture Manager, Northeast Georgia Health Ventures
- Lygeia Ricciardi, Founder and CEO, AdaRose, Inc.
- Caitlin ("Cait") Riccobono, Privacy Counsel, CRISP Shared Services

- Dina Ross, Attorney, Dina B. Ross Law Offices
- Abby Sears, CEO, OCHIN
- Susan M. Smith, RN, MSN, Certified Professional in Healthcare Information and Management Systems, Director Clinical and IT Applications
- Lindsay Stratton, Vice President of Operations, Eye Med Management Solutions
- Susan Solinsky, Co-Founder, Ellipsis Health
- Jill A. Towns, Electronic Health Record Specialist, Community Care of North Carolina
- Sally Trnka, Executive Director, Breakwater Health Network
- Shannon Vogel, Associate Vice President, Health Information Technology
- Dana Ann Williams, MSBA, RHIA, Lead Health Economics Analyst, ProgenyHealth, LLC
- Leah Wittus, Software Training Consultant
- Rebecca Woods, Founder and CEO, Bluebird Tech Solutions

# Tayyeba K. Ali, MD, Physician, Stanford University, Department of Ophthalmology

**Please provide a brief overview of your professional experience.**

Tayyeba K. Ali, MD, a Board-Certified adjunct faculty member at Stanford University's Department of Ophthalmology, specializes in complex corneal disease and uveitis. She sees patients at the Palo Alto Medical Foundation/Sutter Health in Sunnyvale, CA. Dr. Ali also works as a subject matter expert on contracts for Google.

Prior to completing two fellowships in cornea, external disease, refractive surgery, and uveitis at the Bascom Palmer Eye Institute, ranked #1 eye hospital in the United States by *U.S. News & World Report*, Dr. Ali finished her ophthalmology residency at the Jones Eye Institute/UAMS. She earned her medical degree from the Emory University School of Medicine and completed her undergraduate training in English literature and creative writing at Agnes Scott College.

Dr. Ali has received many academic and teaching awards, including the Bascom Palmer Fellow of the Year Award and the Jone's Eye Dean's Faculty Award. She has delivered dozens of lectures on national and international levels and published numerous meeting abstracts and peer-reviewed journal articles.

As a second-generation American, Tayyeba finds herself dwelling on migrant and refugee stories, their need for ethnic and religious identity, and the repercussions of these journeys. She is keenly interested in international medicine, resident education, health technology, and taking a closer look at the moral crossroads we face in healthcare. She is the Associate Director and Senior Fiction Editor of the Pegasus Physician Writers at Stanford.

**Professional licenses and/or certifications:**

American Academy of Ophthalmology Board Certification

**Other education or training relevant to your position:**

Education

Emory School of Medicine (doctor of medicine); Atlanta, Georgia

September 2002–May 14, 2007

Agnes Scott College (bachelor of arts); Atlanta, Georgia

September 1998–May 2002

Major: English/creative writing with a concentration in pre-medicine

Honors: Magna Cum Laude; Agnes Scott College Honor Scholarship (1998–2002)

Medical Training

Uveitis Fellowship, Bascom Palmer Eye Institute; Miami, FL

September 1, 2014–August 31, 2015

Cornea/External Disease/Refractive Surgery Fellowship, Bascom Palmer; Miami, FL

July 8, 2013–July 6, 2014

Ophthalmology Residency

Jones Eye Institute/University of Arkansas for Medical Sciences (UAMS); Little Rock, AR

November 1, 2009–November 30, 2012

"Staggered start" system, thus dates do not coincide with traditional academic year start dates

Internship in Medicine

UAMS; Little Rock, AR

July 1, 2008–June 30, 2009

**LinkedIn profile:**

https://www.linkedin.com/in/tayyebaalimd/

**Were you referred to this project by a colleague? If so, who?**

Rebecca Hepp, Editor-in-Chief, Retina Today.

# HCIT Questions

1. **What led you to pursue a career in the HCIT industry?**

   The changing face of healthcare and a desire to leverage technology to re-humanize medicine motivated me to join the HCIT space.

2. **What is the best professional advice given to you that you can share with aspiring women who wish to work in HCIT?**

   Clearly define your personal and professional goals. This is particularly important in a field that is evolving and undergoing dramatic shifts. Knowing your own priorities will help you decide which opportunities to pursue and which to let go of.

3. **What is one of your proudest work-related accomplishments?**

   Receiving the Fellow of the Year Award at the Bascom Palmer Eye Institute. I was voted in by my junior colleagues, who, since that time, have become my peers and surpassed me in their accomplishments. Knowing that this group of doctors deeply valued my contributions was humbling and remains a privilege I honor.

4. **In preparation for a job interview, what type of questions should the candidate consider asking, and in what ways can the candidate set themselves apart?**

   There are countless avenues to join the HCIT space. As a subject matter expert, you don't have to have the same technical prowess that an engineering or hybrid role may require. This means being honest with what you can contribute is important. You can set yourself apart by emphasizing your commitment to the team, the project, the evolving field, and your ability to be resourceful.

5. **Would you say there are additional barriers for women to overcome in this industry? If so, what has your experience taught you about navigating these challenges?**

   I'll copy my own answers from a previous interview on this very topic:

   Women are not given the same respect as men, period. In my experience, it takes women, especially minority women, about 2 years to establish any validity—and that is only awarded if the woman performs above and beyond, nonstop. I still see male medical students and trainees enter a space and immediately be given the mic, a spotlight, and the entire stage. Without using a massively broad brush, this often comes down to three factors: (1) self-confidence (i.e., do

I believe in myself, and can I overcome imposter syndrome?), (2) accountability (i.e., will I be held accountable for what I say, and, if what I'm saying isn't truthful or accurate, will there be consequences?), and (3) fear of consequences (i.e., do I care about being truthful, about my reputation, and about the outcomes of my interactions with my patients and peers?).

Generally, men tend to express greater confidence, be held less accountable, and face fewer consequences than women.[1] Society still has a lot of work to do because this lack of accountability has a deep and negative impact. Although this plays into the difficulties women face in healthcare, it extends far beyond our professional lives. Obviously, not all women think one way and men another, and the entirety of a thought process is not all good or all bad. Still, I have come to appreciate my own thought process and wouldn't want to live my life without accountability or an appreciation for consequences. I can see the benefits of doing so, but it wouldn't bring me joy, so I'm content befriending my imposter self.

6. **How have you navigated instances of inequality that may be experienced by women in the workplace?**

Yes, I've faced many instances of chauvinism and prejudice. I recently published an op-ed with Analyst News about this topic, where I talk about a series of on-call shifts after which I found myself in preterm labor. I go on to describe how, as the chief resident in my program, I was in charge of the call schedule, so I should have heeded my obstetrician's advice to lighten my workload. Instead, I was trying to save my free nights for my postpartum months when I was sure to get no sleep and would need to be home to breastfeed. With a 3-year-old at home and a newborn on the way, I knew how grueling the upcoming months would be. I was also avoiding rising conflict with my co-residents, who were grumbling about the importance of "carrying your own weight" and not getting "special treatment." From their perspective, prioritizing my health and that of my unborn child made me selfish. That time was distressing, and figuring out how to have candid, useful, and pointed conversations about how inequalities impact women, and especially women of color, is challenging. The full article can be found here (https://www.analystnews.org/posts/viewpoint-supporting-women-in-medicine-isnt-simply-about-diversity-its-a-matter-of-life-and-death).

7. **When it comes to traveling on the job (such as for attending conferences or performing on-site tasks), what tips may you share when it comes to safety as well as tips that are convenient for travel?**

   What an important question! Many women, myself included, are so accustomed to solo travel that we don't often pay enough attention to safety when it pertains to work. As you would in any other setting, try to travel with a partner. Avoid being in isolated, closed, dark places alone. Travel can be made more convenient by having a bag that's already packed with toiletries and your must-have travel items (for me, it's my tea kettle and my teas). I only have to throw in my clothes. It also makes unpacking easier since I don't need to pull out all the toiletries to use at home.

8. **How do you maintain a healthy work–life balance?**

   I love words, language, communication, and medicine. Therefore, I try to keep my mission of using the written word to advocate for equitable, just healthcare, as well as setting an example of what it means to devote yourself to conscientious, hard work for my daughters, at the forefront. Reminding myself of this often helps me focus on work that's impactful, but it also integrates it with our family values. More practically, I seek out solitude. Having grown up in a Muslim home, I was taught to be part of this world but also to intentionally self-retreat and to use this isolation to connect with a higher purpose, to better understand human nature, and to even think through how to achieve certain dreams. Although many faiths and traditions promote these practices, they are not uniquely religious acts, and science has shown the benefits of seeking solitude. I also journal and write creatively daily. If you're a visual or auditory artist, then pick a creative medium that speaks to you and practice it for 10 to 15 minutes per day.

9. **Are there any specific books or videos you may recommend as it relates to HCIT?**

   [No answer provided].

10. **What is your advice for women to obtain the best opportunities and to negotiate competitive salaries in this career path?**

    First, do your research. Know what your skill set is worth. Then decide what your non-negotiables are. You may be willing to forgo a full-time salary and benefits in order to have more autonomy and flexibility, or you may choose to work full-time, have access to the perks of "always" being present at the table, and outsource the tasks that aren't worth your time. There is no right or wrong answer. While nothing is free in this world, you should ALWAYS negotiate. Apply for multiple jobs and play one contract against the other. I mentored an ophthalmology fellow who was able to increase her offer by over $100k by systematically working through the process described above.

11. **What are some recommendations for networking and continued education?**

    [No answer provided].

12. **Looking back to the beginning of your career, can you share some lessons learned? Would you have done anything differently?**

    Don't chase someone else's dreams. If you want to work part-time and raise a family, do it. If you want to be persistently at the podium, do it. If you want to have a robust clinical and surgical practice without any research, do it. If you want to pursue a non-clinical path, do it. But remember that nothing is free in this world. In the end, you should strive for balance over a lifetime. Also, keep in mind that your dreams may change, and what you learn while chasing them is part of who you are; it wasn't wasted time or energy. Be ready to embrace that change and to recruit the resources needed to transition through the different stages of your life and career.

# Pam Arlotto, MBA, LFHIMSS, President and CEO, Maestro Strategies

**Please provide a brief overview of your professional experience.**

Pam Arlotto advises CEOs, boards, and senior healthcare leaders in the development of digital transformation and innovation strategies. She is a recognized healthcare industry thought leader and has orchestrated the transition to consumer-centric, connected care for more than 35 years. She combines a background in systems engineering with healthcare strategy to create new value and return on investment across the healthcare ecosystem.

Her specific areas of expertise include business model design, virtual care, advanced analytics, population health, consumer engagement, and emerging digital health strategies. Pam's consulting clients include large integrated delivery systems, academic and community-based healthcare providers, accountable care organizations, software and services vendors, and other healthcare companies. She has facilitated highly visible collaborations across care delivery organizations, public–private partnerships, employers, health-care startups, emerging firms, and technology vendor giants.

Pam facilitates the Innovation in Healthcare Management certificate course for Dignity Health Global Education. She previously served as National President of the Healthcare Information and Management Systems Society (HIMSS) and Chairman of the Center for Healthcare Information Management. She has held positions on the advisory boards of the Wallace H. Coulter Department of Biomedical Engineering at the Georgia Institute of Technology, Emory University School of Medicine, and the Scheller College of Business at Georgia Tech. She is currently a member of the Georgia Tech Foundation Board, serves on the Advisory Board of the University of Alabama at Birmingham Health Informatics program, and is on the board of several privately held companies.

Frequently quoted in publications such as Modern Healthcare, HFMA, and Healthcare Innovation, Pam authored her fifth book, *Orchestrating Value: Population Health in the Digital Age* in 2020. She is a frequent speaker at healthcare industry meetings and podcasts. She has been featured on National Public Radio and in *The Wall Street Journal*.

She has received multiple awards and recognitions, including the AMDIS Award for excellence and outstanding achievement in applied medical informatics, the HIMSS Top 50 in 50, the HFMA Helen Yerger/L. Vann Seawell Best Article Award, the HIMSS Book of the Year, the Georgia Tech Alumna of the Year, and the Georgia Tech Industrial Engineering and Young Alumni Awards.

**Professional licenses and/or certifications:**
N/A.

**Other education or training relevant to your position:**
Master of business administration, Georgia State University
Bachelor of science in health systems, Georgia Institute of Technology
Coursework in Design Thinking at the University of Virginia and with IDEO

**LinkedIn profile:**
https://www.linkedin.com/in/pamarlotto/

**Were you referred to this project by a colleague? If so, who?**
Kristine Rynne Mednansky, Senior Editor, Business & Management, Healthcare Management Routledge and Christy Summers, Manager Digital Events, Medical Group Management Association (MGMA).

# HCIT Questions

**1. What led you to pursue a career in the HCIT industry?**

I received an undergraduate degree in health systems engineering at Georgia Tech. My work as a high school student in hospitals paved the way for me to apply for this program. I also worked at Grady and Northside hospitals in Atlanta in my early career as a healthcare consultant. As Quint Studer says, "once healthcare is in your DNA, it's hard to work anywhere else."

**2. What is the best professional advice given to you that you can share with aspiring women who wish to work in HCIT?**

STEM-based degrees, plus medicine and informatics, provide a great foundation for working in this industry. Opportunities abound within health systems, vendors, payers, and other adjacent spaces within the industry. Look for a team that invests in talent and find a culture that fits your strengths.

**3. What is one of your proudest work-related accomplishments?**

As the first woman Chair of the HIMSS, my Board put the "I" in the organization's name. Previously, the Healthcare Management Systems Society built a strategy to bring information technology professionals into the organization. We set the stage for the growth of the organization and the impact it has today.

**4. In preparation for a job interview, what type of questions should the candidate consider asking, and in what ways can the candidate set themselves apart?**

I recommend that candidates do their homework. Focus on 1–3 subjects and research the specifics of those topics (ideally if they are unique to the company you are interviewing with). For example, if you are interviewing with a telehealth company, research trends in virtual care, challenges in adoption post-COVID, and offerings across the different companies. Be able to have a conversation about specifics. This will help differentiate you from other candidates.

**5. Would you say there are additional barriers for women to overcome in this industry? If so, what has your experience taught you about navigating these challenges?**

According to a study done by Rock Health, although women make up the majority of the healthcare workforce, they hold only 19% of hospital CEO positions, and they head only 4% of healthcare companies.

As a woman leader who has served in this industry since the early 1980s, I've learned that barriers will always be there, but perseverance is the key. Early on, finding like-minded allies, mentors, and collaborators helps ensure your visibility. As you grow in your career, soft skills like relationship building and changing leadership help others feel comfortable with your capabilities and knowledge. Later career opportunities exist for those who help others and provide "wisdom" to those who might find it helpful.

**6. How have you navigated instances of inequality that may be experienced by women in the workplace?**

Early in my career, there were many, from inequal access to leaders during consulting engagements to harassment, a lack of promotion opportunities, etc. There is a "story" and a lesson learned behind each situation. For me, it just made me stronger and more determined. For example, a lack of opportunity for promotion resulted in me launching my own consulting company.

**7. When it comes to traveling on the job (such as for attending conferences or performing on-site tasks), what tips may you share when it comes to safety as well as tips that are convenient for travel?**

Travel has always been essential as a healthcare industry consultant. I recommend five practices to ensure safety:

1. *Preparation*: think through your schedule in advance and make sure you are booking times, locations, services, and other aspects of the travel that are reasonable and secure.

2. *Awareness*: be aware of your surroundings and activate your "Spidey senses." If something doesn't feel right, don't ignore it.

3. *Communication*: make sure others know your schedule and hear from you regularly—family, team members, friends, etc.

4. *Scheduling*: when possible, schedule your trips with others. If that is not possible, make sure you enlist the help of others in situations that are less safe. Hotel workers, transportation staff, and others will often help you if asked.

5. *Action*: be flexible and adapt based on the reality of your situation. Be cautious, think through risks, and change your plans if needed to be sure you put safety and security first.

**8. How do you maintain a healthy work–life balance?**

I have found that my goals change daily. Some days I have a very important trip or consulting assignment that comes first. Other days, it's a family event or personal activity that takes precedence. As a consultant, I am able to manage these different days fairly effectively.

9. **Are there any specific books or videos you may recommend as it relates to HCIT?**

   My own, of course!
   - ***Orchestrating Value***: *Population Health in the Digital Age*
   - ***Beyond Return on Investment***: *Expanding the Value of Healthcare Information Technology*

10. **What is your advice for women to obtain the best opportunities and to negotiate competitive salaries in this career path?**

    Be brave. Recognize your own worth, accomplishments, and value. Step out of your comfort zone and ask for the next opportunity, increase your salary, and step up in responsibility.

11. **What are some recommendations for networking and continued education?**

    Get involved in professional organizations at a local and national level. Learn to "intentionally network"—do your homework before attending an event and pick 1–5 people who would make it a successful event if you met and interacted with them—and think about helpful networking—how can you help others?

12. **Looking back to the beginning of your career, can you share some lessons learned? Would you have done anything differently?**

    Patience: Healthcare is slow to change, and sometimes it feels like failure if your recommendations, work efforts, or ideas are not immediately accepted.

    Act on Opportunity: Over the years, I have had many opportunities that I didn't act on quickly and lost momentum. Even if you are unsure, hesitant, or fearful, opportunities present themselves for a reason; take them seriously.

    Connect: Always deepen your healthcare industry connections and relationships. Don't get busy and forget to stay in touch. We all care very much about making a difference in healthcare, and we can only do it together!

# Samantha Baun, Director, Salesforce

**Please provide a brief overview of your professional experience.**

Samantha Baun began her IT journey as a general support technician at a charter school. She was hands-on with desktop management, the school's network, and the VoIP system, among other common IT infrastructure needs. While working at the school, she became a Cisco-Certified Network Associate.

After a couple of years, with a desire to continue growing her skill set, Ms. Baun became a business systems engineer for a large security organization. She was responsible for application server management, collaborated with developers on homegrown applications, and became the internal Salesforce expert.

Her passion for implementing business solutions on the Salesforce platform led her to the healthcare industry, where they use Salesforce to accomplish many things. Salesforce has been especially rewarding in healthcare because it's a powerful, adaptable tool that is able to keep up with the unique needs of systems in healthcare.

**Professional licenses and/or certifications:**

Certified Administrator

Certified Advanced Administrator

Certified Platform App Builder

**Other education or training relevant to your position:**

Member of the Society of Information Management, Southeast Florida

Regional Leadership Forum (RLF) graduate (RLF is a rigorous six-session leadership class that challenges IT professionals to not only hone their business acumen but also lead with empathy and kindness).

**LinkedIn profile:**

https://www.linkedin.com/in/samantha-baun-735155b9/

**Were you referred to this project by a colleague? If so, who?**

Max Baldinger, Unified Women's Healthcare.

# HCIT Questions

### 1. What led you to pursue a career in the HCIT industry?

HCIT blends the best of two worlds. In technology, you get to deliver solutions to help people perform their jobs more effectively and customers receive the best service possible. In healthcare, you support a mission that benefits the wellbeing of others. It's a win–win.

2. **What is the best professional advice given to you that you can share with aspiring women who wish to work in HCIT?**

You may occasionally find yourself in a room where you feel like the least experienced or the most underestimated; this is when you will shine the brightest. Follow what excites you, study the technology that sparks passion in your heart, and always believe in yourself.

3. **What is one of your proudest work-related accomplishments?**

I'm proud that I've been able to draw upon my years of experience in both infrastructure and application development to become a strong business leader in HCIT. I have a passion for "big picture" solutions that benefit the organization long term. I've been able to design and roadmap solutions that save money, smoothly meet the needs of the business, and readily scale with growth and operational changes.

4. **In preparation for a job interview, what type of questions should the candidate consider asking, and in what ways can the candidate set themselves apart?**

Ask what the expectations during the first 90 days of the role are, what challenges the team you'd join is currently facing, and where the interviewer believes their organization will be in 5 years. Follow up on their responses with conversational curiosity.

5. **Would you say there are additional barriers for women to overcome in this industry? If so, what has your experience taught you about navigating these challenges?**

Women tend to be underestimated in both technical skills and industry knowledge. This does not mean you need to fake or misrepresent your background or experience. Rather, be confident in what you do know, and don't be afraid to ask questions. You will quickly gain respect for admitting a knowledge gap and build a reputation for trustworthiness.

6. **How have you navigated instances of inequality that may be experienced by women in the workplace?**

Inequity isn't a noticeable barrier for me anymore, but I certainly dealt with it early in my professional journey. I had to put a gender-neutral name on my resume to get called for interviews. Of course, some of the callers hung up the phone on me or found excuses not to consider me for the role. In the workplace, I found that the men would leave me out of discussions or direct dialog around me, even though I had the most technical expertise among the group. At the time, I did not have the confidence to speak up. Instead, I would quietly produce quality work, document the process, and share my knowledge. People noticed the results, appreciated my transparency, and began to respect me more. It started to get easier then.

Over the years, I have learned how to speak up. This is something that takes time and practice, as you need to deliver your message in a way that is professional and conscientious. You'll find that people are responsive to thoughtful feedback.

7. **When it comes to traveling on the job (such as for attending conferences or performing on-site tasks), what tips may you share when it comes to safety as well as tips that are convenient for travel?**

When possible, travel with or arrange to meet with a trusted business acquaintance. If you must be solo, make sure your itinerary is available to multiple people so that there's awareness of your schedule. Be mindful of any events or activities that may occur outside standard business hours; treat these with the same mindfulness you would outside the workplace.

8. **How do you maintain a healthy work–life balance?**

Since I work from home and because HCIT never sleeps, it's important to set boundaries around my availability. I don't answer the phone or email when I'm not working. If I am working extra hours to support a go-live or in response to an outage, I try to balance those hours with a shorter or more relaxed day the next time it's reasonable to do so. I also keep up with hobbies outside the workplace to ensure that I don't feel that work is all I do.

9. **Are there any specific books or videos you may recommend as it relates to HCIT?**

N/A.

10. **What is your advice for women to obtain the best opportunities and to negotiate competitive salaries in this career path?**

Apply for any job that sounds interesting to you, even if you don't meet all the listed requirements. Job postings are more like a wish list; just be ready to emphasize your willingness to learn and fill the gaps if you do get an interview! When negotiating a salary, research the market rate against your level of experience and ask for a bit more. This helps ensure a counteroffer still aligns with your value, and there's always a chance they'll agree to the higher rate.

Additionally, it truly helps to network with local professionals. Check out LinkedIn and find local societies that are related to your career ambitions. Word-of-mouth is a great way to learn about opportunities and find established professionals who may be helpful referrals for you.

**11. What are some recommendations for networking and continued education?**

The Salesforce ecosystem is robust, with a virtual Success Community and local user groups that host meetups. Look around LinkedIn and generally search for professional communities in your area. You may also find it helpful to find workshops on your preferred topic(s); these are a great way to network.

**12. Looking back to the beginning of your career, can you share some lessons learned? Would you have done anything differently?**

I wouldn't change anything (I know that sounds cliché). The challenges that I encountered and my missteps motivated me to stay focused on my goals and personal growth. I strongly recommend seeking out a female career mentor. Find a woman who inspires you, who holds a position you aspire for, or who has accomplished things in her career that you would also like to achieve. Ask her questions, share your struggles, and learn from her own hard-earned wisdom. If you cannot find a mentor in person, you can read books and learn about the journey of successful women. The key thing, above all, is to know that you have something special to offer the world, something that only you can uniquely do, and that the journey will be worth the effort.

# Miranda Bender, Senior Director, Digital Solutions

**Please provide a brief overview of your professional experience.**

Miranda Bender, Senior Director of Digital Solutions, began her career as a Data Analyst at the Medical Group Management Association (MGMA) directly out of college. She pursued a double major in Sociology and English: Creative Writing, so HCIT was clearly not a career she had originally considered. However, she gained entry into the data analytics role after completing a Sociology honors thesis based on quantitative analysis of US Census data.

Miranda did not initially enjoy her data analyst role. She found it to be too monotonous, and it wasn't as challenging as she would have liked it to be. As she began looking for other jobs, she was given the opportunity to use a trial license of a new software development tool MGMA was piloting to begin building their resale data analytics software platform internally. She loved diving into the more technical side of data and, shortly after, was offered a position on a newly formed business intelligence (BI) team within MGMA.

Miranda thrived working in the technical space and database side of MGMA's analytics tools. She enjoyed the creative aspect of user experience design as she spearheaded the launch of new features within their data tools. The BI team eventually grew within the IT Department, and Miranda was promoted to a management role. She worked full-time throughout college as a movie theater manager and enjoyed people management and leading teams. While this management role was much different than the ones previously fulfilled in the service industry, Miranda thrived in a leadership role. She was quickly promoted to a senior leadership role, overseeing a larger team within the IT Department that extended beyond data analytics software and into the entire database management team.

A couple of years later, after helping lead the organization through a complete database rebuild project and launching a new user interface for the flagship data analytics products, Miranda had the opportunity to step into the Director of IT role. This expanded her leadership to include overseeing additional development and infrastructure teams and managing people as leaders. Her predecessor left the organization in March of 2020. Miranda was in the Director role for about a week before moving her entire organization to remote work for the next year and a half.

The COVID-19 global pandemic provided Miranda with the unique opportunity to learn her new role very quickly. The IT department was in a time of immense change and turnover. She reimagined the dynamics of the team culture and began creating processes and procedures that enabled the department to collaborate more than they had before. The company successfully got numerous projects back on track and improved its internal satisfaction scores throughout the pandemic.

In 2022, Miranda had the opportunity to move to a Senior Director role, overseeing a new division that includes IT and its data analytics and survey collection departments. This division, called Digital Solutions, is the largest in the organization and owns the development of its highest-revenue, flag-ship product. The Senior Director role provides Miranda with the opportunity to focus on the operational side of the organization as well as product development and innovation.

**Professional licenses and/or certifications:**

Certified ScrumMaster° (CSM°)

**Other education or training relevant to your position:**

Currently enrolled in the Executive MBA program at the University of Denver, graduating in March 2024.

**LinkedIn profile:**

https://www.linkedin.com/in/mirandabender/

**Were you referred to this project by a colleague? If so, who?**

Christy Summers, Medical Group Management Association (MGMA).

# HCIT Questions

**1. What led you to pursue a career in the HCIT industry?**

Candidly, I never pursued a career in the HCIT industry and more so fell into my career path. While it has taken a lot of hard work and dedication to get where I am in my profession, I have also benefited quite a bit from being in the right place at the right time. I have also had amazing professional mentors who have helped me discover what I am passionate about and the kind of work that makes me happy.

**2. What is the best professional advice given to you that you can share with aspiring women who wish to work in HCIT?**

Everyone experiences imposter syndrome from time to time. Sometimes the best way to overcome those doubts is the cliché "fake it 'till you make it." You have every right to carry yourself with confidence, even when you're still learning. You also don't owe anyone an explanation. I attended a conference years ago that was focused on women in technology and other male-dominated industries. A takeaway I will never forget is from one speaker who pointed out that, typically, men do not provide unnecessary explanations in the workplace, whereas women constantly feel the need to explain themselves. For example, it is less likely for a man to describe in detail that he has to leave early because his daughter has a soccer game and he has to do pick-up and drop-off, whereas a woman will almost certainly provide this level of detail.

Another helpful piece of advice that extends to all aspects of my life is being intentional about reducing or eliminating passive language. Adding passive words like "just" or "sort of" to my speech inadvertently downplays my work or opinion. Use the contrast of these sentences as an example: "I just worked with our vendor partners to sort of address the problem" compared to "I worked with our vendor partners to address the problem." Women are typically more likely to include passive voice in their speech patterns, and it's a tough but impactful habit to break.

3. **What is one of your proudest work-related accomplishments?**

When I first stepped into the Director of IT role, I proposed a website rebuild project that would extend for 18–24 months and entail stakeholder involvement across the entire organization. I wrote a business case for this project proposal with an estimated $700,000 total investment for the 2-year-long project. The proposal was approved by my executive team and board. I led my team through a complete reimagination of our website and brand, including the implementation of an enterprise data warehouse and a new back-end content management system. The project ended up involving over 80 stakeholders across the organization and was a herculean effort for our teams. I am so proud of the ways we were able to innovate, question the way we were doing things, and create a new and improved experience for our members and customers. Beyond the technical complexity of this project, the dozens of stakeholders made our processes and communication plan almost more important than the work being done to ensure everyone was moving forward toward the same vision.

4. **In preparation for a job interview, what type of questions should the candidate consider asking, and in what ways can the candidate set themselves apart?**

The following types of questions are ones I appreciate candidates asking when interviewing for positions in my team. These questions show an interest in the company and position that extends beyond just scoring a new opportunity. I want to see that someone is culture- and team-focused because I believe those elements drive success far more than pure technical skill set or acumen.

- What characteristics are you looking for in the ideal candidate for this role?
- How does this position contribute to the team's and organization's success?
- What are the biggest challenges that I might face in this position?
- What gets you most excited about the company's future?
- How would you describe the team's culture?

- Why do you love working here?

  To set yourself apart, I recommend the following:

- Always dress nicely, regardless of the industry or if the company appears laid-back.
- Bring a printed copy of your resume with you to the interview (if it's in-person).
- Shake hands with all interviewers upon arrival and at the end of the interview.
- Answer questions with specific examples vs. describing "what-if" scenarios.
- Don't be afraid to be a little vulnerable and tell a story about yourself. You will be more memorable if you aren't providing a cookie-cutter answer to questions and are willing to be more personal and specific to who you are.
- Send a thank-you email or written note to the people you interviewed with.

5. **Would you say there are additional barriers for women to overcome in this industry? If so, what has your experience taught you about navigating these challenges?**

   Yes, HCIT is still a male-dominated industry. I find people often make assumptions about me based on my gender, and it's something women will contend with constantly. I often have to work harder to make sure my voice is heard. This can also span across any sort of business-type scenario, not specific to HCIT. For example, the server typically still hands the bill to the oldest man at the table when I take my department out for a meal.

   My experiences have taught me to advocate for myself. I am not responsible for making other people feel comfortable when I note a mistake or assumption they've made. However, what I am responsible for is doing this with kindness and acting as an example for the change I hope to see in my industry. I will often try to defuse potentially awkward or tense situations or conversations with a bit of humor.

6. **How have you navigated instances of inequality that may be experienced by women in the workplace?**

   When I first stepped into a leadership role, I found that one of my male direct reports was paid over $10k more than my salary in a management position. Our credentials, experience, and education were comparable, and I had also been at the company for a year longer than he had. I approached this situation by gathering as much data as I could find about salary ranges for my position and having a tough conversation with my direct supervisor. He and my HR team acknowledged the discrepancy, and I ended up getting a significant raise. This was not a comfortable conversation to have. But the truth is, you'll never get what you don't ask for. As much as possible, I recommend driving these conversations with facts and data. People also don't like to feel under attack for their (potentially unconscious) gender biases, so supporting your point with concrete information can help relieve tension in these discussions. And at the end of the day, especially in moments of inequality, remember that you are not a burden and have the right to ask for clarification or more information. You may feel like it's easier to sweep conversations like this under the rug, yet I recommend stepping outside your comfort zone and advocating for yourself whenever possible. Posing questions like "Can you help me understand how you came to this decision?" can also force others to reconsider their standpoint and thought process, which will help everyone move toward better equality in our industry.

7. **When it comes to traveling on the job (such as for attending conferences or performing on-site tasks), what tips may you share when it comes to safety as well as tips that are convenient for travel?**

   I find there is an unspoken bond between women, especially in male-dominated professional situations. I was once at a conference where I felt uneasy because I was one of only a handful of women in attendance at an evening networking event. I specifically sought out another woman there and candidly said something like, "I am so glad to have another woman here. Do you want to grab a drink and find a couple other women to chat with?" She expressed relief that I had come up to her, and we ended up finding a little "girl gang" to hang out with for the rest of the event. While we certainly talked with other male attendees at the event, it certainly felt better with "safety in numbers." We all ended up walking back to our hotel together as well. I found a lot of value in learning from peers who I had more in common with from a professional standpoint.

   Otherwise, typical safety advice absolutely applies when traveling for work. Be aware of your surroundings, make eye contact to create a more personal connection so someone can't hide in anonymity, and be cautious about sharing too much detail with strangers, even when you meet them in a professional setting. For example, there is no need for someone you just met to know what floor of the hotel you're staying. From both a professional and a safety standpoint, be conscious of your alcohol intake at work events as well. While I often find my old college ways kicking in when there's free alcohol available (haha!), it's important to enjoy in moderation and represent yourself well. Others, especially men, may inherently take you less seriously. I suggest avoiding giving people other opportunities to make that assumption, like drinking too much at a professional gathering.

**8. How do you maintain a healthy work–life balance?**

Setting boundaries is extremely important to maintain a healthy work–life balance. Ensure your team has what they need to manage workloads and issues that come up without you when you're on vacation or generally out of the office. Identify the things that are important to your mental health and intentionally protect them in your schedule and make sure your work calendar is up to date so others can respect your availability. For example, physical activity is very important to my mental and physical health, so I commit to making time before going to work each morning to attend a workout class. If someone wants to schedule an early meeting with me that conflicts with this priority, I politely recommend a different time.

Leading by example is also a great way to create a positive culture for your teams at work. For instance, if you want to be able to take time off without needing to hop online to do work, don't create an expectation with your team members that you contact them when they're on vacation. I wholeheartedly believe that working more or longer hours to the point of burnout actually counteracts your ability to do good work. Turn work notifications off on your phone when outside your working hours. If you are someone who balances family obligations as well, remember how important being present with your partner and children is. I often put things in perspective this way: in a year, what will I remember? Responding to that email at 9 p.m. vs. 9 a.m., or the quality time I am spending with my partner?

**9. Are there any specific books or videos you may recommend as it relates to HCIT?**

My book recommendations are more specific to leadership, business, and personal growth than HCIT. These are books that have helped me learn the best ways to lead teams, create a positive culture at work, and love what I do:

- *Leaders Eat Last* by Simon Sinek

- *Four Thousand Weeks: Time Management for Mortals* by Oliver Burkeman
- *Dare to Lead: Brave Work. Tough Conversations. Whole Hearts.* by Brené Brown
- *The Subtle Art of Not Giving a F\*ck* by Mark Manson
- *Radical Candor* by Kim Scott

10. **What is your advice for women to obtain the best opportunities and to negotiate competitive salaries in this career path?**

    Become your biggest advocate. Know that you are capable of hard things and that we're all faking it a little. You don't have to feel 100% comfortable before doing it anyway. Confidence is one of your biggest and most underutilized tools. Talk to and about yourself like you would a best friend or someone who has your utmost respect. In an industry where you are likely already going to have to work harder to gain the respect and trust of your peers, it's important that you respect and trust yourself first.

    Especially in conversations about salary and pay, drive the discussion with data. There are numerous sources for pay-grade comparisons out there. And remember, you will never get what you don't ask for. The worst they will say if you ask for more money during a job negotiation is no.

11. **What are some recommendations for networking and continued education?**

    Most cities have numerous free networking groups that I encourage you to join. In Denver, we have both tech-specific and general women in business groups to participate in. Make reasonable goals for yourself, especially if you are introverted like me and struggle with networking events and having to make small talk. An example of these goals is one networking event per month or making one new connection per quarter. Don't be afraid to reach out to people on LinkedIn who may have similarities to you.

    There are so many inexpensive and free continuing education opportunities to take advantage of. Many libraries offer free subscriptions to LinkedIn Learning, where you can find hundreds of courses to grow your knowledge on almost any topic. Ever since the COVID-19 global pandemic, Microsoft has offered the majority of its conference content for free online. Search YouTube for tutorials on new technology or topics you're interested in.

12. **Looking back to the beginning of your career, can you share some lessons learned? Would you have done anything differently?**

Looking back to the beginning of my career, I wish I'd been more diligent about networking and growing my professional connections. I have been at the same company for the majority of my professional career. While I have gained a lot of opportunities to grow both personally and professionally as I have moved to elevated positions at MGMA, I know I will also benefit from perspectives outside my organization. I am diligent about expanding my network now, yet I wish I'd started earlier.

Throughout my career, I have always benefited from speaking my mind and being candid with my supervisor in a respectful and professional way. There have been numerous moments when I have been unhappy and started looking for new opportunities. Each time, when I was honest with my manager about how I was feeling, I was provided new opportunities to move to different roles, try new things, or learn something different. In some cases, early in my career, I wish I'd spoken up sooner because I likely would have further minimized the time I spent feeling dissatisfied in my job.

# Heather Bettridge, Associate Vice President, Practice Management Services

### Please provide a brief overview of your professional experience.

Heather Bettridge, Associate Vice President, is a healthcare professional with 25+ years of diverse healthcare experience in medical practice administration, healthcare consulting, project management, and business development activities. As a medical practice administrator, she functions as a high-trust, enthusiastic team leader responsible for juggling multiple projects alongside a diverse team of staff members while aligning outcomes with the organization's vision and business strategies. In her current role at a membership association in Texas, she directs all practice management consulting, reimbursement, and educational products, services, and initiatives. While having worked in or with practices of all types—small and large, primary and specialty care, independent physicians and groups, rural and urban settings—her focus has always been on hands-on practice operations, technology and workflow optimization, financial analysis, human resource management, clinical documentation improvement and audit activities, and policy and procedure development.

**Professional licenses and/or certifications:**
Certified Professional Coder, credentialed by AAPC
Certified Professional Medical Auditor, credentialed by AAPC
**Other education or training relevant to your position:**
A double major in English and Sociology, with a minor in Mathematics, University of Texas. (Note: I am sharing this information to demonstrate that it does not always matter in which primary fields of study your degrees are. If you are passionate about a subject and you wish to make a difference, put in the work, gain experience, make yourself known, and success will follow. While degrees are largely considered a prerequisite to being competitive in today's market, your field of study does not necessarily need to align with the industry.)
**LinkedIn profile:**
N/A.
**Were you referred to this project by a colleague? If so, who?**
Jeffery Daigrepont, Senior Vice President, Coker.

# HCIT Questions

**1. What led you to pursue a career in the HCIT industry?**

While I did not explicitly pursue a career in technology, HCIT went hand in hand with medical practice administration. Initially, I was a practice's one-person IT department, changing toner cartridges and troubleshooting misprints and lost network connections. My technological responsibilities evolved organically with the onset of the digital age and all the specialized software programs, electronic health record (EHRs)/electronic medical records (EMRs), opportunities for telehealth, etc. that accompanied it. Today, I experience the best of both worlds: I get to work with a variety of practices that have varying levels of technology and integration all across the state.

**2. What is the best professional advice given to you that you can share with aspiring women who wish to work in HCIT?**

Approach every problem with a question: How can I turn this obstacle into an opportunity? because addressing a problem with a quick fix is sometimes not a solution at all. Rather, a problem can be an opportunity to tackle a much bigger underlying or snowballing issue that could achieve an even greater outcome.

**3. What is one of your proudest work-related accomplishments?**

During the COVID-19 pandemic, medical practice viability was a multifaceted issue. Many physicians on the front lines had to quickly augment their practices with telemedicine platforms while navigating compliance and payment challenges. As the COVID curve rose, practice revenue and cash flow were trending downward. To help physicians take decisive actions to shore up practice operations for the months (or years) to come, I successfully coordinated efforts association-wide and published two comprehensive guides on the steps they could take to have a meaningful impact on a practice's viability and bottom line. The guides received numerous commendations nationwide.

4. **In preparation for a job interview, what type of questions should the candidate consider asking, and in what ways can the candidate set themselves apart?**

To set myself apart from other candidates, I have found it beneficial to make a purposeful connection with the person with whom I am interviewing. When scheduling an interview, ask for the name of the interviewer and look for commonalities by perusing their company biography and profiles on professional and social websites (e.g., LinkedIn and Facebook)—past employers, schools, hometowns, friends, hobbies, sports teams, etc. Delicately pepper those details in your responses, as appropriate, so that it's not bothersome or obvious to the interviewer that you stalked them online. It's important to come across as being genuine to build a rapport because, in the end, they will decide if they (1) need you and the skills and experience you bring to the table and (2) can see themselves working with you day in and day out as part of the team.

Another fun tip: wear a bold accent color. Interview candidates typically wear an outfit that is predominantly navy, black, or gray. Make your interview even more memorable by dressing professionally with a subtle yet bold accent color that speaks to your personality.

My favorite questions to ask interviewers:

- What are the current goals of the company, and how does this team work to support achieving those goals?
- What metrics will my performance be evaluated against?
- What are common career paths in this department, and where have successful employees moved on to?
- What do you wish you would have known about the company when you first joined?

5. **Would you say there are additional barriers for women to overcome in this industry? If so, what has your experience taught you about navigating these challenges?**

Although barriers exist for women in almost every industry, it is evident that many companies are making diversity a priority and taking steps to have more diverse populations and perspectives in the workplace. However, there is still a lot of work to be done, especially for top leadership positions. A good first step toward combating this would be to encourage females to pursue their interests in technology, science, engineering, and mathematics at a much younger age. While I loved math and excelled in math competitions in grade school, I do not recall anyone telling me, "If you like math this much now, you could do this as a career, have fun doing it, <u>and</u> make money."

6. **How have you navigated instances of inequality that may be experienced by women in the workplace?**

Let's face it: with all the incredible creams, lotions, and serums at our disposal, oftentimes women look younger than expected for their age. Silence sweet talkers who call you "Darlin" and "Sweetie" with professional yet authentic and firm responses. If they seem to have good intentions but you would like more respect moving forward, you might be able to simply steer the conversation in another direction. However, if their words feel condescending, stand up for yourself and set clear boundaries by keeping a neutral facial expression and speaking calmly while informing them how they may refer to you.

7. **When it comes to traveling on the job (such as for attending conferences or performing on-site tasks), what tips may you share when it comes to safety as well as tips that are convenient for travel?**

As a consultant, I travel frequently and have done so for many years. My top five tips for convenience and safety are as follows:

- Research extensively the area to which you are traveling—not just where you will be working or sleeping but also the surrounding area as well. This will help ensure that restaurants, parking garages, and gas stations are close by and easily accessible.
- Look for lodging that has sleeping rooms accessible only from the inside. Avoid accommodations with exterior access points.
- Travel with a power bank and several different charging options for electronics. Some hotels provide wireless charging stations,

and some have USB outlets built into their furniture, while others require the use of wall plugs.

- Sleep with your cell phone powered on, within reach, and the ringer volume on (not muted or on vibrate).
- Purchase a portable door alarm so that you are alerted if someone tries to enter your room while you are in the shower or asleep.

**8. How do you maintain a healthy work–life balance?**

My work–life balance can be directly attributed to two lessons learned:

1. Saying no with a smile. Learning to say no professionally yet politely has allowed me to stop doing things out of guilt, gain more time for my family, and participate in activities that I truly enjoy.
2. Working remotely whenever possible. Be aware, though, that this requires great discipline to set priorities, stay focused, and ignore the full dirty clothes hamper and kitchen sink.

**9. Are there any specific books or videos you may recommend as it relates to HCIT?**

I found *Project Management for Healthcare Information Technology* by Scott Coplan to be incredibly helpful. It provides insight into and best practices for effective project management—management of the project itself, the technology involved, and the change that people will experience—all of which are required for implementation to be successful.

**10. What is your advice for women to obtain the best opportunities and to negotiate competitive salaries in this career path?**

While negotiating a competitive salary is never comfortable or easy, do not be intimidated or hesitant to negotiate if an initial offer is underwhelming. If you are unsure, ask for time to carefully consider the offer, and then research the position and your professional worth using free online tools and resources. Also, research the potential employer because you may learn that the company has fixed, non-negotiable pay grades; if you accept the offer, your starting pay grade becomes the baseline for future earnings. Whenever possible, carefully consider the entire employment package (e.g., paid time off, retirement, insurance, and perks), not just the salary.

**11. What are some recommendations for networking and continued education?**

Staying abreast of emerging technologies and networking with peers is critical for working in an industry that is constantly changing. Enhance software knowledge by attending conferences and participating in user groups. Both will help you acquire technical information and education for optimal software utilization. User groups, in particular, are inexpensive and allow for discussions of real-life examples and experiences online with peers. Also, never ever burn bridges. Healthcare is a small world, so regardless of how much you may dislike a person, the likelihood of you running into them again in the future is extremely high.

12. **Looking back to the beginning of your career, can you share some lessons learned? Would you have done anything differently?**

Don't be afraid to fail. Instead, fail fast! Meaning, don't waste valuable time continuing down the same path when something is not working as anticipated. Instead, accept that failure, revisit your initial plan and thought process, and adjust your strategy to achieve success.

# Durga S. Borkar, MD, MMCi, Vitreoretinal Surgeon & Director of Clinical Data Science at Duke Eye Center and Assistant Professor of Ophthalmology at Duke University

**Please provide a brief overview of your professional experience.**

Dr. Borkar has always enjoyed analytics and clinical informatics. During her residency, she participated in a research program/project and used a lot of her time curating data and working with complex health data. This is how she got her start in data analytics, and she always found herself becoming involved in data research projects. It became clear to Dr. Borkar that her data were not always easy to use and interpret, so this was her driver to make the data useful. Soon after, Dr. Borkar began her faculty position at Duke University. She pursued her degree in Clinical Informatics and became board-certified in clinical informatics. This then opened the door for many opportunities at Duke as well as within the industry. Currently, Dr. Borkar spends a lot of time as a medical advisor to Verana Health, an

AAO Technology Partner for the IRIS registry. Outside of clinical informatics work, Dr. Borkar is a board-certified vitreoretinal surgeon at the Duke University Medical Center.

**Professional licenses and/or certifications:**

Board-Certified Surgeon of American Board of Ophthalmology, Retina-Vitreous Surgery

**Other education or training relevant to your position:**

Master of management in clinical informatics

**LinkedIn profile:**

https://www.linkedin.com/in/durgaborkar/

**Were you referred to this project by a colleague? If so, who?**

Rebecca Hepp, Editor-in-Chief, Retina Today.

# HCIT Questions

**1. What led you to pursue a career in the HCIT industry?**

A lot of what drives me to do this is that everyday, providers are collecting so much data, and there is a story to be told, and we need to figure out a way to curate it and make it applicable. It's an important mission because we need to have real-world patient data. For example, clinical trial data show a small subpopulation of patients and are also limited in regard to the participants of clinical trials. So, to me, it's important to tell the story of all patients.

**2. What is the best professional advice given to you that you can share with aspiring women who wish to work in HCIT?**

Oftentimes, we think of this field as extremely technical, but there are so many facets to HCIT. Personally, I believe that having good communication skills is key, no matter what pathway you may be pursuing. For me, I have strong clinical expertise, and while I may not be an expert in programming, I have the ability to bridge the gap between the clinical and programming sides. I believe this is a skill that can open up a lot of doors.

**3. What is one of your proudest work-related accomplishments?**

[No answer provided].

**4. In preparation for a job interview, what type of questions should the candidate consider asking, and in what ways can the candidate set themselves apart?**

Look for the opportunity to showcase the ways in which you can improve the company as a whole. I think a lot of times, we focus our time on identifying how you can make a position better, but what really makes you stand out is the way in which you can influence change and positively impact the overall process. It shows that you see the big picture.

5. **Would you say there are additional barriers for women to overcome in this industry? If so, what has your experience taught you about navigating these challenges?**

I think we need to focus on the skills that women are traditionally thought to be strong in, for example, communication. Men traditionally dominate the HCIT field because, inherently, men are more technical. But I think it's important to focus on the soft skills that women bring to these positions and how they can dramatically improve results.

I do think that there is an aspect of self-perpetuating this belief because many times women are more afraid to speak up when they are the only woman at the table because you are conscious of that. So, for me, the way I have navigated these situations is by not being afraid to lean into the softer skills and by not being afraid to speak up and contribute my opinions at the table.

6. **How have you navigated instances of inequality that may be experienced by women in the workplace?**

There were definitely inequalities in medical training and in HCIT in general. One of the things that have helped me get through is surrounding myself with people who understand inequality and who support me. My advice would be to identify supportive mentors and fellow peers who are experiencing the same thing. It's going to be hard to break those barriers, and you won't be able to erase them with ease, but by surrounding yourself with the right people, you can overcome them.

7. **When it comes to traveling on the job (such as for attending conferences or performing on-site tasks), what tips may you share when it comes to safety as well as tips that are convenient for travel?**

[No answer provided].

8. **How do you maintain a healthy work–life balance?**

I am constantly working on this. For me, there are times when you have to focus more on home life versus work life, and having a support system at home is key. There's a philosophy out there that, as you begin your career, you should say "yes" to everything because that is how you become successful. I don't necessarily agree with that. I think you should say "yes" selectively to things that you are excited about and that will further your career/path.

9. **Are there any specific books or videos you may recommend as it relates to HCIT?**
   - *Lean in: Women, Work, and the Will to Lead* by Sheryl Sandberg
   - *Four Thousand Weeks* by Oliver Burkeman

10. **What is your advice for women to obtain the best opportunities and to negotiate competitive salaries in this career path?**

    I think there needs to be more pay transparency. Women often don't feel that they are entitled to more. But if we knew what others were making in that role, we would be more empowered to ask. My advice would be to ask around and do your research. And if you can, try to create a group of likeminded individuals that support this idea.

11. **What are some recommendations for networking and continued education?**

    Networking is so important. You should have a very open mind to meeting new people in different roles and industries.

12. **Looking back to the beginning of your career, can you share some lessons learned? Would you have done anything differently?**

    I would have focused less on inequalities. Using up time mulling over inequalities does not really get you any further than where you are. Many times, we limit ourselves when we think about inequalities, and we let that stop us. Overcoming "imposter syndrome" and recognizing your own value and what you bring to the table is so important.

# Cathy Bryan, Health IT Strategist/ Innovator/Collaborator

**Please provide a brief overview of your professional experience.**

With over 35 years of experience and a career spanning a variety of sectors in the industry, Cathy brings a broad and diverse set of knowledge and skills in healthcare and HCIT to the table. From her start as a neonatal staff nurse, to managing home infusion teams serving AIDS patients in the early 90s, to co-founding a clinical software company in the 2000s, being immersed in the ACO and value-based care world and leading operations for a large, nonprofit provider group, Cathy has enjoyed being on the forefront as an industry leader throughout her career, always working toward innovative approaches to drive quality-focused, evidence-based care delivery to serve patients and communities.

After working as a neonatal ICU nurse and then moving into the expanding field of home infusion therapy during the AIDS crisis, Cathy transitioned from direct patient care into consulting in the early 2000s, simultaneously with healthcare's move from a focus on quality assurance to quality improvement. In leading clients through accreditations in Joint Commission on Accreditation of Healthcare Organizations (JCAHO) and Utilization Review Accreditation Commission (URAC), she was on the frontlines as the industry began to embrace these new concepts around quality. With this evolution of the industry, it became evident there was a need for more robust data, thus the impetus behind the formation of the clinical software company CINA, later to rebrand as QED Clinical, where she served as Co-Founder and Chief Clinical Officer for 15 years.

CINA/QED Clinical, a clinical software solution company established in 2003, created one of the first extraction–translation–loading solutions and clinical data repositories with a point-of-care clinical decision support tool using only clinical EMR data. The QED Clinical Point-of-Care tool became one of the first, near-real-time solutions on the market that used evidence-based guidelines to generate actionable data in a usable format for busy providers. With over 5000 physicians nationally and being still in use today, the system that was conceived and developed in the mid-2000s has proved invaluable to many providers, allowing participation in quality data reporting and revenue generation (PQRS/PQRI/GPRO/MU/PCMH/HEDIS) prior to the formation of ACOs and value-based care. Additionally, the federated data model allowed for the support of professional research networks and, subsequently, the creation of the nationally recognized DARTNet Institute (http://www.dartnet.info.)

After leaving QED Clinical, Cathy utilized her experience as a software vendor to join UT Southwestern in 2015 as Director of Care Coordination and Director of Post-Acute Utilization Management for the ACO that would become Southwestern Health Resources (SWHR), one of the largest and most successful Medicare NextGen ACOs in the country. During the time she was at SWHR, the ACO grew to serve over 700,000 covered lives across all payors, saving Medicare over $140M and leading the nation in NextGen ACO savings for 2 consecutive years.

Cathy then moved to the role of Executive Vice President Patient Services & Operations for Prism Health North Texas in 2020, leading the clinical, facility, and IT operations for the nonprofit serving both an insured and uninsured population focused on HIV management, prevention, sexual health, and LGBTQ primary care. With an annual budget of $120MM, over 60,000 encounters per year, 250 employees, and over $10 million in state and federal grants, Cathy managed teams that provided services in clinics and community settings, including medical, dental, behavioral health, and case management, and was responsible for oversight of all IT functions and physical facilities, overseeing significant enhancements in IT and physical security, and initiating the move to a single EMR, plus significant physical moves and expansion. Additionally, Cathy volunteers on the Board of VNA Texas, the ACHE North Texas Mentor Committee; has been published in peer-reviewed journals; and participated in funded research grants.

**Professional licenses and/or certifications:**

Registered Nurse (RN)

**Other education or training relevant to your position:**

Bachelor of nursing, Baylor University

Master of healthcare administration, University of Missouri-Columbia

**LinkedIn profile:**

https://www.linkedin.com/in/cathy-bryan-0720b12/

**Were you referred to this project by a colleague? If so, who?**

Jeffery Daigrepont, Senior Vice President, Coker.

# HCIT Questions

### 1. What led you to pursue a career in the HCIT industry?

I did not so much pursue a career in HCIT as much as it became necessary for achieving a goal. As a nurse, I was already in healthcare but had absolutely no background or experience in IT. But I happened to be in the right place at the right time, as they say. In the early 2000s, the shift to measuring outcomes was just starting to be recognized in healthcare, borrowing from Deming's work in manufacturing around total quality management, with the recognition that we could derive consistency in healthcare—that there was more than just the "art" of medicine.

During this time, I was consulting with several home care and home infusion companies that were trying to make this switch to generating outcomes, but to derive outcomes and the reporting, we needed data. EMRs were just starting to become mainstream with the most for-ward-thinking providers, and since in my consulting business, I quickly discovered you could not ask busy providers, or even staff, to provide duplicate data entry into a Microsoft Access database, it became evident we needed the EMR as the means to the end. We needed to capture the data within the course of business in order to have the (mostly) discrete data available to be able to analyze and understand patient and process variables in order to achieve desired outcomes.

So, I co-founded a company (CINA/QED Clinical, Inc.) that started as an EMR reseller and then emerged into a clinical software solutions vendor that was founded with a single purpose in mind: to be able to produce the same level of evidence-based, quality clinical outcomes in a solo primary care practice as was being produced in large, fully integrated health systems with a robust, single EMR. In other words, when you have access to all the data, a robust EMR, and a large team of IT staff, you can create some impressive clinical outcomes. We believed this should be available to patients and providers regardless of where they lived, what EMR they used, or the level of IT support and analytics at their disposal.

**2. What is the best professional advice given to you that you can share with aspiring women who wish to work in HCIT?**

The industry is so much more evolved today than it was when I came into it. When I started, most of the women in HCIT were in sales, with very few in programming, leadership, and the like. That is certainly no longer the case, and aspiring women, regardless of age or where they are in their career journey, have many avenues to seek out mentors, education, certifications, experience, and the like.

If you have an idea of the area you want to work in, great—start to navigate and seek out experiences in that area. But if you don't have a clue what area you are most interested in, or even if you think you know, be open to being surprised! Don't be afraid to take a chance and try something that you may not feel completely prepared for! Remember, men never think twice about taking on new roles or new challenges that they might not be experienced in, and neither should we! You are smart, talented, and a quick learner! You can and will learn and lead your way through to the next step on your career ladder, and then the next, and the next. It may not be the path you expected, but that is half the fun!

**3. What is one of your proudest work-related accomplishments?**

Co-founding a company that created a new solution for providers that was truly "cutting edge" technology, was unique in the industry at the time, and provided practical benefit to providers is an accomplishment I carry with pride. Despite not realizing the financial gains from that company that we had hoped, the product we designed and implemented was a tremendous success, with providers still using tools built on the original architecture and design we created over 20 years ago. In a time before value-based care and ACOs were even conceived, we were engaging providers in using evidence-based guidelines to inform decision-making at the point of care and, in doing so, impact the health and lives of many patients.

4. **In preparation for a job interview, what type of questions should the candidate consider asking, and in what ways can the candidate set themselves apart?**

Interview prep should always include a review of the company or organization's services, target market, and mission/vision, especially if you are interviewing with a company in an industry that is new to you. You do not need to spend countless hours researching the company—unless you are maybe in a second or third round for a management or senior leader role—but you should at least be conversant in the company's or organization's work and be able to ask questions about how the role you are applying for impacts the overall purpose of the organization.

Setting yourself apart in a market where it is so easy to apply to jobs via LinkedIn, services like Indeed, or even an organization's website is certainly a challenge. It is not uncommon to see hundreds of applicants for entry-level or mid-management positions and trying to determine the correct "key words" to include in your application to get past the automated screening devices is often a futile effort! As a hiring manager, I spend the most time on the first page of the resume and specifically on the initial section that summarizes the candidate's skills, experience, and interests. I would recommend keeping your introductory summary concise and impactful, focused on your skills and ambition, followed by your experience that is most in line with the role for which you are applying. By the time a hiring manager turns to page 2 of a resume, they are generally looking for additional information that supports or extends something of interest that caught their eye on page 1.

Finally, keep submitting resumes; you will have many more "no response" or "thank you, but we are not interested in you at this time" than you will have a request for an interview. Do not be discouraged!

Keep at it! And anytime you can find a colleague, former classmate, or networking contact that works at the company or organization, let them know you have applied and ask them to notify the hiring manager to be on the lookout for your resume.

5. **Would you say there are additional barriers for women to overcome in this industry? If so, what has your experience taught you about navigating these challenges?**

There are certainly segments of IT where men are represented in higher numbers, and often, organizations may gravitate toward hiring a male over a female because they believe the male will "fit in" better with the team. I think the best thing for females in IT to do is to just keep showing up—at conferences, at interviews, in the classroom, at local and national association meetings—and speak out and show that we are capable, that we do "know our stuff," and that we can integrate into teams that have historically been male-dominated. It is already starting to evolve, and women are being acknowledged as serious and effective leaders in health IT. We need the next generation to continue to step up and speak up to carry on the work of our foremothers, who have forged the path for the next generation of female leaders, such that health IT teams of the future are gender-neutral at all levels of all organizations.

6. **How have you navigated instances of inequality that may be experienced by women in the workplace?**

N/A.

7. **When it comes to traveling on the job (such as for attending conferences or performing on-site tasks), what tips may you share when it comes to safety as well as tips that are convenient for travel?**

The secret to successful travel is a great laptop workbag, ideally one that isn't that boring black rolling bag that all the men use, comfortable shoes, and basic pants that can be worn with multiple shirts or jackets—think the equivalent of how men will take one pair of slacks, several shirts, and one jacket—and no one ever realizes they have worn the same pants and jackets multiple days straight! Nothing says women have to have a completely different outfit for each day. Remember, you are there for your knowledge and what you bring to the meeting/client/conversation. There is no fashion police, and if there is, who cares? Buy a quality pair of slacks and shoes that can be multi-purposed with various shirts, sweaters, and/or jackets. And make sure they all pack easily and are wrinkle-resistant! As to the perfect laptop workbag for women, most of us are always on the hunt for one!

**8. How do you maintain a healthy work–life balance?**

I realized way too late in my career the importance of maintaining a healthy work–life balance, especially during the years I was traveling around 40–50% of the time. It is necessary—not important, but essential—to schedule time in your week for exercise, quiet time/meditation/prayer/self-reflection—you have to recharge in order to continue to give back to your job, your family, and the other components of your life that are important to you. You are not superhuman. You will burn out. You will take it out on those you care the most about. It will impact your work. Others will notice. So, be kind to yourself and to those around you, and take care of yourself throughout your career. You are in this for the long haul!

**9. Are there any specific books or videos you may recommend as it relates to HCIT?**

*Effortless* by Greg McKeown. It is not specific to health IT, but it teaches how to be more effective in approaching work in general.

**10. What is your advice for women to obtain the best opportunities and to negotiate competitive salaries in this career path?**

[No answer provided].

**11. What are some recommendations for networking and continued education?**

Look for networking groups and associations focused on women in health IT and health management because all areas of healthcare involve IT, so even organizations and associations that are not focused on IT will have a lot of good networking opportunities with colleagues in IT roles and disciplines. And don't just join an association; get involved—volunteer for a committee or task force, show up at events, get to know other members—even if you absolutely HATE networking; it will be one of the best things you can do for your career!

The American College of Healthcare Executives is a great organization for anyone interested in IT in the hospital or health system industry, and many metropolitan areas have local chapters in addition to the national association. The HIMSS is the industry's premier association, but the annual trade show is massive and expensive to attend. But again, many areas have a local or regional HIMSS chapter that is a good place to start networking and gain access to educational offerings.

12. **Looking back to the beginning of your career, can you share some lessons learned? Would you have done anything differently?**

At this point in my career, having moved from being solidly rooted in health IT for so many years to moving over to the ACO and provider space for the past 10 years, I wish I had kept more of a footprint in health IT. The industry changes so rapidly, so even if your career path takes you away from being fully rooted in health IT, it makes sense to stay engaged at some level—by attending conferences, staying involved in local or national organizations, continuing to receive news updates on the industry, and staying in touch with your industry connections and colleagues, etc.—so that if/when you decide to return more fully to health IT, you are not so far behind the curve and can re-enter more seamlessly!

# Serena Bryson, Senior Information Security Program Manager

**Please provide a brief overview of your professional experience.**

Serena Bryson's role in IT evolved from a career change from research into compliance by way of Home Healthcare Administration via DHS and CMS audits. Through the years, she has designed and developed team building and communication strategies in an effort to smooth the rough edges of those around her by emphasizing their strengths. Serena possesses the motivational skills to help boost confidence and provide motivation to the team in a positive manner.

During her career, Serena has created and assisted in the development and design of training programs, technology platforms, and technology applications for storing and distributing data within multi-site organizations. Her area of focus includes compliance with regulatory requirements and the security of company data, assets, and information. These areas have always been a cornerstone of her projects and have stemmed from a consumer research base that has continued throughout all development and infrastructure projects.

**Professional licenses and/or certifications:**

Systems Security Certified Practitioner (SSCP), Security +

Certified Information Systems Security Professional (CISSP) (in process)

**Other education or training relevant to your position:**
MSM in IT and Project Management
**LinkedIn profile:**
https://www.linkedin.com/in/serena-bryson-74191752/
**Were you referred to this project by a colleague? If so, who?**
Caitlin L. Riccobono, Esq., HCISPP, Privacy Counsel, CRISP Shared
Services (CSS).

# HCIT Questions

1. **What led you to pursue a career in the HCIT industry?**
   I have always been pulled toward healthcare and public health since
   college, and HCIT was a natural fit.
2. **What is the best professional advice given to you that you can share
   with aspiring women who wish to work in HCIT?**
   Try it, you may like it!
3. **What is one of your proudest work-related accomplishments?**
   My proudest work-related accomplishment is changing the relationship between the development, networking, and security/compliance
   departments from what has usually been tug-of-war battles between
   the departments to collaborative, meaningful discussions that propel
   the organization forward.
4. **In preparation for a job interview, what type of questions should
   the candidate consider asking, and in what ways can the candidate
   set themselves apart?**
   [No answer provided].
5. **Would you say there are additional barriers for women to overcome in this industry? If so, what has your experience taught you
   about navigating these challenges?**
   The barriers are similar to other STEM roles that women are in,
   and my advice is the same. There may be pushbacks on your ideas,
   concepts, or projects. Keep the focus on the facts, data, and direction
   of the project, not on the social/political/interoffice relationships that
   may be brought up. Do not be afraid of defending your position with
   facts and data; it becomes a supported opinion rather than just an idea.

6. **How have you navigated instances of inequality that may be experienced by women in the workplace?**

I've navigated instances of inequality my entire life, and I'm not sure that a brief statement would change this. Depending on the organization you are working for and the state you are working in (if in the US), the instances of inequality may be different. I have been underestimated regularly. I have been talked over, talked down to, degraded, and demeaned by colleagues, co-workers, vendors, and some management positions. Take the high road every time. Do not let the small-mindedness of others change your behavior or make you drop your head. Rely on the facts, data, and supporting and corroborating evidence to speak on your behalf. Support your position every time with more than enough evidence and bring solution options when discussing problems.

7. **When it comes to traveling on the job (such as for attending conferences or performing on-site tasks), what tips may you share when it comes to safety as well as tips that are convenient for travel?**

I only travel to areas where I feel safe. I try to stay in the hotel that is hosting the conference, and I usually tell someone every time I am traveling. They know when I am scheduled to land where I am staying, and I check in with that person regularly (at least daily) to let them know I am safe. If possible, travel with a co-worker. Happy hours are usually well stocked at conferences; know your personal limit and stay well below it so you are aware of your surroundings at all times.

8. **How do you maintain a healthy work–life balance?**

Still trying to learn how to do that!

9. **Are there any specific books or videos you may recommend as it relates to HCIT?**

[No answer provided].

10. **What is your advice for women to obtain the best opportunities and to negotiate competitive salaries in this career path?**

[No answer provided].

11. **What are some recommendations for networking and continued education?**

Join your local (ISC)2 Chapter. Engage in your local tech communities, and don't be afraid to exchange information at conferences. There are several great sites for continuing education, but the cornerstone of continuing education is to always have a desire to learn more. Whether it is the latest components created by your favorite vendor, the changes in policy, or the ins and outs of AI, the world of HCIT is expanding, changing, and growing. There is always something new to learn.

12. **Looking back to the beginning of your career, can you share some lessons learned? Would you have done anything differently?**

I would have started earlier in HCIT instead of following the research path out of undergrad, but I am thankful and grateful for the road that brought me to where I am now. All the bits of information that I've gathered, collected, and retained from past positions, careers, and opportunities have built the toolbox I use regularly. Including the conflict redirection techniques, I learned them early on as an Early Childhood Educator.

# Roz Cordini, JD, MSN, RN, CHC, CHPC, Senior Vice President/Director of Coding and Compliance, Coker

**Please provide a brief overview of your professional experience.**

Roz Cordini, Juris Doctor (JD), MSN, RN, CHC, CHPC, has had a tremendous career in healthcare. She started as and remained an RN, having practiced in clinical areas such as the cardiovascular and emergency departments. Roz served in a variety of leadership roles in hospitals and health systems including quality/peer review, critical care, and emergency services. Later, at age 40, she returned to school for her law degree and practiced healthcare regulatory/compliance law for a regional law firm. Ms. Cordini ended up moving to an in-house associate general counsel and chief compliance officer position for a health system. She now works at Coker, leading and further developing the compliance service line.

**Professional licenses and/or certifications:**
RN
KBA Law License
Certified Healthcare Compliance
Certified Healthcare Privacy Compliance
**Other education or training relevant to your position:**
Juris Doctor
Master of science in nursing

# HCIT Questions

**1. What led you to pursue a career in the HCIT industry?**

My career naturally evolved into the Health Insurance Portability and Accountability Act (HIPAA) privacy and security space. Over time, cybersecurity concerns have moved to the forefront and have made that experience all the more relevant.

**2. What is the best professional advice given to you that you can share with aspiring women who wish to work in HCIT?**

Stay connected to your professional organizations and seek to become an expert in your area. Read, stay current with what's going on in the industry, seek relevant education and certifications, and put yourself out there in terms of writing and speaking.

**3. What is one of your proudest work-related accomplishments?**

Getting my JD at 40 with three kids at home in order to further expand into the healthcare compliance/regulatory space.

**4. In preparation for a job interview, what type of questions should the candidate consider asking, and in what ways can the candidate set themselves apart?**

I recommend setting yourself apart by giving concrete examples when asked a question. Doing so highlights your experience and provides insight into your strategic thinking and problem-solving mindset.

**5. Would you say there are additional barriers for women to overcome in this industry? If so, what has your experience taught you about navigating these challenges?**

Anytime a field or industry is dominated by a particular sex, there are perceived barriers, but my recommendation is to not let such perceptions become your reality. Surround yourselves with others who value your contributions and who complement your skill set.

**6. How have you navigated instances of inequality that may be experienced by women in the workplace?**

[No answer provided].

**7. When it comes to traveling on the job (such as for attending conferences or performing on-site tasks), what tips may you share when it comes to safety as well as tips that are convenient for travel?**

N/A.

8. **How do you maintain a healthy work–life balance?**

I do yoga and cycling. Both give me social and fitness interactions, and getting outside reminds me that it's okay to sign off and take care of myself. I am more focused and content while working because of this balance.

9. **Are there any specific books or videos you may recommend as it relates to HCIT?**

[No answer provided].

10. **What is your advice for women to obtain the best opportunities and negotiate competitive salaries in this career path?**

Know the market and accept nothing less.

11. **What are some recommendations for networking and continued education?**

Join your professional societies, both nationally and locally. Speak, write. Be involved.

12. **Looking back to the beginning of your career, can you share some lessons learned? Would you have done anything differently?**

Probably my best advice is to remember that there are a lot of gray areas in the compliance/regulatory space. Try to facilitate a positive response when faced with a need or request. Consider those asking, even co-workers, as your clients. Listen. Seek to understand their needs and try to get them where they want to be (while staying compliant!). Doing this will solidify your place as a trusted partner.

# Marinda Costabile, Senior Account Executive, AdvancedMD

**Please provide a brief overview of your professional experience.**

Marinda Costabile has 25 years of healthcare experience. She began her career as a medical biller and then transitioned into a Practice Administrator role where she oversaw the largest neurology practice in the panhandle of Florida. Upon relocating to Atlanta, Georgia, Ms. Costabile worked as a revenue cycle consultant for 6 years, where she had her first taste of sales. After the first deal she closed, Ms. Costabile knew she had found her passion! Since that time, she has worked in enterprise account executive roles and has sold a full suite of solutions including EHR, Project Management (PM), telehealth, patient engagement tools, Revenue Cycle Management (RCM) services, and charge capture technology. In most recent years, her focus has been on Artificial Intelligence (AI)/Machine Learning (ML)/natural language processing/Optical Character Recognition (OCR) technology.

**Professional licenses and/or certifications:**
Certified Billing and Coding Specialist
Certified Patient Account Representative
**Other education or training relevant to your position:**
Six Sigma Yellow Belt
Gulf Coast State College
**LinkedIn profile:**
https://www.linkedin.com/in/atry12678/
**Were you referred to this project by a colleague? If so, who?**
Jeffery Daigrepont, Senior Vice President, Coker.

# HCIT Questions

**1. What led you to pursue a career in the HCIT industry?**

First and foremost is my passion for healthcare. I always thought I would be a nurse until I realized I nearly fainted at the first sight of blood! HCIT plays a pivotal role in improving patient care and streamlining healthcare processes. I have a strong aptitude for technology and an understanding of how it can be leveraged to enhance healthcare operations. The HCIT field is characterized by innovation and constant technological advancements. I have a desire to be a part of an industry that is continually pushing boundaries and improving healthcare outcomes!

**2. What is the best professional advice given to you that you can share with aspiring women who wish to work in HCIT?**

The best piece of career advice that I have been given was from my former VP of sales early in my sales career. She told me that she wanted me to run my day-to-day processes just as I would if I owned my own business, and that is the advice that I have taken with me throughout my sales career.

**3. What is one of your proudest work-related accomplishments?**

I successfully closed the first healthcare opportunity at my former company in record time (less than 60 days when the typical sales cycle is 6–9 months), and it was purely self-generated from my personal network. It was also the largest COVID laboratory in the state of

California, and they had an urgent need as this happened right in the middle of the pandemic. It was a great win for me professionally, but to feel like I was really helping to make a difference in the fight against COVID was a feeling I will never forget.

4. **In preparation for a job interview, what type of questions should the candidate consider asking, and in what ways can the candidate set themselves apart?**

   The most important thing is to not only answer questions effectively but also to ask thoughtful questions. (1) Company-specific questions: Can you tell me more about the company culture and values? What are the company's short-term and long-term goals? What recent achievements or projects are the team proud of? (2) Roles and responsibilities: What are the key responsibilities and expectations for this role? Can you describe what a typical day or week in this position will look like? How does this role contribute to the overall success of the team and company? (3) Team dynamics: Who will I be working closely with, and what is the team's structure? How would you describe the management style of the team leader or supervisor? (4) Company's challenges and industry trends: What are the current challenges the company is facing? How does the company stay updated with industry trends and innovations? How does the company plan to address future challenges and opportunities? Performance metrics and success criteria: How is success measured in this role? What are the Key performance indicators (KPIs)? What opportunities for growth and advancement does this role offer?

   To set themselves apart in an interview, a candidate should consider the following:

   1. *Showcase Research*: Demonstrate that you've thoroughly researched the company, its industry, and the specific role. Mention your knowledge and understanding during the interview.
   2. *Highlight Achievements*: Provide specific examples of your accomplishments and how they align with the company's needs and values.
   3. *Ask Unique Questions*: Craft questions that show genuine interest in the company and role, rather than asking generic questions that can contribute to your success.

4. *Share Your Vision*: If appropriate, share your vision and ideas for the role or the company's growth. Show how you can contribute to their success!

5. *Emphasize Your Soft Skills*: Highlight your soft skills, such as adaptability, teamwork, and problem-solving, as these are often as important as technical skills.

6. *Follow-Up*: After the interview, send a personalized thank-you email or note that summarizes your enthusiasm for the role and your appreciation for the opportunity to interview.

By asking insightful questions and showcasing your unique qualifications and enthusiasm, you can leave a lasting impression and increase your chances of standing out as a candidate!

5. **Would you say there are additional barriers for women to overcome in this industry? If so, what has your experience taught you about navigating these challenges?**

Absolutely, there are often additional barriers. These barriers include gender bias, lack of representation, and stereotypes. Navigating these challenges successfully requires a combination of strategies and approaches. Here are some key strategies:

1. *Self-Confidence*: Building self-confidence is crucial. Believe in your skills and your abilities! Seek out mentors and sponsors who can provide guidance and support.

2. *Networking*: Establish a strong professional network. Connect with other women in the industry and allies who can provide advice and opportunities.

3. *Membership and Sponsorship*: Find mentors who can offer guidance and sponsors who can advocate for your career advancement. They can help open doors and provide valuable insights.

4. *Skill Development*: Continuously invest in your skills and education. Stay updated with industry trends and technologies.

5. *Advocate for Inclusivity*: Promote diversity and inclusion within your workplace. Be an advocate for positive change and challenge stereotypes and biases.

6. *Work–Life Balance*: Recognize the importance of work–life balance. Be vocal about your needs and seek employers who support this balance.

7.  *Negotiation Skills*: Develop strong negotiation skills, particularly in terms of salary and career advancement. Don't be afraid to negotiate for what you deserve.

8.  *Resilience*: Understand that challenges may arise, but resilience is key. Learn from setbacks and use them as opportunities for growth.

9.  *Community Involvement*: Engage in organizations and initiatives that support women in tech. These can provide a sense of community and resources.

10. *Set Goals*: Clearly define your career goals and create a plan to achieve them. Break down your goals into management steps.

Navigating these challenges often requires a proactive and persistent approach. Many successful women in the technology industry have faced and overcome gender-related obstacles. By drawing inspiration from their experiences and taking these steps, women can work toward achieving their career aspirations in this field!

6. **How have you navigated instances of inequality that may be experienced by women in the workplace?**

   Yes, I have. At one of my previous companies, I was the mother of two young children at the time. I was working in an account management role and had a strong desire to transition into a quota-carrying role. I was pulled aside by this manager who told me, "Let's just face it. You're just not cut out for sales. What about all of the traveling that you will have to do with two kids at home." I do not believe that comment would have ever been made to a male employee. I left that company shortly after that comment and became a president's club winner the following year. I made sure he saw it on my social channels!

7. **When it comes to traveling on the job (such as for attending conferences or performing on-site tasks), what tips may you share when it comes to safety as well as tips that are convenient for travel?**

   1. *Safety First*: Research and choose accommodations in safe areas. Share your travel plans with a trusted contact. Do not walk alone at night. When in doubt, call an Uber even if it's a short walk from the hotel. Request hotel rooms that are near elevators and on higher floors for added security.

   2. *Stay Connected*: Keep your phone charged and use location-sharing apps with trusted contacts. Remember that your safety is a

priority, and taking precautions can help ensure a secure and successful business trip!

**8. How do you maintain a healthy work–life balance?**

Set boundaries and communicate them. I prioritize self-care and make time for it. I try to take breaks from my desk every few hours, and when I walk away from my workstation at my home office, I leave my cell phone behind as well. TAKE THE PTO and unplug!

**9. Are there any specific books or videos you may recommend as it relates to HCIT?**

- *The Challenger Sale: Taking Control of the Customer Conversation* by Matthew Dixon and Brent Adamson
- *The Psychology of Selling: Increase Your Sales Faster and Easier Than You Ever Thought Possible* by Brian Tracy
- *The New Strategic Selling* by Robert Miller

**10. What is your advice for women to obtain the best opportunities and to negotiate competitive salaries in this career path?**

- *Build Expertise*: Continuously update your knowledge and skills in HCIT to stand out in a competitive field.
- *Network*: Connect with mentors and colleagues to gain insights and opportunities.
- *Confidently Negotiate*: Be assertive in salary negotiations, backed by research on industry standards and the value that you bring.
- *Advocate for Yourself*: Don't hesitate to express your accomplishments and value during performance evaluations and discussions about promotions.
- *Seek Support*: Lean on mentors and allies for guidance and support throughout your career journey.
- *Stay Informed*: Stay up to date on industry trends as HCIT is dynamic, and this knowledge can lead to better opportunities.
- *Work–Life Balance*: Prioritize work–life balance to maintain wellbeing and career sustainability. By proactively developing your skills, network, and negotiation abilities, you can position yourself for success and equitable compensation in the HCIT field.

**11. What are some recommendations for networking and continued education?**

Actively participate in industry conferences, webinars, and local HCIT events to connect with professionals. Join HCIT forums and LinkedIn groups to engage in discussions and build a strong network. In terms of continued education, consider pursuing relevant certifications such as health informatics, HCIT management, or data analytics. Depending upon what type of software you end up pursuing, even having a medical billing certification, such as myself, has proven to be extremely helpful in my position.

12. **Looking back, to the beginning of your career, can you share some lessons learned? Would you have done anything differently?**

1. *Continuous Learning*: It is important to continuously update skills and knowledge to adapt to a rapidly evolving industry like HCIT.

2. *Work–Life Balance*: Early on, it's essential to establish healthy work–life boundaries to avoid burnout and maintain overall wellbeing.

3. *Resilience*: Early career experiences come with setbacks, but resilience and a growth mindset can help you overcome challenges and learn from them.

4. *Flexibility*: Being open to taking on various roles and projects can lead to unexpected career paths and opportunities for growth.

5. *Communication Skills*: Effective communication, both written and verbal, is crucial for success in HCIT, where collaboration and clarity are key.

These early career lessons can serve as a foundation for long-term professional growth in the HCIT field.

# Leigh Cox, Business Owner and Founder, Medical Group IT INC

**Please provide a brief overview of your professional experience.**

Leigh Cox is an executive with 30+ years in health information management. She is experienced in leading IT within large health systems as a CIO and is currently the owner of Medical Group IT, a boutique consulting company in Atlanta, GA. Leigh's healthcare career started as a management engineer in a hospital, observing how care is delivered to vendor supporting applications to a large healthcare organization for implementation, and currently as a consultant. Experiences at the help desk, as a trainer, an analyst, a desktop tech, a project leader, and a CIO have provided experience at every level of the delivery of care leveraging technology.

**Professional licenses and/or certifications:**
N/A.
**Other education or training relevant to your position:**
MBA
**LinkedIn profile:**
https://www.linkedin.com/in/leigh-cox/
**Were you referred to this project by a colleague? If so, who?**
Jeffery Daigrepont, Senior Vice President, Coker.

# HCIT Questions

**1. What led you to pursue a career in the HCIT industry?**

My first real post-college job was as a management engineer for a large hospital. The position was to observe and document patient flow. At the time, very few applications/systems were in place. Systems were limited to appointment schedules and claims. Charges were still key punch. I realized I was more interested in pursuing how it could be better (i.e., being part of the needed change than documenting and timing tasks). It was clear that information systems were going to be the long-term solution to improving patient and clinical workflows. The next natural step was a position with HBOC (now McKesson) as an application support analyst. Both of these early introductions to healthcare allowed me to apply my process background to supporting and leveraging IT as I continued my career path.

**2. What is the best professional advice given to you that you can share with aspiring women who wish to work in HCIT?**

Attending engineering school provided me with my first exposure to a male-dominated field. The best advice given is not so much as direct advice but a collection of observations and intentionally seeking out (male and female) peers and leaders who share the same professional interests. Healthcare is personal. HCIT is broader than coding, development, and networks. Females are the #1 consumers of healthcare services. As a patient, mother, spouse, friend, and possible future caregiver, you are in a unique position to inherently know how to apply technology. Use it.

**3. What is one of your proudest work-related accomplishments?**

I need to begin by providing background. In 1999, the Institute of Medicine released a report, *To Err is Human: Building a Safer Health*

*System.* In 2000, *Saving Lives and Saving Money* was published in the *Harvard Business Review.* In the late 1990s and early 2000s, technology vendors were releasing round two of clinical applications built on scalable and reasonable-cost platforms. My healthcare system approved a 5-year capital plan to transition from paper to clinical documentation, computerized order entry, and medication administration across four hospitals. Barriers were numerous; clinical staff did not want to move from paper to a "computer," and most did not own a computer and were afraid. Physicians were against the change. The network infrastructure was not stable. Using a computer on wheels was not yet a thing. Scanning bar codes was still new in the consumer market, much less being used in healthcare. My accomplishment was the following: I built a campaign and developed a brand titled "Safety First." The intent was to ensure all levels/roles of the organization knew what was happening; their roles; both clinical and non-clinical, such as pharmacy techs who labeled medications and stocked cabinets; and why reducing errors was important. While there were several overall accomplishments, the one I am personally most proud of was medication administration. Meds were labeled, cabinets filled, armbands were printed with barcodes, med orders were entered electronically by the MD, and 3000+ nurses were trained on bedside medication administration. Medication errors were reduced, and this began a positive technology culture change.

4. **In preparation for a job interview, what type of questions should the candidate consider asking, and in what ways can the candidate set themselves apart?**

    The questions below will provide:

    - Candidate insight into the company's structure and how involved the level of person she is interviewing with is engaged at the executive level. The answers also allow for dialog and could identify a more interesting opportunity.
    - Demonstrates the candidate's interest in the bigger picture, not just the position being interviewed for.

        **Vendor/Payer**

        1. What is the percentage of investment in R&D and support?
        2. What sets your company and/or product apart from your competitors?

### Healthcare Organization Providing Services

1. How is capital allocated?
2. What are the three most important projects for the next 24 months?
3. What do you see as the major challenges in healthcare? How are these challenges being discussed?

5. **Would you say there are additional barriers for women to overcome in this industry? If so, what has your experience taught you about navigating these challenges?**

   My observation of a primary barrier is confidence. Women are less likely to speak up in a group setting. I have found that being prepared for meetings, knowing the participants, and listening with intent give me confidence.

6. **How have you navigated instances of inequality that may be experienced by women in the workplace?**

   Inequality exists in all aspects of our lives. Professionally, I have focused on the long game. Not the short one. Assess the situation. Determine if the instance of inequality is personal or if it is part of the workplace culture. Use the event as a learning opportunity for next time or with a future employer.

7. **When it comes to traveling on the job (such as for attending conferences or performing on-site tasks), what tips may you share when it comes to safety as well as tips that are convenient for travel?**

   If traveling alone, do not put yourself in a situation where there is no one around you. Always be aware of your surroundings. If on-site, do not stay after hours. Leave when others do. Ask other women for recommendations for meals, places to avoid, etc.

8. **How do you maintain a healthy work–life balance?**

   Reduce talking shop post-work hours. Also, have friends who are not in healthcare or IT.

9. **Are there any specific books or videos you may recommend as it relates to HCIT?**

   I recommend seeking out news streams/podcasts related to healthcare policy, reimbursement, and technology. It is important to stay aware of what is current.

10. **What is your advice for women to obtain the best opportunities and to negotiate competitive salaries in this career path?**

    [No answer provided].

11. **What are some recommendations for networking and continued education?**

Align networking with something of interest. Research what additional education or certifications are needed in advance of any career change. Always take advantage of education opportunities with your employer. When possible, make it a performance goal.

12. **Looking back to the beginning of your career, can you share some lessons learned? Would you have done anything differently?**

My one regret is not maintaining some relationships. Through our professional interactions with co-workers or meeting a peer at a conference, each interaction is an opportunity. I treated them as transactions and not relational relationships.

# Aleta Daria, Senior National Sales Director, ModMed

**Please provide a brief overview of your professional experience.**

Aleta Daria began her career in HIT at 17 with a college internship. She worked her way up from there to be the Events Coordinator, Software Trainer, Consultant, Salesperson, and, ultimately, National Sales Director. Ms. Daria has held similar titles since 2014 and has worked at four HIT companies since she began her career in 1995. She has won numerous awards and has made a positive impact in the lives of the team members that she's mentored, not to mention the practices that she has helped.

**Professional licenses and/or certifications:**
N/A.

**Other education or training relevant to your position:**
N/A.

**LinkedIn profile:**
https://www.linkedin.com/in/aletadaria/

**Were you referred to this project by a colleague? If so, who?**
Jeffery Daigrepont, Senior Vice President, Coker.

# HCIT Questions

**1. What led you to pursue a career in the HCIT industry?**

My uncle was a plastic surgeon, and he and my aunt started a CRM company for plastic surgeons in 1993. I admired them greatly and wanted to follow in their footsteps.

**2. What is the best professional advice given to you that you can share with aspiring women who wish to work in HCIT?**

Be yourself. Be sincere. Find a role that aligns with your talents and ethos. Look for a company that has cutting-edge technology. There are a lot of dinosaurs in HIT, and you won't be as happy at one of those companies because you won't be helping practices as much as you could elsewhere.

**3. What is one of your proudest work-related accomplishments?**

Seeing my colleagues, whom I mentored in their 20s, now have leadership positions where they are mentoring others.

**4. In preparation for a job interview, what type of questions should the candidate consider asking, and in what ways can the candidate set themselves apart?**

What is your management style? What is the company culture like? What do customers like most about your tech? What are the areas where the tech needs enhancement? Whom do you compete against? How well are you funded? Are you hoping to be acquired in the next 5 years or do you see yourself as the acquirer?

**5. Would you say there are additional barriers for women to overcome in this industry? If so, what has your experience taught you about navigating these challenges?**

I'm in sales, and I wouldn't say that there are additional barriers for women as individual contributors. In fact, we've done a study at our company, and there are more women who are top performers in our sales organization than men.

**6. How have you navigated instances of inequality that may be experienced by women in the workplace?**

At one employer, I had a great track record of success and was passed over several times for leadership roles. Ultimately, I left that company for that reason.

7. **When it comes to traveling on the job (such as for attending conferences or performing on-site tasks), what tips may you share when it comes to safety as well as tips that are convenient for travel?**

I've been in the field, both visiting practices and exhibiting at trade shows, innumerable times. I generally feel perfectly safe, although I always make sure to close the latch on my hotel door. With that said, I have dealt with sexual harassment on several occasions. My best advice for avoiding uncomfortable situations like those is to limit alcohol consumption when around colleagues.

8. **How do you maintain a healthy work–life balance?**

I make sure to work out 3–5 times per week. That helps keep my endorphins high and requires me to carve out time to take care of myself physically.

9. **Are there any specific books or videos you may recommend as it relates to HCIT?**

N/A.

10. **What is your advice for women to obtain the best opportunities and to negotiate competitive salaries in this career path?**

Don't be afraid to negotiate your compensation. Never accept the first offer.

11. **What are some recommendations for networking and continued education?**

[No response provided].

12. **Looking back to the beginning of your career, can you share some lessons learned? Would you have done anything differently?**

I don't think I would have. My career has been incredibly rewarding.

# Jessica Feigen, Director of Provider Success, Geode Health

**Please provide a brief overview of your professional experience.**

Jessica Feigen spent the first 7 years of her career at Epic, an EMR software company, managing software implementations for hospitals and clinic healthcare systems. During that time, she had the opportunity to grow her skills in project management, operational change management, and people and team management. In this role, Ms. Feigen developed and provided expertise to customers on healthcare workflows and industry best practices, technical software configuration, training, and go-live strategies.

Ms. Feigen left Epic to join Geode Health, a mental healthcare startup that provides outpatient psychiatric and therapy services, as one of the first fifteen employees. As the Director of Provider Success, she has created and managed the department that implements, trains, and supports all clinical software applications across the organization. This entailed hiring a team and creating all the department's processes from scratch, including implementation methodology, support protocols, vendor selection, and structure for ongoing decision-making and change control.

**Professional licenses and/or certifications:**
N/A.

**Other education or training relevant to your position:**
Bachelor of science, Psychology

**Were you referred to this project by a colleague? If so, who?**
Jeffery Daigrepont, Senior Vice President, Coker.

# HCIT Questions

**1. What led you to pursue a career in the HCIT industry?**

I wasn't aware of the HCIT industry until I graduated from college, when I was lucky to have a friend forward me a job application at Epic, the EMR software company. I joined the company as an implementation project manager and quickly learned that healthcare project management sits at a unique intersection of people skills, analytical skills, organizational skills, and communication skills. The HCIT industry presents rewarding challenges that require creative approaches, teamwork, and, most importantly, a tangible impact on patients' lives. Knowing that the effort you're putting in every day is improving the delivery of healthcare is a strong "why" that can get you out of bed in the mornings, even on your hardest days.

**2. What is the best professional advice given to you that you can share with aspiring women who wish to work in HCIT?**

Seek first to understand, then to be understood. Practice becoming a great listener and aim to fully understand a problem or perspective before trying to solve it; this can save you from spending a lot of time and heartache going down the wrong path.

Early in your career, be curious and ask good questions to continue to expand your understanding of the industry. Seek to understand why projects go well as well as why projects don't go well. Asking good questions will greatly increase your knowledge and allow you to adopt other's lessons learned without needing to make the same mistakes yourself.

3. **What is one of your proudest work-related accomplishments?**

   [No answer provided].

4. **In preparation for a job interview, what type of questions should the candidate consider asking, and in what ways can the candidate set themselves apart?**

   Set yourself apart by explaining the measurable ways that your efforts have produced positive outcomes. Whether you have professional or more informal experience (school or internships), think about ways that you changed something for the better. The HCIT industry needs go-getters that care about outcomes and can follow through to deliver results, even in the face of challenges. Whether you led teammates to meet a tough deadline, came up with a creative way to make a process more efficient, or organized a chaotic situation, you'll stand out if you can help demonstrate to an employer that by hiring you, they'll be hiring someone who can solve their challenges.

5. **Would you say there are additional barriers for women to overcome in this industry? If so, what has your experience taught you about navigating these challenges?**

   N/A.

6. **How have you navigated instances of inequality that may be experienced by women in the workplace?**

   N/A.

7. **When it comes to traveling on the job (such as for attending conferences or performing on-site tasks), what tips may you share when it comes to safety as well as tips that are convenient for travel?**

   In my first job, I was traveling 2–3 times a month. My top tips are:

   - If you're traveling somewhat regularly, keep your essentials "pre-packed" in organizers so you can just toss the pack into your luggage and not worry about remembering each individual item. For example, I created a travel toiletry kit where I kept a travel toothbrush, toothpaste, shampoo, conditioner, etc. Unpacking and repacking those kinds of items each time eventually lead to forgetting something!

- Find something non-work-related to try in each new place you travel to, whether that's a restaurant, an exercise class at a nearby gym, or walking to a local landmark. I found that if I didn't make a plan, I would just work in my hotel at night and wind up feeling burned out. Find at least one activity outside of work that you can look forward to and that gets you out of the hotel in the evenings.

**8. How do you maintain a healthy work–life balance?**

If you're someone who tends to just let the workday keep sliding into your evenings, make plans or commitments that start at a specific time, so you're forced to put the work away for the day and jump into your personal life. Whether that's a happy hour plan with a friend, signing up for a workout class, or a FaceTime date with a family member, having plans keeps you accountable to being efficient and getting your work wrapped up by a certain time.

**9. Are there any specific books or videos you may recommend as it relates to HCIT?**

[No response provided].

**10. What is your advice for women to obtain the best opportunities and to negotiate competitive salaries in this career path?**

[No response provided].

**11. What are some recommendations for networking and continued education?**

[No response provided].

**12. Looking back to the beginning of your career, can you share some lessons learned? Would you have done anything differently?**

I wish I would have understood that almost everyone feels like an imposter when they first enter a new role or position; nerves and uncertainty are normal and are not signs that you're in the wrong place or that you can't succeed. Aim to continuously learn and improve and put in your best efforts, and the rest will fall into place over time!

# Michelle Fox, Director Medical Staff & Information Services

**Please provide a brief overview of your professional experience.**

Michelle Fox, as a nurse by training, worked in multiple areas, including med-surg/telemetry, home health, hospice, and rural health clinics. She started working in the informatics area and then branched into information technology as well when the former CIO was moving to COO and asked Ms. Fox to take on the role of IT Director.

**Professional licenses and/or certifications:**
RN

**Other education or training relevant to your position:**
I've learned a lot of informatics items from the EMRs we have had. As for IT, it has been a lot of learning on the job.

**Were you referred to this project by a colleague? If so, who?**
Jeffery Daigrepont, Senior Vice President, Coker.

# HCIT Questions

1. **What led you to pursue a career in the HCIT industry?**

   I was asked by our then-CEO to consider taking on the role of Informaticist when the hospital decided to create a new department/role. When our then-CIO was moving to the COO position, he asked me to take the IT Director position that he would be vacating due to my director-level skills with budgeting, problem-solving, etc. from having been a director for years in multiple areas and already having the clinical informatics department under my umbrella.

2. **What is the best professional advice given to you that you can share with aspiring women who wish to work in HCIT?**

   Don't think you cannot do it. Although I do not come from a trained IT background, I have learned a lot over the years in the IT arena, and having a competent IT team that has deep-level knowledge works. Sometimes you just need to be the problem-solver, the deep thinker, the person who throws out questions, etc.

3. **What is one of your proudest work-related accomplishments?**

   In the IT arena, the entire new network and phone system installation for all of our buildings.

4. **In preparation for a job interview, what type of questions should the candidate consider asking, and in what ways can the candidate set themselves apart?**

   Always ask what the expectations are related to hours, overtime, daily/weekly functions, opportunities for advancement, etc. Knowing pay rates and benefits at the time of an interview is important as well.

And make sure you know what your strengths and weaknesses are before the interview and touch on them.

5. **Would you say there are additional barriers for women to overcome in this industry? If so, what has your experience taught you about navigating these challenges?**

   I am sure that this can happen in some areas. I do not feel that I have experienced it, though.

6. **How have you navigated instances of inequality that may be experienced by women in the workplace?**

   N/A.

7. **When it comes to traveling on the job (such as for attending conferences or performing on-site tasks), what tips may you share when it comes to safety as well as tips that are convenient for travel?**

   Always watch your surroundings!

8. **How do you maintain a healthy work–life balance?**

   I work more than 40 hours a week, and as my kids were growing up, that was usually the case. However, I made a point to get out of the office timely and spend time with my kids, go to their events, etc., and then I may work from home later (after they went to bed, after home from their game, etc.). Luckily, my employer would let me take off early for their events when needed, knowing that I was still going to put in the time and complete what needed to be done but I could be creative with the hours I worked.

9. **Are there any specific books or videos you may recommend as it relates to HCIT?**

   N/A.

10. **What is your advice for women to obtain the best opportunities and to negotiate competitive salaries in this career path?**

    Know your worth! Get things in writing and don't just settle!

11. **What are some recommendations for networking and continued education?**

    Having a pool of people in your area is a huge asset. Take advantage of having a pool of resources so you can reach out to them with questions! And if listservs are an option, sign up for them. Sometimes someone else might pose a question that you haven't thought of yet or have already fixed the issue that you are struggling with!

12. **Looking back to the beginning of your career, can you share some lessons learned? Would you have done anything differently?**

When I look back to the beginning of my career, I definitely could not have predicted where my career path would go. I started out working as a floor nurse on a med-surg/telemetry unit. From there, I moved to home health as a staff nurse and worked my way up to Clinical Supervisor and then Director. I then was the Director when my hospital started its hospice program. I implemented the EMR in our home health and hospice departments. I then moved to the Director of our Rural Health Clinics. I was Director when we upgraded our EMR to include points of care in the clinics. Having a higher level of understanding of the EMR prompted our CEO to ask me to work in informatics. That led to adding the IT department under my umbrella a few years later. You never know what door is going to open! Healthcare is vast and provides so many opportunities! Allow yourself to grow as you are given options!

# Linn Foster Freedman, Partner, Chair Data Privacy + Cybersecurity Team, Robinson & Cole LLP

**Please provide a brief overview of your professional experience.**

Linn Freedman focuses her practice on compliance with state and federal data privacy and security laws and regulations, emergency data breach response, mitigation, and litigation. She counsels clients on state and federal investigations and enforcement actions. She has a particular focus on health information technology (HIT) and has assisted clients with navigating laws governing the access, use and disclosure of protected health information, and substance use disorder information and HIPAA compliance.

Ms. Freedman is an Adjunct Professor at the Roger Williams University School of Law teaching privacy law and a former Adjunct Professor in Brown University's Executive Masters of Cybersecurity Program. She has been globally (since 2019) and nationally (since 2012) ranked in *Chambers USA: America's Leading Lawyers for Business* in the area of privacy law; was named among *Becker's Healthcare*'s Women in Health IT to Know in 2020, 2022, and 2023; was selected by her peers for inclusion in *The Best Lawyers in America©*; has been recognized by the *National Law Review* as a "Go-To Thought Leader" and by Lexology as a "Legal Influencer," named a Top Author and the #1 author in Cybersecurity in JD Supra's *Reader's Choice* awards since its launch in 2016–2023; was named *Health Data Management*'s "Top 50 Healthcare IT Professionals in the US"; and is frequently interviewed and quoted in numerous publications, including *The Wall Street Journal*, National Public Radio, *Modern Healthcare*, Reuters, and *Bloomberg Law*.

**Professional licenses and/or certifications:**
JD
Certified Information Privacy Professional

**Other education or training relevant to your position:**
N/A.

**LinkedIn profile:**
https://www.linkedin.com/in/linn-freedman-447a51b/
R+C bio: http://www.rc.com/people/LinnFFreedman.cfm

**Were you referred to this project by a colleague? If so, who?**
N/A.

# HCIT Questions

**1. What led you to pursue a career in the HCIT industry?**

My initial exposure to the HCIT industry was as a founder of one of the first five statewide Health Information Exchanges in the United States in 2000. Through that experience, I became knowledgeable and experienced about data privacy and security issues relating to the access, use, and disclosure of health information. That led me to become experienced in HIPAA compliance and data privacy and security state laws applicable to the exchange of health information. As more security incidents occurred from 2003 to the present, I have focused on cybersecurity, including prevention, responding to security incidents, and mitigation following security incidents.

**2. What is the best professional advice given to you that you can share with aspiring women who wish to work in HCIT?**

Don't be intimidated by a roomful of men in this industry. Women are making headway, so stay the course. Wow them with your knowledge and experience, and you will gain credibility and trust. Be practical and a team player. Find ways to solve problems instead of contributing to them. Don't be afraid to get over your skis a bit. If you have the reputation of being a problem-solver and a team player, any man will want to be on your team.

**3. What is one of your proudest work-related accomplishments?**

Being recognized nationally in Data Privacy and Security by *Chambers USA: America's Leading Lawyers for Business* since 2012. One of the proudest and most heartfelt moments was when a client told me that if I had not helped him through a ransomware attack, he would have gone out of business—a business he started 35 years ago. He said I was his "guardian angel." To be able to help a small business stay in business after a devastating cyberattack was so very meaningful to me.

**4. In preparation for a job interview, what type of questions should the candidate consider asking, and in what ways can the candidate set themselves apart?**

How do you want me to fit into your team? What do you see as my role in enhancing your team? What kinds of projects would you assign me to, and how do you envision that my knowledge and experience can assist with those projects? What gaps do you want me to fill? What kinds of projects or assignments would you want me to take the lead on? How does your team integrate new members?

I think a message to the interviewer that you are a team player and that you want to fit into an existing team is important. Showing that you don't want to step on toes and want to work side by side with the existing team is advantageous, especially if the team is primarily composed of men.

**5. Would you say there are additional barriers for women to overcome in this industry? If so, what has your experience taught you about navigating these challenges?**

Because the industry is composed of mostly men and has been so for many years, if you are the first woman on the team, it is important to dispel long-standing attitudes and assumptions about working with women. Establish your place on the team and don't bow down or be meek, but don't be too strong so you are viewed as a bully or can be seen as the "b" word. It may take extra time to establish credibility and trust, but be patient. Once your team members see that you have their back and that you are smart, practical, and a team player, they will embrace you. I also think it is helpful to find someone on the team or in the organization (I suggest a man who has been in the company for some time, has succeeded, and has historical knowledge) to help you navigate issues that you are experiencing with others on your team or in the organization. Find someone you can trust to go to with questions and to seek advice. I have always had male mentors in my life, and I have learned a tremendous amount from them.

**6. How have you navigated instances of inequality that may be experienced by women in the workplace?**

I have experienced inequality in both elevation in position and compensation in the past (not presently). Despite appealing both decisions, the decisions were not reversed, so I decided to terminate my relationship with that organization. Equal pay seems to be getting better in the workplace, but sometimes the only option is to leave. Having the courage to leave an organization that is not treating you fairly is difficult, but sometimes necessary.

**7. When it comes to traveling on the job (such as for attending conferences or performing on-site tasks), what tips may you share when it comes to safety as well as tips that are convenient for travel?**

Always be aware of your surroundings, and don't put yourself in a position of risk. I try to pack very lightly so I don't have to check a bag and worry that the bag will get lost, so I don't have proper attire for meetings. It is easier to move around with a small bag. I tend to stay close to the hotel where I am staying, but I like to eat meals at the hotel bar and chat with others who are traveling. I have met incredible people while eating dinner at the bar. It is a great place to network. If colleagues are with you or you meet someone from another organization, ask them to join you for dinner at the bar.

**8. How do you maintain a healthy work–life balance?**

I don't! That said, I work hard and play hard. That is and has always been my mantra. I love to fish, ski, and golf. When I am not working, I can be seen enjoying those three activities.

**9. Are there any specific books or videos you may recommend as it relates to HCIT?**

*The Immortal Life of Henrietta Lacks* by Rebecca Skloot. If you haven't read it yet, you simply must.

**10. What is your advice for women to obtain the best opportunities and to negotiate competitive salaries in this career path?**

Wait for the employer to make an offer, and don't take the first offer. Figure out what the range of salaries is for the position and your experience before you go into a negotiation. Determine what your target is before the first interview or evaluation. Write out a plan for why you believe you are worth your target amount. When they come in with their first offer, even if it is at or above your target, ask for more! As women, we don't ask, but men do. If you don't ask, you don't get!

11. **What are some recommendations for networking and continued education?**

Join local and national organizations that are not only relevant to your job and profession but that you are interested in. Embrace the concept of lifetime learning. I started my career in this area in the year 2000, and 23 years later, it is amazing how much I have grown professionally, how much more I know now, and how that knowledge has allowed me to predict what's to come. Never stop learning.

12. **Looking back to the beginning of your career, can you share some lessons learned? Would you have done anything differently?**

I am very satisfied with the decisions I have made. I had great mentors and support along the way, and I am very grateful looking back at my career. I think, looking back, if I could change anything, it would be to leave organizations where I wasn't treated as I should have been quicker. I was too loyal and stayed too long. I don't know now whether it was a sense of loyalty or a lack of courage to go out and find a new position, but I wish now that I had seen the writing on the wall, accepted it, and moved on to the next position quicker than I did. I feel like I lost some valuable time in establishing a better work situation, and I would have been happier sooner if I had transitioned to the new opportunities. There's always doubt about leaving an organization—doubt about whether the new one will be better, giving up the time and credibility that you have established at the organization and knowing that it will take time to establish it at the new organization, and leaving a situation that is comfortable. The lesson learned for me is that if you know the organization is not treating you well, the chance that it will all of a sudden change is unrealistic, so getting the courage to leave and having confidence in yourself that you will make the new situation work are valuable.

# Chelsea Gambino, Director of Administration, Comprehensive Family Health

**Please provide a brief overview of your professional experience.**

Over the past 18 transformative years, Chelsea's journey through the healthcare realm has been inseparably intertwined with technological progress. Rooted in a specialization in nuclear medicine technology from Keiser

University, her career narrative has been shaped by the symbiotic relationship between healthcare and technology. Following her academic tenure, Chelsea stepped into the role of Lead Nuclear Medicine Technologist at a new hospital. This position demands not only clinical expertise but also an acute grasp of complex equipment and systems. From cameras to Picture Archiving and Communications (PAC) systems and processing software, she navigated the intricacies of troubleshooting, ensuring the flawless execution of patient procedures. Seeking to expand her horizons, Chelsea embraced the opportunity to receive specialized training from Philips Healthcare in Chicago, IL, which profoundly amplified her technological acumen. By immersing herself in their nuclear medicine program, she not only refined her technical skills but also imbibed the latest industry practices. This training catalyzed her journey into a realm where technology became both a tool and a canvas for innovation.

Chelsea's trajectory converged with the dynamic domain of radiology, particularly within the mobile landscape. It was at this time that she realized the pivotal role technology played in not just streamlining healthcare processes but also in catalyzing on-the-spot problem-solving. This stint in the mobile environment significantly advanced her prowess in technology and troubleshooting. Chelsea grasped that technology was more than an aid—it was the linchpin upon which effective healthcare hinged. This understanding led her into sales, providing firsthand insight into the synergy between medical technology and business dynamics. Yet, a pivotal juncture beckoned, guiding her to a primary care practice spread across three Florida counties.

Since 2016, Chelsea has been deeply immersed in this multifaceted role within these practices. Her responsibilities have included everything from working as a medical assistant to answering phones at the front desk to troubleshooting network and firewall problems. Throughout her journey, technology has been the compass guiding her path. From mastering complex equipment to adapting to mobile setups, her narrative underscores the fusion of technology and healthcare. Chelsea states that as she looks ahead, "my purpose remains steadfast: to leverage the profound technological insight to elevate healthcare experiences. By seamlessly integrating technology and troubleshooting into the realm of care delivery, I endeavor to forge a path where innovation seamlessly aligns with compassion."

**Professional licenses and/or certifications:**
Nuclear Medicine Technologist License
AART(N) Certification
**Other education or training relevant to your position:**
N/A.

**LinkedIn profile:**
[Optional, not provided.]
**Were you referred to this project by a colleague? If so, who?**
Jeffery Daigrepont, Senior Vice President, Coker.

# HCIT Questions

### 1. What led you to pursue a career in the HCIT industry?

Since my early experiences with HTML coding as a child, it became evident to me that I possessed a natural aptitude for troubleshooting and IT-related tasks. Throughout my journey, my fascination with healthcare persisted, largely due to my admiration for the fusion of science and artistry inherent in the field of medicine. This affinity for healthcare initially led me to explore nuclear medicine, where the convergence of compassionate care and cutting-edge technology intrigued me.

As I delved further into my career, my current role has granted me the privilege of not only influencing but also steering the technological landscape within our practices. This empowerment to shape technology decisions and spearhead the implementation of novel advancements for the betterment of patient care resonates profoundly with me. Witnessing the tangible impact of technology on healthcare outcomes fuels my passion to drive innovation and contribute to the HCIT industry.

In essence, it is the harmonious blend of my inherent IT skills, an enduring interest in healthcare, and the opportunity to merge technology with compassionate patient care that propels me forward in my journey within the HCIT industry.

### 2. What is the best professional advice given to you that you can share with aspiring women who wish to work in HCIT?

First and foremost, trust your instincts—that innate wisdom that sets you apart. In the dynamic world of tech and healthcare, your intuition can be your guiding light. Also, keep in mind that challenges are part of the journey. And when they show up (which they surely will), be relentless. Your persistence acts as your superpower. By forging ahead, you can uncover solutions that truly transform healthcare.

### 3. What is one of your proudest work-related accomplishments?

I'm really proud of introducing ambient AI for our providers to use in charting. It's made our work more efficient, patients and providers happier, and boosted overall productivity. Furthermore, this innovation has led to enhanced proficiencies across the board, enabling our team to allocate more time and resources to other critical tasks.

4. **In preparation for a job interview, what type of questions should the candidate consider asking, and in what ways can the candidate set themselves apart?**

   When exploring opportunities in HCIT, it's crucial to inquire about the key aspects of your role in addition to the scalability of the IT solutions. I also feel it's imperative to ask about the work–life balance and the company's goals to ensure they align with yours. To distinguish themselves, a candidate should showcase their adeptness in problem-solving, highlight their skill in communicating technical ideas to non-technical healthcare staff, and emphasize their patient-centered approach to technology.

5. **Would you say there are additional barriers for women to overcome in this industry? If so, what has your experience taught you about navigating these challenges?**

   Absolutely. I believe there are additional barriers for women to overcome in any competitive, male-dominated industry. From my experience, these challenges have taught me the importance of relentless determination and presenting myself with confidence. It's crucial to trust in my abilities and, regardless of others' perceptions, to consistently show up and stand my ground. I firmly believe that no one can make you feel inferior without your consent. By adopting this mindset, I've been able to navigate these barriers and forge a path that not only challenges stereotypes but also contributes to positive change in the industry.

6. **How have you navigated instances of inequality that may be experienced by women in the workplace?**

   N/A.

7. **When it comes to traveling on the job (such as for attending conferences or performing on-site tasks), what tips may you share when it comes to safety as well as tips that are convenient for travel?**

   I have a passion for both personal and professional travel, and safety is always a top priority. Whenever possible, I opt to travel with a companion. Additionally, I invest time in thoroughly researching my destination to ensure I'm well prepared. To enhance safety, I often choose to pre-book transportation through the hotel or venue rather than relying solely on ride-sharing services. If I do use ride-sharing, I make sure to share my route details with someone I trust. Another safety measure is refraining from using devices while walking around to stay alert. These practices not only prioritize my safety but also contribute to a smoother and more enjoyable travel experience.

**8. How do you maintain a healthy work–life balance?**

Maintaining a healthy work–life balance has been a journey for me, primarily through setting and respecting boundaries. While I thrive on deadlines and pressure, I've come to realize the importance of balance. Although there are instances where staying late is necessary, I ensure I log off at an appropriate time. Learning to differentiate genuine emergencies from situations that can wait until regular hours has been pivotal. Interestingly, many issues I once deemed urgent turned out to be manageable during the workday. I've also come to appreciate the value of utilizing vacation time. Taking these breaks not only rejuvenates my engagement, creativity, and energy levels but also enhances my overall performance. It's a reminder that looking after oneself is a crucial foundation for delivering optimal results.

**9. Are there any specific books or videos you may recommend as it relates to HCIT?**

N/A.

**10. What is your advice for women to obtain the best opportunities and to negotiate competitive salaries in this career path?**

For women seeking to excel in HCIT and secure competitive salaries, two essential strategies stand out. Firstly, it's crucial to have a clear grasp of your own values. Take the time to research prevailing industry standards and earnings for similar roles. Armed with this knowledge, you can confidently advocate for a salary that aligns with your skills and experience without settling for less than you deserve.

Moreover, showcasing your value is paramount. During salary negotiations, spotlight your past accomplishments that directly relate to the role you're pursuing. By illustrating how your expertise can contribute to the success of the HCIT team and the organization, you build a compelling case for a higher remuneration package.

**11. What are some recommendations for networking and continued education?**

When it comes to networking and learning more, remember to get out there and meet people. Attend events and connect with professionals in and outside your field. Also, always keep learning. Take every chance to gain knowledge, even if it doesn't seem important at the time. No one can take away what you've learned, and you never know when it might be useful in the future.

12. **Looking back to the beginning of your career, can you share some lessons learned? Would you have done anything differently?**

Looking back on my career journey, I'm torn between two perspectives: yes and no. On the one hand, I wouldn't change a thing about my past choices and experiences. Each step I've taken and every challenge I've conquered have played a role in shaping the confident and self-assured professional I am today. On the other hand, I now realize that genuine growth arises from pushing boundaries and embracing new opportunities. I regret not taking more chances outside my comfort zone in the past. I've come to understand the value of welcoming discomfort and exploring uncharted territories early in my career to foster growth and transformation.

# Leshia Garrett, Director of Health Information Technology

**Please provide a brief overview of your professional experience.**

Leshia Garrett has been in healthcare for 30 years. She has worked in anesthesiology, internal medicine, pediatric home health, chiropractic, home health, hospice, palliative care, skilled nursing, and assisted living. While the majority of Ms. Garrett's career has been in revenue cycle management, she has years of experience in operational and financial support, as well as EMR implementation and training. So, combined, all of her years of experience polished her for her venture into IT. Currently, Ms. Garrett is the Director of Health Information Technology. In addition, the following are some of the roles she has held: Director of Operational Support, Revenue Cycle Manager, Accounts Receivable Manager, Regional Financial Counselor, and Practice Manager.

**Professional licenses and/or certifications:**

MatrixCare Skilled Nursing and Senior Living, Revenue Cycle Management and Clinical

**Other education or training relevant to your position:**

N/A.

**LinkedIn profile:**

https://www.linkedin.com/in/leshia-g-061a761a8

**Were you referred to this project by a colleague? If so, who?**
Lindsay Rowlands, MHA, Project Coordinator.

# HCIT Questions

1. **What led you to pursue a career in the HCIT industry?**

   It was during an unsettling time, but it's important to remember that great stories sometimes come from hard beginnings. My position was eliminated. It was an anxious time. But I kept my faith and knew I would land exactly where I was supposed to, and that's exactly what happened. Within the same company, a position opened in health information technology! I had extensive experience with the EMR system they needed support, so I was transferred to that team as a Health Information Technology Specialist! In less than a year, I was offered the Director role, and I'm blessed to lead one of the best teams in the industry!

2. **What is the best professional advice given to you that you can share with aspiring women who wish to work in HCIT?**

   Network. It's a word that is thrown around a lot, but connections are so important. Always have pride in your work, keep a strong work ethic, and build those professional relationships. Healthcare is a small world, and you never know how important a connection will be or what doors it can open for you.

3. **What is one of your proudest work-related accomplishments?**

   The easy answer would be the cash goals I've met during my time in Revenue Cycle Management or the successful EMR implementations. But I would say I am most proud of the teams I've had the privilege to lead. To mentor and watch others grow and go on to accomplish career and personal goals makes me proud.

4. **In preparation for a job interview, what type of questions should the candidate consider asking, and in what ways can the candidate set themselves apart?**

   Questions to ask:
   - What is their management style? This will give you the opportunity to determine if this is a style that fits your personality.
   - Do you currently have any special projects the team or individual position will be responsible for, and what are the deadlines for those projects? This will let you know their expectations and whether it is

a team effort or individual responsibility. You will be able to expand on how you handle special projects and/or deadlines.
- What experience or qualities are you looking for when filling this position? This will give you the opportunity to sell yourself and explain how you fit their needs.

5. **Would you say there are additional barriers for women to overcome in this industry? If so, what has your experience taught you about navigating these challenges?**

   Recently, I read that women make up 25% of the technology sector, and there are even fewer in leadership roles. While this may seem like a barrier, I do see that changing. More and more women are entering the HCIT industry and are bringing new ideas and perspectives. It's taught me that it is no longer the "best man" for the job, but the best person.

6. **How have you navigated instances of inequality that may be experienced by women in the workplace?**

   N/A.

7. **When it comes to traveling on the job (such as for attending conferences or performing on-site tasks), what tips may you share when it comes to safety as well as tips that are convenient for travel?**

   I have traveled a lot in my career, and safety is always important. I would advise you to be mindful of the hours you are traveling. Try not to fly or drive late at night. You should always research where you are going and be familiar with the area. As for convenience, check-in online, try to only have a carry-on, and always have a charger! You can get a lot accomplished while waiting for your flight or if you arrive early to your destination.

8. **How do you maintain a healthy work–life balance?**

   This is an important question. It's not always easy, but it's a must for your mental health and your personal relationships. I think if you have a high work ethic, then you will apply yourself each day so that when you are "off the clock," you will be able to relax and enjoy that time. It comes with respecting others' time but also your own time. There will always be special projects or emergency situations that require after-hours attention, and that's ok. But finding balance is key.

9. **Are there any specific books or videos you may recommend as it relates to HCIT?**

   I do not have any specific to HCIT, but I do believe in having mentors and following people who inspire you.

10. **What is your advice for women to obtain the best opportunities and to negotiate competitive salaries in this career path?**

Know your worth. Know your goals. Put in the work. Pursue your education, but also get the experience. As you are doing both, you will gain professional relationships. Those relationships will open doors for you.

11. **What are some recommendations for networking and continued education?**

Join social media groups, committees, or participate on advisory boards or discussion groups.

12. **Looking back to the beginning of your career, can you share some lessons learned? Would you have done anything differently?**

This is another great question. I've learned many lessons, but the biggest one is that you must believe in yourself. That may sound like the simplest or hardest one for most, but it is vital for success. You will make mistakes, but learning from and owning those mistakes is where you will grow. As for doing things differently, I think we are products of our environment, so make sure you gravitate toward healthy environments and lean on mentors. I wish I had learned this earlier in my career.

# Mary P. Griskewicz, Director, Federal Government Affairs, MS, FHIMSS

**Please provide a brief overview of your professional experience.**

Mary P. Griskewicz, Director, Federal Government Affairs, MS, FHIMSS, is a specialist in government affairs and industry relations. She manages policy strategies for HCIT, covering areas including telehealth, cybersecurity, artificial intelligence, interoperability, and privacy and security. She has held leadership positions at Cigna, HIMSS, GE Healthcare, Yale New Haven Health System, and TEKsystems, with management responsibilities at Aetna and Anthem, and Blue Cross Blue Shield.

Throughout her career, she developed relationships with key health policy-makers and industry leaders, leading to opportunities to contribute and advise the White House, members of Congress, CMS, ONC, the U.S. Government Accountability Office, the Medicare Advisory Payment Commission, and the U.S. Department of Commerce on key policy HCIT issues.

Ms. Griskewicz also leads the HIMSS Public Policy Committee and is the former Chair of the New England HIMSS Chapter Advocacy Committee for the second time in her career. She has served as Vice Chair for the HIMSS Public Policy Health Equity Workgroup, raising awareness and providing a voice to ensure health IT policies are shaped to provide equitable care for all. She is currently the Chairperson of the American Telemedicine Association's Policy Council.

As a member of the Walking Gallery and patient advocate, Ms. Griskewicz works to build awareness about the need for patients to access their health information to achieve health and wellness. Her patient advocacy work has resulted in the roles of author and ghostwriter and Associate Editor to HIMSS, *Participatory Healthcare: A Person-Centered Approach to Healthcare Transformation*. She has also served on many industry boards, leveraging her HCIT experience.

Ms. Griskewicz has taken an active role in mentoring future HCIT leaders and has served as a professor and guest lecturer at the NE HIMSS Mentoring Committee, Northeastern University, the University of New Haven, and Yale University. She has received several awards for her leadership in HCIT and has been recognized by the HIMSS as *One of the Most Influential Woman in Health IT (2021)*.

**Do you hold any professional licenses and/or certifications? If so, please list.**

HIMSS Fellow

Certified Master Gardener

**Other education or training relevant to your position:**

BA, Political Science, MS Industrial Relations

Negotiating, Mendoza School of Business, Notre Dame

**LinkedIn profile:**

https://www.linkedin.com/in/mary-griskewicz-ms-fhimss-6aa496126/

**Were you referred to this project by a colleague? If so, who?**

Jefferey Daigrepont, Senior Vice President, Coker.

# HCIT Questions

### 1. What led you to pursue a career in the HCIT industry?

My mother encouraged me to create an opportunity for myself to make a difference and help others. HCIT has provided me with many opportunities to help others. I am truly blessed.

2. **What is the best professional advice given to you that you can share with aspiring women who wish to work in HCIT?**

    Have no fear. Believe in yourself no matter what, as only you can define your success.

3. **What is one of your proudest work-related accomplishments?**

    Being named HIMSS, Most Influential Woman in Health IT (2021) by my peers.

4. **In preparation for a job interview, what type of questions should the candidate consider asking, and in what ways can the candidate set themselves apart?**

    • What challenges/problems can I assist in resolving that no one else has been able to accomplish? (Remember, the interview is about what you can do moving forward, not what you did.)

    • How will I know I have achieved success in this role?

5. **Would you say there are additional barriers for women to overcome in this industry? If so, what has your experience taught you about navigating these challenges?**

    Bias against women is still an issue today in the workplace. Oftentimes, bias is unintentional, though sometimes it can be intentional. Taking the time to express your intent to be included in your thoughts, actions, and words is important. You must listen to others, redirect them, and educate them toward the inclusion of women and others in HCIT.

6. **How have you navigated instances of inequality that may be experienced by women in the workplace? Type N/A if this question is inapplicable to you.**

    I have, when necessary, directed the issue head-on and educated those above me and around me about the environment or actions that I observed in others. I then had very direct discussions in an effort to educate those who are not seeing that their words or actions are resulting in inequality in an effort to correct the issue.

7. **When it comes to traveling on the job (such as for attending conferences or performing on-site tasks), what tips may you share when it comes to safety as well as tips that are convenient for travel? Type N/A if this question is inapplicable to you.**

    Always tell someone where you are. Use text to keep in contact with your family and colleagues. When possible, have a travel buddy and exchange family contact information as appropriate for emergencies.

Use technology to enhance safety, i.e., set the safety mode for ride shares.

**8. How do you maintain a healthy work–life balance?**

I exercise by gardening, swimming, and walking my dog. I became a certified Master Gardener during the pandemic. You need to challenge your mind, body, and spirit.

**9. Are there any specific books or videos you may recommend as it relates to HCIT?**

*Participatory Healthcare: A Person Centered Approach to Healthcare Transformation* by Jan Oldenburg, FHIMSS and Mary Griskewicz, MS, FHIMSS.

**10. What is your advice for women to obtain the best opportunities and to negotiate competitive salaries in this career path?**

Know the value/worth of your position by market segment. Always ask for more of whatever it is you need. Culture and benefits are often just as important as salary.

**11. What are some recommendations for networking and continued education?**

Build your network early in your career and keep up your network. Join the local chapter of your professional society and get engaged. Go as far as you can with formal education, but remember, you never stop learning; you must become a lifelong learner.

**12. Looking back to the beginning of your career, can you share some lessons learned? Would you have done anything differently?**

Travel internationally as the world is your oyster and you can learn from other people, cultures, and approaches to work.

# Lisa Grisim, Vice President and Associate Chief Information Officer

**Please provide a brief overview of your professional experience.**

Lisa Grisim is an RN by background who has worked at Stanford Medicine for over 35 years, with the past 25 years spent working in various positions in the information services department at Stanford Medicine Children's Health. Starting her IT career as an analyst, she quickly became a Lead and then a Project Manager. During her time in the project management role, Ms. Grisim has led a number of multi-million-dollar, complex system implementations, including four electronic health record (I) implementations. After the second implementation, she became the first Director of Applications for Stanford Children's and built the first production support team. Other notable experiences are her role as Director of the Project Management Office (PMO), where she started the first PMO for the organization, implementing a project management methodology, tools, and templates that are still in use today. In her current role as Vice President and Associate Chief Information Officer, Ms. Grisim leads a team of over 150 staff, overseeing all clinical, revenue cycle and business systems applications, enterprise imaging services, web services, and the PMO. Passionate about supporting, mentoring, and promoting women in health IT, she also serves on the board of Women in Healthcare Information Technology (WHIT) as the President Elect for 2023–2024. WHIT is a volunteer organization dedicated to developing talent and supporting tomorrow's female leaders in HCIT. As part of my role on the WHIT board, I also function as the Chair for WHIT's Mentorship Program, designed to connect experienced HCIT leaders with women seeking career guidance, coaching, and advancement.

**Professional licenses and/or certifications:**
RN License
Certified Healthcare CIO
Certified Digital Health Executive
**Other education or training relevant to your position:**
Stanford University Leadership Academy
Introduction to Cybersecurity course
LEAN Leader training course
**LinkedIn profile:**
https://www.linkedin.com/in/lisam-grisim
**Were you referred to this project by a colleague? If so, who?**
Lindsay Rowlands, MHA, Project Coordinator.

# HCIT Questions

**1. What led you to pursue a career in the HCIT industry?**

I started my career as a nurse, became a nurse educator, and then a nurse manager. Feeling burned out in my nursing management position, I was offered the opportunity to be involved in the implementation of my organization's first EHR. At first, I felt very out of my league and had horrible imposter syndrome. However, the more I learned, the more excited I got about being in the world of HCIT, with so many opportunities to positively impact the lives of clinicians and the patients and families that we serve. I have never regretted my decision to leave nursing and go full-time into HCIT.

**2. What is the best professional advice given to you that you can share with aspiring women who wish to work in HCIT?**

Push yourself out of your comfort zone and take risks. Have confidence in your skills, abilities, and what you have to offer. You do not need to know it all or have all the answers. Ask lots of questions and be a lifelong learner. Set goals for yourself and work hard to achieve them. Oh, and find a great mentor(s) to help you!

**3. What is one of your proudest work-related accomplishments?**

Building the highly competent, talented, and engaged leadership team that I have. I am successful because of them.

**4. In preparation for a job interview, what type of questions should the candidate consider asking, and in what ways can the candidate set themselves apart?**

Ask the interviewer how they will measure the success of the person selected for the role. It will give you all kinds of insights into their values, priorities, and expectations. To set yourself apart, be enthusiastic, let your passion shine through, and highlight your unique skills and abilities.

**5. Would you say there are additional barriers for women to overcome in this industry? If so, what has your experience taught you about navigating these challenges?**

HCIT is heavily dominated by men, especially in leadership positions. This makes it all the more important to find strong female role models and mentors who can share with you their lessons learned regarding how to successfully navigate in a male-dominated profession. Work–life balance is another area that can be particularly challenging for women who aspire to advance their careers in HCIT. Understanding and honoring your values and priorities is key to maintaining a healthy work–life balance and ensuring your success and happiness in the workplace as well as in your personal life.

**6. How have you navigated instances of inequality that may be experienced by women in the workplace?**

It is critical that you learn how to advocate for yourself and learn effective negotiation skills.

7. **When it comes to traveling on the job (such as for attending conferences or performing on-site tasks), what tips may you share when it comes to safety as well as tips that are convenient for travel?**

   My best advice is to plan ahead and be organized. Know the specifics of your travel plans, such as how you will get from the airport to your hotel or conference location, places in the area to eat, how you will get around while you are on the trip, etc. Travel in pairs or find a buddy that you can go out with, particularly at night. Walk in areas that have lots of people around, and always be aware of your surroundings.

8. **How do you maintain a healthy work–life balance?**

   I have the attitude that working hard and playing hard make me the most productive and happy, both at work and at home. I take time for myself to do the things I love, and I always prioritize regular vacations and time away from work.

9. **Are there any specific books or videos you may recommend as it relates to HCIT?**

   [No answer provided].

10. **What is your advice for women to obtain the best opportunities and to negotiate competitive salaries in this career path?**

    Be open to opportunities and say yes, even if you think you are not fully qualified for a role. Take a class on negotiation and start higher than you think they will accept. You won't get it if you don't ask for it.

11. **What are some recommendations for networking and continued education?**

    Consider every encounter you have with someone in the field of HCIT as an opportunity to network. Connect on a personal level first and find the things you have in common outside of work. It will make the connection feel more authentic and give you something to build on for the future. Ask people for their advice and assistance. Almost everyone welcomes the opportunity to help someone else along their career path. And in terms of continued education, be a lifelong learner. Never stop growing and developing. If something interests you, take a class and learn more about it.

12. **Looking back to the beginning of your career, can you share some lessons learned? Would you have done anything differently?**

    I would have believed in myself the way others believed in me. People always thought I was more capable than I thought I was.

# Marcia Howard, Director, Enterprise Project Management Office, Springfield Clinic, LLP

**Please provide a brief overview of your professional experience.**

Early on in Marcia Howard's career, she spent her years at a technology company in the finance department. It was there that Ms. Howard started as a Credit Analyst and found herself working her way to become a Senior Systems Integration Financial Manager. Within this role, she managed large project financials from pre-sales to full implementation. Oftentimes, she was working directly with project managers and engineering teams to implement integrations between local, state, and federal government entities.

After this experience, Ms. Howard made the transition into HCIT. Initially, she started as an Analyst, supporting the EMR and other ancillary systems. From there, she became a Project Manager after the company began to scale to a nationally recognized PMO. Ms. Howard ran IT projects involving new software implementations, upgrades, new interface engines, and new provider affiliations. As fate would have it, the company continued to show more value and transitioned into an Enterprise PMO supporting all projects company-wide. At that time, she was promoted to Program Manager, supporting several portfolios of projects and multiple project managers. Soon after, she was promoted to the Director of the EPMO and currently manages two program managers and six project managers.

**Professional licenses and/or certifications:**

Project Management Professional (PMP)

**Other education or training relevant to your position:**

Bachelor's degree in business administration and management, Eastern Illinois University

**LinkedIn profile:**

https://www.linkedin.com/in/marcia-howard-pmp-43103357/

**Were you referred to this project by a colleague? If so, who?**

N/A.

# HCIT Questions

### 1. What led you to pursue a career in the HCIT industry?

Honestly, it kind of fell into my lap. I was looking to relocate to the Springfield, Illinois area, and was visiting the area when I ended up having a conversation with my future boss. She mentioned some opportunities at Springfield Clinic, LLP, and really wanted to hire someone who wanted to work hard and was eager to learn. As I talked with her more, the job seemed really interesting. Healthcare was attractive to me, knowing it's a pretty stable industry and a need that will always be there. Once I started in healthcare, I knew it was the perfect fit for me. I fell in love with being part of the healthcare journey. Technology is always changing, so every day is a challenge and a day to learn something new. It never gets old or stale.

2. **What is the best professional advice given to you that you can share with aspiring women who wish to work in HCIT?**

Work hard, educate yourself, and diversify your resume. The longer I have worked, the more I realize the importance of every role I have taken. I always tell people, even if it's not your job, do it. Nothing bad has ever come from adding a new skill or acquiring additional knowledge.

3. **What is one of your proudest work-related accomplishments?**

Leading a project that brought the local School of Medicine onto our EMR. This was a collaborative effort with the school, Springfield Clinic, LLP, and two local hospitals to integrate 500+ providers into our shared EMR. Seeing 4+ organizations working together for the betterment of our community (full patient sharing) was something to be very proud of.

4. **In preparation for a job interview, what type of questions should the candidate consider asking, and in what ways can the candidate set themselves apart?**

I am always looking for candidates who are invested in getting to know our company and culture. I remember candidates who want to understand our strategic goals or how our IT team collaborates with other departments. Be creative in your questions and be prepared to ask questions.

5. **Would you say there are additional barriers for women to overcome in this industry? If so, what has your experience taught you about navigating these challenges?**

I think there are always barriers in the work industry for women, regardless of the industry. Even if they are small, they still exist. I have always navigated these barriers by being the hardest worker in the room. I make sure I am prepared and educated on the topic.

6. **How have you navigated instances of inequality that may be experienced by women in the workplace?**

    N/A.

7. **When it comes to traveling on the job (such as for attending conferences or performing on-site tasks), what tips may you share when it comes to safety as well as tips that are convenient for travel?**

    N/A.

8. **How do you maintain a healthy work–life balance?**

    One way I have been able to balance work and personal life is by working from home a couple of days a week. This has allowed me to be present for my kids for their daily activities, whether that is running carpool or popping in for lunch at the school. Next, I spend a few minutes a day prioritizing tasks based on what needs to be accomplished during the day versus what can be done after my kids are in bed. This has allowed me to manage my time more effectively, ensuring that both work-related responsibilities and personal activities receive the attention they deserve.

    I also remind myself to take the vacation, go for a jog, and be present with my kids. Work will be there tomorrow. It's also been beneficial for me to communicate to my managers how important my family/personal time are. I am lucky that Springfield Clinic, LLP supports this balance.

9. **Are there any specific books or videos you may recommend as it relates to HCIT?**

    N/A.

10. **What is your advice for women to obtain the best opportunities and to negotiate competitive salaries in this career path?**

    Don't be afraid to ask. I have learned that there is nothing wrong with asking for what you deserve. There is nothing wrong with being direct and setting expectations from the start of a conversation or negotiation.

11. **What are some recommendations for networking and continued education?**

    I encourage every opportunity to network. I have built so many relationships through a happy hour or golf outing that have led me to a new job or opportunity. Having a network to call on makes the professional world so much easier to navigate. Education is key in IT, and making sure you are keeping up with where technology is and is going is crucial to success in this industry.

**12. Looking back to the beginning of your career, can you share some lessons learned? Would you have done anything differently?**

Most things I would not change for me personally because it's led me to the job I want to be in. I do wish I would have taken another job or two in different departments outside of IT and finance to get a better understanding of the entire business.

# Heather Hudnall, BSN, RN, Chief Nursing Informatics Officer, NTT DATA

**Please provide a brief overview of your professional experience.**

Heather Hudnall is an RN and the Chief Nursing Informatics Officer at NTT DATA. She is a pioneer for clinicians at the company and the first ever to hold this title. In this role, she is focused on providing leadership around strategic healthcare decisions and direction for the organization, along with helping clients solve their biggest challenges using a clinical lens and innovative technologies to deliver quality outcomes.

Heather has over 15+ years of experience in the healthcare industry, with a background in the clinical setting, informatics, solution consulting, and designing and implementing healthcare-specific technology. Her real-world bedside experience has given her a unique perspective on the needs and challenges clinicians and health systems face every day. This experience and drive to create better health technology led her to develop and design clinician-friendly technology to address the needs of clinicians, making them more efficient and reducing fatigue. She's designed solutions around clinical mobility and collaboration, workforce management, smart hospitals, digital front doors for nurses, ERP, and healthcare enterprise analytics.

Heather is an advocate for the voice of the nurse as well as an industry thought leader and has been published in the Financial Times as *"Edge computing delivers healthcare beyond the clinic."* She's helped to evolve the field of nursing informatics and has been on the planning committee for nursing informatics certification programs. Heather has also been focused on solving nationwide nurse staffing concerns and is a member of the Commission on Nursing Reimbursement. The commission advocates for fair reimbursement policies for nursing services and collaborates with nursing associations and healthcare organizations on the development of a solution to address the nurse staffing shortage. She is also a member of the Missouri

Nurse's Association (MONA) Political Action Committee as a nurse liaison, representing the voice and interests of all professional nurses in Missouri to advance MONA's legislative and regulatory agendas.

Heather's clinical experience as a bedside nurse combined with her health IT background has enabled her to bridge the gap and break boundaries by connecting clinical and IT ecosystems, leading to a better healthcare experience for all. Saving lives is her passion!

**Professional licenses and/or certifications:**
Bachelor of Science in Nursing (BSN)
RN
**Other education or training relevant to your position:**
Nursing Informatics Training and Certification
**LinkedIn profile:**
https://www.linkedin.com/in/heatherhudnall/
**Were you referred to this project by a colleague? If so, who?**
N/A.

# HCIT Questions

**1. What led you to pursue a career in the HCIT industry?**

I began my healthcare career as a bedside nurse but transitioned into health technology a decade ago. While at the bedside, I experienced firsthand everything that was broken in healthcare, and technology was part of the problem. Many times, technology that was supposed to make my job easier did the exact opposite and caused me more issues and workarounds. So, instead of complaining about technology, I decided I was going to be part of the solution and saw the move to HCIT as an opportunity to make a big impact as the voice of the nurse and a chance to help countless patients and my fellow clinicians. My driver and ultimate goal were to make health technology easier for nurses to use and provide value in their workflow, so they actually wanted to use it and enjoyed using it. I'm proud to say that I've been able to do just that!

**2. What is the best professional advice given to you that you can share with aspiring women who wish to work in HCIT?**

To dream big and believe in your ability to accomplish whatever you set your mind out to do! Focus on what inspired you to go into healthcare in the first place and let that passion shine through in everything you do. Strive to bring your best self to work each day because the work you do is extremely important and might 1 day help to save someone's life.

**3. What is one of your proudest work-related accomplishments?**

In one of my previous roles, I was part of the team that designed, implemented, and brought to market a new clinical mobility and communication solution for healthcare. I was the voice of the nurse, leveraging my real-world bedside experience in the design and implementation of the solution to ensure that clinicians had everything they needed to be more efficient and deliver better quality care. The most rewarding part of that entire journey was seeing my fellow clinicians enjoy using the solution that I helped design for them and hearing their positive feedback and appreciation for finally making their voices heard in the development of healthcare technology!

**4. In preparation for a job interview, what type of questions should the candidate consider asking, and in what ways can the candidate set themselves apart?**

Ask the interviewer about team dynamics and the biggest challenges for the organization and position and specifically ask, "What do you like most about working here?" I believe this is one of the most impactful questions a candidate can ask in an interview. It's a great way to create a connection with the interviewer and gain some insight into the culture of the organization.

One of the best ways a candidate can set themselves apart for a role in healthcare is to talk about their personal reasons for entering the field. Sell yourself by sharing what inspired you to go into healthcare and why you are passionate about helping others.

**5. Would you say there are additional barriers for women to overcome in this industry? If so, what has your experience taught you about navigating these challenges?**

Yes, I believe so. Overall, the industry is dominated by men in leadership positions, and even though women continue to outnumber men in the nursing profession, men are typically promoted into leadership positions faster and paid more. Be aware of these dynamics in the industry and continue to fight for fair wages and advocate for more women in leadership positions. As women in this industry, we must band together, inspire, lift each other up, and make our voices heard!

**6. How have you navigated instances of inequality that may be experienced by women in the workplace?**

I personally experienced inequality at one of my previous companies. I was not given the same opportunities as one of my male counterparts and was paid less, even though I had double the amount of and more relevant experience for the position. I eventually reached out to my all male leadership, advocating for myself and requesting that I be given bigger deals and more opportunities to prove what I could do and the knowledge I had. I did prove what I could do and how successful I could make the company in those opportunities, and I was eventually promoted into a leadership role with a big raise that was well deserved and much overdue. You must have confidence, believe in yourself, and be your own advocate if you want to be taken seriously and given the same or even better opportunities as your male counterparts.

7. **When it comes to traveling on the job (such as for attending conferences or performing on-site tasks), what tips may you share when it comes to safety as well as tips that are convenient for travel?**

When traveling for business, you must always be aware of your surroundings, especially when you are not with a group. Share your travel plans, itinerary, ride share information, and location with a family member or a friend so someone is aware of where you should be at all times. There are a lot of great travel apps available that allow you to easily share your travel plans with others. I have also found that using a digital business card instead of the traditional paper business card is an easy way to network and share your contact information at conferences and events.

8. **How do you maintain a healthy work–life balance?**

A healthy work–life balance is extremely important and is something that I didn't always maintain until it started affecting my health. I now start my day by meditating, drinking coffee, and taking a walk BEFORE checking my work email. I also take breaks by going outside for fresh air throughout the day and shut down work at a decent time to eat dinner with my family each night without the distraction of constantly checking my email and messages.

9. **Are there any specific books or videos you may recommend as it relates to HCIT?**

*The Patient Will See You Now. The Future of Medicine Is in Your Hands* by Eric Topol. For anyone wanting to go into this field who does not have a clinical background, I'd recommend reading the book "*The Comfort Garden: Tales from the Trauma Unit*" by Laurie Barken to gain some insight from the perspective of a nurse taking care of patients on the worst day of their lives. Gaining an understanding the experiences of the caregivers who use technology to deliver lifesaving care to patients is key to delivering real value to the world of healthcare technology.

**10. What is your advice for women to obtain the best opportunities and to negotiate competitive salaries in this career path?**

Network as much as you can and create a brand for yourself as a thought leader in the industry, and the best opportunities will start to come your way. When it comes to negotiating a competitive salary as a woman, it's wise to understand that there's still a gender wage gap that exists today, and you deserve to be fairly compensated for your work! You must first believe in yourself and know your worth. Research the market value for your role and consider your academic background, years of experience, qualifications, proven achievements, and any specialized knowledge or skills you have. Be confident in your request and be willing to negotiate, no matter how uncomfortable it feels. It will be worth it in the end.

**11. What are some recommendations for networking and continued education?**

LinkedIn, HIMSS, and the American Nurses Association are all great places to network with others in the industry and find opportunities for continuing education. Attending some of the big HCIT conferences, such as HIMSS, CHIME, and HLTH, is also a great way to network and find educational opportunities.

**12. Looking back to the beginning of your career, can you share some lessons learned? Would you have done anything differently?**

Looking back at the beginning of my career, I believed that people with more experience or more degrees somehow had more knowledge and better ideas than I did. Having less experience doesn't mean you bring less knowledge and value to the table. You know way more than you think you do, and your thoughts and ideas are just as important. So, be confident, speak up, and make your voice heard because your knowledge and contributions are no less valuable or important than the next person's.

# Erin Jamal, Senior Manager of Implementations, M&A

**Please provide a brief overview of your professional experience.**

As a brief overview of Erin Jamals's professional experience, she was an undergraduate in medical sociology and interned at a medical software company doing market research in an effort to push continuous improvement with the product. Afterward, she graduated and started full-time work as a Customer Service Analyst with athenahealth, which is a larger medical software organization. Ms. Jamal quickly transferred to the professional services department and became a Project Associate and continued to move upward with athenahealth as a Project Manager over enterprise accounts. She later accepted a position at Unified Women's Healthcare as a Technical Project Manager and continued growing in her career as a Manager of Implementation with Unified and then as a Senior Manager of Implementation over the M&A pipeline.

**Professional licenses and/or certifications:**

PMP

**Other education or training relevant to your position:**

Continuous learner reading relevant industry updates, taking courses on communication, stakeholder management and leadership.

**LinkedIn profile:**

http://www.linkedin.com/in/erin-jamal

**Were you referred to this project by a colleague? If so, who?**

Lindsay Rowlands, MHA, Project Coordinator.

# HCIT Questions

**1. What led you to pursue a career in the HCIT industry?**

I became very passionate about pursuing a career in which technology is embraced and leveraged to improve our struggling healthcare system.

**2. What is the best professional advice given to you that you can share with aspiring women who wish to work in HCIT?**

Don't give up because you think you can't do the job or task at hand. Give it your best shot, keep trying, and you might surprise yourself with how far your persistence takes you.

3. **What is one of your proudest work-related accomplishments?**

Creating a team that was able to be self-organized, and for me, becoming their champion.

4. **In preparation for a job interview, what type of questions should the candidate consider asking, and in what ways can the candidate set themselves apart?**

Do research on the company so you can speak their "lingo" when you ask your questions. It will make the interviewer aware of your preparation and interest in the company. In addition, ask about where they struggle in their processes today and how you would be able to make an impact in your future role.

5. **Would you say there are additional barriers for women to overcome in this industry? If so, what has your experience taught you about navigating these challenges?**

Absolutely, have confidence when speaking about things you know for sure! When you don't have an answer, it's perfectly ok to say you aren't sure and take the question back for further research. This approach is greatly appreciated, rather than providing wrong answers just to be able to provide an on-the-spot answer.

6. **How have you navigated instances of inequality that may be experienced by women in the workplace?**

N/A.

7. **When it comes to traveling on the job (such as for attending conferences or performing on-site tasks), what tips may you share when it comes to safety as well as tips that are convenient for travel?**

Plan your customer onsite trip like you would any other personal trip, review flight logistics and travel logistics to ensure you're arriving in your destination during the day if possible, and clearly know where you're going from there. If it's to the rental car center, make sure it's open for when you're planning to arrive.

8. **How do you maintain a healthy work–life balance?**

I'm a fierce advocate for time management and believe that in order to be our best, we need to allocate time to customer activities, corresponding follow-up activities, and continuous improvement.

9. **Are there any specific books or videos you may recommend as it relates to HCIT?**

- *Quiet* by Susan Cain
- *Emotional Intelligence* by Daniel Goleman
- *Girl, Stop Apologizing* by Rachel Hollis

10. **What is your advice for women to obtain the best opportunities and to negotiate competitive salaries in this career path?**

Constantly bring up career growth opportunities and advances that you're interested in and document major wins for you in a OneNote or note pad.

11. **What are some recommendations for networking and continued education?**

I cannot recommend the PMP enough; the leadership and project management methodologies learned through this certification set a solid foundation for several different role types beyond just project managers. Additionally, I recommend becoming a member of Women in Technology; there are so many networking events and career fairs to help promote connections between women in tech!

12. **Looking back to the beginning of your career, can you share some lessons learned? Would you have done anything differently?**

No, I made a lot of mistakes, and each misstep helped me learn, grow, and ultimately get to where I am now in my career.

# Karen Jaw-Madson, Principal, Co.-Design of Work Experience

**Please provide a brief overview of your professional experience.**

Karen Jaw-Madson has 20 years of experience working with IT leaders, including women in pharma and healthcare in the midst of organizational change/transformation—as a business partner, advisor, consultant, and/or coach. In addition, she collaborated with Sherri Douville, industry thought leader and CEO of Medigram, as a co-author in her Taylor & Francis book series on healthcare and technology, including mobile medicine and advanced health technology. Please see below for her biography:

Ms. Jaw-Madson is principal of Co.-Design of Work Experience, author of *Culture Your Culture: Innovating Experiences @ Work* (Emerald Group Publishing, 2018), founder of Future of Work platform A New HR, executive coach, and instructor at Stanford University's Continuing Studies Program and LinkedIn Learning. She enables decision-makers to address organizational challenges that affect business performance through

1. Coaching and developing LEADERSHIP and their TEAMS
2. Enabling organizations to leverage CULTURE, DIVERSITY (DEIA&B), and EMPLOYEE EXPERIENCE
3. OPTIMIZING TALENT by aligning people with strategy
4. Driving CHANGE MANAGEMENT and TRANSFORMATION

A former corporate executive Karen is known as a versatile leader across multiple industries with experience developing, leading, and implementing numerous organizational initiatives around the globe. She has been featured in Inc., Fast Company, Fortune, Thrive Global, and MarketWatch, as well as written for publications such as *Forbes*, Greenbiz, SHRM's HR People+Strategy, TLNT.com, HR.com's *HR Strategy & Planning Excellence* magazine, and *HR Professional* magazine. Other publications where she appears as a contributor include *Mobile Medicine: Overcoming People, Culture, and Governance*, *Punk XL (Experience Leadership)*, *The Secret Sauce for Leading Transformational Change*, and *Advanced Health Technology: Managing Risk While Tackling Barriers to Rapid Acceleration*. Karen has a BA in ethnic and cultural studies from Bryn Mawr College and an MA in social-organizational psychology from Columbia University.

**Professional licenses and/or certifications:**

A variety of certifications in assessments, including Center for Creative Leadership, Hogan, Organizational Culture Inventory, Organizational Effectiveness Inventory, Predictive Index, and Burke Learning Agility Inventory.

**Other education or training relevant to your position:**

MA, Organizational Psychology (Organization & Leadership), Columbia University

**LinkedIn profile:**

https://www.linkedin.com/in/karenjawmadson/

**Were you referred to this project by a colleague? If so, who?**

Sherri Douville, CEO, Medigram.

# HCIT Questions

### 1. What led you to pursue a career in the HCIT industry?

Though not exclusive to the industry, working with women leaders in HCIT especially supports my personal mission to deliver/enable positive social impact at scale. I was blessed to be exposed earlier in my career and never really left, knowing the stakes (and therefore potential) are very high.

2. **What is the best professional advice given to you that you can share with aspiring women who wish to work in HCIT?**

In the interest of brevity, I will summarize that the best things an aspiring woman leader in HCIT can do is to (1) seek out multiple mentors who serve different purposes at different phases in one's career, and (2) as an executive coach, I've observed that those with a support system generally achieve greater success and faster progress than those who do not. Having your own braintrust/board of directors is priceless. Build and continually cultivate a strong network with equally strong relationships. (3) Years ago, I fretted about the possibility of being laid off to a colleague who is now the Chief Digital Information Officer for a biopharmaceutical company. What he said to me has stuck with me for decades: "Don't worry about your job security. Focus on building your career security." We have to stop trying to force-fit ourselves into the roles defined by a single company when our careers span beyond our tenures there. We should widen our lenses to consider each role within the context of our entire career. Another sage piece of advice was from the VP IT infrastructure in Big Pharma: "Your peers can take you down. Manage across." Managing ups and downs is critically important, but forgetting to manage relationships with peers could also be risky.

3. **What is one of your proudest work-related accomplishments?**

I am proud of establishing my own business, and sustaining it for 10 years, and being in a position where I can share my thought leadership through multiple publications and teaching opportunities. However, I am most proud to see the accomplishments of those I have coached and supported to great success over the years.

4. **In preparation for a job interview, what type of questions should the candidate consider asking, and in what ways can the candidate set themselves apart?**

Of the senior leaders, some of the questions include the following:

- You've achieved great success in your career. From where you are today, what do you still want to learn?
- What would others tell me about what it's like to work with you?
- What do you find to be the most meaningful aspects of your leadership/work/working here?

- What aspects of the culture support or challenge the vision and strategies that need to be achieved?
- What have you changed your mind/perspective about lately?
- What are the core competencies needed to be successful here?
- Can you tell me more about the gap between where the company is and where it wants to be?

5. **Would you say there are additional barriers for women to overcome in this industry? If so, what has your experience taught you about navigating these challenges?**

At a certain level, technical know-hows, industry knowledge, and good old-fashioned experience are givens. What differentiates is leadership, and the standard for women is higher. Some nuggets of wisdom I'd like to share:

- The glass cliff is real. Be aware of what conditions need to be in place in order for you to be successful and what might derail you. Always be aware of what could erode people's confidence in your leadership and address it on time.
- Manage up, manage down, and don't forget to also manage across.
- It's challenging enough already. Do the work to ensure you are not working against yourself/self-sabotaging. Be your own best advocate instead. Collaborate with a coach if needed.
- Advocate for and build up other women (and those who do the same) and avoid perpetuating the barriers to other women coming up.
- Reframe and reset your relationship with failure—learn from and take value out of every setback.
- Be careful not to be too internally focused and lose sight of what is going on in the industry or those in your network.
- Continually build your leadership capabilities, starting with emotional intelligence (EQ) and learning agility.
- Lead with your values—they will help you make the decisions and remain steadfast and consistent for those that follow you.

I also wrote about the three interdependent super-capabilities needed for certifications, standards and quality assurance in *AI & Cybersecurity: For Healthcare Boards*, edited by Sherri Douville. I believe these are especially important for women in HCIT: Strategic Follow-Through, Change Leadership, and Partnership.

6. **How have you navigated instances of inequality that may be experienced by women in the workplace?**

   I've navigated inequality by

   - Cultivating my self-awareness and social awareness. Experiences with inequality have a way of compelling us to question ourselves. The more we know about ourselves and where others stand, the more accurate and self-assured we can be.
   - Learning to steer through organizational dynamics and politics without losing my soul nor my reputation, and in turn being able to help others navigate as a result of my experiences
   - Reframing the oppression I've experienced, challenging myself to overcome it as a personal achievement, and refusing to be a scapegoat or in the crossfire.
   - Finding the support systems and networks I could rely upon.

7. **When it comes to traveling on the job (such as for attending conferences or performing on-site tasks), what tips may you share when it comes to safety as well as tips that are convenient for travel?**

   I don't usually travel where I don't already know people or without the support of an established organization with a local presence. I can be comfortable with my sense of independence and be out with others, never alone except in the hotel room. In the past, my work has taken me to places that are not altogether safe, and I realized that there are some close calls. Had it not been for the protocols I had in place (working with drivers who have long served the organization as an example), things might have been different.

8. **How do you maintain a healthy work–life balance?**

   I have maintained a healthy work–life balance by doing the following:

   - Continuously calibrating/adapting is how I work toward balanced work–life integration. Flexibility is key.
   - Being aware of and actively managing my resilience level along with what erodes or enhances it.
   - Empowering myself where possible to make things happen, allowing things to happen to me.
   - Leveraging my support system, knowing when to call out what's happening, and breaking unproductive patterns.

9. **Are there any specific books or videos you may recommend as it relates to HCIT?**

   All books edited by Sherri Douville.

**10. What is your advice for women to obtain the best opportunities and to negotiate competitive salaries in this career path?**

Do not rely only on applying for jobs. Network, network, network to open yourself to other opportunities you otherwise wouldn't have. Don't let your pride get in the way. Know your worth, and don't undervalue yourself. Get and leverage resources to ensure you accept the most competitive packages (there are market data and even coaches for negotiating contracts). Pre-negotiate the financial terms of your eventual exit if possible.

**11. What are some recommendations for networking and continued education?**

1. Clients have benefited from my Mentoring Strategy Template (see Exhibit II), a process for creating individualized networking/mentoring plans I developed and facilitated. It answers the following questions:
   - What?
   - Why?
   - How will I know?
   - What do I need to get there?
   - Who can help?
   - Where can I find them?
   - What will I do and by when?

2. We can't possibly maintain relationships with everyone, so we also need to be strategic about who would have the most importance to our success and how often we need to cultivate them.

3. Anyone can learn to network better and become a master connector. One of the first steps you can take is to simply look out for networking opportunities in everyday interactions. Think of who you can connect with—based on interests, needs, capabilities, shared experiences, etc. Ask others if they can recommend anyone in their network based on your needs too. This is one thing you can actually affect directly, so don't hold back.

4. When it comes to achieving full potential, also aim for lifelong learning of all varieties and channels. Allow space and time for exploration that brings about new connections and insights. Reflect to solidify, integrate, and demonstrate learning. Challenge yourself to become an expert by teaching or sharing with others. Knowledge isn't power unless you use it.

**12. Looking back to the beginning of your career, can you share some lessons learned? Would you have done anything differently?**

I am not one to have many regrets. I am grateful that even my most challenging experiences taught me, shaped me, and changed my trajectory. That being said, I have learned through myself and others that our mental health is paramount and should be protected. We are socialized to give too much of ourselves, sometimes to the point of depletion or beyond. Know when your emotional bank account balance is getting too low so you can address it before there's a problem. Leverage everything available to you—breaks and time off, your friends, family, network, employee assistance and other programs, counselors, therapists, and psychiatrists. Oftentimes, people regret not seeking support sooner. Having a career is challenging enough. We need to set the conditions for our success where possible.

Establish goals you want to achieve, for you are more likely to make progress if you have something to aim toward. When you get there, set new goals to continually learn, challenge yourself, and increase your impact. In "Career Advice for Recent Graduates (And Everyone Else)," I encouraged the possibility of forging our own paths when the established ones aren't right for us. It took me 1 year to question my former career path and another to figure out my transition to a portfolio career made up of where I thrive and contribute the most: coaching, consulting, research, writing, teaching/speaking, and a space for other pursuits. To do this, I needed to reframe my identity (which was tied to my previous career) and open my mindset to new possibilities. It can be profound when we stop pursuing individual jobs and shift our focus toward collecting meaningful experiences. This reverses the sequence and breaks the bad habit of trying too hard to force fit ourselves into less-than-ideal situations: "First consider what's most important according to your own ambitions and in what environment, and *then* seek the endeavors that might align with that, if only *for now*." I hope that my experiences, challenges, lessons learned, and advice have a positive impact on others; it makes my journey up to this point even more worth it.

# Leah S. Jones, Chief Financial Officer, Allscripts

**Please provide a brief overview of your professional experience.**

Leah S. Jones is an executive with a unique and valuable blend of business acumen, finance expertise, software industry experience, and sales/revenue operations skills. She leverages an innate ability to distill information, translate complex issues into relatable solutions, and create actionable insights that address and achieve the objectives of all stakeholders. Ms. Jones has a deep understanding of the full business cycle, financial impacts, and the levers that trigger business development and operational success. She excels at structuring and negotiating deals, aligning client requirements with the goals of the business, and maximizing revenue, profit, and competitive advantage.

Ms. Jones is a trusted advisor and resource to the senior executive team, as well as cross-functional business leaders, colleagues, clients, and team members. She is an influential leader who bridges gaps, promotes open communication, and fosters a culture of integrity, collaboration, empowerment, and accountability. She is also a skilled mentor and coach who develops individuals to excel, creates teaching moments to reinforce learning, sets high expectations, and puts them into roles of greater scope and responsibility.

**Professional licenses and/or certifications:**
Certified Professional Accountant

**Other education or training relevant to your position:**
Bachelor of business administration, Accounting Major

**LinkedIn profile:**
https://www.linkedin.com/in/leah-jones-50b4822/

**Were you referred to this project by a colleague? If so, who?**
Jeffery Daigrepont, Senior Vice President, Coker.

# HCIT Questions

### 1. What led you to pursue a career in the HCIT industry?

My expertise was in accounting for technology, which was agnostic to industry. I had experience in the manufacturing and point-of-sale industries before my introduction to HCIT. The attraction for me was seeing where my expertise contributed to the betterment of my own healthcare journey as well as enabling an improved experience for the vast population of patients and healthcare providers. What started as just a new employer transitioned to a passion to grow my career while influencing the success of our vision of "Building open, connected communities of health' and a mission of 'Transforming health, insightfully."

**2. What is the best professional advice given to you that you can share with aspiring women who wish to work in HCIT?**

There are a few and they are not specific to HCIT:

- "Stop looking for a box on an organizational chart. Be amazing at what you do, and the box will find you."
- "Strive for perfection. You will make mistakes. When you do, your focus on perfection will most likely result in a minor mistake vs. what could have been a material error."
- "Be nice! There is no reason not to be."

**3. What is one of your proudest work-related accomplishments?**

Consistent upward growth—all the way to a C-level position—while never sacrificing my core personal passion of being a wife and mom!

**4. In preparation for a job interview, what type of questions should the candidate consider asking, and in what ways can the candidate set themselves apart?**

- What characteristics are common in those that are most successful in this organization?
- Are there items on my resume beyond specific technical/specialized skills that spiked your interest in me as a candidate for this role?
- Is there a career path here that could keep me challenged and growing beyond the next 3 years? And if so, are there examples of individuals who have evidenced internal growth and promotions?
- What is the process for iterative feedback in the first year to ensure proper alignment between expectations and performance?
- What ability do you see for me to make valuable contributions and impact the company's performance?

**5. Would you say there are additional barriers for women to overcome in this industry? If so, what has your experience taught you about navigating these challenges?**

I would say the technology industry is probably more welcoming to women than many other industries. However, there are biases in all fields, and it's not just toward women. I have found that if I perform at my best and do not make gender or race an issue, it typically isn't an issue for those around me either. When I have encountered what I felt was bad behavior in that regard, I typically call it out relatively quickly and have an element of self-confidence in doing so, which is helpful in overcoming the perceived threats. In most cases, the aggression from others comes as a defense mechanism because THEY feel pressure or threat from others. It's not really anything I/YOU are doing wrong.

If the bad behavior persists after your efforts to address it, take it to your advocate in human resources and get it addressed quickly. The key is to remember that we are all co-workers hired to do a job. That job and team should not be focused on the personal elements of each individual. That includes me; I do not advertise all my female characteristics at work. I come as a contributor first and foremost.

6. **How have you navigated instances of inequality that may be experienced by women in the workplace?**

    N/A.

7. **When it comes to traveling on the job (such as for attending conferences or performing on-site tasks), what tips may you share when it comes to safety as well as tips that are convenient for travel?**

    Research the venues, modes of transportation, and environment well before you travel. Plan out your trip with safety always as a priority. If safety is a concern, express such to those involved to suggest alternatives to meet the same objectives. As for normal business travel, pack as much as you can into each trip with multiple meetings or visits. Make the most of the time away so you reduce the number of trips and maximize the value of your invested time and the company's money.

    On the packing front, I try to stay with one main color, typically black or navy. This reduces the number of shoes you have to pack! Also, if you are a road warrior, duplicate your toiletries and cosmetics. This eliminates the need to take those things in and out of your suitcase and reduces the risk that you will forget something important. Also, make it a priority to populate your calendar with important personal things. This protects those dates from travel as much as possible. This is a huge key to balance! Additionally, invest in a good suitcase! There is nothing worse than crappy luggage to wear you out while traveling. Try to maintain your workout routine while on the road. I attend a national chain fitness place, which I can normally find in the cities where I travel.

8. **How do you maintain a healthy work–life balance?**

    The first was having a mutual understanding with my family about my career requirements. When everyone is aware, there are fewer misunderstandings about expectations. Next, keep your personal/family time sacred. You can work around events, but don't miss events! With my kids, when I knew I was going to be late or not be present for something, I would ask permission and gain alignment. Amazing how much this helped relieve my guilt!

I share with my family what I do for work. It's at an appropriate level in each stage of life. But when they understand more, they respect more of the intersections of life and work. It also helps them better understand corporate America and what work is like for their future.

9. **Are there any specific books or videos you may recommend as it relates to HCIT?**
   - *Emotional Intelligence 2.0* by Dr. Travis Bradberry
   - *Daring Greatly* by Berne Brown
   - *The Fred Factor* by Mark Sanborn

10. **What is your advice for women to obtain the best opportunities and to negotiate competitive salaries in this career path?**

    You are responsible for your career. Do your research on the market dynamics. Test your value with a recruiter occasionally. When you feel that you are not paid fairly, make it about you and no one else. Take your fact-based, objective research results to your management in a scheduled discussion. (Do not surprise them with a topic on salary.) Anchor the discussion around career development, personal contributions, value added, and THEN salary. Be open to an iterative dialog. Ultimatums do not typically work. Help develop a plan of progression that takes time and contribution into account and gains agreement. Then work out the plan and revisit it on a pre-determined schedule to monitor progression and adherence from both sides.

11. **What are some recommendations for networking and continued education?**

    [No answer provided].

12. **Looking back to the beginning of your career, can you share some lessons learned? Would you have done anything differently?**

    I would have requested to sit in on more discussions to simply listen and learn about new or complex topics. The dialog involved in strategic planning and issue resolution is a wonderful learning experience!

# Andrea L. Kamenca, MBA, CEO

**Please provide a brief overview of your professional experience.**

Andrea Kamenca, MBA, CEO, began her career early in sales, which expanded into marketing. Later, she found herself working her way through the operations, finance, and technology sides of healthcare. By working with large corporations, she gained an invaluable asset: a professional perspective and a template for excellence. Ms. Kamenca led a $4 million clinical research organization partnered with the VA. In addition, she has founded, led, and grown a successful digital marketing company ranked in the top 7% nationwide. Ms. Kamenca has published 35 books and numerous technical and expert articles.

Today, Ms. Kamenca is a result-driven healthcare executive who stabilizes and grows organizations to be operationally and financially successful. She has a proven track record of demonstrating excellence in strategy, management, finance, operations, marketing, and telemedicine. She currently serves as the CEO of a 90-person gastroenterology clinic and ambulatory surgery center.

**Professional licenses and/or certifications:**

N/A.

**Other education or training relevant to your position:**

Master of business administration, post-graduate certificate in healthcare informatics

**LinkedIn profile:**

https://www.linkedin.com/in/andreakamenca/

**Were you referred to this project by a colleague? If so, who?**

Jeffery Daigrepont, Senior Vice President, Coker.

# HCIT Questions

**1. What led you to pursue a career in the HCIT industry?**

I love technology and its capacity to improve healthcare. Technology has always fascinated me. Its power to improve clinical outcomes, the patient experience, and overall organizational success is a compelling and worthy career focus.

**2. What is the best professional advice given to you that you can share with aspiring women who wish to work in HCIT?**

Believe in yourself. Be resilient. Constantly re-tool and keep your knowledge base and skills current.

**3. What is one of your proudest work-related accomplishments?**

Mentoring high-potential individuals and witnessing their career successes!

**4. In preparation for a job interview, what type of questions should the candidate consider asking, and in what ways can the candidate set themselves apart?**

Asking the question, "What does success look like?" or "How can I immediately add value to your organization?" signal that you are interested in immediately contributing to the team.

**5. Would you say there are additional barriers for women to overcome in this industry? If so, what has your experience taught you about navigating these challenges?**

Yes. You must prove yourself the moment you enter a technical conversation or room of technology professionals. Don't overreact to the (often) unflattering assumptions. Have confidence and learn how to communicate with authority. Keep your personal life separate from your dating or romantic life.

**6. How have you navigated instances of inequality that may be experienced by women in the workplace?**

Worked harder. Learned more. Never gave up. (Highly recommend working for large corporations with training programs and formal mentoring.)

**7. When it comes to traveling on the job (such as for attending conferences or performing on-site tasks), what tips may you share when it comes to safety as well as tips that are convenient for travel?**

Ask the hotel clerk to write down your room number and not announce it. Walk with confidence. Ask a colleague to escort you if you don't feel safe.

**8. How do you maintain a healthy work–life balance?**

N/A.

**9. Are there any specific books or videos you may recommend as it relates to HCIT?**

There are many important books to read. Patrick Lencioni is great. Simon Sinek, too.

10. **What is your advice for women to obtain the best opportunities and to negotiate competitive salaries in this career path?**

Start your career with a large corporation. It develops your experience and gives your resume credibility. Also, know your worth. Find a mentor. Always watch the macro trends. That will help you know how to navigate your career. Be an early adopter, but not on the bleeding edge!

11. **What are some recommendations for networking and continued education?**

An under-recommended strategy is volunteering for state, county, or city boards and commissions. It widens your perspective, gives you additional places to learn, and exercises your leadership skills.

12. **Looking back to the beginning of your career, can you share some lessons learned? Would you have done anything differently?**
   - I shouldn't have worried so much.
   - Invest in your 401(k) early and keep investing. Pay yourself first.
   - I wish I had majored in computer sciences or finance in college, not general business.
   - I should have avoided marketing and stuck with technology or other technical fields.

# Erica Kaplan, Senior Manager, Clinical Applications

**Please provide a brief overview of your professional experience.**

Erica Kaplan began her career in healthcare as a front desk staff person and, not long after, stepped into a supervisory role. As the organization grew and changed, so did Ms. Kaplan. She went from being a front desk staff member to supervising the team. Opportunities presented themselves as technology advanced, and she was included in those changes. As the company acquired organizations, Ms. Kaplan was an integral part of their onboarding, and this taught her a whole new set of skills. She was blessed with two children in the midst of all of this and continued to grow in her career upon returning. As the organization went through a drastic change of going from private to public, Ms. Kaplan was able to progress with the ongoing organizational changes, landing her where she is today as the Senior Manager of Clinical Applications.

**Professional licenses and/or certifications:**
N/A.
**Other education or training relevant to your position:**
N/A.
**LinkedIn profile:**
[Optional, not provided].
**Were you referred to this project by a colleague? If so, who?**
N/A.

# HCIT Questions

**1. What led you to pursue a career in the HCIT industry?**

It was destiny. I started my career at Summit as a PSR/Front Desk member and have been lucky enough to continue to grow within this ever-changing organization.

**2. What is the best professional advice given to you that you can share with aspiring women who wish to work in HCIT?**

Never be afraid to speak up, make recommendations, and always be willing to admit that you are wrong or that you've made a mistake. People respect you for being a genuine person versus always trying to be the best person.

**3. What is one of your proudest work-related accomplishments?**

Earning the respect and trust of my teammates.

**4. In preparation for a job interview, what type of questions should the candidate consider asking, and in what ways can the candidate set themselves apart?**

I would recommend they ask about the team they are joining and the support model for learning the ins and outs of the organization. Even if you know a system, you don't necessarily know how the institution you are attempting to join utilizes it.

**5. Would you say there are additional barriers for women to overcome in this industry? If so, what has your experience taught you about navigating these challenges?**

Unfortunately, in work as in life, there are times where you are not going to be liked, no matter how you present yourself, what you offer, how much you know, etc. Do not let that stop you from being yourself and giving it your all.

6. **How have you navigated instances of inequality that may be experienced by women in the workplace?**

   N/A.

7. **When it comes to traveling on the job (such as for attending conferences or performing on-site tasks), what tips may you share when it comes to safety as well as tips that are convenient for travel?**

   Sharing my hotel information with my family and checking in a few times a day to make sure they know I've arrived and returned safely.

8. **How do you maintain a healthy work–life balance?**

   I think working remotely has made this even more challenging, so I try to dedicate myself to starting a workout by 5:30 p.m. most nights a week. It forces me to walk away from my desk and helps me to work out any frustrations that I might have accrued during the day.

9. **Are there any specific books or videos you may recommend as it relates to HCIT?**

   N/A.

10. **What is your advice for women to obtain the best opportunities and to negotiate competitive salaries in this career path?**

    Know your worth.

11. **What are some recommendations for networking and continued education?**

    Learn from anyone and everyone around you. I've always felt learning from experience does so much more for someone than watching a video or reading a textbook does.

12. **Looking back to the beginning of your career, can you share some lessons learned? Would you have done anything differently?**

    It's okay to not know the answer. It's okay to try and fail, as long as you tried.

# Rachel Kent, Clinical Informatics Manager, Clarify Health

**Please provide a brief overview of your professional experience.**

Rachel Kent graduated from university thinking that her career would be in communications and marketing. She also graduated at the beginning of a recession, so the universe had another plan in store.

Rachel ended up working for her parents' company, QED Clinical dba CINA, a software company that had a software package consisting of clinical decision support and gaps in care analysis tools. These tools were based on data aggregated and standardized directly from practice electronic health records. Her parents got into this business in the late 90s/early 2000s, so they really were ahead of the game. Working for them in account management, clinical content development, and data element mapping was where Rachel first cut her teeth in healthcare informatics. Being that CINA was a small company, she was given a long leash to learn by trial and error how to map clinical data elements and write algorithms that would be used in the CINA software.

Rachel realized in her role at CINA that she had a deep interest in, even a passion for, health informatics and how software can be used to put more value into provider care practices. She quickly found that she had a knack for data element mapping and for turning clinical guidelines into detailed algorithms. It became clear at CINA that health IT would be her career path. So, thanks to the economic recession, she was forced into an industry that she may never have thought to enter.

Rachel spent approximately 4 years with CINA, then moved to the DARTNet Institute, a spinoff research arm of the American Academy of Family Physicians (AAFP). She was the first full-time employee with DARTNet once it became its own entity outside of the AAFP. DARTNet was a client of CINAs, so the professional relationship was there when she made the move. Rachel spent the next 9 years at DARTNet, growing skills and experience in project and client management, data standardization and detailed data element mapping, clinical content development, coding and querying skills, team development, and leadership. She worked with incredibly smart people and will forever be grateful to those who took the time to sit on hours-long Zoom calls, puttering through data, thinking through the problems, and developing thoughtful solutions for their clients.

The team at DARTNet often felt like a family, and it was a special place to spend so many formative years in her early career. DARTNet was an organization of fewer than 25 employees, and, because they were small, the team was constantly fighting to keep up with the workload and projects. It was an easy place to get as much responsibility as she was willing and able to take on. Rachel took full advantage of this, which often led to poor work–life balance but gave her the space and encouragement to get her hands into as many areas as she was willing to take on. This led to a great breadth of experiences and tons of hands-on, pressure cooker learning, which is how she learns best.

One of the most notable things that Rachel took from DARTNet was confidence and comfort in saying, "I do not know the answer, but let me work on figuring it out from someone who does." Out of necessity and an overburdened workload, she became very comfortable in the space of not knowing everything and being okay with that. Rachel commented, "The older I get, the more I realize that what I don't know far exceeds what I do know. And that is OK!"

A commonality of her experiences at both CINA and DARTNet was that they were very small companies with big workloads, and due to this, she was able to gain meaningful, real-world experiences that would not have been available if she worked for larger, more traditionally organized companies. She was given space and freedom to take chances, to sometimes mess up, and to always to learn—every single day.

While at DARTNet, Rachel became a mom to two little girls. At some point, the chaos, heavy burden, and responsibility of working as a strong figure in a small company became too overwhelming. That style of work–life balance was not working out any longer. At this point, Rachel started working with a coach to help her identify her next career move and figure out the path to making this change.

It was a much easier and quicker process than Rachel expected, and she took a position as Clinical Informatics Manager at Clarify Health in September 2022.

A year into her time at Clarify Health, and she is still very happy with her decision. The culture at Clarify fits her personality, and the position matches her experience and interests (passions) so well. She is working with a team of incredibly bright and talented people, and challenges arise daily to keep her interested, engaged, and sprinting just a bit.

Her biggest takeaway in her short time at Clarify has been the importance of finding a company culture that feels right and even delights and also being in a position that you have fun doing.

**Professional licenses and/or certifications:**
PMP
**Other education or training relevant to your position:**
BA in Communication from University of Missouri, Columbia
**LinkedIn profile:**
https://www.linkedin.com/in/rachel-bryan-kent-31146963
**Were you referred to this project by a colleague? If so, who?**
Cathy Bryan, Health IT Strategist/Innovator/Collaborator.

# HCIT Questions

**1. What led you to pursue a career in the HCIT industry?**

I graduated from university thinking that my career would be in communications and marketing, but the timing of my graduation was at the beginning of a recession, so the universe had another plan for me. I ended up working for my parent's company, which was a HCIT company, which is where I cut my teeth in clinical algorithm development and clinical data element mapping. I was also exposed to working with all sorts of clients, from private practices to health systems to university-based research organizations. We were a small enough company that I was able to go to these kinds of meetings and gain both customer and back-end informatics work. It became clear at CINA that health IT would be my career path, which was absolutely not the original plan. So, thank you economic recession for forcing me into an industry that I may never have thought to enter.

**2. What is the best professional advice given to you that you can share with aspiring women who wish to work in HCIT?**

Try lots of things to find what you really love doing—the types of things that you truly find fun. Also, look for positions that will highlight your natural talents. There is something to be said for trying things that make you uncomfortable, but I believe that even more can be said for leaning heavily on the talents that you naturally have and shining in an area that you already feel confident in. For instance, I hate speaking and presenting to large groups. I CAN do it, and I HAVE done it... a lot. But leading up to a presentation, I would spend hours preparing out of fear of being a screw up and then be a ball of stress on top of that. At some point, I decided that I COULD take on presentations, or I could lean into the work that comes more naturally—organizing, motivating, and interpersonal relationships—and take tons of stress out of work while also adding IN lots of fun.

**3. What is one of your proudest work-related accomplishments?**

In my 8th year at DARTNet, I was considering starting to look for a new job, but at work, one of our main software partners had to shut their doors, meaning that our mutual clients would lose their software. I put my job search on hold because I did not want to leave my DARTNet clients up a creek. Over the next 9 months, I led that team through an insane amount of work to get new decision support and population management software developed. Over those 9 months, I built and tested between 70 and 90 clinical metrics for Family Medicine (FM)/ Internal Medicine (IM) providers. I held off on my job search until I felt like our software was in a good enough spot for me to move on. I am proud of myself for sticking around when things were hard and for delivering for clients that I cared about.

4. **In preparation for a job interview, what type of questions should the candidate consider asking, and in what ways can the candidate set themselves apart?**

A way to set yourself apart would be to ask more questions of the interviewer than they ask of you. This indicates your interest in and excitement for a position. Also, do not be afraid to be yourself and show yourself, and try to make a connection with your interviewer. Remember that if you have made it to an interview, you likely meet the basic job needs, and your interviewer is trying to determine who they want to work with and who they most want on their team. Anything personal you can add will be something to remember and make you potentially more interesting than someone else.

Come prepared with about 20 questions (way more than you would ever ask, but just so you have a good bank of questions available to you). Some questions I like are included below:

- What is the biggest need of the team that I would be joining?
- If I were to start working today, what project would I be working on, and what would my high-level deliverables be?
- If applying for remote work: What opportunities does our team have to connect since we are working remotely? How does the company support colleagues in building relationships?

5. **Would you say there are additional barriers for women to overcome in this industry? If so, what has your experience taught you about navigating these challenges?**

Tech has historically been a bit of a boys' club. In fact, most of the people that I work the closest with on more technical work have also been men. I have built strong relationships with the men that I work with by being a vulnerable and personal version of myself, making lots of jokes, laughing, and bringing my personhood to the relationship while also encouraging reciprocation. I am able to build really great relationships with the men that I work with, and I like to think that they really enjoy working with me as well. I also believe that the more you can connect with those that you work with, the better you will be and the better products we will build. We want to work hard for people that we really like working with.

6. **How have you navigated instances of inequality that may be experienced by women in the workplace?**

I believe that in my final year at CINA, there was some inequality in pay. I came across a printed email with salaries, and mine was not on par with others at my level. Over the years, I became aware that I could ask for more money in raise/promotion conversations. However, I always had a lot of beef with this, as it seems really unfair that those who are bolder are able to get higher salaries. I very much appreciated that at DARTNet, once I was in a place where I was asking for more money, that I often did not get what I asked for, but it was explained that this was for equity reasons and that others were making below their education level and that they needed to be brought up. So, I can appreciate the transparency of that company's salary equity.

7. **When it comes to traveling on the job (such as for attending conferences or performing on-site tasks), what tips may you share when it comes to safety as well as tips that are convenient for travel?**

N/A.

8. **How do you maintain a healthy work–life balance?**

This is an ever-evolving challenge. It is easy to make that a gray area in a post-COVID-era remote-work world. I have had an awful work–life balance for most of my career, but I have seen a real change since moving to my most recent position at Clarify Health. Here are some things that are different:

- CINA and DARTNet were much smaller and more chaotic.
- I worked with customers at CINA/DARTNet and my people-pleaser personality was not suited to customer service in the sense that I wanted to make everyone happy, so I would agree to things and then work around the clock to make it happen. Not Healthy!
- I remind myself that the work will be there tomorrow.

9. **Are there any specific books or videos you may recommend as it relates to HCIT?**

I subscribe to Data Camp. It is software with training in a variety of programming languages. It is a good program that has helped me as I come across different languages or different questions about how to query data.

10. **What is your advice for women to obtain the best opportunities and to negotiate competitive salaries in this career path?**

Spend time thinking about what you want to do and looking for that role. If you are new to the field, then maybe consider starting at a smaller company where you may be able to wear a lot of hats and learn a ton. Then, once you have a better idea of where your niche is, you can take on a future role in that area or grow within your company.

Also, do not be afraid to "not know" something. Ask lots of questions. Reach higher than you want on your salary. If you get it, cool. If not, you will likely land a little higher than you expected. Also, check the salaries for positions like the one you are looking at Glassdoor or other sites. You will also be able to see if the company tends to have equitable and competitive salaries.

11. **What are some recommendations for networking and continued education?**

Get involved in some industry-specific groups. Many have chat room programs where you can chat with others in your industry, see job boards, and keep tabs on industry-specific news. I spent some time at one called Health Tech Nerds. I am also a member of the Project Management Institute, and they offer opportunities for continued education and networking.

12. **Looking back to the beginning of your career, can you share some lessons learned? Would you have done anything differently?**

It is hard to say because without the mistakes and missteps, I would not be where I am today. I wish I had asked for higher salaries earlier in my career. I wish I had been kinder to and more patient with people working under me in my earlier career. I wish I had figured out what my passion was earlier. All of that. But the experiences I have had, the people I have worked with, and the story my career steps have told are what make me who I am. I am most glad that I have become a gentler person to work with as I have grown in my career.

# Laurice Rutledge Lambert, Founding Partner

**Please provide a brief overview of your professional experience.**

After graduating college, Ms. Lambert began her career in healthcare consulting in Washington, DC. After a few years of consulting, she made her way down to Atlanta for law school. After graduating in 2010, Ms. Lambert spent over a decade at large firms as a healthcare regulatory and transactional attorney. She ultimately became a big law firm partner, but like most people, the COVID-19 pandemic brought her life into focus. In late summer 2021, after having her third child, Ms. Lambert realized it was time for a change and took a leap of faith to join a healthcare tech-enabled services company as the General Counsel and Chief Compliance Officer. They took that company, Trellis Rx, through a sale in June 2022, and from there, she had to decide what she wanted to be when she grew up! Ms. Lambert decided she wanted to be a CEO and joined forces with her former law partners to launch Health Law Strategists (HLS), a boutique healthcare law firm. At HLS, they are building a law firm geared toward servicing founder-led/investor-backed digital health companies, while also supporting women attorneys on their career journeys.

**Professional licenses and/or certifications:**
JD
**Other education or training relevant to your position:**
N/A.
**LinkedIn profile:**
https://www.linkedin.com/in/lauricelambert/
**Were you referred to this project by a colleague? If so, who?**
Jeffery Daigrepont, Senior Vice President, Coker.

# HCIT Questions

1. **What led you to pursue a career in the HCIT industry?**

   I have always been fascinated by medicine. When I was young, I wanted to be a doctor. Ultimately, I realized that I didn't like blood but found my way to law school and a career helping all types of healthcare companies, from providers to digital health companies.

2. **What is the best professional advice given to you that you can share with aspiring women who wish to work in HCIT?**

   Outlast: don't give up. Even if you scale back to navigate your family and other life demands, always keep your foot in the door.

3. **What is one of your proudest work-related accomplishments?**

   Making partner at an AmLaw 100 law firm.

4. **In preparation for a job interview, what type of questions should the candidate consider asking, and in what ways can the candidate set themselves apart?**

Questions that show a long-term interest and commitment to growth with the company as well as curiosity about the company's values and guiding principles. For example, what opportunities do you see for my growth with the company?

5. **Would you say there are additional barriers for women to overcome in this industry? If so, what has your experience taught you about navigating these challenges?**

Find allies in both other women and men. Look to others who can help show you how to pave a path that works for you and who will help open doors for you along the way.

6. **How have you navigated instances of inequality that may be experienced by women in the workplace?**

Do not be afraid to ask for what you deserve, whether it be compensation or a work schedule that works for your needs. If you don't speak up for yourself, no one else will. I recently just told my 5-year-old daughter that I waited too many years to speak up for myself and am trying to teach her to advocate for herself at a young age.

7. **When it comes to traveling on the job (such as for attending conferences or performing on-site tasks), what tips may you share when it comes to safety as well as tips that are convenient for travel?**

Stay in on-site hotels; travel with a buddy when possible. Otherwise, make sure someone at home generally knows your whereabouts.

8. **How do you maintain a healthy work–life balance?**

I have three young children and a full-time job. I have realized there is no true balance. I think work–life integration is the appropriate term. I try to reserve certain hours of the day for time just with my kids. However, I have also learned to lean in to my husband and accept that I don't have to be superwoman. My children love me; they know I am here for them, but sometimes mommy has to work, and that's ok.

9. **Are there any specific books or videos you may recommend as it relates to HCIT?**

N/A.

10. **What is your advice for women to obtain the best opportunities and to negotiate competitive salaries in this career path?**

Do not be afraid to ask for what you deserve, and always negotiate. Ask for a salary that makes you uncomfortable; if you aren't uncomfortable, the number is too low of an ask.

11. **What are some recommendations for networking and continued education?**

Be genuine in all your relationships, be curious about others' paths, and follow through on what you say you'll do.

12. **Looking back to the beginning of your career, can you share some lessons learned? Would you have done anything differently?**

I would have demanded higher compensation and advocated for myself earlier in my career.

# Naomi Lenane, Chief Information Officer, Vice-President, Information Services

**Please provide a brief overview of your professional experience.**

Naomi Lenane's first HCIT role was with Medical Information Technology, Inc. (MEDITECH) as an implementation consultant. She spent 6 years at MEDITECH implementing clinical modules and later, as part of the sales cycle, as a marketing representative demonstrating the full suite of the EHR. Moving to Dana-Farber Cancer Institute allowed her to focus her workflow analysis and problem-solving skills on the needs of end users providing direct patient care. Clinical systems work overlaps with all other aspects of HCIT, which led to her involvement in a variety of projects. Ms. Lenane moved into project management as the technology lead, opening regional campus locations. This exposed her to the business of healthcare, including revenue cycle, ERP, hardware, networking, space, and philanthropy. Learning how it all comes together as a business was invaluable for her career. Ms. Lenane was able to create new management opportunities and build teams over the next few years. She thought her largest project would be leading the tech design and implementation of a new 14 floor cancer center in Boston, but then Epic came along. Epic was the opportunity to truly show her understanding of this organization and the healthcare industry. Ms. Lenane was a true change agent in her role, leading teams of technology and operational staff to rethink how they worked together. They created an Epic program that continues today. It has shown countless departments that what they do has an impact up and downstream of their task. This understanding allows the organization to deliver a better patient experience. In 2017, after 15 years at Dana-Farber, Ms. Lenane became CIO.

**Professional licenses and/or certifications:**
N/A.
**Other education or training relevant to your position:**
Gartner Leadership development program, CHIME CIO Boot Camp
**LinkedIn profile:**
www.linkedin.com/in/naomi-rapoza-lenane-0477302
**Were you referred to this project by a colleague? If so, who?**
N/A.

# HCIT Questions

**1. What led you to pursue a career in the HCIT industry?**

The stability of hospitals is what brought me to healthcare. Streamlining workflows and automating tasks for clinicians is what kept me in healthcare. It is fulfilling to witness technology making a real difference in clinical care. In my role as CIO, I see the impact of technology in all aspects of the hospital business and how that ties directly back to the patient's experience. It is this continuous reinforcement of the good that we do that keeps me in this industry.

**2. What is the best professional advice given to you that you can share with aspiring women who wish to work in HCIT?**

Understand the value you bring to your role and the industry. At one point in my career, I thought I should work on the healthcare operations side. I wasn't sure I fit into the technology department. I was reminded that my understanding the patient care workflows and appreciation for the business of healthcare are what make me so valuable in the technology department. I evaluated technology for what it brought to the experience, not for being cool technology. So, think about what you bring, how your perspective will be different from others, and how that will bring success.

**3. What is one of your proudest work-related accomplishments?**

There are many accomplishments to be proud of after two decades in this industry. I am also proud of the one time that I stopped a project and the product was never put into production. We were halfway through building an in-house electronic medication administration tool when it was decided to implement Epic. It took a month of meetings, resource and budget analysis, and just conversations to finally decide to stop the project. It felt like a true accomplishment to understand the financial impacts, depreciation factors, consulting contracts, and other components of undoing a multi-million dollar project.

4. **In preparation for a job interview, what type of questions should the candidate consider asking, and in what ways can the candidate set themselves apart?**

Ask about the culture of the organization and the management style of the leader. It is important to understand how they expect the work to get done, not just what the work is. Is there a training program, or is there autonomy in how to learn and onboard? What does success look like for this role and for the team? What is expected in the first 90 days vs the first year? Candidates who can speak beyond the buzz words and articulate a vision for themselves at my organization will stand out. I would also like to share how you participate in the industry of HCIT. There is so much collaboration in our industry that it is surprising when candidates are not engaged in industry groups.

5. **Would you say there are additional barriers for women to overcome in this industry? If so, what has your experience taught you about navigating these challenges?**

There are barriers for women in this industry. Women in technical career paths often find ceilings where they continue to be the only woman or would be the first woman to do a job or get a title. There are many places where the women leaders in HCIT are in non-technical areas or not in the executive suite. It is important to look at companies and hospitals to see if women are in a variety of roles and levels of leadership. Know that there are "traditional" leadership roles for women like HR, Customer Success, or Marketing. Look for women in Research and Development or Strategic Direction roles and know that those may be organizations to work for or with.

The only way I have learned to navigate these barriers is to address them head-on and discuss them. I have worked with colleagues who deserved to be promoted but weren't. I helped her with job descriptions, presentations, or whatever she needed to bring to her boss to push for the promotion. In addition to this mentoring, I was her advocate for other leaders when she wasn't in the room. It is important to highlight the efforts and successes of other women in the presence of more senior leaders. I take every opportunity to bring up their successes so that they are front of mind when those promotions come up for discussion.

6. **How have you navigated instances of inequality that may be experienced by women in the workplace?**

   Navigating the experience hasn't always resulted in righting the wrongs of inequality. Naming the inequality and saying it out loud has decreased its power, but it does not right the wrong. It is important to raise the issue with leadership. If you are in a position to speak for others, do so. As a manager, I have raised examples to HR and organizational leadership. For salary-related inequality, I recommend asking for a market adjustment. Market adjustments mean that you are at a minimum at market rates. This forces the manager, HR, and leadership to look at salaries across their organization and the market. It will highlight a gap if you know it exists. Then you will know if they are truly ignoring the inequality with your male colleagues.

7. **When it comes to traveling on the job (such as for attending conferences or performing on-site tasks), what tips may you share when it comes to safety as well as tips that are convenient for travel?**

   As with any work event, keep the alcohol to a minimum. You are representing your organization at the conference. There is also still a bit of a double standard where a woman drinking too much is seen as making bad choices when the man drinking too much probably just had a long day. Also, know that there are people who will trick you into thinking they've met you before. They may pretend to know you or use information like the hotel name on your bottle of water or the conference lanyard on your neck to start a conversation. It could be an overly aggressive salesperson or a predator. Trust your gut.

8. **How do you maintain a healthy work–life balance?**

   Schedule your fun. If you do not plan your life outside of work, it will feel like all you do is work. Realize that work is part of life, and not only certain hours of the day. If you realize that you can be doing the "life" part at lunchtime, where you break from work to spend time with a friend, then cleaning up your inbox after dinner won't seem wrong or unbalanced. The focus should be on managing stress, not worrying about balance. There will not be a 50/50 split every day. You do need to find time to breathe in your day. Block calendar time every day to go outside for some fresh air or turn away from a computer screen/device.

9. **Are there any specific books or videos you may recommend as it relates to HCIT?**

   *Picture a Scientist* is an amazing documentary focused on women in STEM. I highly recommend it to any woman thinking of a STEM career.

10. **What is your advice for women to obtain the best opportunities and to negotiate competitive salaries in this career path?**

    Do your research. Understand what the best opportunity for you is and what a competitive salary would be. Look at your competitors' job descriptions and understand what the roles are at the level you are looking to achieve. And talk to people in the industry. If there is a job in your current organization that you wish you had, go talk to the person who has it. What did it take for them to get there, and what would it take for you to get there? Once you've done research, you need to ask for it, whatever it is for you. You need to know your salary number and say it out loud. Advocate for yourself. Know that what you are asking for is in line with the industry, and then say it out loud.

11. **What are some recommendations for networking and continued education?**

    Especially early in your career, always find the free stuff—webinars, newsletters, podcasts. It won't all be good, but there is so much free content that you'll definitely learn from some of it. Join local industry groups within HCIT and within technology generally. Ideas from other industries are a great way to bring new ideas to your own organization.

12. **Looking back to the beginning of your career, can you share some lessons learned? Would you have done anything differently?**

    I would have focused on industry-specific certifications earlier in my career and focused more energy on working with industry groups. I did not balance what I was learning "on the job" with what I could have also been learning within the industry.

# Elise Levine, Director of Business Development, Eye Med Management Solutions

**Please provide a brief overview of your professional experience.**

Elise Levine has worked or volunteered in some human services or healthcare field for over 30 years, from Medicare benefits to workforce development and practice management to clinical research. Ms. Levine spent the majority of her career as a practice administrator and clinical research director in Ophthalmology. She now continues to stay connected to this field, working part-time as the Director of Business Development of Eye Med Management Solutions, a concierge medical billing firm specializing in Ophthalmology.

Ms. Levine is an alumna of Mount Saint Mary's University, holding a bachelor's degree in gerontology and liberal studies and a master's degree in gerontology from the University of Southern California. She has also completed advanced certificate work in DEI in the Workplace and Ethical and Inclusive Leadership from the University of South Florida.

**Professional licenses and/or certifications:**

N/A.

**Other education or training relevant to your position:**

Master's degree in gerontology, University of Southern California

Bachelor's degree in gerontology and liberal studies, Mount Saint Mary's University

Advanced Certification, DEI, Workplace and Ethical and Inclusive Leadership, University of South Florida

**LinkedIn profile:**

https://www.linkedin.com/in/eliseglevine/

**Were you referred to this project by a colleague? If so, who?**

Jeffery Daigrepont, Senior Vice President, Coker.

# HCIT Questions

**1. What led you to pursue a career in the HCIT industry?**

My career has all been happenstance. HCIT fell into my lap with every job I have had. From choosing software for our medical practice to retail software for our optical shop as well as software for clinical research, I have been forced to keep up with the times and offerings.

**2. What is the best professional advice given to you that you can share with aspiring women who wish to work in HCIT?**

Network, network, network. Grow your connections on LinkedIn and keep in touch; you never know when you can put those to work for you. In addition, when a door is opened for you, don't be afraid to step through it. Don't succumb to imposter syndrome; remember that someone thought enough of you to open the door for you!

**3. What is one of your proudest work-related accomplishments?**

Over the years, multiple software and hardware conversions (while keeping the practice up and running with little to no downtime!)

4. **In preparation for a job interview, what type of questions should the candidate consider asking, and in what ways can the candidate set themselves apart?**

Remember that interviews are like a first date; you need to like the company as much as they like you. Ask where they would see a successful candidate in 30 days, 90 days, 1 year. Does it seem reasonable? Gut feelings go a long way. If you are interviewing your potential boss, ask them how long they have been at the company and what their favorite thing about their job is? Don't ask questions that are easily answered on the company's webpage but do research and ask probing questions that have shown you have done your research.

5. **Would you say there are additional barriers for women to overcome in this industry? If so, what has your experience taught you about navigating these challenges?**

As older generations are retiring, I am hoping that women are more fully embraced in leadership roles. Particularly women of color, who traditionally have filled entry-level roles in large measure while being hardly represented in the C suite. Find mentors and leaders in the space and educate yourself. Also, having a mentor doesn't mean someone older; if you wish to stay on the cutting edge of things, find a mentor even younger than you!

6. **How have you navigated instances of inequality that may be experienced by women in the workplace?**

Absolutely. From inequal pay to microaggressions, from being called difficult to being passed over for things. After being in the workforce for almost 40 years, I feel like I have seen and experienced it all. Much of it has gone away with better laws and protections, but there are still instances that occur to this day.

7. **When it comes to traveling on the job (such as for attending conferences or performing on-site tasks), what tips may you share when it comes to safety as well as tips that are convenient for travel?**

- Always have someone to call on speakerphone in the cab from the airport to let them know you are on your way to the hotel.
- Don't engage in anything to dull your senses. Ginger ale and cranberry juice are my go-to drinks.
- It's okay to say no to anything that doesn't make you feel comfortable. (I'd rather not have dinner in your room; can we eat in the restaurant?)

- Sign up for every hotel/airline affinity program. Free Wi-Fi is always a good thing, and if you are traveling a lot, you can benefit from loyalty.
- Bring one spare work outfit, just in case.
- High heels (unless you are one of the anomalies who are really comfortable in them) will cause you nothing but grief later. There are plenty of sensible cute shoes.
- Have several extra charging cords (for home, for work, for the car/travel) that way, when you leave one behind, you are never without one.
- Network, collect business cards, and connect on LinkedIn or send an email after a meeting. Don't wait too long to follow up.

8. **How do you maintain a healthy work–life balance?**

Meditation, self-care (regular massage/facials, therapy). I spent too many years making work my life; now I ensure that my cup is full first before I can share with others.

9. **Are there any specific books or videos you may recommend as it relates to HCIT?**

Not as it relates to HCIT, but I highly recommend *The Four Agreements: A Practical Guide to Personal* Freedom by Don Miguel Ruiz as a guide path for life. If you can master these four agreements for daily living in both work and life, it gets to be pretty easy.

10. **What is your advice for women to obtain the best opportunities and to negotiate competitive salaries in this career path?**

Network and follow trends. Watch websites like Indeed and Glassdoor to see what is happening in the real world. Also, a referral to a job from a friend will go much farther than a blind submission online. Work with a career coach to help you develop an elevator pitch and to be comfortable selling yourself, because no matter what your resume says, ultimately you are your best commercial in the interview.

11. **What are some recommendations for networking and continued education?**

LinkedIn is still one of the best for industry networking. Follow and engage with those you admire or who are leaders in the field. Ask for help; you will be amazed at how helpful people will be if you just ask. Join industry-specific organizations related to your passion. Join women's empowerment groups as well. Look at EVERYTHING as an opportunity to network. Always have your contact information available. I have networked in more airport terminals, supermarkets, or standing in-line at concerts than I can remember. Be open to every opportunity.

12. **Looking back to the beginning of your career, can you share some lessons learned? Would you have done anything differently?**

I would have listened more to the people who thought I could and less to the people who thought I couldn't. I realized many years later that folks who held me back or down were jealous and not knowledgeable about my talents. Don't work in a field or for people who don't spark joy in your life. If you are just beginning your career, that's going to be a long time of being miserable.

# Marissa Maldonado, CEO, Proda Technology

**Please provide a brief overview of your professional experience.**

Marissa Maldonado created Proda Technology in 2010 when she discovered a gap between honest but fast-managed IT and cyber security services. Founded alongside her brother in his basement, Proda Technology has grown into one of the most well-respected businesses in their industry and continues to aggressively grow across the nation. Proda Technology keeps their commitment to people and leading with soul at the core of who they are and how they provide service. Marissa attributes her success to being a first-generation college graduate. Her vision for how to create a great organization was inspired by her immigrant parents, who instilled in her the importance of higher education.

With both the dedication of her parents and the numerous community outreach programs tailored toward minority students graduating college, Marissa completed her degree from Terry College of Business at the University of Georgia in 2010. Marissa focuses on identifying key resources ranging in finance, specialists, strategy, and policy for a healthy IT environment for her clients. Marissa is passionate about upholding an approachable and friendly culture to improve the experience of employees when it comes to technology and foster the best in the engineers who are a part of Proda Technology. Marissa is a national speaker at conferences across multiple industries, leveraging Cyber Security and Technology to drive operational strategy and success. Marissa has remained passionate about community outreach and serves on the board of Meals on Wheels Atlanta and Bluebird Leaders, a nonprofit focused on empowering women in HCIT.

**Professional licenses and/or certifications:**
N/A.
**Other education or training relevant to your position:**
Bachelor of business administration
**LinkedIn profile:**
https://www.linkedin.com/in/mmmaldonado/
**Were you referred to this project by a colleague? If so, who?**
Jeffery Daigrepont, Senior Vice President, Coker.

# HCIT Questions

**1. What led you to pursue a career in the HCIT industry?**

Once I finished college, I went to pursue a career as an IT Business Analyst. It triggered a fun passion of mine for automation. At that point, my brother had built a book of business and building relationships, so he asked me to join him. From there, it was a fun journey to feminizing HCIT. In the beginning, there were times when I tried to "blend in," and then there was a turning point where I realized that, as a woman in IT, I had a lot of strengths to bring to the table, and it was empowering for the end users and customers. Working with many women as end users, I realized that we could create a better experience if we put emphasis on the soft skills, i.e., empathy, communication, and listening. It has helped propel my story and my experience in HCIT.

**2. What is the best professional advice given to you that you can share with aspiring women who wish to work in HCIT?**

Be yourself. Embrace who you are and all your amazing qualities. You may not fit in with everyone, and that is okay. When I became a mother, it was such a turning point for me. I realized how intense it is to be a mother and still be great in my career. It's a badge of honor. It's in those moments when you embrace who you are and just be you. In addition, find a group of women at work (or create one!); there is strength in numbers! It's important to support one another and lift each other up.

**3. What is one of your proudest work-related accomplishments?**

Achieving Woman-Owned Business of the Year in 2020! In addition, I am proud of navigating and keeping everything together while becoming a mother and still maintaining a successful business. There were a lot of naysayers who said I couldn't do it. I had to work hard to find a balance between being present at home and at work.

4. **In preparation for a job interview, what type of questions should the candidate consider asking, and in what ways can the candidate set themselves apart?**

Be yourself; be authentic.

5. **Would you say there are additional barriers for women to overcome in this industry? If so, what has your experience taught you about navigating these challenges?**

We have made a lot of progress from past generations. As a woman, it's important to align yourself and find an organization that gives you the balance, the time, etc. One of my biggest challenges as a woman is that many organizations don't embrace all the responsibilities that women have and don't allow them the flexibility to do so. For example, not being able to pick children up from school means they leave the workforce. There needs to be more flexibility. Traditionally, we also tend to underestimate ourselves. My hope is that the new generation of women will be empowered and continue to make strides in this industry to pursue whatever they want to do.

6. **How have you navigated instances of inequality that may be experienced by women in the workplace?**

N/A.

7. **When it comes to traveling on the job (such as for attending conferences or performing on-site tasks), what tips may you share when it comes to safety as well as tips that are convenient for travel?**

Use your technology as your protector! Always have your location on and share it with family and/or friends. Use air tags for bags, etc. Share your calendar and travel arrangements with family and trustworthy co-workers. When possible, identify travel buddies or friends that you can rely on so you are not alone. Create a buddy system with fellow women in attendance at the conference or event. Also, in a male-dominated industry, we tend to want to fit in and be "one of the guys." Stand up for yourself when you are uncomfortable in a conversation, and learn to set boundaries, and learn to walk away when you recognize these situations.

8. **How do you maintain a healthy work–life balance?**

It's a cultural thing within an organization. At Proda Technology, I encourage everyone to focus on their family, and we support one another when something comes up. The work will be here when you get back.

In addition, I encourage the following:

- Create non-negotiables. For example, dropping children off for school or being home for dinner every night.
- Enjoy the weekends and unplug to take time with family and friends.
- Read for pleasure in the evenings if reading is something you love to do.

9. **Are there any specific books or videos you may recommend as it relates to HCIT?**
   - *Radical Candor* by Kim Scott
   - *Nice Girls Don't Get the Corner Office* by Lois Frankel
   - *Bossy Pants* by Tina Fay
   - *Atlas of the Heart* by Brené Brown

10. **What is your advice for women to obtain the best opportunities and to negotiate competitive salaries in this career path?**

    Role-play the interview, mid-year reviews, and negotiation with another woman, particularly one that is in the position you're aiming for. A conversation with another woman like this is empowering and uplifting in a high-pressure situation.

11. **What are some recommendations for networking and continued education?**

    One that comes to mind is BlueBird Leaders.

12. **Looking back to the beginning of your career, can you share some lessons learned? Would you have done anything differently?**

    I would not have felt the need to become a chameleon. I wish I hadn't done that at the beginning of my career. I tried to fit in, and I wish I realized it was okay to be me. Being comfortable with my feminine side and recognizing earlier that it was a strength of mine and not that I was "emotional," as some would say.

# Julie McGovern, CEO and Founder, Practice Wise, LLC

**Please provide a brief overview of your professional experience.**

Julie McGovern obtained her degree in Health Care Administration, and in 1999, she managed a multi-site pediatric group while at the same time building two new replacement clinics and prepping for Y2K. At the time, Ms. McGovern felt her understanding of technology was lacking, and with the impending Y2K, two new clinic sites were being opened that had to be connected via a Frame Relay. She was tasked with explaining to her board of 16 doctors what the technology was, what the price quotes were, and the design implementation plans, but this was all very challenging.

Shortly after, Julie left that job and became a practice management software implementer. It was there that she identified the missing link between the software, hardware, and IT services industries and the clients supported: ambulatory medical clinics. Ms. McGovern found that she was capable of quickly synthesizing information and picking up IT skills smoothly. She began assisting her implementation clients with other IT issues on-site and provided guidance, which resulted in her clients asking her to become a consultant. Although it took some convincing, Ms. McGovern entered the industry, though initially consulting was not something she had considered in a favorable light.

One of her more memorable experiences include one of her first clients, who was an implementation customer. The customer's IT vendor did not heed her advice when she told them their grandfather/father/son backup scheme would not work well for the type of practice management database needed and recommended doing a full backup nightly. Ultimately, this clinic lost a hard drive and 28 days' worth of data. The client called her at 8 p.m.; their IT vendor had been onsite for 27 hours and still did not have the server backup, and the client begged her to come in and save the day.

Ms. McGovern was able to reinstall the Windows Server OS, then install all the programs and restore the backup for the practice management software, which was 28 days old. She then helped them file an insurance claim to cover their hard costs for her, their IT, and their staff overtime needed to re-input 28 days of data. And with the practice management software, there was plenty of data not captured in reports; they needed to wait for patients to call and complain to find the missing payment plans, etc. It was at this time that the lightbulb went off. She knew this was the role for her as an IT consultant for ambulatory medical clinics.

**Professional licenses and/or certifications:**
N/A.

**Other education or training relevant to your position:**
When I restored that first server, I hired an IT guy who was my neighbor, and he shadowed me for months in the evenings and taught me the basics of Windows network management. I took that first client from a pure Novell network for Windows network. Through this period, I learned how to build a server, build out terminal servers, and stand up a full network. You cannot consult on what you don't know.

**LinkedIn profile:**
https://www.linkedin.com/in/julie-mcgovern-24551510/
**Were you referred to this project by a colleague? If so, who?**
N/A.

# HCIT Questions

1. **What led you to pursue a career in the HCIT industry?**

   It really came out of a need to know more and help my clients more.

2. **What is the best professional advice given to you that you can share with aspiring women who wish to work in HCIT?**

   Get as much education and experience as you can, and never stop. HCIT is an ever-changing industry; you have to continually learn to stay current. Also, believe in yourself! Don't listen to the naysayers. I got a lot of grief early on; I was in my early forties and blonde, and there were not a lot of women in my space. I had a lot of resistance from the male IT community.

3. **What is one of your proudest work-related accomplishments?**

   I changed my core focus from consulting to selling and supporting an EMR application. I realized in 2007 that EMR was going to happen (I had 2 clients who were early adopters) and that the best way for me to support my clients fully I would need to be the provider of the app. I am the longest-running Value Added Reseller in my application's history, to date.

4. **In preparation for a job interview, what type of questions should the candidate consider asking, and in what ways can the candidate set themselves apart?**
   - What are the growth opportunities for them personally and for the company as a whole?
   - How does the company support its staff?
   - What does ongoing education and advancement look like?

5. **Would you say there are additional barriers for women to overcome in this industry? If so, what has your experience taught you about navigating these challenges?**

   It is still a bit of an old boys' network, but it's getting better. To navigate the roadblocks, you must know your stuff. If you are un/under prepared, it will show. Do your homework and show them who you are and what you know. Actions speak louder than words.

**6. How have you navigated instances of inequality that may be experienced by women in the workplace?**

Being a woman in IT in the early aughts was a struggle on a daily basis. Everyone in IT wrote me off! It was my clients who had belief in me and continued to push back against their vendors.

I recall having a client meeting with a client's IT vendor. The discussion was about their EMR software upgrade and the need for a new server. As we were reviewing their server quote, I noticed that it was being built to the minimum specs from the vendor. As we discussed the lifespan of the server, I suggested they beef up some of the components on the initial build when it's cheaper for the client and not significantly more expensive on the initial order. After I left that meeting, they told the clinic administrator I didn't know what I was talking about and that their server was scalable (a.k.a., more money for them in the future). She fired them on the spot! That was a pivotal moment in my career; having a client believe in me to that level, it was a first.

**7. When it comes to traveling on the job (such as for attending conferences or performing on-site tasks), what tips may you share when it comes to safety as well as tips that are convenient for travel?**

This was one of my biggest hurdles. I have a lot of anxiety about traveling alone. I love to do it but hate the hotel experience. Here's my process:

- Never let the hotel front desk announce your room number. Most of the big hotels already know this, but I've traveled to some very small towns and have had to educate the front desk when I refused the room they offered in earshot of others.
- Invest in hotel door locks.
- Don't connect your devices to free Wi-Fi, anywhere!
- Stay alert to your surroundings.
- I rely on my clients for advice about where to stay, etc.

**8. How do you maintain a healthy work–life balance?**

Well, that's the big question. For the first 15 years, I worked ridiculous hours and the fear of failure was intense. As a consultant, the big question near the end of every project is: where will my next dollar come from? That feeling takes a long time to overcome. I have encouraged several other women to branch out on their own, and everyone seems to go through that fear of no new business.

This year is my 20-year anniversary, and I work fewer than 40 hours most weeks. For me, this is possible because I've hired a good team, and we have consistent recurring revenue outside of our consulting projects.

9. **Are there any specific books or videos you may recommend as it relates to HCIT?**

    I read a lot of industry blogs and newsletters. The most important blog that I read daily is HISTalk2.com.

10. **What is your advice for women to obtain the best opportunities and to negotiate competitive salaries in this career path?**

    Know your worth and be the most competent person in the room. Stand your ground for the salary and work–life experience that work best for you. There is no point in having a great salary if you are expected to sacrifice your life on the altar of your job.

11. **What are some recommendations for networking and continued education?**

    This landscape has changed a lot in 20 years. There used to be a lot of networking opportunities in the form of networking breakfast groups, etc. Since the pandemic, those opportunities are not as great. Find your tribe. Build relationships with clients and vendors. My relationships are the key to building my business and my success.

12. **Looking back to the beginning of your career, can you share some lessons learned? Would you have done anything differently?**

    I would not take such personal offense to what others say, whether vendors or disgruntled clients. I would say that early in my career, I was hurt and offended whenever doctors blamed me or made bad decisions against my advice. I had to earn a thick skin and believe that I can't please everyone, and if they pay their bills, it's fine; move on.

# Karen Murphy, PhD, RN, Executive Vice President, Chief Innovation and Digital Transformation Officer, Geisinger

**Please provide a brief overview of your professional experience.**

Karen Murphy, PhD, RN, Executive Vice President, Chief Innovation and Digital Transformation Officer, has worked to improve and transform healthcare delivery throughout her career in both the public and private sectors. Before joining Geisinger, she served as Pennsylvania's secretary of health, addressing the most significant health issues facing the state, including rural health challenges and the opioid epidemic. Prior to her role as secretary, Ms. Murphy served as director of the State Innovation Models Initiative at the Centers for Medicare and Medicaid Services, leading a $990 million CMS investment designed to accelerate healthcare innovation in state governments across the United States. She previously served as president and chief executive officer of the Moses Taylor Health Care System in Scranton and as founder and chief executive officer of Physicians Health Alliance, Inc., an integrated medical group practice within Moses Taylor.

As chief innovation and digital transformation officer, Ms. Murphy leads Geisinger's efforts to transform healthcare delivery by improving patient experience and outcomes. An integrated health system, Geisinger includes ten hospital campuses, a health plan with more than half a million members, a Research Institute and the Geisinger Commonwealth School of Medicine. Its 25,000 employees and more than 1,700 employed physicians care for more than one million people across central and northeast Pennsylvania.

Ms. Murphy earned her doctor of philosophy in business administration from the Temple University Fox School of Business. She holds a master of business administration from Marywood University, a bachelor of science in liberal arts from the University of Scranton, and a diploma in nursing from the Scranton State Hospital School of Nursing.

An author and national speaker on health policy and innovation, Ms. Murphy also serves as a clinical faculty member at Geisinger Commonwealth School of Medicine. She has been recognized by Modern Healthcare as one of the "50 Most Influential Clinical Executives" in 2021 and one of the "Top 25 Women Leaders" in 2023. She has been included in Becker's Hospital Review's list of "Women Power Players in IT" and "30 Great Chief Innovation Officers to Know." In 2021, Ms. Murphy was named a "Changemaker in Health" by the HIMSS, and in 2023, she was recognized as an "Innovation Leader" by the Sharp Index.

**Professional licenses and/or certifications:**
N/A.
**Other education or training relevant to your position:**
N/A.
**LinkedIn profile:**
https://www.linkedin.com/in/karen-murphy-58094638/
**Were you referred to this project by a colleague? If so, who?**
N/A.

# HCIT Questions

**1. What led you to pursue a career in the HCIT industry?**

My goal was transformation, and I felt that technology was an enabling strategy to be able to actually transform the way we deliver healthcare. After spending many years in the clinical space, and as the digital world advanced, I became very interested in learning more about how IT could accelerate this transformation.

**2. What is the best professional advice given to you that you can share with aspiring women who wish to work in HCIT?**

Be authentic, have a solid knowledge base, and treat people well.

**3. What is one of your proudest work-related accomplishments?**

Operationalizing our AI Lab at Geisinger. In 2018, we established a steering committee to study AI, evaluate some use cases, and determine if we could use it to improve both healthcare and business efficiency. We developed a successful partnership with Medial EarlySign, through which we developed a machine-learning algorithm that was able to detect potential signs of colorectal cancer in high-risk patients who had missed a routine colonoscopy. We were able to save lives and save money, too. We've also been able to implement AI in other areas of healthcare, including risk stratification of patients. Aside from AI, another career accomplishment has been working with our team to develop a new model of care for patients with chronic diseases that includes remote patient monitoring.

**4. In preparation for a job interview, what type of questions should the candidate consider asking, and in what ways can the candidate set themselves apart?**

Always ask about the organization's mission, vision, and values and evaluate how they align with your own.

**5. Would you say there are additional barriers for women to overcome in this industry? If so, what has your experience taught you about navigating these challenges?**

There are barriers for women in every industry. To navigate these challenges, you have to be both competent and confident: fully understand what the job role is and believe that you can do a good job.

**6. How have you navigated instances of inequality that may be experienced by women in the workplace?**

N/A.

7. **When it comes to traveling on the job (such as for attending conferences or performing on-site tasks), what tips may you share when it comes to safety as well as tips that are convenient for travel?**

   N/A.

8. **How do you maintain a healthy work–life balance?**

   I think the balance sometimes swings depending on where you are in your career. When my children were young, I had a job that allowed me to be home more. As they got older, my jobs were more demanding, but I never had to feel like I was taking from one part of my life or the other.

9. **Are there any specific books or videos you may recommend as it relates to HCIT?**

   *Glaser on Health Care IT: Perspectives from the Decade that Defined Health Care Information Technology* by John P. Glaser is a good read.

10. **What is your advice for women to obtain the best opportunities and to negotiate competitive salaries in this career path?**

    Take time to research and understand what the market rate is for the job and be confident and assertive when asking for it. If you're not getting what the market rate is, you may need to reevaluate whether this is an organization you want to be a part of.

11. **What are some recommendations for networking and continued education?**

    Continuing education has to be self-education: read, read, read. Also, when it comes to industry conferences, some are better than others. Identify the ones that will give you the best value based on what you want to take away from them.

12. **Looking back to the beginning of your career, can you share some lessons learned? Would you have done anything differently?**

    Hindsight is always 20/20. In reality, you can't change anything. Your journey was your journey. It's important to accept that the only day you can change is today and tomorrow.

# Robin Ntoh, Vice President, Aesthetics

**Please provide a brief overview of your professional experience.**

A recognized expert in the business of elective healthcare and aesthetics, Robin Ntoh has seen success in the launch of both her own consulting company and the addition of consulting services for Nextech, serving more than

400 clients. Her 35+ years include small-mid business management as well as executive leadership for one of the leading Aesthetic Health Care Platforms, Nextech. Throughout her career, Robin has driven strategy focused on practice optimization, workflow efficiency, excellence in patient engagement, and improved financial management. Robin often serves as faculty and national speaker for many aesthetic national meetings. She has served as a lecturer on faculty at ASCRS-ASOA, AACS, VCS, VAS, ADAM, AAFPRS, and ASAPS. Additionally, she has authored numerous papers and articles and is a member of Women in Tech.

**Professional licenses and/or certifications:**
N/A.

**Other education or training relevant to your position:**
Bachelor of science, biology, and chemistry

**LinkedIn profile:**
https://www.linkedin.com/in/robin-ntoh-48b00723/

**Were you referred to this project by a colleague? If so, who?**
Jeffery Daigrepont, Senior Vice President, Coker.

# HCIT Questions

### 1. What led you to pursue a career in the HCIT industry?

Working for Mirror Software (now Canfield Scientific) was on-the-job training in installing turn-key systems. This gave me an early start in HCIT, which evolved into consulting and finally working with Nextech.

### 2. What is the best professional advice given to you that you can share with aspiring women who wish to work in HCIT?

As a female in a leadership role for a software IT company, I find that innately, we often want to do everything. Cook, cleaner, and bottle washer, I think is the phrase my mother often used. We as females are multi-taskers and oftentimes lack the singular focus that is required to really understand strategy and prioritize what really needs to get done. A mentor taught me "critical few verses, important many." We don't have to do it all to get the most done.

### 3. What is one of your proudest work-related accomplishments?

Nextech approached me about developing a consulting division for the company. This allowed me the opportunity to use both my healthcare technology knowledge and consulting skills to create a department that started as one employee and is now 10 employees, servicing more than 400 clients. It has evolved into two arms: MIPS-regulatory and Practice Management. Generally, consulting is not offered a service inside a technology company. Many times, third parties are certified or partnered with the HCIT company to provide those services.

4. **In preparation for a job interview, what type of questions should the candidate consider asking, and in what ways can the candidate set themselves apart?**

     Questions to consider in your interview:
   - What metrics or success criteria are measured for my role?
   - What career-pathing opportunities has your company provided for females in this role?
   - What employee belonging groups are represented in your company?
   - What priorities do you envision for this role for the next 30, 60, and 90 days?
   - What long-term goals do you see for this role?
        Setting yourself apart:
   - Make sure you include your tech knowledge; this can often be a primary differentiator between you and someone else.
   - Be prepared to share how you support a company initiative and how you prioritized this in your previous role.
   - If your current/previous role was measured quantitatively, provide that information in your interview.
   - What "big ideas" did you bring to the table to generate a new revenue stream for the business?

5. **Would you say there are additional barriers for women to overcome in this industry? If so, what has your experience taught you about navigating these challenges?**

     Many senior leaders are still managing with "old school" thinking. Be prepared to be adaptive and supportive. But always look for ways to contribute and/or support when appropriate. It does not mean you have to be in every conversation; be an active listener who is sometimes the last one to provide feedback or commentary.

6. **How have you navigated instances of inequality that may be experienced by women in the workplace?**

     N/A.

7. **When it comes to traveling on the job (such as for attending conferences or performing on-site tasks), what tips may you share when it comes to safety as well as tips that are convenient for travel?**

- In general, do not engage with your seatmate on a plane. You never know who a predator may be or may misunderstand your friendliness as something else.
- Always park very close to the front door if you are arriving late at night, even if it means you park in the portico.
- Using a known driver from home to and from the airport is always better than the stress, safety risk, and sanity in your marriage when traveling.
- Never take the last flight. If it cancels or delayed, you create an unwarranted risk.
- Pick up water at the airport cone through security. You never know what may or may not be open once you arrive, and hotels may not always be provided.
- Pack snacks! You never know when you need emergency food or if you can always depend on the food provided in a boardroom meeting.
- Pick one hotel, one airline, and one car rental company. If you travel, you take on so much additional stress for your body and life. You should at least get the reward of free trips with your significant other or a fun girl's trip! Furthermore, the status once again reduces unnecessary stress and inconvenience.
- TSA and Clear are well worth the less than $200 investment!
- If at all possible, live in a city that is a hub for an airline. I have seen more co-workers change jobs because of the connections required for travel.

**8. How do you maintain a healthy work–life balance?**

I don't always. I must schedule the time to make it happen. Scheduling a weekend away from home, even if I travel, works for me. Working partly from home makes it hard for me to disconnect at around 5 p.m. Adding reminders on my calendar for going on a walk or to the gym helps. Sometimes, I schedule mid-day appointments that require me to disconnect. Creating disruptors that require me to disconnect has helped as well.

**9. Are there any specific books or videos you may recommend as it relates to HCIT?**

- *Crucial Conversations: Tools for Talking When Stakes are High* by Kerry Patterson
- *Digital Body Language: How to Build Trust and Connection, No Matter the Distance* by Erica Dhawan

**10. What is your advice for women to obtain the best opportunities and to negotiate competitive salaries in this career path?**

- Put the ego aside and find the smartest person in the room to gain advice or mentorship from. Finding an executive to be your mentor also gives you the advantage that they are suddenly very aware of your desire to learn, consume, and grow.
- There is no replacement for experience. Find opportunities to gain experience. Shadow other people, especially recognized leaders, not necessarily managers.
- Ask for career pathing and make sure it is in writing with clear objectives and timelines.
- When negotiating the salary, make sure you provide clear success in your current role and tie it back to the company or department initiatives, showing your support for the business.
- Always ask for more but know your floor. You cannot live below your standard means.

**11. What are some recommendations for networking and continued education?**

- Participate in employee belonging groups if they are available in your company.
- Look for continuing education courses that you can take remotely and ensure you get them added to the budget.
- Look for a mentor. Be a mentor.
- Look for areas to contribute to the community.

**12. Looking back to the beginning of your career, can you share some lessons learned? Would you have done anything differently?**

Nothing different than above!

# Jamie M. Nelson, Senior Vice President and Chief Information Officer, Hospital for Special Surgery

**Please provide a brief overview of your professional experience.**

Jamie M. Nelson, MBA, is Senior Vice President and Chief Information Officer at the Hospital for Special Surgery (HSS) in New York City. Ms. Nelson's career in healthcare includes extensive experience in Information

Technology Leadership and Consulting, Hospital Operations, and Performance Improvement.

Ms. Nelson's accomplishments at HSS include developing and implementing an IT strategy in support of the HSS strategic roadmap, and, most notably, led the hospital's decision and implementation process to install Epic across inpatient and ambulatory settings for all clinical and revenue cycle applications. Based on these efforts, HSS has been recognized by Epic as being in the top 6% of successful EMR implementations. Under her leadership, HSS has been awarded at HIMSS level 7, a recognition achieved by 5% of hospitals in the United States, and the prestigious HIMSS Davies Award.

In her 10-year tenure at HSS, Ms. Nelson rebuilt the IT function, nearly doubling the number of staff and creating key leadership positions including Chief Medical Information Officer, Chief Technology Officer (CTO), Chief Information Security Officer, and VP applications and AVP BI and analytics. Another major area of her focus and accomplishment was the complete re-architecting of HSS's technical and security infrastructure, including a new data and voice network, establishing a network operations center, moving to an off-site data center, and implementing a state-of-the-art cybersecurity program. Ms. Nelson's leadership also includes building a strong HSS-wide analytics team and developing the plan around the Digital and Patient Consumer Experience. Ms. Nelson was named one of the Most Powerful Women in Healthcare IT in 2017, 2018 and 2019 by Health Data Management and most recently, she was named one of Crain's New York top women in Information Technology in 2019.

Prior to her work at HSS, Ms. Nelson's professional employment included Norwalk Hospital, New York Presbyterian Hospital, Memorial Sloan Kettering Cancer Center, First Consulting Group, Ernst & Young, and Innovatix.

An active member of her community, Ms. Nelson was recently appointed as a Trustee to the Board of the Devereux Foundation, a national, non-profit behavioral health organization. Ms. Nelson also supports the annual Sprinternship Program—Break Through Tech New York, which provides technology internships to CUNY undergraduate female students during their winter breaks at HSS. She is also a major donor to the New York City Ballet.

Ms. Nelson earned an undergraduate degree from the University of Pennsylvania and received her MBA from Cornell University.

**Professional licenses and/or certifications:**
N/A.

**Other education or training relevant to your position:**
MBA with concentration in Health Care Administration, Cornell University, Johnson School of Management
**LinkedIn profile:**
www.linkedin.com/in/jamiemnelson
**Were you referred to this project by a colleague? If so, who?**
N/A.

# HCIT Questions

**1. What led you to pursue a career in the HCIT industry?**

I began my career in hospital administration. Early on, I was assigned to work on a Revenue Cycle system implementation, and my interest in IT began there. There was a career opportunity that I pursued working as a management consultant supporting software implementations for hospital clients.

**2. What is the best professional advice given to you that you can share with aspiring women who wish to work in HCIT?**

Be fearless. With nearly every position that I have taken, there has been a nagging sense of doubt that I was fully qualified. And each time, I realized that the doubt was wrong and that I was indeed up to the new challenge presented. So, quelling those doubts and moving forward without fear is my advice.

**3. What is one of your proudest work-related accomplishments?**

Managing through the pandemic while working in an acute care hospital in New York City is my proudest accomplishment. It was a time of great uncertainty. I chose to go to the hospital every day to support the IT team members who had to work onsite due to the nature of their responsibilities. At the same time, I had to support the rest of the team, who were suddenly working from home in an extremely unfamiliar work and family environment. On top of that, we had to help the hospital physically transform to take care of very sick COVID patients and support all of the other hospital staff who are also suddenly working from home. This work made me very proud and gave me a great sense of accomplishment, knowing that my work and that of my team contributed to vital patient care during those terrible times. I was part of the executive leadership team making minute-by-minute decisions and was so very honored to be part of that experience.

4. **In preparation for a job interview, what type of questions should the candidate consider asking, and in what ways can the candidate set themselves apart?**

   Candidates should always ask how their role contributes to the mission of the hospital and of the IT department. It is important that candidates are interested in and want to connect themselves to the larger organization. They should also have good knowledge about the hospital itself and the interviewer as well.

5. **Would you say there are additional barriers for women to overcome in this industry? If so, what has your experience taught you about navigating these challenges?**

   HCIT is still very much a male-dominated profession; this is just a current reality. On top of that, there is the other reality of unconscious bias. Finally, many more of the men in our field have technical backgrounds than women. All of these are minor roadblocks, though. By focusing on one's core strengths and not being afraid to be the "only," these can absolutely be overcome. Also, help the women around you. Don't be a bystander to bad behavior toward female colleagues. Speak up.

6. **How have you navigated instances of inequality that may be experienced by women in the workplace?**

   Inequality is felt in subtle ways. For example, male colleagues in my world will get together to play golf, for example, and not invite female colleagues. What this does is limit social and networking opportunities. Take control here and invite a male colleague to lunch. Build those relationships in your own way.

7. **When it comes to traveling on the job (such as for attending conferences or performing on-site tasks), what tips may you share when it comes to safety as well as tips that are convenient for travel?**

   A woman traveling alone should always be aware of her surroundings. If something doesn't feel right, change the situation as soon as possible. Dress professionally, and wear shoes that you can walk quickly and comfortably in (every time I see a woman traveling in high heels, I cringe).

8. **How do you maintain a healthy work–life balance?**

   I raised three children while working full-time, on site, including business travel. Having excellent childcare is critical, and this is where I spent my money. Also, housekeeping help is a must. This really allowed me to focus on my family in a positive and relaxed way when I was home. I also prioritized exercise, but this meant rising before the children did and getting my exercise in then. I also realized that it was ok to get some family administrative small tasks done during the workday when needed, and this was counterbalanced by doing some work-related tasks at home when needed. This enabled me to have a healthy work–life balance.

9. **Are there any specific books or videos you may recommend as it relates to HCIT?**

I don't usually read books or view videos about HCIT.

10. **What is your advice for women to obtain the best opportunities and to negotiate competitive salaries in this career path?**

Build professional networks so that you can be made aware of a wide array of interesting work opportunities. And don't be afraid to look at opportunities that you don't feel 100% qualified for. In terms of salary negotiations, aim high. I see issues when you start at a low salary for a given position—you will always be behind.

11. **What are some recommendations for networking and continued education?**

I really like professional organizations. Much of my learning through-out my career has been at professional conferences. Conferences check several boxes: networking, socialization, and a brief respite from the home-front responsibilities that many women shoulder. I also love pod-casts. Harvard Business School (HBS) has some great podcasts about a variety of business and leadership subjects. A great starting point.

12. **Looking back to the beginning of your career, can you share some lessons learned? Would you have done anything differently?**

When I was a management consultant, I witnessed some awful harassing behavior by my direct supervisor. When I brought this to the head of our division, I was thanked and then asked what other office I would consider working out of. Instead of continuing to escalate the issue, I chose to just move on from the organization. In hindsight, I should have continued up the chain of command. Lesson learned.

# Anna Nyegaard, MISM, Client Software Manager, BrinsonAnderson Consulting

**Please provide a brief overview of your professional experience.**

Anna Nyegaard, MISM, began working at an orthopedic practice, Proliance Surgeons, in Lakewood, WA in 2010, filing charts and scanning records. The clinic was fast approaching the move to EHR, and Ms. Nyegaard was hired to "prep" charts for the upcoming visit and scan in paper charts for the providers moving to Phoenix Ortho EHR. During her time at Proliance Surgeons, she led the IT committee and became the liaison between IT and the clinic. Ms. Nyegaard's IT responsibilities included troubleshooting all computer equipment, telephones, and internet bandwidth issues. She was very fortunate to have mentors that took her under their wing and helped her learn and discover how to "fix" problems.

During her time at Proliance Surgeons, Ms. Nyegaard was working on her bachelor of science in technical management and completed a thesis project that included a process map of how and what to train providers transitioning from paper charts to Phoenix Ortho EMR. Her practice administrator then sent her thesis to the CEO of Phoenix Ortho, Paul McCune. She was hired as a Project Manager at Phoenix Ortho about 6 months later, with the role of managing the entire life cycle after selling the product to customers and implementing the Phoenix Ortho EHR. Ten years ago, much of the landscape of EHR implementation looked very different. Clients were mainly concerned about MIPS incentive dollars and less concerned about implementing proper workflows that would ultimately help their providers succeed. Over time, her role changed when the MIPS incentives diminished and people were changing from one EHR to another, and they wanted a successful "all-in-one" solution that included a Practice Management system and X-ray integration. During the last several years of her time with Phoenix Ortho, Ms. Nyegaard worked to implement large practices that had 25+ providers and therapy departments. She learned quickly that she would need to change her mindset about implementation. Training went from small groups approximately once a week to 3–5 hours a day training large super-user groups that were then responsible for their own teams.

This led to another passion in technology for her: being a liaison between developers and the client. It was very important that (1) she was able to explain the issue and all the moving parts so that the developers could get it right the first time, and (2) then be able to translate what was developed and why (that became the biggest part, the why?). Ms. Nyegaard began to learn to use Microsoft SQL to determine and fix issues in the software as well as understand the coding, which she could translate into customer knowledge and better workflows. In 2021, she had reached her peak at Phoenix Ortho (after 8 years). Ms. Nyegaard was also very healthcare fatigued due to the pandemic and decided to try something new. She took a job with Cylynt as a Customer Success Manager/Interface Specialist. Cylynt provides actionable insights on how compliance and piracy are affecting your software business. During her time there, she was able to receive training on C++ programming and helped software companies integrate Cylynt code. In May 2022, Ms. Nyegaard decided her true passion was working with providers and their teams in healthcare. She reached out to Cheyenne Brinson at BrinsonAnderson Consulting after having worked on several projects together during her tenure at Phoenix Ortho. Much to her surprise, she and Amy Anderson had a place for her as their Client Software Manager at BrinsonAnderson Consulting. Ms. Nyegaard's role is to be the Super-User/Trainer for assigned clients for their EMR's and PM systems. She takes care of creating templates, preparing for software releases, creating and delivering training to customers, and being the liaison between the software companies' support and the client.

**Professional licenses and/or certifications:**
HTML, CSS, and JavaScript Certification—Nucamp Coding Bootcamp
**Other education or training relevant to your position:**
Bachelor of science degree, technical management
Master's degree, information systems management
**LinkedIn profile:**
https://www.linkedin.com/in/anna-nyegaard-mism-a9819aaa/
**Were you referred to this project by a colleague? If so, who?**
Cheyenne Brinson and Amy Anderson of BrinsonAnderson Consulting.

# HCIT Questions

### 1. What led you to pursue a career in the HCIT industry?

I just fell into it. I was pursuing a BS in Geology at Central Washington University when I became ill and had to return home from college for treatment. After about 6 months, I was offered a job at Proliance Surgeons. I was quickly introduced to the corporate IT team and became friends with most of the team. They started teaching me to troubleshoot software and hardware issues, and it became very exciting! I decided to go back and complete my bachelor of science, and I was able to transfer all my BS college credits into technical management and begin taking more focused classes in project management. My love for technology just grew with more and more education and projects I took on.

**2. What is the best professional advice given to you that you can share with aspiring women who wish to work in HCIT?**

Walk through the door of opportunity. The best advice I have received (and have given) is to, no matter how small or large the opportunity is, TAKE IT! I didn't realize at the time that this meant much more than just a job or a small project. This meant everything: relationships, networking, education, and career development. The magic lies in the hard things you didn't think were going to make you better. I have used this logic to guide most of my career path when calculating risk and reward.

**3. What is one of your proudest work-related accomplishments?**

In August 2018, my best friend and co-worker was diagnosed with Stage 4 breast cancer during our largest project. Her battle was short but courageous, and she passed away in December 2018. Gina and I worked together, traveling the country for 3+ years. We had each other's back and were literally the other's right arm. Unfortunately, when she died, there were several people at my company who believed that I would not be able to complete projects or do the important work we had been doing together any longer. One of the big projects Gina was working on was helping our CEO and Development Team overhaul our Physical Therapy and Occupational Therapy software suite. I was determined to take this on and prove everyone wrong. I put my head down and traveled the country from 2018 to 2020, talking to over 30+ PT's and OT's, determining what their needs were, and then translating this back to the development team. Once those items were developed, I then quality-controlled them, created online training materials for them, and trained customers. Because I had learned so much in the research and development stages of this project, I was also able to become the lead on sales calls by showing off the software and its capabilities. I helped sell 30+ therapy licenses all over the US. The adversity taught me that I can overcome anything with hard work, determination, and research.

**4. In preparation for a job interview, what type of questions should the candidate consider asking, and in what ways can the candidate set themselves apart?**

Questions to ask:
- What are your 5-year goals with this company/department?
  I have asked this question a few times to see if the hiring manager is going to be with the company for the next 5 years. I would often

get the feeling that they were leaving a big piece of the puzzle unsaid, and that would worry me.

- How do you plan to leverage new technologies? Does the department have adequate funding?

  Having the right tools for the job is essential. I have been in multiple organizations where the IT and CSM's were left to mitigate 4–5 systems for documenting day-to-day client tasks.

- What are the 30, 60, and 90-day goals for the position I am applying for?

  This taught me if the hiring manager had a plan, the goals for the position, and were they measurable. I like to know ahead of time what the expectations are.

5. **Would you say there are additional barriers for women to overcome in this industry? If so, what has your experience taught you about navigating these challenges?**

   The biggest barrier that I face/faced is people automatically thinking that I don't have the skills to "talk the talk" with other members of the IT industry. I often felt that I needed to walk up and introduce myself as "Hello, I'm Anna. I have a BS in Technical Management, a master's in information systems management, and have coded in C++, JavaScript, and HTLM." Although I never actually took that exact approach, I did befriend many male IT colleagues who have helped me. For example, when I would get a new project, a co-worker would ask for a private meeting with the IT group to tell them my credentials and how much of an asset having me on their team to help facilitate the project and the client needs was. The biggest thing that I have learned is that I have to always keep learning what is new in the industry to be able to "talk the talk." I have felt more judged than my male peers, but I have learned to work harder and navigate this with education and kindness.

6. **How have you navigated instances of inequality that may be experienced by women in the workplace?**

   It was all about never quitting, no matter what. One of my favorite quotes is "If you want something, go get it, period" from the book, *Pursuit of Happyness*. I had many experiences where I was looked over for promotions, pay raises, etc. for being a woman, but I just kept showing up, getting more education, creating lasting client relationships, and gaining experiences. This led to opportunities that I could have only dreamed of.

7. **When it comes to traveling on the job (such as for attending conferences or performing on-site tasks), what tips may you share when it comes to safety as well as tips that are convenient for travel?**
   - Have a packing list to make sure you always have what is needed.
   - Preview the area/town you are going to.
   - If I travel alone, I pre-plan food.
   - Have directions for airports, hotels and rental cars with you.
   - I always pack an extra dress shirt and pants in case I spill morning coffee or an extra day/event is scheduled.

8. **How do you maintain a healthy work–life balance?**

   Trying to maintain regular work hours has helped me schedule in time for workouts and other activities that I enjoy. When I am not at the computer working, I try to be working on projects outside and away from the computer. This helps my brain to stop trying to "fix" the daily problems with any project that I am working on. I have found that having an outlet away from the computer and work project tasks allows my brain to focus during working hours and not carry work into my personal life.

9. **Are there any specific books or videos you may recommend as it relates to HCIT?**
   - YouTube: https://www.youtube.com/@KevinStratvert Podcast
   - Healthcare IT Today Books
   - *Dare to Lead* by Brené Brown (Really anything Brené Brown)

10. **What is your advice for women to obtain the best opportunities and to negotiate competitive salaries in this career path?**

    My best advice would be to look for a company with your same values and work ethic. Until I found a company that was aligned with those things, I always felt out of place, like a square peg in a round hole. Negotiating a fair salary is difficult, but do your research and look at national, state, etc. wages for the job title. Knowing your worth is extremely important, and don't fear the negotiation process. More than likely, the first number is not the top number the employer is willing to pay. Last year, I made a value list when I was interviewing. I made the list before I started negotiating the salary. I asked myself the following questions:
    - What is your worth?
    - What do you bring to the table?
    - What pitfalls did you have the last time you negotiated salary?
    - What wins did you have the last time you negotiated salary?
    - Do you have a bottom-line salary number?

It is important to prepare your list and have the answers to the questions prior to negotiating. This allowed me to not bring emotion into the process.

11. **What are some recommendations for networking and continued education?**

Networking: follow influencers on LinkedIn and other platforms that are in companies or positions where you desire to work. Reach out and ask them questions about how they were able to get the role. Meet other people in HCIT who have different interests than you do. This creates a network of people that can help you with problems that you may not be able to solve on your own.

Continued Education: HCIT has many facets, anywhere from security to the latest EMR release. I make sure that I am continuing my education in each of the areas that I want to focus on for my clients, and I also watch where the industry is moving. Healthcare and IT move quickly, so you have to always be up to speed on regulations and new technologies. I am currently getting a full certification as a Software Engineer with a focus on AI. I want to help current and future clients take advantage of these new technologies.

12. **Looking back to the beginning of your career, can you share some lessons learned? Would you have done anything differently?**

1. *Negotiating Pay and Raises*: Early in my career, I rarely asked for pay raises and was excited about very minimal raises. Make sure you are constantly understanding your value and the value of your industry.

2. *Communication with Management*: Having an open line of communication with managers and leaders in the organization so they always know what your goals are and how they align with the company goals. Having these conversations leads to a better work experience.

3. *Not Listening to Everyone's Advice*: I am an introvert, and a lot of people in my career have tried to push me in directions that were for their benefit and not my own. I would be more cautious about the advice I took, from whom, and their motivations vs. mine.

4. *Not Staying Too Long*: I would have changed companies and paths more quickly to try new things. Making sure that I am valued where I go and am living/working to my potential. I think my biggest lesson was waiting until my career stagnated. Working for a company that is always forward-thinking is very important to me.

# Carol Olsen, RN, BSN, MSHI, Retired, Previous Director of Population Health EMR Integration

**Please provide a brief overview of your professional experience.**

Carol Olsen was a clinical nurse and advanced into education and ultimately management for the same hospital system. It was in this position that she assisted in the early version of an EMR in 1994, and that's when she was "bitten" by the IT bug. She became focused on people, processes, and technology for the next 27 years, always with the driving philosophy that we "have to make this better." Ms. Olsen worked for two large health systems as a clinical informaticist, leading large initiatives in designing workflows, training, and supporting/optimizing EMR systems for nurses, physicians, and other care providers. She fulfilled various roles, leveraging her vast clinical background, management skills, and executive leadership skills.

**Professional licenses and/or certifications:**

Bachelor's-prepared RN with a master's in science in health informatics

**Other education or training relevant to your position:**

I completed my graduate degree in informatics while working in the field.

**LinkedIn profile:**

https://www.linkedin.com/in/carol-olsen-rn-bsn-mshi-60bb024/

**Were you referred to this project by a colleague? If so, who?**

Kelly Raffel, MBA, Senior Manager, Coker.

# HCIT Questions

## 1. What led you to pursue a career in the HCIT industry?

As a clinical director for clinical care units, I provided leadership to our team to navigate the significant change of moving from paper to computerized documentation back in 1994. I was absolutely captivated by the impact of this technological change on the processes that nurses and physicians had adopted over time. As technology changed, becoming more robust and complex, I saw the value of clinical informatics in the role of process/workflow assessments, design, training, and adoption of the technology. Any implementation of technology, specifically EHRs, MUST consider people, processes, and the tech solution to achieve adoption/optimization success and ultimately safe, high-quality patient/person care. I knew I could make a difference because of this passion. I feel privileged to be able to work in this industry, leveraging my clinical background with knowledge and know-how to optimize the technological tools to improve care.

2. **What is the best professional advice given to you that you can share with aspiring women who wish to work in HCIT?**

There were a couple of key things that led to my success that I would advise women who are entering HCIT. First, identify a really good mentor: someone who you can learn from, who will support you and push you out of your comfort zone while providing a safety net. Second, pursue your passion. HCIT provides so many opportunities for someone just entering the field and for seasoned professionals aspiring to be in key leadership roles. There is no better time than now for women working in HCIT; don't let anything hold you back from what your passions are!

3. **What is one of your proudest work-related accomplishments?**

There are many, but what stands out for me is building a team of diverse individuals with different educational backgrounds and professional experiences to work together on the development and delivery of a complete EHR solution for a healthcare system. Understanding the goal and identifying and mitigating the risks to achieving it together in partnership with the users was simply outstanding. Everyone brought value to the team; communication was excellent, and there wasn't anything we couldn't do together! It's still so gratifying to see individuals coming together as a cohesive, effective, and valuable team!

4. **In preparation for a job interview, what type of questions should the candidate consider asking, and in what ways can the candidate set themselves apart?**

What is the culture of the company/division/team? What are the challenges they're navigating, and what are their strengths? Is it a team with a shared vision? This will help you determine your fit in the group. Be prepared to discuss your professional goals and passions, and in the course of the conversation, determine if this opportunity will support your development. You want to be and feel valued within the team. If you are a person who is a lifelong learner as I am, it would be important to know that you can continually learn in the environment, whether through formal education support or great mentoring programs. Ask what the philosophy is for professional development and what specific programs are available.

5. **Would you say there are additional barriers for women to overcome in this industry? If so, what has your experience taught you about navigating these challenges?**

My answer today is different than it would have been 25 years ago; today there are many strong, talented women leaders in HCIT that serve as role models for women, whereas 25 years ago there were far fewer. That said, I've learned that mutual respect, knowledge, confidence, excellent communication skills, and a sense of humor can overcome many barriers.

6. **How have you navigated instances of inequality that may be experienced by women in the workplace?**

N/A.

7. **When it comes to traveling on the job (such as for attending conferences or performing on-site tasks), what tips may you share when it comes to safety as well as tips that are convenient for travel?**

I did travel a fair amount in my career, most times with a colleague but occasionally solo. I always had a charged phone and a main point of contact at the conference or organization I was visiting. When making hotel reservations, make sure they know you're traveling alone; reputable hotel chains will place your room with safety in mind. When going to dinner, ask the hotel where you can go that would be safe for a single female and the best way to get to the location. Share your travel information (flight, hotel, telephone numbers, etc.) with a family member or friend so they can track you and stay in good communication. Lastly, pay attention to your surroundings; don't have ear buds in or look at your phone when on the street in public.

8. **How do you maintain a healthy work–life balance?**

I've always thought that there should be a life-work balance rather than the reverse, indicating that life has to come first. It took me 20 years, but I figured this out finally! Practically speaking, I set and revisited priorities daily (in HCIT they change often!) and put due dates and estimated effort (an hour, day, week, etc.). I would take 5–10 minutes every day to identify my priorities for the day. While there will be those critical times when you work crazy long hours, those periods are generally not the norm. Set your work hours, block time for mealtime, and stretch/walk a few times a day. It's amazing what 3–4 minutes of some deep breathing and good stretches can do for your attitude. From a human factor's perspective, whether for yourself or co-workers, remember that life comes before work.

9. **Are there any specific books or videos you may recommend as it relates to HCIT?**

The text *Health Care Information Systems* by Wager, Lee, and Glaser is a terrific manual for all things HCIT; I used it in graduate school and wish someone had suggested it for me when I was starting out in HCIT. Another book is *Engaging Physicians* by Beeson MD; it applies not only to physicians but other clinicians as well. Other books applicable to any role in or out of HCIT include *Radical Candor* by Kim Scott, and to help assess what your strengths are, check out *Strengths Finder* from Gallop/Tom Rath. The latter is a great tool for professional development and specifically helps with interviewing, team building, etc. And there are always TED Talks, which, in my opinion, are undervalued!

10. **What is your advice for women to obtain the best opportunities and to negotiate competitive salaries in this career path?**

Know what the climate is in the area you're pathing into. Certainly, consider regional influences, research organizations salary ranges by role, division, etc. Spend time researching salary disparities, changes in the past 3–5 years, and compensation packages other than salary. The best thing to advocate for yourself is arming yourself with data; this will help mitigate this risk of under/overvaluing your skill sets and value to the organization.

11. **What are some recommendations for networking and continued education?**

I had a great mentor who taught me the value of building and maintaining a network. Join LinkedIn, subscribe to groups/memberships that support your career path with like-minded professionals, attend related conferences, and establish and keep up with the contacts that result. And as for my personal bias, social media platforms are not the platform for professional growth. I've unfortunately seen promising careers abruptly stop because of the misuse of social media.

12. **Looking back to the beginning of your career, can you share some lessons learned? Would you have done anything differently?**

I used to hold back from taking my career to the next step, whether due to a lack of confidence and/or comfort with the norm: "I don't know enough yet." I wish I would have been more active in advocating for myself, stretching goals, and planning for what I wanted next. I learned that it's okay not to know everything, and mistakes are lessons learned, not failure points.

# Melissa Paczos, Clinical Informatics Supervisor

**Please provide a brief overview of your professional experience.**

Melissa Paczos, Clinical Informatics Supervisor, has over 12 years of experience in healthcare. She began working as a receptionist in the cardiology department, eventually transitioning to the learning and development team, and finally into HCIT.

**Professional licenses and/or certifications:**

Post-Baccalaureate Certificate in Teaching, Learning, and Curriculum

**Other education or training relevant to your position:**

Bachelor of arts

**LinkedIn profile:**

https://www.linkedin.com/in/melissa-paczos-09992496/

**Were you referred to this project by a colleague? If so, who?**

Christopher Torregosa, Certified Professional in Healthcare Information and Management Systems (CPHIMS), PMP, Vice President, Coker.

# HCIT Questions

1. **What led you to pursue a career in the HCIT industry?**

   Prior to working in IT, I was a part of the learning and development team at Summit Health. I was able to partner with the Clinical Informatics Support team to troubleshoot the EMR and implement new clinical workflows. The process of troubleshooting and understanding how to build all components of the EMR was like solving a puzzle, and I loved every part of it.

2. **What is the best professional advice given to you that you can share with aspiring women who wish to work in HCIT?**

   Never be afraid to ask a question, or twelve.

3. **What is one of your proudest work-related accomplishments?**

   I transitioned four high-acuity urgent-care centers to a more efficient model of documenting in the EHR while being mindful to adapt the new documentation so that the high-acuity centers would be successful.

4. **In preparation for a job interview, what type of questions should the candidate consider asking, and in what ways can the candidate set themselves apart?**

   Be sure to ask about the team structure and the types of projects that the team is currently working on.

5. **Would you say there are additional barriers for women to overcome in this industry? If so, what has your experience taught you about navigating these challenges?**

   I do think that there is potential for the IT industry to be harder for women, but I would recommend candidates think outside the box and ask as many questions as needed. Don't sit quietly, and always share thoughts and ideas.

6. **How have you navigated instances of inequality that may be experienced by women in the workplace?**

   N/A.

7. **When it comes to traveling on the job (such as for attending conferences or performing on-site tasks), what tips may you share when it comes to safety as well as tips that are convenient for travel?**

   Always be aware of your surroundings and park in a well-lit area. When choosing a hotel, look at the surrounding community, not just the hotel reviews.

8. **How do you maintain a healthy work–life balance?**

   I make sure to use my PTO! I make family time a priority, and I take time for myself—to exercise and to listen to an audiobook.

9. **Are there any specific books or videos you may recommend as it relates to HCIT?**

   I found *The Emerging Healthcare Leader* by Natalie Lamberton and Laurie Baedke helpful.

10. **What is your advice for women to obtain the best opportunities and to negotiate competitive salaries in this career path?**

    I recommend doing your research, getting comparisons from online sources, and most importantly, knowing your worth.

11. **What are some recommendations for networking and continued education?**

    Do your best to attend onsite events and foster relationships with co-workers as well as outside representatives and colleagues.

12. **Looking back to the beginning of your career, can you share some lessons learned? Would you have done anything differently?**

    I wish I had transitioned into the IT world sooner. I dreamed about being a teacher, only to discover that it wasn't for me.

# Dipti Patel-Misra, PhD, MBA, Professional Certified Coach, Principal Consultant

**Please provide a brief overview of your professional experience.**

Dipti has over 20 years of experience working across the healthcare spectrum. She has significant experience in healthcare leadership, specifically in driving technology, data, and analytics vision. She was named as a top 50 data and analytics professional in North America by Corinium in 2018 and to Becker's Hospital Review's 2017 Women to Know in MedTech. In her career, Dipti has worked with payors, providers, pharma, and software vendors. Dipti holds a PhD in Chemistry from Johns Hopkins University and an MBA from Kenan-Flagler, UNC Chapel Hill.

**Professional licenses and/or certifications:**

Professional Certified Coach

**Other education or training relevant to your position:**

PhD, MBA

**LinkedIn profile:**

https://www.linkedin.com/in/diptipatelmisra

**Were you referred to this project by a colleague? If so, who?**

Joshua Tamayo-Sarver, MD, PhD, FACEP.

# HCIT Questions

1. **What led you to pursue a career in the HCIT industry?**

   I am very passionate about making a meaningful impact in healthcare and enjoy the use of technology and data to drive improved outcomes, efficiency, and patient and physician satisfaction.

2. **What is the best professional advice given to you that you can share with aspiring women who wish to work in HCIT?**

   Start by answering the questions: How will this drive impactful change? What would motivate the end user to adapt to the new technology/product? How does this simplify healthcare or drive meaningful change?

3. **What is one of your proudest work-related accomplishments?**

   Building products and solutions that have made a significant impact.

4. **In preparation for a job interview, what type of questions should the candidate consider asking, and in what ways can the candidate set themselves apart?**

   It is critical to ask about the culture and team, how success is measured, and what the overall expectations of the role will be in the organization.

5. **Would you say there are additional barriers for women to overcome in this industry? If so, what has your experience taught you about navigating these challenges?**

   There are many barriers for women in this industry. The best way to overcome this is to have a strong network, work with a mentor, be genuine, be a learner, and not let the barriers prevent you from seeking a fulfilling path.

6. **How have you navigated instances of inequality that may be experienced by women in the workplace?**

   Yes.

7. **When it comes to traveling on the job (such as for attending conferences or performing on-site tasks), what tips may you share when it comes to safety as well as tips that are convenient for travel?**

   Try to book a hotel close to or where the conference is being held. It allows for good networking opportunities and is potentially safer. Build a strong network and find folks who are connectors.

8. **How do you maintain a healthy work–life balance?**

   I love what I do, but my family knows that they come first. Enjoying my work makes it easy for me to balance (it feels less like work).

9. **Are there any specific books or videos you may recommend as it relates to HCIT?**

   [No response provided].

10. **What is your advice for women to obtain the best opportunities and to negotiate competitive salaries in this career path?**

    Educate yourself on the market, speak with colleagues, and be objective.

11. **What are some recommendations for networking and continued education?**

    [No response provided].

12. **Looking back to the beginning of your career, can you share some lessons learned? Would you have done anything differently?**

    [No response provided].

# Katie Pellish, Venture Manager, Northeast Georgia Health Ventures

**Please provide a brief overview of your professional experience.**

Before joining Northeast Georgia Health Ventures (part of the Northeast Georgia Health System, NGHS) in June 2023, Ms. Pellish was the director of operations in the merchant services industry. In that role, she was a jack of all trades, managing the sales, operations, and marketing teams. Ms. Pellish joined the company when it was just 2 months old as the second employee, and she helped grow it for over 7 years, which provided her with experience in the startup space. She also formed strategic partnerships for the company, which was useful experience for her current job as venture manager at NGHV. Now, she helps accelerate the piloting process of getting health-tech startup companies into the health system. She enjoys helping bring innovative technologies into the healthcare system.

**Professional licenses and/or certifications:**
N/A.

**Other education or training relevant to your position:**
N/A.

**LinkedIn profile:**
https://www.linkedin.com/in/katie-pellish-89366759

**Were you referred to this project by a colleague? If so, who?**
Johanna Dutton, PhD, Venture Director, Cone Health Ventures.

# HCIT Questions

1. **What led you to pursue a career in the HCIT industry?**

   Whether it's patient experience and outcomes, staff engagement, or improving the technology that is available, there is always a way to improve efficiency, and I am looking forward to how I can help facilitate these improvements at the NGHS.

2. **What is the best professional advice given to you that you can share with aspiring women who wish to work in HCIT?**

   "There's room for everyone at the table" is probably the best advice given to me. That quote has allowed me to change my perspective on what's possible in this industry for women. So many opportunities, and opportunities to work with other women, exist in all aspects of HCIT.

3. **What is one of your proudest work-related accomplishments?**

I think the proudest accomplishment has yet to come in this field since I began in June, but I can say that every step, every partnership secured, has been its own accomplishment. These moments take time to achieve, which makes the end result all the more rewarding.

4. **In preparation for a job interview, what type of questions should the candidate consider asking, and in what ways can the candidate set themselves apart?**

Ask what the main pain points are in the system that they are working with. This question shows you are interested in fixing problems and finding solutions. This also gives you good insight into the types of companies you would be working with and what you are up against in terms of existing issues.

5. **Would you say there are additional barriers for women to overcome in this industry? If so, what has your experience taught you about navigating these challenges?**

HCIT is definitely a male-dominated industry. I think it's important to seek out different networking opportunities with other women in the field so you can build new connections and partnerships.

6. **How have you navigated instances of inequality that may be experienced by women in the workplace?**

N/A.

7. **When it comes to traveling on the job (such as for attending conferences or performing on-site tasks), what tips may you share when it comes to safety as well as tips that are convenient for travel?**

N/A.

8. **How do you maintain a healthy work–life balance?**

I make sure that I stick to a schedule in the morning: I go to the gym and then get myself ready for the day. Obviously, there will be days where there are obligations after normal working hours, but I try to still make time for family and friends throughout those busy weeks.

9. **Are there any specific books or videos you may recommend as it relates to HCIT?**

N/A.

10. **What is your advice for women to obtain the best opportunities and to negotiate competitive salaries in this career path?**

Research the average salary and benefits for the position you are looking for. Know your worth and be confident when negotiating. Hiring managers almost always expect there to be some sort of negotiation, but you also need to have the facts to back up why you are looking for a specific salary. Don't be afraid to reference your past experiences, even if they are in another industry entirely; your skill set is valuable and transferable, and you can speak to what you have accomplished (especially your past experience, even if it was not in this specific field).

11. **What are some recommendations for networking and continued education?**

See if there is a local Healthcare Information and Management Systems Society chapter in your area, join LinkedIn networking groups, and keep an eye out for any in-person networking events near you. There are also so many free resources, as well as online courses, to learn about the industry or upskill.

12. **Looking back to the beginning of your career, can you share some lessons learned? Would you have done anything differently?**

Oh, the power of patience! There are so many moving parts in the healthcare system. Bringing in new technology is not like flipping a switch. Be patient with the process, set up meetings with who you need to, and don't take it personally if you get a "no." The process is a learning experience, and there are always plenty of other deals out there!

# Lygeia Ricciardi, Founder and CEO, AdaRose, Inc.

**Please provide a brief overview of your professional experience.**

Lygeia Ricciardi is the Founder and CEO of AdaRose, Inc., a startup that helps busy people fit realistic moments of wellness into their lives. AdaRose, Inc. works with companies that prioritize the wellbeing of their employees, offering them wellness experiences that include a combination of physical products mailed to home, guidance from experts, and digital engagement. She has been named among the Top 30 Voices Transforming Wellness for 2023, the Most Influential Women in Health IT, and the 50 Most Influential Voices in Healthcare. While outward recognition is an honor, it is secondary to the satisfaction of making a difference in something one is passionate about.

Before founding AdaRose, Ms. Ricciardi spent more than 20 years at the vanguard of the patient engagement movement in digital health in both the public and private sectors. In the federal government, she established and led the Office of Consumer eHealth at the Office of the National Coordinator for Health IT (ONC) within the US Department of Health and Human Services. Previously, she helped to develop the first telehealth policies at the Federal Communications Commission (FCC). In the private sector, Ms. Ricciardi served as the Chief Transformation Officer at Carium, a virtual health company. She was also a Director of the Health Program at the Markle Foundation and ran a consulting practice focused on consumer e-health.

Through AdaRose, Ms. Ricciardi applies what she has learned about consumer engagement in health to holistic wellness. She is excited about how technology can be utilized to help people "own their health." She is a frequent speaker and has appeared in *The Wall Street Journal, Forbes*, and Consumer Reports. Ms. Ricciardi has a master's in technology in education from Harvard with extensive study at the MIT Media Lab, and a BA from Wellesley College. She lives in Washington, DC, with her husband, two daughters, and two Siamese cats.

**Professional licenses and/or certifications:**
Bachelor of arts in history
Italian Language and an EdM in Technology in Learning

**Other education or training relevant to your position:**
I've completed several executive education and online learning programs, including a program on corporate governance through Kellogg Executive Education and some design and marketing courses via IDEO and Wharton (through Coursera). In addition, last year, my business partner at AdaRose and I graduated from the Founder Institute startup accelerator. I believe learning is a life-long journey!

**LinkedIn profile:**
https://www.linkedin.com/in/lygeiaricciardi/

**Were you referred to this project by a colleague? If so, who?**
Lindsay Rowlands, MHA, Project Coordinator, Coker.

# HCIT Questions

### 1. What led you to pursue a career in the HCIT industry?

My first job out of college was writing case studies for HBS. The professor I worked for, Dr. Richard Tedlow, is a business historian. As I learned about business history through a wide lens, I was inspired by the potential power of information technology to shape every aspect of our society. While at HBS, I wrote some case studies on the FCC, which was at the time (in the 1990s) trying to figure out whether and how to regulate the internet and how related technologies might impact health and education. At the FCC, I worked on those issues and have been focused on shaping the impact of technology on people ever since. I believe passionately in the power of technology to empower people and give them agency if it is applied well.

2. **What is the best professional advice given to you that you can share with aspiring women who wish to work in HCIT?**

Don't let the perfect be the enemy of the good. Push forward, even if you're not sure exactly what you're doing. As I progress through my career, it becomes increasingly evident that everyone faces uncertainty. So, by all means, do your due diligence and make informed decisions, but don't let doubt slow you down too much—the world needs your unique skills and contributions! On a related note, don't assume the job landscape of today will look like the landscape 10 or 15 years from now. Be flexible, curious, and open to learning.

3. **What is one of your proudest work-related accomplishments?**

I am especially proud of being part of the movement in support of patient and consumer empowerment. In part because of the work I did with my colleagues in the public and private sectors, the majority of Americans now have electronic access to their own medical information. In addition, it is common for people to use health data from a variety of apps, tools, and trackers to manage and inform their daily health-related choices.

4. **In preparation for a job interview, what type of questions should the candidate consider asking, and in what ways can the candidate set themselves apart?**

It's important to understand the culture of the place you'll be working in, in addition to the substance of the work you'll be doing. Are there opportunities to learn and grow? Is the management supportive of new ideas and initiatives? Would you want to be stuck in an airport with the people on your team, and do they share your values?

You can set yourself apart by doing background research on the place and the people in the interview. Ask informed questions that actually interest you, not just basic ones that could be answered through a Google search. Also, follow up with personal thank-you notes. It's important that you recognize that the people interviewing you have taken their precious time to meet with you and that, in many cases, they are just as concerned as you are about finding a great fit.

5. **Would you say there are additional barriers for women to over-come in this industry? If so, what has your experience taught you about navigating these challenges?**

Women face barriers to professional success across most industries; it's hard to say which may be particular to health and healthcare technology. For your own benefit and that of the team, try to envision other women as partners and potential allies, not as adversaries fighting over limited slots —grow the pie. Amplify the contributions of other women and celebrate their successes. Seek mentors who can teach you and will also go to bat for you. Try to create win–win situations wherever possible, but at the same time, if you feel you are being treated unfairly, speak up about it. Finally, as you become more senior, take junior women under your wing and help them succeed.

6. **How have you navigated instances of inequality that may be experienced by women in the workplace?**

Sure. Part of the problem is that it can be hard to spot or define. For example, if you float an idea that people don't consider seriously only to hear it restated by a senior male colleague, at which point everyone responds positively, it can be frustrating, even though no one else may notice. I just get out there and try again. Often, people don't even realize that they have biases.

7. **When it comes to traveling on the job (such as for attending conferences or performing on-site tasks), what tips may you share when it comes to safety as well as tips that are convenient for travel?**

I think most women are aware that we have to consider safety differently from the way many men do. So, for example, there are times when I've exercised by running up and down the stairwell of a hotel because I didn't feel safe jogging in the open streets in some neighborhoods.

8. **How do you maintain a healthy work–life balance?**

It's a life-long challenge. It's part of why I started the company AdaRose: to make wellness easier for busy people, including career-oriented women who also bear heavy family responsibilities.

9. **Are there any specific books or videos you may recommend as it relates to HCIT?**

[No answer provided].

10. **What is your advice for women to obtain the best opportunities and to negotiate competitive salaries in this career path?**

Try to seek as much information as possible so you can make a concrete case for why you should have a particular salary or other opportunity.

11. **What are some recommendations for networking and continued education?**

Yes! Do it. Use social media as well as in-person opportunities to connect with others.

12. **Looking back to the beginning of your career, can you share some lessons learned? Would you have done anything differently?**

Stay curious. Follow ideas and people you are excited about. If something isn't working and you've made a serious and unsuccessful attempt to fix it, move along. Keep learning and growing, and don't be afraid to color outside the lines!

# Caitlin ("Cait") Riccobono, Privacy Counsel, CSS

**Please provide a brief overview of your professional experience.**

After graduating from college, Caitlin ("Cait") Riccobono worked as a skilled nursing and long-term care social worker at a large post-acute company that had more IT infrastructure than most post-acute settings. After several years, she transitioned to a smaller organization where actual charts were utilized that needed to be lugged around the building. One of the things she most enjoyed at the job was understanding and navigating the compliance aspects of the industry, while the most frustrating aspect was the way in which technology was behind and how lacking communication was around transitions of care.

Cait realized that she desired to work with compliance and policy in the healthcare industry and thus applied to law school. She graduated from the University of Richmond School of Law, passed the Virginia Bar Exam, and has been working as a healthcare attorney ever since.

She began doing contract work for a health law firm where she law clerked during school, but no full-time position was available. As a result, Cait began to network by going to local industry events. To further her networking efforts (and with a name that always required spelling out), she decided to order "business" cards with her contact information. She then had the idea of coming up with a cool domain name instead of a generic e-mail address. Once she had a domain, she then thought it would be fun to see whether she could remember anything from the HTML class she had taken 10 years earlier to custom-build a website. It was the "If You Give a Mouse a Cookie" effect. By late 2016, Cait had managed to stand up her own virtual,

HIPAA-compliant law firm with an operating cost of under $100 per month (including the home internet her partner and she were paying for).

After doing this for some time, Cait accepted an employment offer with a two-attorney virtual health law firm. Her first big health IT/health information security project was managing the Qualified Entity Certification Program application and completing the security review for one of the firm's clients. She also worked extensively with a rapidly growing telehealth group.

In 2018, she then had the opportunity to work on a project with Steve Gravely, who had recently started his own digital health law firm. This project was her introduction to Health Information Exchanges (HIEs).

Over the next year, the firm she was with started changing, and she found herself handling corporate/business work for healthcare companies and defending clinicians in complaints before the licensing boards. Cait decided to put in her notice and do some contract work while figuring out whether or not to completely transition into IT. Then, her amazing professional development counselor from Richmond Law reached out to her about a job posting she had seen. Steve Gravely was hiring. They had lunch, and she learned that there was an entire niche dedicated to health IT law and policy. Steve was looking to bring someone on in anticipation of work ramping up for something she had never heard of Trusted Exchange Framework and Common Agreement (TEFCA).

Cait joined Steve's firm in late 2019, serving as legal counsel to the Recognized Coordinating Entity, the Sequoia Project, and the TEFCA. The efforts toward developing and drafting the Common Agreement gave her the opportunity to work closely with ONC and to be involved in the types of policy discussions she had thought about as a post-acute care social worker. As amazing as that experience was, what she most enjoyed was working with health information exchanges and networks, including serving as legal counsel to the eHealth Exchange and Carequality, at the national level and to VHI, which operates her home-state HIE.

The first time Cait was on a call with Nichole Sweeney, General Counsel for CRISP and CSS, she had to fight the urge to blurt out, "Will you please be my friend?" Instead, she reached out later via e-mail and suggested grabbing lunch sometime. Later, when Nichole informed her about a privacy position with CSS, she had to throw her hat in the ring.

Cait joined CSS as Privacy Counsel in January 2023, and her role allows her to work on many of the facets she loves about health IT. She interacts with patients to help them understand how their data are used and exchanged; she works with industry-leading state health information exchanges and health data utilities while also working collaboratively on matters involving and affecting national connectivity and exchange, and she has the privilege of working with some of the most extraordinary engineers, developers, and other "technical folks" in the industry.

**Professional licenses and/or certifications:**

Attorney and Counselor at Law, Virginia State Bar

Health Care Information Security and Privacy Practitioner, (ISC)2

**Other education or training relevant to your position:**

N/A.

**LinkedIn profile:**

www.linkedin.com/in/cait-riccobono

**Were you referred to this project by a colleague? If so, who?**

N/A.

# HCIT Questions

### 1. What led you to pursue a career in the HCIT industry?

Thanks to my upbringing, I have always had an interest in both healthcare and technology. After graduating from college, I got a job as a skilled nursing and long-term care social worker. I started out with a large post-acute company that had more IT infrastructure than most post-acute settings (which was still not saying a lot). After several years, I transitioned to a much smaller company where we did all of our charting on actual charts that we lugged around the building. I found that one of the things I enjoyed most about my job was understanding and navigating the compliance aspects. One of the most frustrating things was how behind the technology was and how terrible the communication was around transitions of care.

That experience led me to realize that I really wanted to do something in healthcare compliance and policy. It also lit the spark for me to hone my focus on health information exchange and interoperability.

### 2. What is the best professional advice given to you that you can share with aspiring women who wish to work in HCIT?

There is not just one seat at the table. More importantly, there is not just one table.

### 3. What is one of your proudest work-related accomplishments?

There was one minor subsection in the Common Agreement that I felt was important from a procedural standpoint, and I went to the mattresses over why it mattered. In the end, that provision survived without any edits. I am sure this will sound trivial and vain, but the Common Agreement went through so much editing and revision, and that one subsection felt like it was completely mine.

I don't know if you can really call it an "accomplishment," but seeing that subsection in the Federal Register when the final version of the Common Agreement was finally published was definitely one of my proudest work-related moments.

4. **In preparation for a job interview, what type of questions should the candidate consider asking, and in what ways can the candidate set themselves apart?**

Classic lawyer answer: It depends. What do you want to know? If you have a question, ask it. Be tactful about it, but ask for it.

Along those same lines, set yourself apart by being authentic. I cannot count how many times I rejected advice to take out my nose ring, make sure my tattoos would not show when I went to shake someone's hand, and get rid of the purple in my hair for job interviews. It is entirely probable that it cost me the high-paying job at that big, fancy firm I interviewed with when I was fresh out of law school. If so, thank goodness. Being turned down for a job is never a relief in the moment, but finding a job where you can be authentic will be a relief every single day.

5. **Would you say there are additional barriers for women to overcome in this industry? If so, what has your experience taught you about navigating these challenges?**

I would say that there are additional barriers for women to overcome in all industries. However, I do think IT (and law) can be particularly challenging for women. I often joke after a conversation that I'm not sure if it was "the attorney thing or the woman thing." In other words, did the person assume I do not understand technology because I am an attorney or because I am a woman? Because one of those assumptions is not entirely unfair.

I think this is another area in which authenticity plays a key role. If I do not know something, I say that. If I am uncertain, I acknowledge that. I will ask questions or say that I need to do some research. When you are open and honest about what you do not know, I think it makes it harder for people to discount your knowledge and expertise when you speak authoritatively about something you do know.

Another really important approach to navigating these challenges is for women to elevate and support each other as professionals, as opposed to treating more limited opportunities for women as a cause for competition. Be helpful. Share what you know. Genuinely want others to succeed. The barriers are for those in this industry who identify as women to overcome, not for one particular woman to overcome. There are women professionals who mentor and nurture others, and there are those who eat their young. There are some who climb the ladder to give others a hand from the top, and there are those who try to kick the ladder out from under them. To overcome barriers for women in this industry, all those who identify as women professionals in this industry need to be the mentors and the elevators.

Lastly, I think it is important that we also avoid the mentality that we are in direct competition with the men in this industry. A conscientious male colleague is a far better ally than a young-eating, ladder-kicking female colleague.

6. **How have you navigated instances of inequality that may be experienced by women in the workplace?**

I think it can be easy to misinterpret instances of inequity as personal ineptitude, or to at least have that concern in the back of your mind. I would not say that I have "navigated" that, as much as I have come to realize that certain "missed opportunities" had nothing to do with me not being good enough or smart enough. Acknowledge the good work of others around you. That should not apply only between female colleagues, but I think it can be especially important in those circumstances.

7. **When it comes to traveling on the job (such as for attending conferences or performing on-site tasks), what tips may you share when it comes to safety as well as tips that are convenient for travel?**

There are probably not any safety tips I can share for work travel that are not already familiar to most women. The key is to not let yourself get so wrapped up in the atmosphere or the feeling of needing to "keep up" that you fail to heed those safety precautions.

8. **How do you maintain a healthy work–life balance?**

It requires a conscious AND ONGOING effort to maintain a healthy work–life balance. Truthfully, I have a terrible habit of saying, "After this project, I will get back to a more normal schedule," when the reality is that there will always be another project to take its place. Therefore, I find it helpful to be very intentional with respect to my schedule. I make sure to block off recurring times on my calendar for focused work. If someone wants to schedule a meeting with me with less than 24 hours' notice, I generally try to make sure that they have to reach out to me directly versus being able to simply add the meeting to my calendar. In health IT, there **will** be situations that arise that are legitimately urgent and/or that warrant exceptions/flexibility. Managing my schedule *absent* such circumstances helps me ensure that I have the bandwidth to deal with them when they *do* occur.

9. **Are there any specific books or videos you may recommend as it relates to HCIT?**

   No. When you find the time, (1) catch up or keep up on world events and (2) read something that has nothing to do with work. The first will naturally benefit your role in HCIT, and the latter will benefit your wellbeing and well-roundedness.

10. **What is your advice for women to obtain the best opportunities and to negotiate competitive salaries in this career path?**

   Push yourself to have uncomfortable or difficult conversations about money. In a niche industry, it can be difficult to find accurate, reliable salary information online. Plus, I was raised in a culture of "you don't talk about money," especially as a woman. It took a while for me to gain the nerve, but I finally started asking trusted colleagues—male- and female-identifying—if they would be comfortable telling me what their compensation is, and I would offer to take the lead by sharing mine. Not one person seemed the least bit offended by the request, and I gained information that I could literally put a price tag on.

   In terms of obtaining the best opportunities, the best advice I can give is to be someone people want to work with. I do not mean that you should be placating. You can and should challenge others while still being supportive of them. Be competent and hardworking, but also be open-minded and collaborative.

11. **What are some recommendations for networking and continued education?**

   Find a form of networking that fits your personality and comfort level. I have significant social anxiety, and trying to participate in "typical" networking activities was an absolute nightmare. For me, a silver lining of the COVID pandemic was that opportunities to network became virtual. I participated in the HIMSS, surrounded only by two snoring beagles. I worked with leaders at ONC from the comfort of my home office. I helped lead workgroups, presented during webinars, and responded to questions from industry leaders—all while mercifully unable to see a crowd of faces staring at me. For informal social networking, I took to social media. I connected with colleagues all over the country via different social media platforms. I still have social anxiety (and always will), but now I can actually look forward to the occasional in-person meeting or event as an opportunity to connect with the people I have gotten to know from a comfortable distance.

12. **Looking back to the beginning of your career, can you share some lessons learned? Would you have done anything differently?**

There is so much I could have—and *perhaps* should have—done differently, but then I would not have learned any lessons worth sharing. I am also extremely grateful for my strange little journey.

I have talked about authenticity, in one respect or another, in response to a lot of these questions. What I have left out is the importance of also being willing to occasionally do something that the best version of yourself would do. I am extraordinarily introverted, and it never feels authentic for me to initiate social interactions. However, the times that I have challenged myself to reach out to other women professionals have predominantly resulted in many of the most professionally and personally rewarding relationships in my life. So, be authentic, but try being authentically bolder every once in a while.

# Dina Ross, Attorney, Dina B. Ross Law Offices

**Please provide a brief overview of your professional experience.**

Dina Ross holds an MBA from the University of Chicago and a JD from Loyola University. She has been a health technology lawyer for almost 30 years. Her national practice is focused on advising and assisting clients in meeting their technology and data legal needs and general commercial transactions in a variety of industries, with an emphasis on startup and mid-cycle companies. Dina focus on helping emerging companies and established multi-national entities solve real problems, in real time, in their commercial and business operations. She prides herself on working creatively, efficiently and within budget to help companies of all sizes manage legal expenses in balance with legal risks.

The practice includes drafting and negotiating software license and services agreements for EHRs, revenue cycle, claims management, and all other functionalities from all major HIT vendors. Dina is also experienced in related regulatory matters such as HIPAA and BAAs, and in the technology issues that arise during mergers, acquisitions, divestitures and other corporate restructurings. She will meet clients wherever they are in their life cycle, by helping clients negotiate license and services agreements, transition services, subscription, cloud computing, financial, customer care and other technology and commercial agreements, including alpha/beta agreements, particularly in relation to artificial intelligence and emerging technologies.

**Professional licenses and/or certifications:**
MBA, JD

**Other education or training relevant to your position:**
MBA

**LinkedIn profile:**
[Optional, not provided].

**Were you referred to this project by a colleague? If so, who?**
Kelly Raffel, MBA, Senior Manager, Coker.

# HCIT Questions

**1. What led you to pursue a career in the HCIT industry?**
   I started doing technology legal work in the mid-90s (before Google!). At the time, healthcare was a major consumer of technology.

**2. What is the best professional advice given to you that you can share with aspiring women who wish to work in HCIT?**
   Ask for what you want. Ask over and over again until you get it.

**3. What is one of your proudest work-related accomplishments?**
   Quitting a perfectly good job (as a partner at a law firm) after 13 years and becoming a solo practitioner. I opened a business checking account with $20 and hoped for the best. That was 17 years ago and I'm still going strong.

**4. In preparation for a job interview, what type of questions should the candidate consider asking, and in what ways can the candidate set themselves apart?**
   My favorite question to ask is, "What DON'T you like about this job?" I once asked this of a female partner at a law firm and her answer was, after she thought about it for a bit, "They don't treat women here very well."

5. **Would you say there are additional barriers for women to overcome in this industry? If so, what has your experience taught you about navigating these challenges?**

It's very hard to balance work and motherhood—and no one asks men to do it. You have to be willing to set and enforce boundaries at home and at work. Put home first.

6. **How have you navigated instances of inequality that may be experienced by women in the workplace?**

I changed jobs. My first law firm was toxic for women.

7. **When it comes to traveling on the job (such as for attending conferences or performing on-site tasks), what tips may you share when it comes to safety as well as tips that are convenient for travel?**

I never really worried about safety, but I definitely do not drink when out with co-workers or clients (or maybe nurse a glass of wine all night). When I traveled a lot (pre-COVID), I always had a second, stocked bag with duplicates of all toiletries, so I never had to think about what to pack.

8. **How do you maintain a healthy work–life balance?**

I put family first. I raised two kids as a single parent, and when I realized that work was getting in the way of that, I quit my job (as a partner at a law firm) and became a solo practitioner. I created the work–life balance I needed, rather than trying to retrofit my law firm.

9. **Are there any specific books or videos you may recommend as it relates to HCIT?**

[No response provided].

10. **What is your advice for women to obtain the best opportunities and to negotiate competitive salaries in this career path?**

Know your worth, above all. And don't settle for less; you have to be willing to walk.

11. **What are some recommendations for networking and continued education?**

HIMSS (of course!), alumni groups and trade associations.

12. **Looking back to the beginning of your career, can you share some lessons learned? Would you have done anything differently?**

I would have left a toxic work environment even sooner than I did. I would have asked for more money EVERY SINGLE TIME, regardless of how much was initially offered.

# Abby Sears, CEO, OCHIN

**Please provide a brief overview of your professional experience.**

Abby Sears is the President and CEO of OCHIN, a nonprofit leader in equitable healthcare innovation and a trusted partner to a rapidly growing national provider network. As a business leader and community advocate, Abby has been with OCHIN since its inception, stewarding its growth from a $7M organization focused on hosting electronic health records for 20 Oregon health centers to a $150M national consultancy. Today, OCHIN supports more than 25,000 providers at over 2,000 care delivery sites across 40 states with the clinical insights, practice-based research, and tailored technologies needed to help more than 5.4 million systemically underserved patients access the quality and comprehensive healthcare they deserve. Under Abby's leadership, OCHIN now employs a diverse virtual workforce of more than 1,000 technologists, clinicians, data scientists, and innovators, two-thirds of whom are women—more than twice the tech industry average.

A prominent speaker and HIT advisor with over 20 years of healthcare expertise, Abby is a member of many regional and national boards. In 2018, Abby was recognized by the Portland Business Journal as a Top 25 Women of Influence award winner. She holds an MBA and MHA, both from the University of Minnesota.

**Professional licenses and/or certifications:**

N/A.

**Other education or training relevant to your position:**

Master of business administration, University of Minnesota

**LinkedIn profile:**

https://www.linkedin.com/in/abby-sears-9ab9889/

**Were you referred to this project by a colleague? If so, who?**

N/A.

# HCIT Questions

**1. What led you to pursue a career in the HCIT industry?**

I wanted to take care of the most vulnerable population in our nation. I used IT because I felt like it lacked cohesion. I did not go to school for IT or federally qualified health centers (FQHCs). But this is my passion: using IT to drive better care for patients.

**2. What is the best professional advice given to you that you can share with aspiring women who wish to work in HCIT?**

You have to follow your passion because you will be able to weather the highs and lows. There will be times that are not optimal. Obstacles will be encountered by those who give you reasons why what you're doing won't work, but I consider the risks and plan to mitigate them. I don't personalize or internalize those comments. It strengthens my strategy because I am able to poke holes in the plans and correct them.

**3. What is one of your proudest work-related accomplishments?**

A Critical Access Hospital go-live which took 15 years to get there. Growing and maintaining the company for so long. It's been challenging and rewarding at the same time.

**4. In preparation for a job interview, what type of questions should the candidate consider asking, and in what ways can the candidate set themselves apart?**

Enter a job interview as a discussion, not an interview. You need to make sure you are the right fit for that company, and vice versa. As an applicant, you want to discern if the values of the company align with yours.

**5. Would you say there are additional barriers for women to overcome in this industry? If so, what has your experience taught you about navigating these challenges?**

There is a business model approach to work and the workforce. The right person and the right attributes are what matter. What does not matter is whether they do the work at 6 a.m. or 8 p.m. at night; what matters is that the work gets done well and the client's needs are met. For example, that working mom who is wrapping up her day after her kids are in bed—that's where we need to be flexible.

The definition of 'how' work gets done needs to change. Success looks different today; it's about the outputs and the accomplishments, not how they are getting it done. Today, women are being left behind. I am very proud to say that here at OCHIN, we have 72% female employees.

In IT specifically, we need to be elbow-to-elbow with the clients. We need to understand what they are going through day-to-day providing care. Hardware technology, cloud engineers—these types of roles are highly male dominated, and we need to encourage more females into these roles. Women do not see themselves in these roles and I would love to be a part of seeing this change.

6. **How have you navigated instances of inequality that may be experienced by women in the workplace?**

   N/A.

7. **When it comes to traveling on the job (such as for attending conferences or performing on-site tasks), what tips may you share when it comes to safety as well as tips that are convenient for travel?**

   N/A.

8. **How do you maintain a healthy work–life balance?**

   I love what I do. I love growing and mentoring people and seeing them succeed. I am creative in how I work, and I may take a few days off but be available to keep a project going. You need time off; you have to have joy; otherwise, you lose inspiration and have a narrow mindset. Finally, I love being onsite with our members and providers because they open my eyes to a lot of new ideas.

9. **Are there any specific books or videos you may recommend as it relates to HCIT?**

   In general, I encourage anyone in this industry to keep up with the recent news, articles and latest happenings. It's important to know what's going on around you.

10. **What is your advice for women to obtain the best opportunities and to negotiate competitive salaries in this career path?**

    Know your own worth.

11. **What are some recommendations for networking and continued education?**

    In HCIT, you need to be well-rounded. In technology, you need to understand the following: the industry and what is going on, and the financial side.

12. **Looking back to the beginning of your career, can you share some lessons learned? Would you have done anything differently?**

    Know what you do, specifically what you do well and have the humility to stay within that. This will serve as a method for success in avoiding risks. My final words of advice/wisdom as a woman are to know your worth and don't feel like you need to make excuses for what you have going on, because it's a lot!

# Susan M. Smith, RN, MSN, CPHIMS, Director Clinical and IT Applications

**Please provide a brief overview of your professional experience.**

Susan Smith, RN, MSN, CPHIMS, is the Director of Clinical and IT Applications at Amsurg. She oversees and manages a team that serves as the IT Support Owner of 12–20 applications utilized by corporate offices and/ or ambulatory surgery centers. She also provides IT support to end users in collaboration with business owners and subject matter experts to multiple clinical and IT applications. Her prior professional experience includes the role of Senior Director of Case Management Clinical Informatics at LifePoint Health, in addition to having served as their Director of Compliance Education and Manager of Clinical Revenue Integrity, Revenue Cycle throughout her 13 years of employment with this healthcare provider network.

**Professional licenses and/or certifications:**

RN

CPHIMS

**Other education or training relevant to your position:**

MSN Clinical Informatics, Middle Tennessee State University

Safety, Quality, Informatics and Leadership Post-Graduate Certificate, Harvard Medical School

HIMSS HIT Accelerator Certificate Program

Immediate Past President 2021–2022 | TN ANIA

Leadership Maury | Class of 2019

**LinkedIn profile:**

https://www.linkedin.com/in/susan-smith-msn-cphims-27497533/

**Were you referred to this project by a colleague? If so, who?**

N/A.

# HCIT Questions

**1. What led you to pursue a career in the HCIT industry?**

The ER I worked in as a nurse documented on paper when I started working there. After a couple of years, the ER became a pilot for an electronic documentation system. I signed up to become a Super User and Trainer. I was always looking for opportunities to learn new things. This was the best decision I have ever made. I fell in love with what I learned and knew I could use that knowledge to help clinicians and providers streamline their daily work and make patient care better. That one decision changed my graduate studies from APRN to Clinical Informatics.

2. **What is the best professional advice given to you that you can share with aspiring women who wish to work in HCIT?**

   The best advice given to me is to never stop learning and to not regret anything!

3. **What is one of your proudest work-related accomplishments?**

   Leading the implementation of the first Enterprise documentation system in a large healthcare company.

4. **In preparation for a job interview, what type of questions should the candidate consider asking, and in what ways can the candidate set themselves apart?**

   Ask what career development opportunities the company offers. Know what you want and ask for it. You may not receive the answer you want, but the prospective employer will know that you have goals and want to work somewhere that will help you move closer to achieving those goals. Additionally, spend the time required to truly understand what type of leader you are and be that leader in everything you do.

5. **Would you say there are additional barriers for women to overcome in this industry? If so, what has your experience taught you about navigating these challenges?**

   There are no barriers that cannot be brought down.

6. **How have you navigated instances of inequality that may be experienced by women in the workplace?**

   I have not experienced inequality.

7. **When it comes to traveling on the job (such as for attending conferences or performing on-site tasks), what tips may you share when it comes to safety as well as tips that are convenient for travel?**

   N/A.

8. **How do you maintain a healthy work–life balance?**

   I don't work extra hours on something that can wait until tomorrow. It's important to keep the phone out of sight when having dinner and other quality time with family. My kids are good at letting me know when I have been on my phone too long, and I encourage them to do that. Open communication is so healthy. I also take time for myself to relax and recharge whenever possible by reading, spending time with friends, walking or growing in my faith. It is not always possible to do everything I mention, especially with children; however, I try very hard to do at least one thing for myself every week. I am a better person mentally and physically when I devote time to myself to recharge and relax.

9. **Are there any specific books or videos you may recommend as it relates to HCIT?**

   I always read books on what I was learning at the time. There were many books. However, now I listen to podcasts on HCIT and lots of TED Talks.

10. **What is your advice for women to obtain the best opportunities and to negotiate competitive salaries in this career path?**

   Get a mentor in your industry that is a good fit for you. A mentor will support you, cheer you on, provide feedback, advice, and help you define and reach your goals. It can be a key relationship in your life and one that has the potential to impact your choices and career trajectory significantly.

11. **What are some recommendations for networking and continued education?**

   Join professional organizations and attend meetings and educational events. Talk to people you don't know and find out what they do and why they like doing that job. Attend conferences and attend education events and networking events. Don't just show up and walk around and eat. Make a plan before walking in the door to meet 2 to 3 people at the least. Connect with people you meet on social media networks and never hesitate to reach out to your network with questions or to ask for advice.

12. **Looking back to the beginning of your career, can you share some lessons learned? Would you have done anything differently?**

   I took a very thoughtful approach at the beginning of my career. I made notes on when I really enjoyed working on different projects and what parts I liked the most. I joined professional organizations and participated in them. It is easy to join, but it is so very important to be an active member and participate in meetings, education and networking events and conferences when possible. If I found something new that I thought I would be interested in learning more about, then I made it a priority to learn everything I could about that subject. This work led me to Clinical Informatics. I continued to dig deeper into Informatics and joined every education event I could join to learn more and more. The more I learned, the more I wanted to do. I said "yes" to every new project I was asked to join, no matter what I would be doing. Just getting a place in the room opens so many doors. Always say "yes." I found that the more I attended meetings with executives, the more I realized that I could also be an executive. So, I made that my plan to accomplish!

# Lindsay Stratton, Vice President of Operations, Eye Med Management Solutions

### Please provide a brief overview of your professional experience.

Lindsay Stratton's first job out of college was working as an assistant for a venture capitalist. She was responsible for scheduling meetings, booking travel, organizing European vacations, stocking the kitchen office with coffee and snacks, organizing political receptions, and purchasing beautiful plants to brighten up the office (her personal favorite)! Lindsay's boss demanded high performance, so she began thinking ahead to the future. Her undergraduate degree was in political science, and she was afforded the opportunity to meet many US senators, congressmen, and presidential candidates. The people she met at this job led to her career as a political staffer. Lindsay worked for a member of the California State Legislature for 6 years. As she puts it, "to say it was an amazing and interesting experience is an understatement. Not many people get an inside look at how the government functions (or lack thereof!), and I am so honored I was given the opportunity to be a part of the staffer club." It was here that she met incredible people, made lifelong friends, and mastered the art of cocktail parties. When the economic recession of 2006 hit, she was a staffer and it got her thinking about which industries would always be in demand. Healthcare is one that stuck out in her mind, and after some research, she decided to go back to school for her master's degree in health administration. Lindsay believes that going to graduate school, in combination with some real-life work experience, helped her tremendously. Lindsay highly recommends taking a few years to work before jumping into graduate school, as it brought a different perspective to her studies.

By the time Lindsay finished graduate school, her boss was termed out and couldn't run for reelection. Subsequently, she got a job as an EHR trainer for a large HCIT company. Travel has always been a passion of hers, and the job was 100% travel! She quickly learned that training doctors on a new technology leaned more on psychology than anything else.

After that job ran its course, Lindsay states, "I decided to pivot hard to the left and help my mom grow her medical billing company, Eye Med Management Solutions." The business was starting to grow, and her mother was looking for some help. She made a pact with her mother that if it didn't work out for any reason, she would get another job. Almost 14 years later, they are still working side by side. Eye Med Management Solutions has been a remote work company since its inception 20 years ago. They were remote working before it was cool to do remote work! Lindsay states that the "company has grown rapidly, and it's been extremely rewarding to do this together with my mom."

**Professional licenses and/or certifications:**
Certified Ophthalmic Coding Specialist, American Academy of Ophthalmology

**Other education or training relevant to your position:**
Master of health administration, Chapman University
Bachelor of arts in political science and history, University of Colorado

**LinkedIn profile:**
https://www.linkedin.com/in/lindsay-stratton-mha/

**Were you referred to this project by a colleague? If so, who?**
Jeffery Daigrepont, Senior Vice President, Coker.

# HCIT Questions

**1. What led you to pursue a career in the HCIT industry?**

During the recession of 2007–2009, so many people lost their jobs. This got me thinking about industries that are always going to be in demand. During this time, HCIT/tech was starting to evolve with EMRs and cloud-based practice management systems. There's the human and humanitarian element of patient care, tied together with forward-thinking, automated technology. The dichotomy between the two is fascinating.

**2. What is the best professional advice given to you that you can share with aspiring women who wish to work in HCIT?**

Grow where you're planted. It transcends both personal and professional life. If you don't understand where you're at during certain times in your career or didn't plan to be where you're at, there's always something to learn in the process.

**3. What is one of your proudest work-related accomplishments?**

Building a successful business and being able to provide jobs as we grow is a very humbling experience. The team we've built motivates me every day.

**4. In preparation for a job interview, what type of questions should the candidate consider asking, and in what ways can the candidate set themselves apart?**

Be yourself and show your personality. Don't give the answer you think the employer wants to hear. One good question to ask is: What would my typical workday look like? Stick to your values and ask questions that are important to you. Don't be afraid of offending someone with your questions if they're important to you.

**5. Would you say there are additional barriers for women to overcome in this industry? If so, what has your experience taught you about navigating these challenges?**

If there are any barriers left, they're coming down daily!

**6. How have you navigated instances of inequality that may be experienced by women in the workplace?**

N/A.

**7. When it comes to traveling on the job (such as for attending conferences or performing on-site tasks), what tips may you share when it comes to safety as well as tips that are convenient for travel?**

One of the great things about my job is that it affords me the opportunity to travel extensively. I always stay in a safe neighborhood, even if it costs me a little bit more money. Pull up Google Maps on your phone and familiarize yourself with the area before you get there. Be aware of your surroundings, and don't put yourself in a vulnerable or compromising position.

**8. How do you maintain a healthy work–life balance?**

Maintaining a work–life balance takes work. It will never be 50/50 all the time; sometimes you give more at work and your personal life takes a back seat. Other times, it's important to put yourself first— take that vacation or have a long lunch with a friend.

**9. Are there any specific books or videos you may recommend as it relates to HCIT?**

*Outliers: The Story of Success* by Malcolm Gladwell. I also love podcasts, especially "How I Built This" with Guy Raz.

10. **What is your advice for women to obtain the best opportunities and to negotiate competitive salaries in this career path?**

Don't settle for less than you're worth, and don't jump at the first job opportunity if it doesn't feel like the right fit. Listen to your gut. If it doesn't work out, it wasn't meant to be. What's meant for you will find you.

11. **What are some recommendations for networking and continued education?**

Get involved! Whether it's the Rotary Club in your city or a professional organization, meet people who have the same interests as you. There are a lot of great online educational programs to further your professional development. Find what interests you and take advantage of those opportunities.

12. **Looking back to the beginning of your career, can you share some lessons learned? Would you have done anything differently?**

Don't be afraid to fail! Everyone fails, and there's so much to learn in those moments. Try that thing you've always wanted to do. I also would have started networking earlier in my career. You never know who you might meet at an event or what you can learn at a conference. Put yourself out there and don't be afraid to ask questions.

# Susan Solinsky, Co-Founder, Ellipsis Health

**Please provide a brief overview of your professional experience.**

Susan Solinsky is a Co-Founder and CGO at Ellipsis Health. Ellipsis Health leverages the unique power of voice—the words one says and how they say them—to identify and monitor depression and anxiety. Susan's passion is to support mental health. She's also an avid supporter of female entrepreneurs. She volunteers as the Director of the Women's Health Tech Initiative at HITLAB, and she's a Founding LP of the How Women Invest Fund, LP at DigitalDx, LP at Coyote Ventures, LP at HIP, and Investing member of Portfolia. Susan is a Strategic Operating Partner with Kayne Anderson Capital and serves on the Board of Directors of Carium, a comprehensive platform to enable virtual care. Prior to joining Ellipsis Health, Susan was Vice President of Enterprise Sales at Phreesia (IPO, 2019). Before, she co-founded Vital Score (acquired by Phreesia), a digital health company that harnessed the evidence-based therapeutic technique, motivational interviewing, to help patients self-identify goals and barriers and drive their own care planning. She also served as Managing Partner at Reditus Revenue

Solutions, a management consulting firm that provided interim/fractional executive leadership across sales, strategy, marketing, product, operations, and fundraising to innovative startups and healthcare companies to develop new business lines with an emphasis on scaling to profitability. Earlier in her career, Susan was SVP and Managing Director as part of the founding team of the Advisory Board (IPO) and the Corporate Executive Board (IPO). Susan received her A.B. from Princeton University.

**Professional licenses and/or certifications:**
N/A.

**Other education or training relevant to your position:**
AB Princeton

**LinkedIn profile:**
https://www.linkedin.com/in/susansolinsky/

**Were you referred to this project by a colleague? If so, who?**
Sherri Douville, CEO, Medigram.

# HCIT Questions

**1. What led you to pursue a career in the HCIT industry?**

After many woman's health issues affecting my mother (two-time cancer survivor, multiple other chronic conditions), as well as my own health challenges, I realized that technology has the ability to dramatically change how we provide care. I believe that there is a mind-body connection with all health-related issues, and my passions are women's health and mental health.

**2. What is the best professional advice given to you that you can share with aspiring women who wish to work in HCIT?**

Lead with your heart and listen; there are many opportunities to change healthcare with technology. We serve our community best by focusing on where we can have the biggest impact.

**3. What is one of your proudest work-related accomplishments?**

Work, now many years ago, supporting HPV vaccines in vulnerable communities in NYC. The impact was significant.

**4. In preparation for a job interview, what type of questions should the candidate consider asking, and in what ways can the candidate set themselves apart?**

Candidates can set themselves apart by giving real word examples of ways that they have used their skills (which could be service-related or an internship). Candidates should ask about the culture of the organization, how team members are evaluated and succeed, the goals of the organization, and how decisions are reached in the company.

5. **Would you say there are additional barriers for women to overcome in this industry? If so, what has your experience taught you about navigating these challenges?**

   There are still many barriers for women to overcome. Women can often overcome challenges in a new role by cultivating relationships with mentors and sponsors in their companies (and understanding the difference), as well as advocating for their goals and needs to achieve their company and professional goals. Communication is key.

6. **How have you navigated instances of inequality that may be experienced by women in the workplace?**

   Yes.

7. **When it comes to traveling on the job (such as for attending conferences or performing on-site tasks), what tips may you share when it comes to safety as well as tips that are convenient for travel?**

   With travel, women have the added risk of making sure that the hotel is safe as well as the area of any after-hours work activities. It's always better to evaluate the situation and react, even if it feels like you are being difficult.

8. **How do you maintain a healthy work–life balance?**

   This applies to men and women; we all need boundaries and self-care. Walks outside are important, and time with family is fundamental to recharging. We are all healthier and better contributors if we are rested and able to perform at the top of our game.

9. **Are there any specific books or videos you may recommend as it relates to HCIT?**

   There are many books; however, I think outside organizations like *WBL* or *How Women Lead* are better than a single book, and I would highly suggest both.

10. **What is your advice for women to obtain the best opportunities and to negotiate competitive salaries in this career path?**

    There's a phenomenal group called Aequitas Partners and Polina Hanin is the principal that's led a lot of salary rankings—also Chasm Partners with Pam Zients in healthcare startups. They are trying hard to provide information so that all of us can understand the salaries being given in our industry.

11. **What are some recommendations for networking and continued education?**

Organizations that support women's health and founder networking are fundamental to our ability to meet sponsors. Csweetner stands out as an easy way to be a mentor or mentee; how women lead; Hitlab; I can go on and on.

12. **Looking back to the beginning of your career, can you share some lessons learned? Would you have done anything differently?**

I didn't appreciate early in my career the power of having a male or female sponsor and didn't understand the term "mentor," so I would have found one earlier. A mentor has no relationship to the person they are mentoring (not a boss, not in the same company). I am very grateful for the men and women who have corrected my path. I had many sponsors, and I would have sought out a mentor or coach earlier in my career.

# Jill A. Towns, EHR Specialist, Community Care of North Carolina

**Please provide a brief overview of your professional experience.**

Jill Towns has been in patient care (emergency medicine/oncology) for over 28 years. At a time during these years, she was asked to support the providers as the company implemented a new EHR. It was at this time that her journey in IT began. After diving in headfirst, she transitioned into a role focusing on physician advocacy, with an emphasis on implementing EHR systems, creating efficient workflows, and customizing systems to fit providers ease of use. Later, she joined an EHR software company advisory board and maintained that seat for 19 years. In addition, Jill participated in the first-time CMS grant for oncology and assisted with the rollout of the oncology Medical Home implementation of a triage dashboard across the country. Jill was also a co-creator of the triage dashboard user interface. Currently, she continues to forage her career in EHR technology, working as an EHR Specialist.

**Professional licenses and/or certifications:**

Certified Medical Assistant (CMA)

Emergency Medical Technician (EMT)

Advanced Emergency Medical Technician (AEMT) II (Paramedic)

Board Certified Patient Advocate
Certified Electronic Health Record (CEHR) Specialist
BS Biology
**Other education or training relevant to your position:**
N/A.
**LinkedIn profile:**
N/A.
**Were you referred to this project by a colleague? If so, who?**
Lauren Leopard, MSN, RN, CCM, Director of Value Solutions at Community Care of North Carolina.

# HCIT Questions

**1. What led you to pursue a career in the HCIT industry?**

I had a forward-thinking boss who was the CEO and physician champion at the cancer center where I worked. This boss ended up being president of the AMA in 2018, Dr. Barbara McAneny. She saw that I had additional skills in seeing issues before they happened, troubleshooting effectively, and transcribing workflows that needed to take place in the EHR.

**2. What is the best professional advice given to you that you can share with aspiring women who wish to work in HCIT?**

Be open to any opportunity that comes your way, even if it may seem challenging. Most likely, you were meant to be challenged. and that challenge will grow you.

**3. What is one of your proudest work-related accomplishments?**

Implementing the Oncology Medical Home triage dashboard across the country, with an emphasis on creating small urgent care clinics. Teaching cancer centers how to keep patients out of the ED by bringing them back into the cancer centers (using the urgent care setting at the center) allows the experts (oncologists) to treat the patient and lower any additional financial burden for the patient.

**4. In preparation for a job interview, what type of questions should the candidate consider asking, and in what ways can the candidate set themselves apart?**

Is there an opportunity to grow?

5. **Would you say there are additional barriers for women to overcome in this industry? If so, what has your experience taught you about navigating these challenges?**

   This industry has been mainly made up of men. However, it's changing. All of us have goals or tasks we must commit to and achieve annually in our jobs. If you ever get the opportunity to create your own goal, think big and ask the company to support you in growing your skills. Look into other aspects of knowledge or learning that will strengthen your position (e.g., coding).

6. **How have you navigated instances of inequality that may be experienced by women in the workplace?**

   N/A.

7. **When it comes to traveling on the job (such as for attending conferences or performing on-site tasks), what tips may you share when it comes to safety as well as tips that are convenient for travel?**

   Before travel begins, have the physical address of the location you are headed to. Have the phone number of the person who is meeting you, preferably their cell phone. If you arrive the day before, after checking into your hotel, drive to the location so you know exactly where you are headed the next day. Log onto your computer and check to see that everything is working as expected before heading to the onsite work.

8. **How do you maintain a healthy work–life balance?**

   Remember that unless you are facing deadlines or an urgent situation that needs your attention, work will continue to be ongoing. Work hard every day, accomplish as much as you can each day, and choose a stopping point that is reasonable.

9. **Are there any specific books or videos you may recommend as it relates to HCIT?**

   I don't know of any.

10. **What is your advice for women to obtain the best opportunities and to negotiate competitive salaries in this career path?**

    Be sure you look at what the national average is for salaries, plus your experience. You have to start somewhere in your career, and you must perform and present your skills, so a higher salary is warranted as you grow with the company.

11. **What are some recommendations for networking and continued education?**

    Podcasts are great e-learning opportunities. Check with your accreditation headquarters; they offer opportunities too.

**12. Looking back to the beginning of your career, can you share some lessons learned? Would you have done anything differently?**

Nothing different. I was open to opportunities and tried them. If they worked out, then great, and if they didn't, I learned something from the experience. You will always take something from the experiences you have as you grow in your career; don't be black/white. Think outside the box and be open to growing many parts of yourself.

# Sally Trnka, Executive Director, Breakwater Health Network

**Please provide a brief overview of your professional experience.**

For more than 8 years, Sally Trnka has the great privilege of serving as the Executive Director of Breakwater Health Network (BHN). At BHN, she leads the strategic, organizational, fiscal, and development efforts for the organization, which is composed of FQHCs and migrant health centers located in four states in the Midwest. Sally also serves on the national leadership team for health center controlled networks for the National Association of Community Health Centers. BHN is often referred to as the "little network that could," where they leverage the collective size, strengths, skills, and insights of these health centers to promote and sustain high-quality, low-cost, patient-driven care in rural and (mostly) small metro areas. Sally works with talented, dedicated, and passionate people; it's their collaborative approaches that have allowed the organization to evolve and thrive for over 20 years.

With an incredibly small team at BHN, they have been able to provide significant, meaningful benefits to its members, which allows them to focus on providing care and support to their patients, staff, and communities. Sally has also been able to provide insight and input into legislative efforts to help policymakers better understand healthcare in rural communities and support innovation that is meaningful to rural healthcare.

While in this role, Sally has also led a robust campaign and ultimately ended up serving on the School Board in Duluth, MN. She was the Chair of the Human Resources and Finance Committee all 4 years of her term and served on the Transportation Committee, the Intergovernmental Committee, and the Community School Collaborative Committee/Board. Her experiences on the School Board were incredible opportunities for which she will be forever grateful.

Prior to that, Sally served as the Director of Network Development for a highly sophisticated rural/critical access hospital (CAH) representing the small, rural hospitals in Colorado and California. They supported the expansion of vital services to over 50 mostly CAHs and provided training to hospital staff, supported the development of revenue-generating lines of business that paid dividends to the network members, supported the launch of a now wildly successful alternative payment methodology structure to support the Quintuple Aim, facilitated Peer Network Groups, guided strategic planning initiatives at the member hospitals, and identified opportunities to provide meaningful services to the network members. She was also charged with helping their internal staff, member hospitals, and key partners digest the impact of legislation on the organizations to better advocate for the unique needs and opportunities in rural areas.

Sally began her career in healthcare, rural health, and HIT as a Senior Program Coordinator at the National Rural Health Resource Center (The Center), working with rural health networks—including the 40 HRSA-designated Rural Health Information Technology Network Development grantees. She also helped lead the team that put on a world-class annual conference that is one of the largest rural health conferences in the country. She provided input to the fabulous team at the Federal Office of Rural Health Policy, as well as state-based partners and programs. Sally was trained in facilitating strategic planning services for organizations and helping leaders see both the macro and micro implications of different strategic endeavors for sustainability and maximum impact. She was also a part of the team that conducted robust activities under the Regional Extension Center (REC) program, supporting the selection, implementation, and optimization of EMRs.

Sally has been wildly blessed to have outstanding, dedicated mentors and nurture a wide network of colleagues and partner organizations that provide richness and support to both her profession and personal life and experiences.

**Professional licenses and/or certifications:**
N/A.

**Other education or training relevant to your position:**
N/A.

**LinkedIn profile:**
https://www.linkedin.com/in/sally-trnka-2490a1a/

**Were you referred to this project by a colleague? If so, who?**
Jeffery Daigrepont, Senior Vice President, Coker.

# HCIT Questions

### 1. What led you to pursue a career in the HCIT industry?

It isn't inspiring or anything you'd find in a blockbuster movie script, but I really didn't actively seek out a career in HCIT. Shortly after being hired at The Center—where I remember telling the Executive Director that I wanted to work in rural healthcare because I truly wanted to improve the world—I began working on a research project in collaboration with the University of Minnesota, Rural Health Research Center, on rural hospital networks across the country. I *immediately* fell in love with collaboratives and networks. When the research work was close to reaching its conclusion, the Health Information Technology for Economic and Clinical Health (HITECH) Act and the Patient Protection and Affordable Care Act were passed, with significant goals of creating opportunities and incentives for healthcare entities to move to electronic platforms to support improved patient safety and care, supporting providers with key decisions, allowing for patient information to be exchanged across healthcare entities, and laying the foundations for the Quintuple Aim.

I began working with rural health networks across the country as they collaborated to assess and implement EMRs to meet the goals outlined in the new legislation, as well as serve as a team member for the REC. Through those opportunities, I not only had the opportunity to understand the HCIT environment but also work with small, rural health organizations in the areas of strategic planning, patient engagement, vendor management and contracting, health information exchange, business development, and community impact. I would not have imagined that I'd still be working in the healthcare IT industry, but it's a passion with a purpose.

### 2. What is the best professional advice given to you that you can share with aspiring women who wish to work in HCIT?

I'd likely answer this question differently depending on the day (or even the moment!). But a dear friend and former Board member of BHN once advised me to "not spend time or energy in trying to understand what someone meant when they made a comment, given you an assignment, introduced criticism, or suggested a change." I find myself playing scenarios over and over in my head, trying to dissect each component of the interaction to understand what someone "*meant*" from their communication rather than taking it at face value. Obviously, this is challenging and requires a certain amount of trust, but her advice has saved me a lot of time, energy, and stress. It also reinforces that "you teach people how to treat you," which is another highly valuable lesson. If people see that you appreciate directness (not to be confused with rudeness) and you expect them to communicate the full picture from the start of a relationship, it'll make those relationships much more meaningful.

**3. What is one of your proudest work-related accomplishments?**

I'm from the Midwest, so identifying accomplishments doesn't come naturally to me! I am extraordinarily proud of the work we did at BHN, with the significant input and leg work done by our members, to rapidly implement telehealth services in meaningful ways at the very start of the COVID-19 pandemic. For patients to be able to continue to receive services during a scary public health crisis, it was vital, and I'm proud to have been a part of that work.

**4. In preparation for a job interview, what type of questions should the candidate consider asking, and in what ways can the candidate set themselves apart?**

I'm highly inquisitive, so my questions often usurp the time allocated in an interview! Do your research before your interview, and not just a surface-level investigation, but dig into some of the details, especially components that align with your passions and interest areas. By asking questions regarding areas that are exciting to you, your energy and commitment will shine. I take notes throughout the interview to try to tie questions back to what those on the interview team have shared to show that you're paying attention and able to think critically on your feet.

**5. Would you say there are additional barriers for women to overcome in this industry? If so, what has your experience taught you about navigating these challenges?**

I recently had a gentleman painfully "mansplain" interoperability to me, and I was furious. I must check myself sometimes to not act/react out of pure emotion and rather take the breaths that I know that I personally need (this certainly doesn't apply to everyone) to look at things with a little less frustration. I have been sitting with male leaders for the entirety of my career, often the only woman in the room, and sometimes folks will disappoint you. Advocating for diverse voices and perspectives around those tables can help reduce some of those barriers, and it's vital that women in leadership roles make room for other women and others who suffer from marginalization or underrepresentation. I still do sometimes find myself wanting to "prove" myself to those who dismiss me after one glance; what helps me is rooting myself in my own beliefs of what I bring to the table and don't allow myself to be silenced or cast aside IF that is important to me in that scenario. Sometimes, you'll simply be dismissed and disappointed, but remember that you have power, and you don't want to give your power away to those who simply aren't worth it! Grounding yourself in your own value and power can make it easier to tease out when it's simply not worth it to pursue further engagement with those that don't recognize your value. It is really, really unfortunate and can be painful. My Mom always says, "What other people think about you is none of your business," which doesn't really apply if those other people are deciding your employment, salary or future opportunities, but your own, authentic confidence in yourself is much more visible to those around us than we often assume.

6. **How have you navigated instances of inequality that may be experienced by women in the workplace?**

    N/A.

7. **When it comes to traveling on the job (such as for attending conferences or performing on-site tasks), what tips may you share when it comes to safety as well as tips that are convenient for travel?**

    As with many other women, I have had unfortunate and, at times, dangerous experiences while traveling and working with entities across the country. Some of those experiences still haunt me. Firstly, it's important that you work for/with an employer that fully recognizes and acknowledges that the safety of their employees is paramount. It can be uncomfortable, but it's important that the culture of the organization/company recognize that engagements can look different for women. And some professional relationships may require that you be reassigned or that you have strong, vocal support from leadership so you don't feel unsafe, threatened, or vulnerable.

    If you can avoid it (which is sometimes impossible in small rural towns!), don't stay in motels that have doors that open directly to the outside. I also almost always stay at a hotel that is close but not the same as conference venues. If it's not possible, I ask the person at registration to try to put me in a different area than most of my colleagues staying at the same hotel, and I ask for rooms that don't have the "feature" of having a pass-through door to make the rooms adjoining. Be sure that the hotel staff don't read aloud your hotel room number when they hand you the keys. Always have a phone charger and charging block with you, and let people know where you are staying and rough estimates of travel times. Finally, get regular feedback from your female mentors. It can sometimes be hard to spot problematic behaviors in our colleagues, but others with an outside vantage point may be able to shine light on relationships or situations that are hard to spot from the "inside." If you feel safe and comfortable, speak up for yourself early and often to set the tone from the start that unsafe, disrespectful, or chauvinistic behaviors won't fly with you or your employer.

**8. How do you maintain a healthy work–life balance?**

Unfortunately, I can't pretend that I have a healthy balance between work and my personal life. (I'm very excited to read what the distinguished women in this book suggest as they answer this question!) When I started my career, I very much wanted to prove myself—and I was truly passionate about the work—so I worked long hours, often times while undertaking other challenges such as graduate school, traveling extensively for work, serving in public office, parenting through COVID-19, and countless other time-intensive pursuits. Seek out employers and colleagues who will help establish and "enforce" boundaries around how much you work and when that work takes place. Unless the project is critical, you don't need to be on your laptop for long hours at night or on the weekends. I try (emphasis on try) to take breaks throughout the day that get my head out of my work, like taking the dog for a walk, going to a lunchtime yoga class, having a dance break, or some other activity that gets me away from my desk and forces me to use different parts of my brain. While progress has been made, we need to set tones and cultures in our workplaces that don't glorify work or hours dedicated to projects outside of work hours. It's hard, especially when you're early in your career, which is part of why a lot of the responsibility to navigate that change of mindset falls on the leaders in this landscape.

I also try to limit the amount of time that I talk about work outside of work (many of my dear friends don't really understand what it is I do for work; they just know that I'm super passionate about technology, collaboration, and rural healthcare!). The most important component, in my opinion, is that you find a job/employer/field that you really, truly love. That foundation takes a great deal of the stress out of seeking the illusive work–life balance.

**9. Are there any specific books or videos you may recommend as it relates to HCIT?**

I like to read books or watch videos that discuss human behavior, cultural impacts and implications, and human-centered approaches to our work. Understanding what motivates people is so important as a colleague and a leader. It's important to not take all of that as gospel, but it is helpful as you set up programs, interact with colleagues, and support change management. Malcolm Gladwell and David Brooks are two of my favorites. I have also been reading a lot about the impact(s) of trauma on human behavior and how to be person-centric in our work. How to be a better ally is also a favorite topic for me to explore.

**10. What is your advice for women to obtain the best opportunities and to negotiate competitive salaries in this career path?**

You MUST speak up for yourself! It can be ridiculously difficult, but the work of HCIT is dynamic and can be difficult and time consuming and it's important that you are recognized for your contributions. Since I work for a nonprofit organization, I can oftentimes find the salaries of my peers by looking at 990 tax information or salary surveys provided by many entities and those are great tools for assessing how your contributions are being financially valued. Money isn't the only type of compensation to seek or consider. I'm fortunate to work for an organization that provides me with flexibility, which is important for me, but that type of "softer" compensation won't show up on a financial spreadsheet. Be thoughtful about knowing your own compensation priorities, and be sure that those are addressed when negotiating a job offer, a promotion, a rebasing, or requesting a raise or additional means of compensation.

**11. What are some recommendations for networking and continued education?**

One of the primary reasons that I have had the career that I have had is because, ultimately, it's all about relationships. Although/because I work remotely, I prioritize opportunities to connect with people in-person whether at a conference, a visit to one of our clinics, engagements with funders and policy makers, and other face-to-face engagements that are meaningful. I am outgoing so I don't feel uncomfortable making new friends or colleagues, and that has been important for not only my professional trajectory but also for how I connect the work that I do to the impact it has on communities and patients. If you're less comfortable engaging with folks you don't know, try sending an email ahead of an engagement to break the ice or ask a colleague, boss, mentor, classmate, etc. to help you establish new relationships.

Maintaining those relationships takes work, but it's crucial. People want to feel seen and heard so listen when they talk and acknowledge what they have to say. Even with professional relationships, we're humans and while you don't need to be best friends with everyone, showing them respect and providing an opportunity for authentic human connection makes an impact on others and they will remember how you made them feel.

As for continued education, it can be easy to move that critical component of our lives to the backburner when we are stressed or overwhelmed so try to build in guardrails or incentives to push yourself to always prioritize growth. For example, I spent the greater part of a decade really understanding telehealth even though it wasn't a priority set by my Board of Directors for a handful of those years. Once the pandemic hit, we were able to stand up telehealth services at all of our clinics over the course of a few days while many other entities took weeks or months, giving our clinics a competitive advantage and assuaging the fears of the patients served by the clinics. Especially if you invest in your own development/education in core principles and not just "sparkly objects," the time dedicated to that development will eventually and inevitably pay off. Continuing education can also help you identify different niches in HCIT where you may want to seek additional responsibilities or career opportunities and can expand your network at the same time!

12. **Looking back to the beginning of your career, can you share some lessons learned? Would you have done anything differently?**

I joke with people that if I were to write an autobiography, it would be titled "What NOT to Do by Sally Trnka!" I've made plenty of mistakes and will continue to do so, but what's important is that you take accountability and identify how you'll learn and grow from the experience.

I am a really curious person, and I ask a lot of questions. For the most part, people are open and willing to share and educate. By setting yourself up early to be comfortable asking questions and recognizing that you don't, in fact, know everything, you'll have more doors open, which will allow you to work with people who have skill sets that complement your own and promote your growth. It's really hard to be honest when you don't know some things, but it'll save everyone time and energy to be honest about that, and it will seriously ingratiate you to team members while cultivating trust with those around you that you will ask for help when needed.

# Shannon Vogel, Associate Vice President, Health Information Technology

**Please provide a brief overview of your professional experience.**

Shannon Vogel, Associate Vice President, did not begin her professional experience with HIT but rather as a project manager overseeing seminars for physicians and administrative staff. The project management experience was a strength when she applied for a job overseeing the fulfillment of a grant that helped physicians adopt electronic health records. At the time, a majority of physicians were still using paper charts. Her knowledge base grew as the HIT industry evolved, and she is now considered a subject matter expert for EHR adoption and transition, telemedicine, interoperability, electronic prescribing, the Medicare Quality Payment Program, and areas impacting health technologies in ambulatory medical practices.

**Professional licenses and/or certifications:**
HIMSS Fellow

**Other education or training relevant to your position:**
Master of science in health informatics

**LinkedIn profile:**
N/A.

**Were you referred to this project by a colleague? If so, who?**
Jeffery Daigrepont, Senior Vice President, Coker.

# HCIT Questions

### 1. What led you to pursue a career in the HCIT industry?

I didn't pursue a career as much as I was ready for advancement when the opportunity presented itself. I'm an eager learner, and I was ready to learn all I could as the industry progressed. My entry into HCIT was timely, as it was during the early stages of EHR adoption. At the time, interoperability was more conceptual than active. This allowed me to grow with the industry professionally and intellectually.

2. **What is the best professional advice given to you that you can share with aspiring women who wish to work in HCIT?**

It's a great career path with lots of opportunities. Even if your degree is not specific to HCIT, you can still learn and grow in the industry. Learn about the various company types and the audience served and determine where you want to work. For example, the startup world may be exciting to some but not a good fit for others. Check the job opportunities with companies you've identified as a good fit. Even if openings are not specific to what you want to do, there is still value in getting your foot in the door with other positions for which you qualify. You can then learn the company culture and make the move when the ideal job opens within the company.

3. **What is one of your proudest work-related accomplishments?**

When the HITECH Act of 2009 was signed into law, there was suddenly a rush of EHR adoption. I had already been helping physicians with EHR adoption for 3 years and had lots of resources ready to go. The work that was done over the following years moved the EHR adoption needle significantly so that now 90% of physicians use an EHR. I realize the incentives offered to physicians were the greatest impetus, but I'm proud of the resources developed and disseminated to help the physician community.

4. **In preparation for a job interview, what type of questions should the candidate consider asking, and in what ways can the candidate set themselves apart?**

Know as much about the company as you can before you walk into the interview. With so much information on the internet, it's easy to obtain company information. Look at the company's social media pages. How does the company respond to critical comments? Does the company have political leanings? If so, are they aligned with your values? If not politically aligned, does that change how you will feel about the work you do? As you peruse the company's website, prepare questions about any strategic plans. It's also good to ask about the company culture and advancement opportunities, especially if you aspire to grow professionally.

5. **Would you say there are additional barriers for women to overcome in this industry? If so, what has your experience taught you about navigating these challenges?**

I sincerely think that women can have a seat at any table. While women may have to work harder to be recognized, other things can set you apart, and this is true regardless of gender. For example, develop your own brand and stay true to it. Lean into the knowledge base you have and the experience you bring to the work you do. Speak up with confidence and contribute to the conversation. Listen to and observe others around you, especially those with more knowledge and experience who can informally mentor you.

6. **How have you navigated instances of inequality that may be experienced by women in the workplace?**

I'm grateful to work for an organization that has a lot of strong women in positions of leadership. Their example gives me the confidence to navigate the industry and to not be timid when sharing knowledge, whether it's through conversations or presentations.

7. **When it comes to traveling on the job (such as for attending conferences or performing on-site tasks), what tips may you share when it comes to safety as well as tips that are convenient for travel?**

When traveling for business, you represent yourself and your employer. This is where staying true to your brand is just as important as if you were in the office. This means maintaining sobriety while attending industry receptions, dinners, and parties. As you anticipate conversations, have words ready in the event a conversation is steered in a direction that is uncomfortable. Always attempt to set yourself apart as an industry professional. You never know what opportunities may come about as a result of networking, and you want to be on your best behavior.

As for safety, if possible, travel with and attend events with a colleague or industry friend who travels in the same circles. Always be aware of your surroundings, and as part of your situational awareness, devise scenarios of what could happen and how you would react. That way, if something actually happens, your brain will pull forward the action you anticipated, allowing you to react more quickly.

8. **How do you maintain a healthy work–life balance?**

I know what I need to do to feel good and be able to live life with a positive outlook. This includes good sleep patterns, time for exercise, self-care, and typically healthy eating. These behaviors impact the work and personal areas of my life. It's important to prioritize your work appropriately and keep a running list of tasks and projects with deadlines so that you do not put yourself in an overly stressful situation by procrastinating. Learn to be a good delegator and use your team appropriately. When exercising or driving, allow your brain to free flow as you think about a challenge and how you can strategically problem-solve.

It's also important to work in a healthy environment. If your workplace is toxic, it may be time to think about your next opportunity. A toxic work environment can definitely impact your personal life. Finally, as you compartmentalize work and personal time, work hard while at work and be present for your loved ones when you are with them.

9. **Are there any specific books or videos you may recommend as it relates to HCIT?**

While I cannot think of anything specific, I recommend that anyone working in the HIT industry stay current with news, events, and research. Always be an eager learner.

10. **What is your advice for women to obtain the best opportunities and to negotiate competitive salaries in this career path?**

To negotiate a competitive salary means knowing your value and the salary ranges of your peers doing similar work. Salary surveys are available, some free and others fee-based. A couple of other things to think about: your work habits will follow you via the references from your previous employers. Make sure you don't burn bridges. Treat others with respect and as you'd like to be treated. Also, know that some employers may have a desired culture but may not pay as well. There are trade-offs that may be important to you and to your work–life balance.

11. **What are some recommendations for networking and continued education?**

It's always good to network and have contacts. Keep your head up and observe what is happening in the industry around you. Look for continuing education opportunities that feed into where you are and where you want to go.

12. **Looking back to the beginning of your career, can you share some lessons learned? Would you have done anything differently?**

I think everyone has things they'd like to do differently as they look in the rear-view mirror. But I can also say that being prepared is the best thing you can do so that you are ready when there are opportunities. Keep a positive attitude. Work hard. Show respect. Help your colleagues succeed. Be the one people want to work with and for.

# Dana Ann Williams, MSBA, RHIA, Lead Health Economics Analyst, ProgenyHealth, LLC

**Please provide a brief overview of your professional experience.**

As a child, Dana grew up with a mother who was a travel RN. She spent her childhood traveling to several countries where her mother worked as a labor and delivery nurse. Her mother would tell her stories of babies being born, and that started her passion for healthcare. Dana grew up and strived to learn more about the "why" and "cost" of healthcare. Later, she graduated with a bachelor of science degree in health administration and a bachelor of science degree in health informatics and information management from the University of Central Florida (UCF). During her time at the UCF, she was very active as a delegate for the American Health Information Management Association (AHIMA)/Florida Health Information Management Association (FHIMA) learning everything she could about the HCIT industry. Shortly after graduating, Dana was offered a position processing requests for federal MAC/RAC audits for over 60 hospitals. It was in this role that she fell in love with claims, as claims tell the medical story of a patient. Over the years, Dana has worked for Progressive Insurance, adjusting auto medical claims and handling specialty pharmacy claims for CVS Health, but she knew she could take her career further.

Dana pursued a master of science in business analytics from the University of Miami. This is where her passion for healthcare technology began. She changed positions and she was offered her first job as a Data Associate at Alegeus. Notably, she was the first ever woman on the healthcare data team at Alegeus. Dana quickly learned SQL and how to configure API endpoints for a healthcare mobile app. As a data associate, she worked for the payer side of analytics, configuring access to a proprietary third-party organization website for large-scale health plans ensuring benefits were being properly paid for members.

Currently, Dana works for Progeny Health as a Lead Health Economics Analyst. Progeny Health is an organization that helps health plans and hospitals save money in Neonatal Intensive Care Unit costs. In this role, she uses healthcare data from health plans and hospitals and develop models in R, Python and Tableau analyzing costs and predicted savings. Dana possesses a strong understanding of SQL server and Health Information Exchange and ensure that health plans can send big data securely. She utilizes the data to conduct pre-sales data analysis using complex SQL queries and create Tableau dashboards to share healthcare costs and areas of improvement for savings. Dana states that "I finally have a position I absolutely love in health data analytics!"

**Professional licenses and/or certifications:**
Registered Health Information Administrator, AHIMA
Azure DevOps Project Management, Microsoft
**Other education or training relevant to your position:**
BS Health Administration
BS Health Informatics and Information Management
MS Business Analytics
**LinkedIn profile:**
https://www.linkedin.com/in/dana-ann-williams-msba-rhia-8160a544/
**Were you referred to this project by a colleague? If so, who?**
N/A.

# HCIT Questions

**1. What led you to pursue a career in the HCIT industry?**
A lifelong passion for science, statistics, and healthcare.

**2. What is the best professional advice given to you that you can share with aspiring women who wish to work in HCIT?**
I would let women know that they are needed in HCIT and healthcare analytics. This industry is often led by men, but this space is open to women! If you are passionate about healthcare and have a desire to work in IT or analytics, all it takes is a little dedication and hard work to get into this field.

**3. What is one of your proudest work-related accomplishments?**
One of my proudest work-related accomplishments was when I was thrown into a project that had been stalling for over a year that and I knew nothing about. The last person handling this project abruptly left the company and obviously was not working on this with attention before I was thrown into the situation. I worked for Alegeus as a new Data Associate, and I had to help a huge health plan get their API configured to be able to hit the endpoint on a web app so that health patient/payer data can be exchanged in real time. When I started the project, I was so new that I didn't even know what any of that meant, let alone how to actually complete the work to get the endpoints written and configured. I ended up studying and taking a course on API online, which greatly improved my understanding. I was able to get

this project completed after being stalled for a year and got rave reviews for my job well done from the health plan and leadership.

4. **In preparation for a job interview, what type of questions should the candidate consider asking, and in what ways can the candidate set themselves apart?**

I help write hundreds of resumes for individuals every year. My suggestion is always simple. Write each resume tailored with your experience to the job you are applying to. Carefully read through the job description and highlight three important skills that you may not be 100% proficient in. When asking interview questions, highlight the skills you do have, then pivot to a skill that you are not as proficient in and ask how your current knowledge can help you improve that skill you lack proficiency in.

Some of the questions to ask include the following:
- What does a typical day look like for the position? What are the typical "fire" situations and how are they handled?
- What are the realistic expectations of the job?

5. **Would you say there are additional barriers for women to overcome in this industry? If so, what has your experience taught you about navigating these challenges?**

I would say that HCIT is a man-led world, but there is absolutely space for women who want to get into the industry. If you are intelligent, passionate, and dedicated to this industry, you can not only work but be a leader.

6. **How have you navigated instances of inequality that may be experienced by women in the workplace?**

As the first woman ever hired on the data and integration team at Alegeus, I can say from experience that I have faced gender inequality in the workplace. This does not have to be a negative impression. My experience as the only woman on a team of men was a positive one. It's not that the company was prejudiced against women who applied for the position; it was that there were not enough qualified women to apply. I would urge women to continue to develop skills in the health technology field they are interested in and not be afraid to apply, even if they don't have all of the skills on the job description.

7. **When it comes to traveling on the job (such as for attending conferences or performing on-site tasks), what tips may you share when it comes to safety as well as tips that are convenient for travel?**

N/A.

**8. How do you maintain a healthy work–life balance?**

I have worked remotely full-time since the beginning of COVID. I know this is the absolute best option for me in life. I will never apply to a position that requires me to work in an office. The most effective way to maintain a healthy work–life balance is though self-discipline. I treat my position as a full-time job as if I were working in an office. During office hours, I make sure to be 100% mentally present at my remote job. When the day ends, I am mentally available for my own life and that of my family. I have set professional expectations that I will not be working during non-business hours. I also think it is important to have a positive professional working relationship with my boss, teammates and other co-workers. Although we do not work in the office together, I make it a priority to help collaborate with my co-workers.

**9. Are there any specific books or videos you may recommend as it relates to HCIT?**

The following are my recommendations (not limited to books):

- Simple SQL
- Python for beginners (super easy for beginners!)
- *The Game of Life and How to Play it* by Florence Scovel Shinn. This is not necessarily a HCIT book, but the principles in the book still apply today and especially for women who are breaking into a career in technology.
- Microsoft offers a free course and certification for people trying to break out into the technology field! Buy the preparation book and get a certification!

**10. What is your advice for women to obtain the best opportunities and to negotiate competitive salaries in this career path?**

I am a huge advocate of fair salary for women in healthcare technology. When helping women write their resume, I always give the following advice:

- Research on Glassdoor the average salary for the company and position you are applying for.
- Find industry standards for your skill level and geographical area.
- If the job has a salary range, always ask for the top of your salary range, and if you have direct resources that prove a higher salary for similar organizations, use it currently. You can always go down and negotiate toward a middle ground, but if you take the least, the organization will most often pay the least.

11. **What are some recommendations for networking and continued education?**

I consider professional development to be a very important aspect of my career. I continue to serve AHIMA/FHIMA. I have been a member of the HIMSS and will continue to be involved in many data science organizations in order to further my career. I would encourage women to network through local organizations and even LinkedIn groups to further their careers.

12. **Looking back to the beginning of your career, can you share some lessons learned? Would you have done anything differently?**

The most important thing I have learned as my career has progressed from health informatics and claims to health data analytics is not to burn bridges. If you take a position just as a steppingstone to learn as much as you can but have intentions to use this knowledge for future opportunities, let your manager know! On the other hand, when you have a manager you do not work well with or a job that is just not for you, always keep a professional attitude and personable mannerism. Sometimes in this industry, it is a very small world, and people know each other across organizations. Maintaining professionalism and poise with leadership and other co-workers no matter the job is my best advice.

# Leah Wittus, Software Training Consultant

**Please provide a brief overview of your professional experience.**

With a background in healthcare, hospitality, marketing, and communications, Leah Wittus decided to take a step in another direction—an industry that could use the skills obtained from her previous experience to improve healthcare and the patient experience overall through technological solutions that work for both the clinical teams and most importantly the patients. This led her to venture out and look for a position at one of the best healthcare/IT/EHR companies out there today, ModMed.

During her time at ModMed thus far, Leah has worked and advanced in two separate roles within the customer success department. She started her journey in the company with the hopes of learning from the bottom up. On day one, she began working as a Software Support Specialist. Leah cannot say enough about this position! This role gave her so much information about the organization as a whole, including how other departments function with one another and what roles are involved, who, when, and how to communicate with individuals. The role also helped her learn how to work remotely, get the job done, and then some. Not only that, as a Software Support Specialist, she was able to gain experience testing and inspecting products and report her findings to development via the JIRA software. In addition, this position gave her the ability to educate clients—with the help of ModMed's amazing internal QRG/Webinar platform, the Lynda/LinkedIn Learning subscription, and the assignment of internal managers, coaches, and mentors—which helped Leah expand her subject matter expertise in compliance, billing, clinical processes and procedures across numerous verticals. The decision to start in this position was the best decision she made. Leah ended up gaining more knowledge than if she had jumped into a different role. This choice has made her more confident, efficient, and effective as she continues to develop professionally.

After spending a bit of time in the Software Support Specialist role, Leah decided to move into a position that involved more hands-on training. She knew the products like the back of her hand, so she figured this would help her excel in her next and current endeavor as a Software Training Consultant for Dermatology Vertical. With an established curriculum and preset lesson plans, Leah is responsible for educating clients before and after the implementation of the software solutions. In this role, she has highly strengthened her public speaking skills and gained a greater understanding of the different methods and paces at which each individual learns.

In some ways, the position involves a bit of project management responsibilities, as cost, scheduling, and resource factors have to be addressed with office leads and internal management. Trainers are required to coordinate travel within a specific budget and ensure appropriate alignment and availability of team members for the engagements within the client's desired timeline to achieve their requested deliverables. This position has allowed Leah to build relations with clients and further establish her credibility and reliability. The hands-on experience has also given her the privilege of observing countless offices, analyzing their setup and current workflows, and discovering any common stresses and areas of concern. In turn, this has allowed her to relay any workflow issues and recommend solutions and implementation approaches that may simplify their day-to-day struggles and make the office work more proficient as a whole.

As the company diversifies and expands into other specialties and continuously enhances the product, there is always room for growth, and with the help of our Internal Certification Programs, it is almost impossible not to grow or learn something new every day. Leah is well on the way to her next endeavor within the company, but she would not change any of her time or choices as they have allowed her to become the business professional she is today.

**Professional licenses and/or certifications:**

Merit-based Incentive Payment System–Medicare Access and CHIP Reauthorization Act (MACRA) Certification

Certified Associate in Project Management (CAPM) Course Certificate

**Other education or training relevant to your position:**

Major: Marketing Minor: Communications, Florida State University

Google Suite, Jira, Microsoft Suite, Salesforce, Cloud Coach

EHR Software Experience and Healthcare Experience

**LinkedIn profile:**

https://www.linkedin.com/in/leahwittus/

**Were you referred to this project by a colleague? If so, who?**

N/A.

# HCIT Questions

1. **What led you to pursue a career in the HCIT industry?**

   After working at a medical spa and a dermatology office, I found that I was extremely passionate about the healthcare industry and knew there had to be a better way to simplify the workload for both clinical teams and patients. I wanted to be a part of that mission.

2. **What is the best professional advice given to you that you can share with aspiring women who wish to work in HCIT?**

   Every day is an opportunity to learn something new. If you are not learning, you are not growing! Ask questions!

3. **What is one of your proudest work-related accomplishments?**

   Achieving the goals I have set since before I started at ModMed, and meeting them ahead of schedule.

4. **In preparation for a job interview, what type of questions should the candidate consider asking, and in what ways can the candidate set themselves apart?**

   Questions to ask: What programs are used? How does cross-departmental communication work? Are we assigned a mentor? What is your favorite part about working for the company?

How to set yourself apart: Be yourself, be passionate about what you do, and show your desire to learn and help people.

5. **Would you say there are additional barriers for women to overcome in this industry? If so, what has your experience taught you about navigating these challenges?**

I have not experienced a barrier in this company. ModMed is all about equality, and the executives work extremely hard to establish equality with each of the affinity groups, including MMwit and ModMed Women in Tech.

6. **How have you navigated instances of inequality that may be experienced by women in the workplace?**

N/A.

7. **When it comes to traveling on the job (such as for attending conferences or performing on-site tasks), what tips may you share when it comes to safety as well as tips that are convenient for travel?**

Try to travel with a buddy, book hotels in areas that you are more familiar with or take recommendations from someone who may be more familiar with the area, have a portable battery and cords to charge your devices, always pack minimally, and place your important belongings in a carry-on. Always be aware of your surroundings. It also helps to prepare yourself and look up the area you will be traveling to prior to arrival.

8. **How do you maintain a healthy work–life balance?**

I try to maintain balance by working within the 8 hour workday Monday through Friday. When the day is done, I am done. I hide my work belongings in my closet over the weekend and take them back out Monday morning. I also avoid communicating with staff over the weekend, as this is also their time to balance their lives as well.

9. **Are there any specific books or videos you may recommend as it relates to HCIT?**

LinkedIn Learning courses and/or books for all of the programs typically used in HCIT.

10. **What is your advice for women to obtain the best opportunities and to negotiate competitive salaries in this career path?**

[No answer provided].

11. **What are some recommendations for networking and continued education?**

Join local groups in your community with like-minded business professionals, join linked-in groups with similar interests, join groups within your company so that you can network with various departments and partake in events in and outside of the company, and look into classes or courses that interest you, but also assist you with your ultimate goals.

12. **Looking back to the beginning of your career, can you share some lessons learned? Would you have done anything differently?**

I would not have done anything differently. The time I have spent and the choices I have made have allowed me to become the business professional I am today.

# Rebecca Woods, Founder and CEO, Bluebird Tech Solutions

**Please provide a brief overview of your professional experience.**

Rebecca is known for her work in helping healthcare organizations utilize their electronic health records in the most efficient way possible. Her impressive record of accomplishments, from Senior Analyst to Chief Information Officer, is a result of her strong engagement skills, extensive operational knowledge, and strength in building teams. Recognized for her excellent leadership, valuable insight, and ability to assist in setting the path for long-lasting success, Rebecca has used her skills and experience to help meet organizations' needs, with a focus on increasing efficiency, transitional changes, and the implementation of sustainable changes. Rebecca received her BS in Communications from Plymouth State University and a master's degree in healthcare administration from the University of Phoenix. She recently relocated to her home state of New Hampshire with her husband and two daughters. Rebecca enjoys an active lifestyle, running road races (including a marathon!), and boating with her family.

**Professional licenses and/or certifications:**
Master of healthcare administration, University of Phoenix
Project Management Certification, Villanova

**Other education or training relevant to your position:**
See above.

**LinkedIn profile:**
https://www.linkedin.com/in/rebecca-woods-mha/

**Were you referred to this project by a colleague? If so, who?**
N/A.

# HCIT Questions

**1. What led you to pursue a career in the HCIT industry?**

I fell into it. I minored in global tourism and began doing sales, but I quickly realized there was no upward mobility. I was introduced to someone at MEDITECH and began my career there doing implementation. Then I moved onto strategic career positions.

**2. What is the best professional advice given to you that you can share with aspiring women who wish to work in HCIT?**

Get out, network, and meet people. Get exposure and learn from them—the good and the bad. Accept a mentor if it's available at your job or in any groups that you are involved in. Don't burn bridges; go out in style; this industry is too small.

**3. What is one of your proudest work-related accomplishments?**

In 2021, I created my own nonprofit called "BlueBird Leaders," which is creating a community for women in HCIT to lift them up and give them the tools to succeed. I built the website and the portal; we have our annual conferences and leadership retreats. I never would have thought this was what I would be doing today.

**4. In preparation for a job interview, what type of questions should the candidate consider asking, and in what ways can the candidate set themselves apart?**

I would ask about financial viability, the turnover rate of the C-suite, upward mobility, and the opportunities for promotions. Understanding if the company is shifting, culture change. What is the company's 3- to 5-year plan? Asking if they are willing to help you learn and network by attending conferences, earning certifications, etc.

**5. Would you say there are additional barriers for women to overcome in this industry? If so, what has your experience taught you about navigating these challenges?**

Women like to second-guess themselves, and our confidence in ourselves is not as good as it should be. We need more mentors and people that other women can trust. We need to create worth in all of our accomplishments and everything we have overcome.

**6. How have you navigated instances of inequality that may be experienced by women in the workplace?**

Be relatable to everyone you work with and identify how you can stay calm in tense situations as a leader. Hold your ground and stand firm for what you believe in or stand for.

7. **When it comes to traveling on the job (such as for attending conferences or performing on-site tasks), what tips may you share when it comes to safety as well as tips that are convenient for travel?**

Surround yourself with a good network; make friends with people you see frequently; and stay in a group as often as you can. Also, be picky when choosing hotel rooms—far proximity to the elevator, no adjoining rooms. Finally, be aware of your surroundings and limit yourself if going out after hours.

8. **How do you maintain a healthy work–life balance?**

"I'll sit still when I'm dead." I am really passionate about what I am doing, so I don't find this to be exhausting. I love what I am doing, so I don't mind staying busy. But I do have two kids, and keeping up with them and staying active is important to me. My Zen time is when I put my running shoes on and hit the road.

9. **Are there any specific books or videos you may recommend as it relates to HCIT?**

- *Blue Ocean Strategy: How to Create Uncontested Market Space and Make the Competition Irrelevant* by W. Chan Kim and Renée Mauborgne
- *Women Mentoring Women: Strategies and Stories to Lift As We Rise* by Michelle Ferguson
- *UNLIMITED: The Seventeen Proven Laws for Success in a Workplace Not Designed for You* by Eugenia Jordan
- Podcast: Gary Vee

10. **What is your advice for women to obtain the best opportunities and to negotiate competitive salaries in this career path?**

Never accept the first offer; always counteroffer. Look for non-monetary benefits such as vacation time, willingness to further your education, flexible schedules, relocation funding, bonus structure, and the ability start healthcare sooner.

11. **What are some recommendations for networking and continued education?**

Attending conferences such as HIMSS or VIVE. Continue obtaining a higher education as much as possible, continue to sharpen your skills, and always look to learn something new.

12. **Looking back to the beginning of your career, can you share some lessons learned? Would you have done anything differently?**

I wouldn't do anything differently because I think everything happens for a reason. Many years ago, I took a job that did not work out favorably, but it ended up pushing me to start my own company. So, I really believe in turning something negative into something positive, and I always keep climbing.

# Note

1  Exley, C. L., & Kessler, J. B. (2019). *The gender gap in self-promotion.* National Bureau of Economic Research. https://www.nber.org/papers/w26345

# Exhibit I

# Approaching and Pitching to Venture Capitalists

By Jeffery Daigrepont,

*Senior Vice President and Stuart Bracken, Managing Director*

The authors of this book would be thrilled if, one day, we found out the next Judy Faulkner (CEO/President of EPIC Corporation) was partly inspired by the content herein. One of the most exciting aspects in the field of healthcare information technology (HCIT) is the abundance of opportunities for innovation and disruption. Despite all the recent technological advancements, HCIT is still rapidly evolving. Much of the innovation we rely on in healthcare today stems from the personal experiences of individuals, such as yourself, who were driven and inspired to find better ways to deliver higher quality patient care. In some cases, this innovation combines your HCIT skills with personal experiences dealing with medical issues or helping family members navigate the complexities of our healthcare system. Either way, you may one day find yourself in a unique position to invent the next big thing. If this happens, venture capital (or a generous rich uncle) will likely be the primary source of financial support, providing funding and expertise.

## The Healthcare Investment Landscape

Venture capitalists are individuals or companies actively seeking investments in various healthcare sectors, including medical devices, HCIT, and healthcare services. Unlike traditional borrowing, venture capitalists invest in your business or product, often at an early stage, in exchange for equity. They often have strong industry connections and relationships that can help accelerate your company or product to market. Moreover, most have successfully taken startups to market over their careers and can act as personal advisors, and in many cases, provide management support until the company gets off the ground. While there is some tradeoff in giving up equity, they are putting their resources and taking considerable risks in the hopes that your company will succeed. In short, they have skin in the game and would be fully aligned with your goals and objectives for going to market.

According to a report by Deloitte Insights,[1] venture funding for health tech innovators almost doubled in 2020 compared to 2019, reaching a record high of $14 billion. The report also suggests that growth will likely continue in 2024 and beyond, with investors viewing the post-pandemic era as the beginning of a multi-year opportunity rather than a bubble.

The thought of approaching an investor may feel overwhelming or intimidating. The truth is most investors are very approachable and enjoy discovering new opportunities. Their entire business model is predicated on finding the next big thing, and many are actively looking for opportunities. You might even be surprised to know that one potential source for private investment could be your local hospital. Yes, your local hospital! Venture capital funds managed within health systems are in a unique position to provide domain expertise and direct access to both providers and patients.

There is a growing trend where venture capital firms partner with local healthcare systems to identify needs and implement innovative technologies. This can address resource limitations in healthcare and help startups gain real-world experience with their technology in hospitals and clinics. An example of this collaboration can be seen between Northeast Georgia Health System (NGHS) and Northeast Georgia Health Ventures, which actively invest in early-stage digital health companies. These partnerships can also be very helpful when it comes to testing and validating the technology in a real-world setting. The term for this is often called "incubation," and it truly means what the word implies. They will help you hatch and develop until you can spread your own wings and fly on your own. We felt it would be beneficial to provide information on this concept of incubation since it was less common. Therefore, we interviewed Mr. Stuart Bracken, the Managing Director of Northeast Georgia Health Ventures, who provided the following advice:

Q: What do you do at Northeast Georgia Health Ventures?

A: **We network with early-stage startups that are looking to solve problems or meet strategic needs of Northeast Georgia Health System (NGHS) in ways that improve outcomes, processes, and revenue—or all three! Because we are part of NGHS, a five-hospital health system with more than 1,300 medical staff members representing more than 60 specialties, caring for more than 1 million people across the state of Georgia each year, there's no shortage of problems to address or strategic opportunities. We see this as a win–win; we get to help early-stage innovators, and they help us solve some of our more complex challenges. We don't lead with capital investments, but we do provide a real-world proving ground and partner with innovators to help validate, license, and take the solution to market.**

Q: How do you engage with innovators?

A: **We work quickly to agree on terms of a working relationship that results in a win-win for the innovator and NGHS. The innovator then gains access to controlled areas of NGHS that include clinical and operational leaders, data, clinical workflow, and whatever other resources they may need. It's a real-world proving ground to quickly refine the solution in partnership with healthcare experts.**

Q: How do you help the innovator go to market?

A: **The primary goal is to help drive value for the innovator by co-developing, validating, licensing, and scaling their solutions/services. We also partner with investors to help them gain access to the funding they need to grow in the market.**

Q: What is the process for innovators to apply?

A: **It's simple. Go to our website and fill out the online form: https://www.nghs.com/nghventures#contact**

Q: Any tips or recommendations for innovators before they pitch their products/solutions?

A:

1. Know your audience. Do background research on the investor to understand what they are looking for, and how you could fit into their portfolio.
2. Know your market. The most important thing an investor looks for is the team. If you aren't a subject matter expert in the space, find one to join the team.
3. Keep it tight. While some investors like creative approaches, most of us are creatures of habit when it comes to format: problem, solution, why you, traction/evidence, vision.
4. Be yourself. An authentic approach is always best.
5. At the end of the day, every pitch is an opportunity. An opportunity to succeed and an opportunity to learn. Approach it as such!

Disclaimer: There is no financial affiliation or conflicts of interest with Northeast Georgia Health Ventures.

# Note

1 Micca, P., Gisby, S., Chang, C., & Shukla, M. (2021). *Trends in health tech investments.* Deloitte Insights. https://www2.deloitte.com/us/en/insights/industry/health-care/health-tech-private-equity-venture-capital.html

# Exhibit II

# Mentoring Strategy Template

### By Karen Jaw-Madson

Many don't know how to go about seeking and finding the right mentor, which is why the Mentoring Strategy Template was created. The principles behind this approach include the following:

- It takes purpose and intention to find the appropriate mentor(s) for your specific need(s) that will yield a mutually beneficial relationship.
- Mentoring and being mentored are not just for early career stages. It can be a lifelong endeavor that benefits both mentor and mentee when "cross-fertilization" occurs, as Dr. R. Michael Scott, Professor of Surgery at Boston Children's Hospital and recipient of their Lifetime Achievement in Mentoring Award, calls it. The template is for those who are seeking mentors, at any stage of their career.
- There are different mentors needed at different stages of one's career. According to Heidrun Stoeger, Daniel Patrick Balestrini, and Albert Ziegler in *"Key Issues in Professionalizing Mentoring Practices* (2021),"
  - Early: focus would be on cultivating love for leadership and the healthcare industry
  - Mid: shift to acquiring the skills, knowledge, and values deliberately
  - Later: requires support from those with the highest levels of knowledge and expertise, to cultivate creativity and innovation

The template's prompts will clarify what a mentee is seeking to achieve through mentoring and how they will go about finding the appropriate mentors.

There are five sections to the mentoring strategy template, built one at a time:

Section 1 articulates the development goals that will be attained through mentoring. Research by Gail Matthews at Dominican University has shown that written goals are more likely to be achieved than those that are not (Gardner & Albee, 2015). What's more, meaningfully written goals can support your motivation to work on them. They should explain the what (specifically), the reasons why they are worth pursuing, and how you would know they've been accomplished.

| 1 | 2 | 3 | 4 | 5 |
|---|---|---|---|---|
| What?<br>Why?<br>How will you know? | | | | |

*With permission from Karen Jaw-Madson, Co.-Design of Work Experience, © 2022*

Section 2 answers, "What do you need to get there?" Come up with at least 3–5 conditions or requirements. If you don't know, your answer may be to explore more, figure it out, or make a few decisions.

| 1 | 2 | 3 | 4 | 5 |
|---|---|---|---|---|
| What?<br>Why?<br>How will you know? | What do you need to get there?<br><br>What<br><br>What<br><br>What<br><br>What<br><br>What | | | |

*With permission from Karen Jaw-Madson, Co.-Design of Work Experience, © 2022*

Section 3 is about naming who can help. List people who are either in your network or those you would like to get to know in your extended network. If you don't have a name, write down characteristics for each person. Be exhaustive. Remember that there are different mentors for different things, so you won't necessarily find everything in any one person.

| 1 | 2 | 3 | 4 | 5 |
|---|---|---|---|---|
| | What do you need to get there? | Who can help? | | |
| | What | Who | | |
| What? Why? How will you know? | What | Who | | |
| | What | Who | | |
| | What | Who | | |
| | What | Who | | |

*With permission from Karen Jaw-Madson, Co.-Design of Work Experience, © 2022*

Section 4 identifies where you can find these types of mentors. It could be where they work or where they spend time (a professional organization, volunteering, or socializing). Not everyone is on social media, and they might not attend formal networking events. You may need to identify the connectors first—those who can and are willing to introduce you to others. Endeavor to become a connector yourself and find other connectors to increase reach.

| 1 | 2 | 3 | 4 | 5 |
|---|---|---|---|---|
| | What do you need to get there? | Who can help? | Where can you find them? | |
| | What | Who | Where | |
| What? Why? How will you know? | What | Who | Where | |
| | What | Who | Where | |
| | What | Who | Where | |
| | What | Who | Where | |

*With permission from Karen Jaw-Madson, Co.-Design of Work Experience, © 2022*

Section 5 puts Sections 1–4 into action with commitment and accountability. What will you do and by when? More than securing the mentors, it includes what you will do to meet your goals. Do you need to investigate, learn, develop, build, practice, or reach out and collaborate with others—or some other form of engagement or involvement? What needs to be done in the short, medium, and long terms? Be creative, experiment, and adjust as needed.

| 1 | 2 | 3 | 4 | 5 |
|---|---|---|---|---|
|  | What do you need to get there? | Who can help? | Where can you find them? | What will you do? By when? |
|  | What | Who | Where | Action |
| What? Why? How will you know? | What | Who | Where | Action |
|  | What | Who | Where | Action |
|  | What | Who | Where | Action |
|  | What | Who | Where | Action |

*With permission from Karen Jaw-Madson, Co.-Design of Work Experience, © 2022*

Now let's connect the dots—this is where the strategy comes to life. Go back to Section 1, where you had your goal. Can you connect the items in Section 2 and validate that those requirements or conditions will help you achieve your goal(s) in Section 1?

| 1 | 2 | 3 | 4 | 5 |
|---|---|---|---|---|
|  | What do you need to get there? | Who can help? | Where can you find them? | What will you do? By when? |
|  | What | Who | Where | Action |
| What? Why? How will you know? | What | Who | Where | Action |
|  | What | Who | Where | Action |
|  | What | Who | Where | Action |
|  | What | Who | Where | Action |

*With permission from Karen Jaw-Madson, Co.-Design of Work Experience, © 2022*

Next, connect the "what" items in Section 2 with the multiple "who" in Section 3 with direct lines. You may have multiple people that can cover a single "what" or you might have one person that can cover multiple "what" items. Perhaps one person can only cover one "what."

| 1 | 2 | 3 | 4 | 5 |
|---|---|---|---|---|
| | What do you need to get there? | Who can help? | Where can you find them? | What will you do? By when? |
| What? Why? How will you know? | What | Who | Where | Action |
| | What | Who | Where | Action |
| | What | Who | Where | Action |
| | What | Who | Where | Action |
| | What | Who | Where | Action |

*With permission from Karen Jaw-Madson, Co.-Design of Work Experience, © 2022*

Now consider the connections between who can help (Section 3) and where you can find them (Section 4). You might find multiple people in one place/channel, one person in multiple places, or one place for every one person.

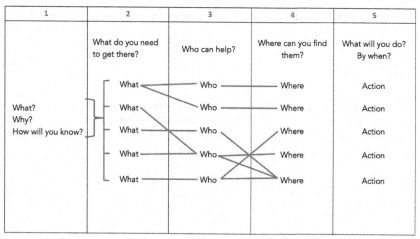

| 1 | 2 | 3 | 4 | 5 |
|---|---|---|---|---|
| | What do you need to get there? | Who can help? | Where can you find them? | What will you do? By when? |
| What? Why? How will you know? | What | Who | Where | Action |
| | What | Who | Where | Action |
| | What | Who | Where | Action |
| | What | Who | Where | Action |
| | What | Who | Where | Action |

*With permission from Karen Jaw-Madson, Co.-Design of Work Experience, © 2022*

By drawing lines across Sections 2–4, you can prioritize and sequence your efforts more efficiently and effectively.

For Section 5, double-check that the actions tie directly back to helping you achieve the goals in Section 1. What you want to make sure of is that there is a direct path that you can connect between what you want to achieve and what you will do to get it. If it doesn't, make some edits to refine the strategy.

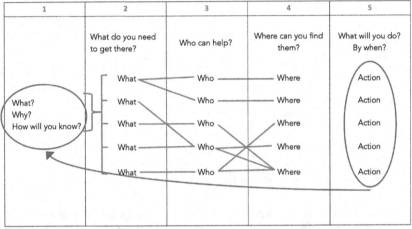

*With permission from Karen Jaw-Madson, Co.-Design of Work Experience, © 2022*

Once completed, you have a strategy to implement with purpose, intention, and a greater chance of success. You are empowered to make it happen!

# References

Gardner, S., & Albee, D. (2015). Study focuses on strategies for achieving goals, resolutions. *Press Releases*, 266, 7. https://scholar.dominican.edu/news-releases/266

Stoeger, H., Balestrini, D. P., & Ziegler, A. (2021). Key issues in professionalizing mentoring practices. *Annals of the New York Academy of Sciences*, 1483(1), 5–18.

# Appendix A

# Healthcare Information Technology Resources

Below will be a list of resources compiled for women desirous of pursuing a career in healthcare information technology (HCIT), or for women already in the field of HCIT who would benefit from having an extensive compilation of such resources available in one convenient place.

## Conferences and Events

- *American Health Information Management Association (AHIMA)*: www.ahima.org
- *American Medical Informatics Association (AMIA)*: www.amia.org/education-events
- *American Nursing Informatics Association (ANIA)*: www.ania.org/events
- *Association of Perioperative Registered Nurses (AORN):* www.aorn.org
- *Becker's Hospital Review*: wwwbeckershospitalreview.com (search "Event")
- *Bluebird Leaders Annual Conference*: www.bluebirdleaders.org
- *Grace Hopper Celebration*: ghc.anitab.org
- *HealthcareIT Connect*: www.healthcareitconnect.com
- *HIMSS Global Conference*: www.himssconference.com
- *Medical Group Management Association (MGMA)*: www.mgma.com
- *Swaay.Health*: www.healthitmarketingconference.com

- *VIVE*: www.viveevent.com
- *Women in Tech Festival*: www.womenintechfestivalglobal.com
- *Women in Tech Summit*: www.womenintechsummit.net

# Education and Training

*Many of the above-listed professional associations also offer education and training. Please note that while this list does not include the name of specific universities, it is advisable to select accredited programs.

- *Ada Developers Academy*: www.adadevelopersacademy.org
- *Center for Creative Leadership*: www.ccl.org
- *Certified Scrum Master (CSM)*: This certification enables an individual to lead teams using the Agile project management approach. Numerous online training programs are available.
- *Commission on Accreditation of Healthcare Management Education (CAHME)*: www.cahme.org
- *CompTIA*: www.comptia.org
- *Girl Develop It*: www.girldevelopit.com
- *Girls Who Code*: www.girlswhocode.com
- *Hackbright Academy*: www.hackbrightacademy.com
- *HITLAB*: www.hitlab.org
- *Isaca Certifications*: www.isaca.org/credentialing/certifications
- *Project Management Institute*: www.pmi.org
- *Skillcrush*: www.skillcrush.com

# HCIT Job Search

*Tip: Some HCIT professional association websites may have a listing of job openings available. Below are some of the more common HCIT-centric job search sites, though there are many other job search sites available.

- *Agile*: jobs.gotoagile.com
- *AHIMA*: www.careerassist.ahima.org
- *CareerBuilder*: www.careerbuilder.com
- *Elite Technical*: www.elitetechnical.com
- *GHR Technology*: www.jobs.ghrtechnology.com

- *Glassdoor*: www.glassdoor.com
- *Han Staffing*: www.hanstaffing.com
- *HIMSS JobMine*: www.jobmine.himss.org
- *Indeed*: www.indeed.com
- *MGMA*: www.careers.mgma.com
- *Monster*: www.monster.com
- *Simply Hired*: www.simplyhired.com
- *ZipRecruiter*: www.ziprecruiter.com

# Organizations and Networking

- *Ada's List*: www.adaslist.co
- *AnitaB.org*: www.anitab.org
- *Bluebird Leaders*: www.bluebirdleaders.org
- *CSweetner*: www.csweetener.org
- *Elpha*: elpha.com
- *Girl Develop It*: www.girldevelopit.com
- *Girls in Tech*: www.girlsintech.org
- *Healthcare Businesswomen's Association (HBA)*: www.hbanet.org
- *Ladies Get Paid*: www.ladiesgetpaid.com
- *MedExexWomen*: www.medexecwomen.org
- *MedtechWOMEN*: www.medtechwomen.org
- *National Center for Women & Information Technology (NCWIT)*: www.ncwit.org
- *Rock IT Women*: www.rockitwomen.com
- *TechLadies*: www.hiretechladies.com
- *TechWomen*: www.techwomen.org
- *Women Business Leaders of the U.S. Health Care Industry Foundation (WBL)*: www.wbl.org
- *Women in Healthcare IT (WHIT)*: www.whittywomen.org
- *Women in Technology (WIT)*: www.mywit.org
- *Women in Tech Council (WTC)*: www.womentechcouncil.com
- *Women in Technology International (WITI)*: www.witi.com
- *Women Who Code*: www.womenwhocode.com

# Appendix B

# General Overview of Acronyms Relevant to HCIT

| Abbreviation | Meaning |
| --- | --- |
| **AAHAM** | American Association of Healthcare Administrative Management |
| **ACA** | Affordable Care Act |
| **ACO** | Accountable Care Organization |
| **AHA** | American Hospital Association |
| **AHIMA** | American Health Information Management Association |
| **AHRQ** | Agency for Healthcare Research and Quality |
| **AMIA** | American Medical Informatics Association |
| **ANI** | Alliance for Nursing Informatics |
| **ANSI** | American National Standards Institute |
| **APHA** | American Public Health Association |
| **API** | Application Programming Interface |
| **APM** | Alternative Payment Model |
| **APRN** | Advanced Practice Registered Nurse |
| **ARRA** | American Recovery and Reinvestment Act |
| **ASC** | Ambulatory Surgery Center |
| **ASP** | Application Service Provider |
| **BAA** | Business Associate Agreement |
| **BHIE** | Bidirectional Health Information Exchange |
| **CAH** | Critical Access Hospitals |
| **CAHPS** | Consumer Assessment of Healthcare Providers and Systems |
| **CBO** | Community-Based Organization |
| **CCD** | Continuity of Care Document |
| **C-CDA** | Consolidated Clinical Document Architecture |
| **CCN** | CMS Certification Number |
| **CCR** | Continuity of Care Record |
| **CDA** | Clinical Document Architecture |

*(Continued)*

| Abbreviation | Meaning |
|---|---|
| CDO | Care Delivery Organization |
| CDR | Clinical Data Repository |
| CDS | Clinical Decision Support |
| CDSS | Clinical Decision Support System |
| CEHRT | Certified Electronic Health Record Technology |
| CFR | Code of Federal Regulations |
| CHC | Community Health Centers |
| CHPL | Certified Health IT Product List |
| CHR | Community Health Records |
| CIO | Chief Information Officer |
| CISO | Chief Information Security Officer |
| CMIO | Chief Medical Information Officer |
| CMO | Chief Medical Officer |
| CMS | Center for Medicare & Medicaid Services |
| CMV | Controlled Medical Vocabulary |
| CPOE | Computerized Physician Order Entry |
| CPRS | Computerized Patient Record System |
| CPS | Composite Performance Score |
| CPT | Current Procedural Terminology |
| DBE | Documenting by Exception |
| DURSA | Data Use and Reciprocal Support Agreement |
| EA | Enterprise Architecture |
| eCQI | Electronic Clinical Quality Improvement |
| eCQM | Electronic Clinician Quality Measure |
| ED | Emergency Department |
| EDIS | Emergency Department Information Systems |
| EHR | Electronic Health Record |
| EHRA | Electronic Health Record Association |
| EHRVA | Electronic Health Record Vendors Association |
| eMAR | Electronic Medication Administration Record |
| EMR | Electronic Medical Record |
| ePHI | Electronic Protected Health Information |
| eRx | Electronic Transmission of Prescriptions |
| FACA | Federal Advisory Committee Act |
| FAST | Federal Adoption Standards for Health IT |
| FFS | Fee-for-Service |
| FHA | Federal Health Architecture |
| FHIR | Fast Health Care Interoperability Resources |
| FIPS | Federal Information Processing Standards |
| FOSS | Free and Open Source Software |
| FQHC | Federally Qualified Health Center |
| FTP | File Transport Protocol |
| GDP | Gross Domestic Product |

(*Continued*)

| *Abbreviation* | *Meaning* |
|---|---|
| **GPRO** | Group Practice Reporting Option |
| **HEDIS** | Healthcare Effectiveness Data and Information Set |
| **HHS** | Health & Human Services |
| **HIMSS** | Healthcare Information and Management Systems Society |
| **HISB** | Healthcare Informatics Standards Board |
| **HISPC** | Health Information Security and Privacy Collaboration |
| **HITAC** | Health Information Technology Advisory Committee |
| **HITRC** | National Health IT Research Center |
| **HITSP** | Healthcare Information Technology Standards Panel |
| **HIT** | Health Information Technology |
| **HITECH** | Health Information Technology for Economic and Clinical Health Act |
| **HITPC** | Health Information Technology Privacy Council |
| **HIQR** | Hospital Inpatient Quality Reporting |
| **HIX** | Health Insurance Exchange |
| **HL7** | Health Level 7 |
| **HRSA** | Health Resources and Services Administration |
| **IAS** | Individual Access Services |
| **ICD** | International Classification of Diseases |
| **ICE** | Integrated Community EHR |
| **IFR** | Interim Final Rule |
| **IOM** | Institute of Medicine |
| **IPPS** | Inpatient Prospective Payment System |
| **ISO** | International Organization for Standardization |
| **IT** | Information Technology |
| **LAN** | Local Area Network |
| **LTPAC** | Long Term Post Acute Care |
| **LOINC** | Logical Observation Identifiers, Names, Codes |
| **MACRA** | Medicare Access and CHIP Reauthorization Act |
| **MCO** | Managed Care Organization |
| **MDDS** | Medical Device Data Systems |
| **MEI** | Medicare Economic Index |
| **MGMA** | Medical Group Management Association |
| **MIPAA** | Medicare Improvements for Patients and Providers Act |
| **MIPS** | Merit-based Incentive Payment System |
| **MITA** | Medicaid Information Technology Architecture |
| **MMIS** | Medicaid Management Information System |
| **MSO** | Management Service Organization |
| **MSSP** | Medicare Shared Savings Program |
| **MTSO** | Medical Transcription Service Organization |
| **MUA** | Medically Underserved Areas |
| **NCQA** | National Committee for Quality Assurance |
| **NCVHS** | National Committee on Vital and Health Statistics |
| **NHE** | Non-HIPAA Entity |

*(Continued)*

| Abbreviation | Meaning |
| --- | --- |
| NHIN | Nationwide Health Information Network |
| NIH | National Institute of Health |
| NIST | National Institute of Standards and Technology |
| NLP | Natural Language Processing |
| NP | Nurse Practitioner |
| NPI | National Provider Identifier |
| OCR | Office of Civil Rights |
| ONC | Office of the National Coordinator |
| ONCHIT | Office of the National Coordinator for Health Information Technology |
| P4P | Pay-for-Performance |
| PA | Physician Assistant |
| PACS | Picture Archiving and Communication Systems |
| PCP | Primary Care Physician |
| PFPM | Physician Focused Payment Model |
| PFS | Physician Fee Schedule |
| PHA | Public Health Agency |
| PHS | Public Health Service |
| PHI | Protected Health Information |
| PHR | Personal Health Record |
| PHSA | Public Health Service Act |
| PMS | Practice Management System |
| POS | Place of Service |
| PPACA | Patient Portability and Affordable Care Act |
| PPS | Prospective Payment System |
| PQRI | Physician Quality Reporting Initiative |
| PQRS | Physician Quality Reporting System |
| QCDR | Qualified Clinician Data Registry |
| QE | Quality Entity |
| QHIN | Qualified Health Information Networks |
| QP | Qualifying APM Professional |
| QPP | Quality Payment Program |
| QRDA | Quality Reporting Document Architecture |
| REC | Regional Extension Center |
| RHC | Rural Health Clinic |
| RHIO | Regional Health Information Organizations |
| RPA | Robotic Process Automation |
| RTLS | Real Time Location Systems |
| RVU | Relative Value Unit |
| SaaS | Software-as-a-Service |
| SDO | Standards Development Organization |
| SGR | Sustainable Growth Rate |
| SMHP | State Medicaid Health Information Plan |
| SMS | Short Message Service |

(*Continued*)

| *Abbreviation* | *Meaning* |
|---|---|
| **SMTP** | Simple Mail Transfer Protocol |
| **SNOMED** | Systematized Nomenclature of Medicine |
| **SOAP** | Subjective, Objective, Assessment, and Plan |
| **SOP** | Standard Operating Procedure |
| **TCPI** | Transforming Clinical Practice Initiative |
| **TEFCA** | Trusted Exchange Framework and Common Agreement |
| **TIN** | Taxpayer Identification Number |
| **TLS** | Transport Layer Security |
| **UCD** | User-Centered Design |
| **UNII** | Unique Ingredient Identifier |
| **UCUM** | Unified Code for Units of Measure |
| **USB** | Universal Serial Bus |
| **USHIK** | United States Health Information Knowledgebase |
| **VLER** | Virtual Lifetime Electronic Record |
| **VNA** | Vendor Neutral Archive |
| **VPN** | Virtual Private Network |
| **XML** | Extensible Markup Language |

# Index

**Note:** *Italic* page numbers refer to figures.

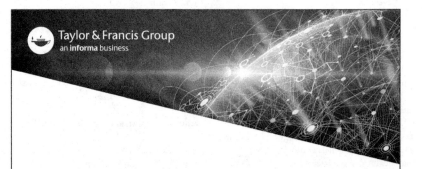

Printed in the United States
by Baker & Taylor Publisher Services